The Centennial History of the Independent Labour Party

*Forthcoming titles of related interest
from Ryburn Publishing include:*

Class and Politics in a Northern Town
A Study of Keighley 1884 to 1914
by David James. Introduced by Lord Briggs

The History of the Social-Democratic Federation
by Martin Crick

Religion and the Rise of Labour
by Leonard Smith

The Centennial History of the Independent Labour Party

A Collection of Essays
edited by
David James, Tony Jowitt
and Keith Laybourn

Ryburn Academic Publishing

First published in 1992
Ryburn Publishing Ltd
Krumlin, Halifax

ISBN 1 85331 037 9

Composed by Ryburn Publishing Services
Printed on Maximus Cream by
Ryburn Book Production, Halifax, England

Contents

Acknowledgements

It is impossible to pay too fulsome a tribute to the many individuals and library and Record Office staffs who have contributed to the essays produced in this collection. In particular, those in Bradford, Bristol, Dewsbury, Glasgow, Leicester, Manchester, Newcastle and South Shields are owed particular thanks. We would also like to thank Richard Clark and his staff at Ryburn Publishing for their encouragement and patience during the preparation of this book. Three of the articles have previously been published. 'The Manningham Mills Strike' has been amended and extended from an article which appeared in *The Bradford Antiquary*, New Series, Part XLI, 1976; 'War and Socialism: The Experience of the Bradford Independent Labour Party 1914–1918', was published in *The Journal of Regional and Local Studies*, volume 4, no. 2, autumn 1984; and 'The Bradford Independent Labour Party and Trade Unionism c 1890–1914', though amended and extended, appeared as '"One of the little breezes blowing across Bradford": The Bradford Independent Labour Party and Trade Unionism', in K. Laybourn and D. James (eds.), *The Rising Sun of Socialism* (West Yorkshire Archive Service, 1991).

Abbreviations

DMA	Durham Miners' Association
ILP	Independent Labour Party
MFGB	Miners' Federation of Great Britain
NAC	National Administrative Council (of the ILP)
NUR	National Union of Railwaymen
SDF	Social-Democratic Federation
UTFWA	United Textile Factory Workers' Association
WEA	Workers' Educational Association
WLL	Women's Labour League
WRCC	West Riding County Council
WSPU	Women's Social and Political Union
YMA	Yorkshire Miners' Association

To the memory of
Jack Reynolds
1915–1988
who inspired a whole generation
of historians to research the
history of the early
British Labour Party and
the Independent Labour Party

Notes on Contributors

MARTIN CRICK is a school teacher in Dewsbury and recently completed his PhD (CNAA) which will be published by Ryburn as *The History of the Social-Democratic Federation* (1993). He has written several articles including 'Labour Alliance or Socialist Unity? The Independent Labour Party in the Heavy Woollen Areas of West Yorkshire c.1893–1902', in K. Laybourn and D. James (eds.), *The Rising Sun of Socialism* (West Yorkshire Archive Service, 1991).

JUNE HANNAM is Principal Lecturer in History at the University of the South West based on Bristol. She has written numerous articles as well as a book on *Isabella Ford 1855–1924* (1989).

JEFF HILL is Principal Lecturer in History at Nottingham Polytechnic. He has written extensively on Labour history and the history of sport for a variety of journals, including the *International Review of Social History*, and is writing a history of Nelson for Ryburn's *Town and City Histories* series.

DAVID JAMES is the Bradford Archivist for the West Yorkshire Archive Service. In recent years he has edited *The Rising Sun of Socialism* (1991) with Keith Laybourn and written many articles and also three books for Ryburn including a history of *Bradford* (1990). In 1991 he obtained his doctorate at Huddersfield Polytechnic on the subject of Keighley politics in the late nineteenth century which is to be published by Ryburn with an introduction by Asa Briggs.

TONY JOWITT is head of the Adult Education Unit of the Centre for Continuing Education, Bradford University. His publications include *Mechanization and Misery* (Ryburn, 1992), *Employers and Labour in the English Textile Industries 1850–1939* (1988, co-editor), *Model Industrial Communities in Mid-Nineteenth Century Yorkshire* (1986, editor), *Victorian Bradford* (1981, co-editor).

BILL LANCASTER is a lecturer in History at the University of Northumberland and is an Associate Fellow at the Centre for the Study of Social History, University of Warwick. He has written numerous articles and *Radicalism, Cooperation and Socialism: Leicester Working-Class Politics 1860–1906* (1987).

KEITH LAYBOURN in Professor of History at the University of Huddersfield. He has published twelve books and more than 30 articles on British Labour history, the history of education, the history of social policy and local history, as well as numerous reviews. His recent books include *The Rise of Labour* (1988), *Philip Snowden* (1988), *Britain on the Breadline* (1990), *The Rising Sun of Socialism* (1991, co-editor with David James), and *A History of British Trade Unionism* (1992). In the mid 1980s he wrote two books with Jack Reynolds on *Liberalism and the Rise of Labour* (1984) and *Labour Heartland* (1986).

BILL PURDUE is a staff lecturer with the Open University, operating in the North East. He has written a number of articles for journals such as the *International Review of Social History* and *Northern History*, and has helped write and edit a number of books for the Open University.

LEONARD SMITH is a Unitarian Minister and the Principal of the Unitarian College in Manchester. He obtained both an MA and a PhD (CNAA) at Huddersfield Polytechnic where he was supervised by Keith Laybourn. He has written a number of articles in Unitarian and Free Church journals and is completing a book on *Religion and the Rise of Labour*, to be published by Ryburn early in 1993.

CAROLYN STEEDMAN is Senior Lecturer in Arts Education at the University of Warwick. She has written many books and articles including *The Tidy House* (1982), *Policing the Victorian Community* (1984), *Landscape for a Good Women* (1986), *The Radical Soldiers' Tale* (1988) and *Childhood, Culture and Class in Britain: Margaret McMillan 1860–1931* (1990).

ANDREW TAYLOR is Principal Lecturer in Politics at the University of Huddersfield. He has written extensively on the politics of mining and trade unionism. His books and numerous articles include *The Trade Unions and the Labour Party* (1987).

BARRY WINTER is political secretary of the ILP.

IAN WOOD lectures at Namier University, Glasgow, and has written many articles and a book on *John Wheatley* (1990). He was also joint editor of *Forward! Labour Politics in Scotland 1888–1988* (1989) with Ian Donnachie and Christopher Harvie.

CHRIS WRIGLEY is Professor of History at the University of Nottingham. He has written and edited many books, including *David Lloyd George and the British Labour Movement* (1976), *A History of British Industrial Relations 1875–1914* (1982), *A History of British Industrial Relations, Vol. II, 1914–1939* (1987), and *Arthur Henderson* (1990).

Introduction

Over the last twenty-five years there has been a remarkable resurgence of interest amongst historians in the history of the Independent Labour Party. This has led to an extensive range of publications in the form of theses, dissertations, articles and books. Part of the work remains unpublished but much has been published over a long period in a range of journals that are sometimes difficult to obtain. It therefore seemed appropriate to mark the centenary of the foundation of the Independent Labour Party at Bradford, in January 1893, by drawing together a range of this work into more accessible book form.[1]

The Independent Labour Party, although never a major quantitative component of the Labour Party, played a crucial and influential role in the forging of the party. In particular, it acted as a powerful inspirational force to convert countless men and women from the political habit of a lifetime, encouraging them to embrace not only new and different patterns of voting but also to conceive and work for a better world. Most particularly was this the case in certain regions, in particular the West Riding of Yorkshire, where this new party had an almost messianic impact. The first section of this work is therefore with a series of studies of the ILP in a number of important regions. These reflect the diversity of the party throughout the country, the different patterns of growth, and the relations with the competing elements within the Labour movement.

Bill Purdue, for instance, suggests that the ILP, and its peculiar brand of socialism, never became truly embedded in the warp and woof of working-class life and culture in the North East where the miners were strongly attached to the Liberal Party until after their formal attachment to the Labour Party in 1909. Jeff Hill, on the other hand, suggests that in Lancashire and the North West there was a well-entrenched and successful socialist tradition built up through the combined efforts of the ILP and the SDF; the ILP could claim no exclusivity in this achievement. Ian Wood focuses upon the strong links between the ILP and the issue of Scottish nationalism, examining the personal contributions of Jimmy Maxton, Thomas Johnston and Roland Muirhead. In contrast, Bill Lancaster focuses upon the industrial and social forces which combined together to crack the established political mould in Leicester in a way which was not achieved in any other major industrial community.

The second section is an attempt to provide a detailed local study – in this case for Bradford which was the birthplace and one of the key centres of the Independent Labour Party up to and during the First World War. These studies examine the social, economic, political and religious nature of late Victorian and Edwardian Bradford, the dramatic Manningham Mills strike which focussed and clarified the underlying tensions and conflict. The strike starkly illuminated the divide between capital and labour in this northern textile community and acted as a powerful catalyst in the foundation of an independent working-class party. The party which emerged out of the Manningham Mills Strike, the Bradford Labour Union, subsequently the Bradford ILP, grew very rapidly in the early 1890s. Thereafter, it declined in the late 1890s but then experienced a steady growth from 1900 to the eve of the First World War, when its membership rose to about 1,600. Indeed, by 1913 it could command more than 40 per cent of the municipal vote. The ILP's 'Coming of Age Conference', in 1914, marked its coming of age as a potent force in Bradford politics. Its growth and development is analysed in detail, and focuses upon the critical alliance forged between the party and the trade union movement. Finally, the impact of the First World War upon the local ILP is examined and the differing strands of thinking in the party delineated. Indeed, it emerges that whilst the official line of the ILP was in favour of peace and pacifist ideas it is clear that the local party was deeply divided on this issue and that a significant proportion of the young male members of the Bradford ILP volunteered to fight. Although on the surface the Party emerged from the War with an enhanced status and authority, this masked a number of fatal weaknesses which were to lead to its decline in Bradford in the 1920s. Attention is drawn to the divisions within the Party and to the demise of the federal structure of the Labour Party, with membership being through constituent parties with individual Labour Party membership.

The third section of the book analyses a number of key issues confronting the Party. Fundamental in the pre-1914 period was the debate about Socialist Unity, which draws attention to the fact that the Independent Labour Party was not the only socialist or labourist organisation operating at the time. In particular it examines the position of the Social Democratic Federation and attempts to forge a united Socialist party embracing all elements. Equally, the position of the miners and the ILP has long been debated. The swiftness of their move from the Liberal Party to the Labour Party in the years between 1904 and 1909 has often been commented upon and Andrew Taylor suggests that in this respect historians have focussed too much on the parliamentary events of these years and have ignored the tensions which, throughout the 1890s, had been developing between the old Liberal-dominated union hierarchy and the new emergent ILP activists amongst some of the pit-head branches. On the issue of religion, there were clearly many contacts between the ILP and religious groups, particularly the Nonconformist religions, although equally there were splits due to the British involvement in the Boer War which was strongly opposed by the ILP but equally strongly supported by some denominational groups. Indeed, in other respects, the international concerns and dimensions of the ILP should not be ignored. Nevertheless, Chris Wrigley suggests that the ILP adopted a rather insular attitude towards the Second International, even though trade union contacts, associations with international socialists, and issues, such as the eight-hour day, began to widen the vision of the ILP's leaders by the early twentieth century.

The relationship between socialist groups and women has also been of rising interest for the last twenty years. It has been suggested that the Social

Democratic Federation's attitude towards women was one in which they paid lip
service rather than took action and June Hannam's article suggests something
similar for the Independent Labour Party – although there was always a close
affinity between socialism and feminism within the ILP. Quite clearly, many
women – such as Isabella Ford, Katherine St. John Conway and Margaret
McMillan – played an immensely important role in the early activities of the
ILP. They lectured, wrote articles and contributed the inspiration required for
the emerging political organisation to widen its appeal. Nevertheless, the ILP
was split on the question of women's suffrage; although many of the ILP leaders,
such as Keir Hardie and Philip Snowden, did accept the Women's Social and
Political Union argument for the limited franchise, others, such as Mary
Macarthur and Fred Jowett, advocated the idea of universal adult suffrage.

Given the importance which the ILP attached to winning membership of
school boards and LEA committees, it comes as a surprise to discover that
there is relatively little discussion of education in ILP records, and very little
concern about the importance of the curriculum. This may well have been
because the ILP placed the abolition of the half-time system, school feeding
and the physical aspects of educational activities to the fore or because the
ILP's attitude towards education was somehow subsumed within that of the
Labour Party whose educational programme was essentially that of the
'Bradford Charter'. Yet the ILP did play a part in the evolution of the Labour
Party's educational policy, even if that role has been somewhat obscured by the
educational experts who took over in the 1920s.

The fourth section provides a Review of Literature and Sources in an
attempt to provide a critical overview of the very disparate writings on the
Independent Labour Party. The main argument is that the study of the ILP
has become increasingly locally orientated in recent years and that our
understanding of the reasons for its growth, its position in the First World
War, and other issues have, consequently, changed dramatically. In addition,
David James, an archivist, has attempted to bring together the sources on the
ILP which are available to the researcher.

Finally, effectively as a postscript, the present Political Secretary of the ILP
has provided a short piece on the party – past, present and future. In polemical
style, he suggests the correctness of ILP thinking in the past and hints at the
ILP's rebirth in 1993.

In any collection of essays, editors are always open to the charge that
certain areas of study have been omitted. Clearly there are areas which have
not been covered in the section on the regions most particularly London, the
South East, the South West or East Anglia. Room and expertise did not permit
this in what is a lengthy book, although there is some justification for
examining areas where the ILP did not take off. Similarly, we could have
incorporated a section on leaders, although the current surge in biographies
on key figures, such as Keir Hardie, Philip Snowden and, in the near future,
George Lansbury, plus the work in the *Dictionary of Labour Biography*, have
made this unnecessary.

13

It could be argued that we have devoted too much space to the years of growth and development before 1914 and give much less space and attention to the years after 1918 which culminated with disaffiliation from the Labour Party in 1932 and the ILP's consignment to the margins of the British political Labour movement. However, we would maintain that the period from the 1920s onwards would require a different book with a different emphasis and this may be attempted in a second volume. Finally, we can only say that we hope that the deficiencies and omissions, which mark any collection of essays, will stimulate other scholars to undertake that research and advance on the understanding of a Party that not only fundamentally changed the lives of countless men and women, but which played a crucial role in changing the face of British politics – even if it was but one, although the most important, of the socialist groups pushing for the changes in British politics at the end of the nineteenth century.

NOTE

1. Most introductions provide an analysis of the literature surrounding the topic of the book, but this has been provided by Keith Laybourn in the chapter on 'Recent Writing on the History of the ILP'.

SECTION I

REGIONAL STUDIES

1. The ILP in the North East of England

A. W. Purdue

The importance of the Independent Labour Party lies in the role it played in helping wean organised labour away from its connections with the Liberal Party and in its success in permeating the Labour Representation Committee and then the Labour Party with a mild degree of socialism. These were substantial but not heroic achievements. They constitute the harvest of what Henry Pelling has seen as 'the fundamental differences between the ILP and the early socialist societies ... the means of political action are regarded as of primary importance,and the theoretical approach gives way to the practical.'[1] Yet, despite its tactful and tactical name, the party was a socialist party and the tension between the need to accommodate a reformist neo-Liberal Labourism and the socialism of party activists was to punctuate its history and to lead finally in 1932 to severance from the Labour Party it had done so much to create. The ILP in the North East of England was not immune from such tensions but its history was, for the most part, one of accommodation to a labourism which gradually parted from Liberal-Labourism.

In the North East the task of challenging Liberalism must have seemed, in the early eighteen nineties, formidable. The region's reputation as a Liberal stronghold was confirmed by the results of the General Election of 1892 which saw the Liberal Party win twenty one out of twenty five seats.[2] Nor was Liberalism the only force to contend with, for North East Conservatism was stronger than the results of 1892 indicated and it had roots in the working-class culture of many towns.[3] Liberalism was indeed in a commanding position but its hold on the major towns, the coastal ports and the heavy industrial areas adjacent to the Tyne, Wear and Tees was never as secure as its hold on its inner keep, the coalfield. The next decade was to witness Unionist successes in Newcastle, Sunderland, Tynemouth, Middlesbrough, Darlington and Stockton. If the strategy eventually adopted by a pragmatic North East ILP, of working with the grain of the Liberal-Labourist tradition while seeking to replace the Liberal Party, was the most straightforward, it was not the only possible strategy in the circumstances of the North East of the early 1890s nor one that was certain to pay equal dividends in every constituency.

The industrial North East has never been the homogeneous region that it can so easily appear from outside. There were in the 1890s social, cultural and political divisions. Even within and between mining communities there were cultural differences, while, between the coalfield, with its concentrated communities dominated by a single industry, and the heavy industrial towns and ports there was a sharp divide. Nor where, as on Tyneside, there were pits close to the riverside towns, did miners and shipyard, dockside and seafaring communities enjoy a common culture or sense of identity.[4] A diversity of employment, a more complex social structure with a larger middle class[5] and a broader popular culture, all contributed to making the towns different from, and less solidly Liberal than, the mining areas. A strategy for a socialist advance in the coalfield might well not be suited to such an advance on industrial Tyneside or Teesside.

The North East had seen the beginning of labour representation when, in 1874, Thomas Burt had been elected MP for Morpeth, one of the first two working-class MPs. Largely because of their members being concentrated in discrete areas, in such numbers that they often made up the bulk of the electorate, the mining unions were effective in securing seats for their officials. In the 1885 General Election four mining MPs were returned in Northumberland and Durham: Thomas Burt (Morpeth), Charles Fenwick (Wansbeck), William Crawford (Mid. Durham) and John Wilson (Houghton-le-Spring). Wilson lost his seat in the 1886 Election[6] but, on Crawford's death, he took over Mid. Durham which he retained from 1890 until 1915. In addition to these mining MPs, John Havelock Wilson, the Secretary to the Seamen's Union, was elected MP for Middlesbrough in 1892.[7]

This considerable achievement by way of labour representation was an obstacle rather than an advantage to the ILP for all the mining MPs were Liberal-Labour, enjoying the backing of their local Liberal Associations as well as their unions. Havelock Wilson had won his seat as an independent Labour candidate but soon made his way back to the Liberal fold.

Certain basic choices faced socialists in the North East as elsewhere. Should socialism see itself as the heir to the liberal radical tradition or should it be firmly independent from both main political traditions and neutral between them? How closely should socialists work with the trades unions and, if they should cooperate with them, were the established unions or the new general unions of the late 'eighties the better partners?

In the event the impact of the ILP was to leaven labourism with an ethical socialism that could be seen as the natural successor to Liberalism. Confrontation with Liberalism and Liberal-Labourism masked cultural and political continuity. Those who supported an independent Labour representation separate from Liberalism were to be successful in proportion to the degree that their stance continued Liberal-Labourist attitudes without the Liberal Party, while the ILP itself managed to fan independent Labourism and to stiffen it only by moderating its socialism and minimising its distinctiveness from the dominant tradition. The ethical socialism that was the essence of the ILP in the North East was well suited to the task of leading the progressive reformist tradition away from the Liberal Party. The ILP's path to success lay in leaving just enough space, and never too much, between it and Liberalism. The fact that ILP influence advanced primarily, not through the autonomous strength of its branches, nor via newly formed general labour unions, but by gaining the support of established unions, the miner's unions, the Amalgamated Society of Railway Servants and the Amalgamated Society of Engineers, reinforced caution and continuity.

Was there an alternative strategy for the ILP in the North-East; one that would have led to a different sort of Labour Party, at once more socialist and divorced from the Liberal-Labour tradition? David Howell has questioned the inevitability of the continuity of the radical tradition into the Labour Party and the ILP and the easy dismissal of the SDF as 'a narrow dogmatic sector' of Henry Champion and Robert Blatchford as mavericks.[8] Surely the Liberal North-East would have been the last place in which a more socialist or even a Tory Socialist path could have been followed with any success! Probably so, but yet, in 1893, a survey of recent socialist activity in the region might have pointed to just such a scenario.

During the bitter miner's strike of 1887 the Socialist League and the Social Democratic Federation had been active. Tom Mann, William Morris, H. M. Hyndman and J. L. Mahon had addressed crowded meetings, occasioning the sarcastic headline in the *Newcastle Courant*, 'The cockney socialists on their holidays'[9].Their efforts did, however, meet with some success and Mahon, in order to avoid rivalry between Socialist League and SDF branches founded the umbrella organisation, the North of England Socialist Federation. One-day wonder though it was, the seeming popularity of socialism among the miners of Northumberland greatly excited William Morris who, after his enthusiastic reception as he spoke from a farm cart in a field near Blyth to an audience of several thousand, complete with banners and brass bands, found these northerners superior to his usual cockney listeners.[10] Henry Pelling has written of the Federation that it, '... was the nearest approach yet made to a mass socialist movement of the working class: but it was a transient success, for with the settlement of the strike its branches, which numbered twenty-four at the peak, rapidly faded away'.[11]

The short-lived success of the Federation had been misleading because the circumstances of a bitter strike had given SDF and Socialist League speakers a temporary popularity among normally Lib-Lab miners as well as some of the urban working class of Tyneside. With the return of industrial peace to the Northumberland coalfield, the miners went back to their normal political allegiance; socialist branches dwindled and subscriptions to *Commonweal* were cancelled. It was unlikely that North-East miners would for long support organisations calling for the eight-hour day,when hewers in the region already worked seven-hour days, nor self-consciously respectable and sexually puritan communities long continue aligned to a Socialist League, which contained an anarchist element which, *inter alia*, recommended 'free love'. The legacy of Tom Mann's work continued, however, to exert a modest influence with the endurance of SDF branches on Tyneside. Where these socialists were singularly unsuccessful was in attempting to influence the growth of general labour unionism in the area. Although much SDF and Socialist League propaganda had been anti-trades unionist, Edward Pease of the Fabian Society had been busy organising labourers on Tyneside into the National Federation of Labour formed in 1886. The more socialist it became, the more it failed as a union, losing the support it had initially received from

Liberal-Labour trades union leaders and becoming largely a front for the SDF. The successful general labour union on Tyneside was the Tyneside and District Labourers Association, later the National Amalgamated Union of Labour. Firmly Lib-Lab and wedded to pragmatism and conciliation, it defied the ethos of the 'New Unionism', might well have modelled itself on the Northumberland Miners under Burt, and flourished. Martin Searles has summed up its impact: 'The Tyneside and District Labourers Association, in defying socialism where socialists felt they could prosper most, amongst the unskilled, played an important role in protecting the strength of Liberalism on Tyneside...'[12]. In contrast to the contempt for unions exhibited by the SDF leadership under Hyndman, many ex-SDF members like Mann, Mahon and Champion realised the importance of working with the labour movement as it was but still tended to view the unions as instruments for socialism.

J. L. Mahon was, in the early 1890s working closely with Harry Champion who, through the Labour Electoral Association, sought an independent party in close liaison with the trades unions. Both were involved in socialist politics in Newcastle as well as Scotland and had a common hostility to Liberalism. The first Newcastle Labour Party set up under their aegis was determined to cut loose from Liberal connections and appeal as much to working class Conservatives as Liberals. That there were plenty of working-class Conservatives to appeal to is demonstrated by election results in Newcastle from 1892 onwards and by the high Primrose League membership especially near the Armstrong munitions factory in Elswick.[13] In 1892 the Newcastle Labour Party attempted to bring about the defeat of that prominent opponent of the eight-hour day, John Morley, by calling on its supporters to vote Unionist. This controversial action, which was supported by Keir Hardie,[14] contributed to the Unionist, Charles Hamond, coming top of the poll, although Morley was also elected in this double member constituency. In the by-election following Morley's appointment as a minister Champion and the Newcastle labour party again called for support for the Unionist but Morley was again elected.

Champion was, of course, widely and almost certainly correctly, believed to be in receipt of 'Tory Gold'. He was closely associated with Maltman Barry who, despite his earlier membership of the first International, was by 1892 the Unionist candidate for Banff and who was, in 1900, to run Thomas Burt to a surprisingly close finish in Morpeth.[15] It is significant that links with Tories were seen as so much more damning than similar links with Liberals by the majority of those who were to make up the ILP. Indeed the ousting of Champion and his supporters from the ILP after the Bradford conference sees the new party, unlike the SDF, set firmly in the Radical tradition. David Howell has argued that: 'The emergence and consolidation of the ILP as a leading vehicle for socialism marks among other things the victory of the Radical variant and the virtual demise of any attempt at "Tory Socialism".'[16] By opting for the Radical variant, British Socialism denied itself support from workers who favoured Protectionism as a safeguard against foreign competition and cut itself off from the pub, the music-hall, the race-course and from popular patriotic sentiment. The Radical variant was not likely to appeal to those Newcastle workers who voted for a populist Tory like Charlie Hamond, a 'Champagne Charlie', given to white waistcoats and the kissing of female supporters as he campaigned in the streets of the town. The gulf between what became the mainstream ILP attitudes and popular culture can be seen in Bruce Glasier's comment when Fred Hammill, ILP candidate for Newcastle in 1895, retired to a pub in Thirsk: ''Twill be hard on us if Lab Agitators descend to the level of prize fighters and footballers'.[17]

Yet, if the example of Newcastle suggests that a socialism, more independent of the Liberal Radical tradition and even set to share the winds that. popular Toryism caught, may have had some hope of establishing itself in the towns and riversides of the region, this would have been an arduous and long-term task. To commandeer labourism and divorce it from the Liberal Party was a more manageable and straightforward enterprise. This was precisely what the ILP in the North East was to attempt, but only after a changed climate in industrial relations had produced an autonomous non-socialist demand for independent labour representation did it meet with a degree of success.

The progress of the party which, immediately after the Bradford conference consisted in the region of a few branches on Tyneside and Teesside, can be measured by its performance in four overlapping areas of activity. These were its own internal organisation, its record in local government, its influence within the trades unions and its parliamentary ambitions. Each helped but could also hinder the other.

There were, in the first place, the members, forming or joining local branches as part of a national party with, at the top, the National Administrative Council, while in between the party attempted, after the first years, to place a structure of district federations and divisional councils. The membership of the ILP in the North East was not, even in the context of a very modest national membership, very high. There were never more than 2,000 members in the region[18] and only the West Country Division had fewer members. Martin Pugh has commented on what he sees as 'the disproportionate share of the attention of researchers ... [gained by] a tiny organisation like the ILP' and has compared this to the lack of attention paid to the Primrose League with its huge membership.[19] Certainly, a consideration of membership figures is sobering and, given that before 1918 the ILP was the largest socialist organisation, casts considerable doubt on claims that. socialism had embedded itself in the warp and woof of working class life and culture. As Deian Hopkin has written, it was, in the last analysis, a very small party indeed.[20]

The ILP was itself conscious of its small membership and put forward the argument that numbers were not everything and that quality could be more important. Thus the NAC in 1918 claimed that 'a large membership is not necessarily a source of strength. The strength of a party depends upon the character and enthusiasm of its individual membership ...'.[2] The party would clearly have liked more members and this argument finds virtue in necessity but it contains the truth that, though small, the membership was usually active and dedicated and was composed of those who were prepared to pay a relatively high subscription and give over much of their time to party work. The ILP in the North East had many such members.

There were in 1893 a handful of independent Labour parties in the region. We have already noted Newcastle's Championite organisation. There was a South Shields independent Labour Party which was very dependent on the enthusiasm of its President, a plasterer, C. H. Reynolds, who with his wife, a delegate of the Jarrow and District Fabians, attended the Bradford conference.[22] Boldon, Hebburn and Jarrow all had ILPs represented at the founding conference, albeit by one man, W. J. Grierson.[23] A branch was swiftly in being at Gateshead and there was from the beginning considerable activity on Teesside with branches being formed at Middlesbrough, Stockton and Darlington. The initial pattern of the ILP in the region was, thus, one of a concentration of branches on Tyneside and Teesside, with a Wearside branch at Sunderland soon following, but this was followed by tentative inroads deeper into the coalfield with Spennymoor, Chester le Street and Washington and Uswort.h active by 1900 and a strong branch at the railway and mining town of Shildon.

Progress was by no means constant. In 1895 there were eighteen branches in the North East but by 1905 the party claimed only eleven in Durham and there were only four in Northumberland. The major advance into the Durham coalfield came with the appointment of M. T. Simm as area organiser in 1905 which was followed by a mushroom growth of branches. In April 1906 the ILP Annual Report announced that: 'Our organiser, Mr M. T. Simm, has been for the greater part of the year in the North East District of England .... As a result of the attention devoted to these counties during the year, the whole area is now covered by branches of the party, and the county of Durham in particular is in the very van of the movement for Labour and Socialism.'[24] By 1909 there were 80 out of a national total of 883 branches in the region.[25]

The party had really too many branches for too few members. Five branches in the Jarrow division in 1906 was perhaps somewhat excessive and eight branches four months later even more so.[26] The party's structure gave branches with a handful of members rather too much autonomy and influence. When, as often happened, local activists had electoral ambitions that ran ahead of their finances and realistic opportunities and when their socialist enthusiasm led them to clash with local trades unionists, the NAC found it difficult to rein them in. Thus branches at Stockton, Darlington and Gateshead were perpetually unhappy with the NAC's view as to parliamentary candidatures, Middlesbrough and South Shields branches were at daggers drawn with local trades unionists and Middlesbrough went ahead with George Lansbury's unsuitable candidacy in 1906.

The party's strength, however, lay in the calibre of its membership and particularly in the fact that it appears to have been, in the region, largely a skilled working-class membership facilitating close links with the unions. The North East membership until 1914 appears to correspond with Deian Hopkin's conclusion for the country as a whole, that 'it was the skilled manual workers, the clerks and supervisory workers who were most attracted to the Labour movement ...'[27] In the county divisions most members were, unsurprisingly, miners with the addition of a few schoolteachers and, around Shildon, railway workers. Membership in the boroughs was more mixed with a greater leavening of lower-middle-class members and a smattering of older artisans such as printers and tailors.

Women were active in the party itself and, from 1904, in the Women's Labour League. They tended to be lower middle class, very often elementary schoolteachers, or to have husbands active in the party, although several prominent female members were from upper middle class backgrounds. Thus, the wealthy feminist Mrs Marion Coates Hansen virtually dominated the Middlesbrough branch and Miss Ruth Dodds from a prominent Tyneside business family was a key figure in Gateshead; Connie Lewcock was an assistant teacher in a mining village, Esh Winning, when she joined the ILP in 1912; Bella Jolley was a miner's wife and both she and her husband were active in the Stanley branch; while Mrs Edith Blacklock and her daughter, Jane, were prominent ILPers in Sunderland.[28] It would of course have been quite foreign to the mores of respectable working-class life for working-class wives or daughters to have become involved with the party without a male member of the family being also involved. Whether the feminist influence women members brought to the party did it much good in gaining votes from the male working-class electorate of the Edwardian North East may be doubted.

The commitment of the party's small membership is illustrated by the vast account of ILP literature produced. Not only did members buy, read and distribute the national ILP press as it came and went, *The Workmen's Times*, *The Labour Leader* and *ILP News*, but also the regional *Northern Democrat* and local publications such as the *Jarrow Labour Herald* and, after 1919, the *Gateshead Herald*.

It is almost impossible to disentangle the ILP's fortunes in local government from those of other socialist groups and the more substantial advance of labour representatives who could be independent trades unionists or Liberal-Labour. Stockton was quick off the mark with three ILPers elected to the borough council in the early 1890s. On Tyneside there were by the end of 1894: 'three trade union backed councillors at Newcastle, five at Gateshead, four at Jarrow, and six at South Shields. Amongst these were several who were members of the newly formed Independent Labour Party (ILP). Unlike some of the earlier socialist candidates, however, none of these ILPers had stood independently; they had all stood as nominees of trades councils'.[29] At Hebburn a trade union party took ten of the twelve seats on the Urban District Council. The phenomenon of working men on school boards, poor law boards and councils was not the advance of a monolith. Such men could not only be Lib-Labs or independent trades unionists rather than ILPers but their first loyalties might be with their Irish catholicism or their militant protestantism or go first and foremost to their trades unions or crafts. Time and again broad labour alliances broke up as did the one at Hebburn. As with the growth of ILP branches, the advance of the party in local government suffered a reverse, along with that of labour representation in general in the later 1890s only to take off again in the early twentieth century.

The 1895 General Election was, in the words of David Howell, 'the death of easy optimism' for the ILP. In the North East the only candidate the party put forward was Fred Hammill at Newcastle, although A. T. Dipper of NAUL withdrew from Jarrow at the last minute. Hammill's candidacy again highlighted the question as to whether the ILP should see itself as a party in the radical tradition, even if it went beyond Liberalism, or as a socialist party outside that tradition. The Championite legacy to the Newcastle branch made it rather more opposed to a Liberal like John Morley than to Conservatives. Tom Mann's monthly report as General Secretary to the National Administrative Council of the ILP warned the Newcastle branch, 'Let none lose sight of the only correct attitude for ILP men in Newcastle and elsewhere. We must not seek the assistance or cooperation of either Liberals or Tories.'[30] Hammill's candidacy may well have contributed to the victory of the Unionists over Morley and his running-mate J. Craig and it is significant that more votes were split between Hammill and Hamond than between Hammill, who was more in the SDF tradition than a conventional ILPer, and any other candidate. Hammill's campaign, which found him on the opposite side to Lib-Labs like Arthur Henderson and Thomas Burt, did much to discredit the ILP with North East trades unionists and was paralleled by a growing distaste for the party among trades councils which were, in the region, often Lib-Lab in sympathy.

The way forward for the party did, however, lie in gaining influence in the trades unions. What was to be far more important than a few branches on Tyneside and Teesside or the occasional success in local government elections for the party's ability to influence the emergence of an independent Labour Party, in the wake of the foundation of the LRC and the Taff Vale judgement, was the progress it made among the officials of certain leading unions. The Labour Party grew out of the unions and the ILP's role in its development in the North East was based upon its influence in the Durham and Northumberland miners' unions, the Railway Servants and the Amalgamated Society of Engineers. It is this ILP position within the unions rather than the small, if vocal, party branches that does much to explain the fact that within five years of the founding of the LRC, to which the ILP brought such slim resources and so few members, three of the six official LRC candidates at the 1906 General Election in the region were ILPers, while two other members of the party stood, but without formal LRC backing. If the formation of the LRC gave the ILP the opportunity to work within and influence a political movement with a broader support, wider appeal and far greater resources than it had by itself, it was the trade unionist records of many of its prominent men rather than their ILP membership that enabled the party to work within an LRC which had so many affiliated members deeply suspicious of socialist propagandists.

To gain influence within the mining unions was the most difficult task, yet one that promised incomparably greater rewards than any other. Influence in other unions meant increased political leverage *pro rata* with the strength and size of the union but only control of the mining unions could seem to promise, given the geographical concentration of miners, a harvest of parliamentary seats as a corollary. The main problems the ILP faced were the entrenched position of the Lib-Lab leadership, the deep cultural roots of Liberalism among the workforce, and the unpopularity of the eight-hour day, to which the ILP was committed, among North East miners. By the late 1890s there were a few ILP branches in the mining villages close to the Tyne and some lodges in the same area were centres of ILP activity. The Durham Miners' Progressive Federation, later the Durham Miners' Reform Association, had moved to a position well to the left of the union leadership. William House, an advocate of independent Labour representation, had been appointed DMA agent, while Tom Richardson, a Washington checkweighman, a county councillor and an ILPer, had been elected to the executive. As R. Gregory has noted, ILP success was not to be measured in mass conversions but by its ability to gain control of union posts and then use the machinery and resources of unions in order to further its own policies.[31] By 1900 it had made a modest but firm start in gaining influence within the DMA though it had as yet hardly a toe-hold in the Northumberland Miners' Mutual Confident Association. The coming of the LRC together with the reluctance of the Northern Liberal Association to provide more seats for miners' candidates were to provide the context for progress.

By 1900 the ILP presence in the coalfield was, in the words of David Howell, '… an irritant rather than a threat'[32] but the next decade was to see many of its industrial and political aims become union policy. This success owed much to small groups of young activists, men like Jack Lawson and the brothers Tom and W. P. Richardson in north Durham and in Northumberland R. Gilbertson, G. Warne and Ebby Edwards.[33] They were the anchormen of small ILP branches, contested County Council and other local government elections (in Durham this was done via the Labour Council formed in 1901) and captured positions in the unions.

From the formation of the LRC, Tom Richardson tried, year after year, to get a resolution passed at the Durham Miners' Council in favour of affiliation. He failed, but the dominant Lib-Lab group was under constant pressure and in 1902 a resolution in favour of the union running independent Labour candidates might well have been passed had it not been that the union's venerable patriarch and general Secretary, John Wilson, threatened to resign if it was. The same meeting, however, voted in favour of more miners' candidates and, in March 1903, it was decided to run two more: John Johnson, an agent of the DMA, and J. W. Taylor, secretary of the Colliery Mechanics.

The response of the Northern Liberal Federation to the miners' claims for more candidates was lethargic and no sitting MPs were prepared to make way for them. in 1904, however, on the death of the Liberal member for Gateshead, Johnson was accepted by the Gateshead Liberals as their candidate in the consequent by-election. The ILP and the LRC in Gateshead were anxious to run a candidate against Johnson. Tom Peacock, a railwayman and secretary of the Gateshead ILP, wrote to Ramsay MacDonald suggesting that either George Barnes or Philip Snowden be rushed up as an emergency candidate but the LRC secretary was determined to avoid an embarrassing conflict, wishing to preserve his understanding with Herbert Gladstone and hoping to eventually win the DMA's affiliation. Johnson was allowed to run and win without LRC opposition.

The other DMA candidate in search of a seat was J. W. Taylor, an ex-Liberal but now a member of the ILP. The DMA under Wilson's leadership did not press his case very hard but at the last moment a county division became available when Sir James Joicey, MP for Chester le Street and a leading Durham pit-owner, was given a peerage in the 1906 New Year Honours list. Taylor was nominated by the DMA and, according to Gregory, the miners in the constituency were almost unanimous in supporting him with votes of confidence in him passed by forty-two lodges in the division.[34] As Taylor refused to stand as a Lib-Lab, had Tom Richardson as his agent and said he was a member of the ILP who would answer to the LRC whip in parliament, the Chester-le-Street Liberals naturally ran a candidate against him. Taylor would almost certainly have been a LRC candidate had time permitted. As a candidate he wore his ILP connections lightly and his election address was a model of cautious neo-Liberalism. His election was, however, a major step forward for those seeking to detach the Durham miners from their traditional loyalties.[35]

The party's growth in the Amalgamated Society of Railway Servants was more rapid. The union was extremely successful in the North East, where it had a large membership and achieved *de facto* recognition from the North Eastern Railway in advance of recognition by other companies. The leading ASRS figure in the region was Walter Hudson, later President of the union. Hudson was a member of the ILP and he was ably supported by Tom Peacock, a railway clerk from Tyneside and also an ILPer, and by the energetic secretary of the Shildon ILP, Z. Cragg. Hudson and Peacock were largely responsible for gaining the union's commitment to parliamentary candidates, independent of the two main parties, at the AGM at Newport in 1894. The ILP made great headway within the union, partly because of industrial tensions and partly because, as Howell has noted, the union's constitution facilitated rapid inroads by a new tendency.[36] It would appear that it was the railway industry's non-commissioned officers, the junior supervisory grades, who were the most enthusiastic ILPers.[37] The transmission of socialist ideas within the union was helped from 1898 by *The Railway Review* having an ILP editor, George Wardle. The 1898 election for the General Secretaryship demonstrated,

26

however, that Liberalism was still strong among the rank and file nationally with the Lib-Lab, Richard Bell, defeating Hudson by 8,000 votes. As is well known, Bell was the union's and the LRC s successful candidate at Derby in the 1900 General Election but his links with Liberalism remained strong, despite the fact that it was an ASRS member, George Wardle, who proposed the motion at the founding LRC conference, defining the independence of its candidates.

As with the miners, one aspect of ILP policy which had considerable appeal to railwaymen was state control of their industry. ASRS members tended to be prominent in some of the most militant ILP branches in the region, Stockton, Darlington and Gateshead. Walter Hudson was, however, a more moderate ILPer. His selection as LRC candidate for Newcastle in 1903 was something of a coup for the party as the Newcastle Trades Council was strongly anti-socialist and at loggerheads with the ILP, which in Newcastle was on good terms with the SDF and cooperated with SDF branches in the Newcastle Socialist Institute. He was the ideal candidate for the uneasy alliance that was the Newcastle LRC; acceptable to the trades unionists because of his ASRS record as well as to the local ILP.[38]

The third union of importance in the region where the ILP achieved significant influence was the ASE. As early as 1891 the Newcastle and Sunderland branches had given Tom Mann large majorities in his unsuccessful bid for the General Secretaryship while Fred Hammill's parliamentary candidacy in 1895 has already been noted. The election of George Barnes as General Secretary brought an ILPer, albeit a very moderate one, to the head of the union. The ASE joined the LRC in 1901 and the socialist background of many of its leading figures seemed to promise that it would influence the new party in a leftwards direction. Two ASE members were to be LRC candidates in 1906, Isaac Mitchell at Darlington and Frank Rose at Stockton. Both these Teesside seats had active and militant ILP branches[39] which were determined to secure LRC and preferably socialist candidates for their constituencies. Isaac Mitchell turned out to be something of a disappointment to the Darlington ILP. He had been a leftish socialist, a De Leonist while in America, but exhibited, what was almost a characteristic of ASE socialists, a tendency to move to the right. Of all LRC candidates in the North East, he was the most determined to work closely with the Liberals. Rose, although he was too much of an individualist to belong to any specific socialist group, was a socialist and entirely acceptable to the Stockton ILP though not to local Liberals.

There was, however, one group of unions in an industry central to the heavy industrial economy of the North East that gave only half-hearted support to independent Labour representation and was also generally impervious to ILP permeation. A feature of the early development of the Labour Party in the region was the lukewarm support given by the shipbuilding unions. Although these unions joined the LRC, their leaders were Lib-Lab, as with the Boilermakers' leader Robert Knight, or Lib-Lab in spirit like Alexander Wilkie, the General Secretary of the Shipwrights. A considerable proportion of the rank and file were Tories, which does much to explain the consistently high Unionist vote in Sunderland and the remarkable strength of Unionism in Jarrow, demonstrated when a Unionist candidate first contested the seat in 1907.

In the 1900 General Election there was only one LRC candidate in the region, Alexander Wilkie, who stood in the two member constituency of Sunderland in close harmony with the Liberal candidate in a contest won by the Unionists. It was because of the shipbuilding workers' lack of interest in even moderately independent Labour representation, their inter-trade rivalries and the fact that, however influential, they did not dominate whole constituencies in the way that miners did, that the one constituency where the ILP placed an ILP sponsored candidates for the 1906 General Election was Sunderland and that the Jarrow candidacy went to the representative of a general labour union, the Gasworkers and General Labourers, who was a leading ILPer. It seems unlikely that, had the shipbuilder' leaders been consistently determined to pace candidates who were both clearly independent of Liberalism and anti-socialist, they would not have succeeded but their vacillation and reluctance to break with Liberalism gave the ILP its opportunity.

The adoption of Pete Curran as LRC candidate for Jarrow demonstrates how numerically small but determined socialist groups and sympathetic union lodges, aided by the ILP's disproportionate influence on the National Executive of the LRC, could have their way in the adoption of a candidate against the wishes of powerful unions, if the latter were tardy and unsure in pressing their case.

As we have seen, there had been some socialist organisation on South Tyneside from the time of the ILP's foundation and in 1900 the Jarrow Labour League was formed. It was intended to bring together all bodies in the division affiliated to the LRC but the organisations which joined demonstrate where its strength lay. They were: the Wardley Miners, Hebburn Miners, Felling Miners, Jarrow Tailors, Felling ILP and Jarrow Socialist Society. It seems clear that the League, led by its Secretary Tom Gibb of the Jarrow Tailors, was determined to adopt an ILP candidate (Gibb's preference was '... first Glasier, second Pete Curran') and by not very legitimate means managed to get Pete Curran, Secretary of the Gasworkers' and General Labourers' Union and a prominent ILPer, selected by the unanimous decision of a meeting called in April 1902. The Shipwrights woke up to the fact that they'd been hoodwinked and, claiming that the meeting which chose Curran was unconstitutional, urged the candidacy of Alexander Wilkie upon the LRC. This was a major embarrassment for the LRC executive not least because both Curran and Wilkie were members of it and the issue revealed fissures that ran from Jarrow to the top of the movement.

The NEC of the LRC sent three members, Frederick Rogers, James Parker and Richard Bell, to enquire into the situation in Jarrow. There could be little doubt that the bulk of Jarrow trades union leaders supported Wilkie but the delegation split and sent in two opposing reports, Bell and Rogers supporting Wilkie, and Parker, Curran. The NEC legitimised Curran's adoption by seven votes to four, the voting being on predictable political lines.

The dispute reveals the division within the LRC between those deeply suspicious of socialism and wishing to cooperate closely with the Liberal Party and those, mainly ILPers, pressing for a socialist and independent political party. These differences existed both on the executive and at the grass roots. In Jarrow the representatives of the skilled workers in the shipbuilding industry had not shifted far from their traditional Liberalism or Liberal-Labourism but had been outmanoeuvred by the socialist groups.[40]

The adoption of Thomas Summerbell as ILP-sponsored candidate for Sunderland was a less contentious business. At first sight it seems surprising that the LRC should have chosen an ILPer to run in a double member constituency where Liberal LRC cooperation was so good and much of the explanation has to do with the personality and record of Summerbell. He owned a printing business in the town, was a Sunderland councillor and had moved across the political spectrum from Conservatism, through Liberalism to the ILP, but he was a pretty moderate ILPer who had worked for Wilkie in 1900 and was on good terms with and entirely acceptable to local Liberals. The Sunderland Trades Council was not, as in most towns in the North East at daggers drawn with the ILP, more because of the moderation of the ILP under Summerbell's direction than to any leftward-leaning on the part of the Trades Council. Despite opposition from the Shipwrights, Summerbell was selected in April 1903 after a series of conferences organised by the Trades Council and Sunderland LRC, from a shortlist which included Isaac Mitchell of the ASE, Arthur Henderson of the Ironfounders, James Conley of the Boilermakers and Alexander Wilkie. Summerbell was, in fact, not originally an ILP candidate but was sponsored by the Trades Council, only being transferred to the ILP list in December 1904. His relations with Sunderland Liberal Party remained cordial.

Sunderland was the only constituency in the North East where the LRC put forward an ILP-sponsored candidate before 1914, though Curran owed his selection for Jarrow more to the ILP than to his union. Oddly enough, the Sunderland branch was not considered a very strong one and the *Northern Democrat* commented in 1907 that as regards Sunderland, 'Well, conditions here do not reflect the rapid growth of the ILP in the North ...'[41]

It would be a mistake to see the NAC as hungry for seats in which to run ILP-sponsored candidates in the North East or anywhere else. It was quite prepared to turn down a branch that desired to run a candidate as it did when North Shields wanted to adopt James Sexton in 1903. The national leadership with its strong representation on the NEC of the LRC had as its priority the election of LRC MPs; second came the desirability of candidates being ILPers; and only third the need for some to be sponsored by the party. It did not have the money to sponsor many candidates and was conscious of the need not to estrange the trades unions by bickering with them in the constituencies or by running the sort of strident and uncompromising candidates that ILP branches often wanted. Arthur Henderson's victory at the Barnard Castle bye-election[42] had strengthened the hand of those trades unionists who wanted to work closely with the Liberals and the ILP would disturb the MacDonald-Gladstone understanding at its peril.

The trouble was that the ILP was running policy from the top with a party with a constitutional structure that gave a great deal of autonomy to the bottom. The party had great difficulty in creating a coherent organisational structure with intermediate bodies between branches and the NAC. From the beginning the regional or divisional structure worked imperfectly: branches tended to communicate directly to the NAC and the development of councils meant. that sub-divisional areas often ignored the divisions. Branches were sometimes unrealistic, both politically and financially, threatening to lead the party into contests it couldn't win and couldn't pay for. The logic of power pointed to a progressive alliance the socialist logic of many local activists to more adventurous policies and even to alliances with socialists outside the Labour Party.

George Lansbury's foray into Middlesbrough as a Socialist candidate at the 1906 General Election provides an example of a numerically small local ILP pressing an unwise candidacy against the advice of LRC candidates in the region, the NRC of the LRC and the ILP's NAC. The sitting MP was a Unionist but the Liberal-Labour candidate, Havelock Wilson, had the support of the Middlesbrough Trades Council. Urged on by the middle-class feminist Mrs Marion Coates Hansen, the ILP branches persuaded Lansbury, a new recruit to the ILP from the SDF, to leave his accustomed London habitat and contest Middlesbrough. The NAC twice advised the Middlesbrough branch to gain the Trades Council's support, which was most unlikely to be forthcoming as it backed Havelock Wilson, before it would give its approval.[43] The Middlesbrough ILP went its own way and, after some prodding from the LRC, the NAC refused to adopt Lansbury as an ILP candidate. It is noteworthy that the strongest of the two Middlesbrough ILP branches that promoted this ill-fated venture had forty-five members. Lansbury got 1,380 votes. It was not his most successful political venture.[44]

The years 1905–1909 were, however, the high water-mark of ILP achievement in the region. The party could claim a significant share of the credit for the LRC's progress and its good performance in the 1906 General Election when, if we include Taylor's victory at Chester-le-Street, it won four seats. It is true that the major reason for LRC success was the electoral understanding with the Liberals but the ILP had provided four candidates and three victors while it had both managed to work within the LRC and stiffen it against relapsing into Liberal-Labourism. At the same time the party had introduced a paid organiser, Matt Simm, into the region whose work was already bearing fruit by late 1905 in the shape of new branches and members especially in the coalfield.

In 1907 the death of Sir Charles Mark Palmer caused a by-election at Jarrow. Unlike the 1906 election this was not a straight fight between Liberal and Labour for the Unionists contested the seat for the first time and the Irish catholics in the constituency, discontented with the government's handling of the Home Rule issue, adopted an Irish Nationalist candidate, J. O'Hanlon, a Jarrow shipbuilding worker.

The election was won by Curran with a majority of 768 votes over his Unionist opponent and was seen by contemporaries as having a more than local significance. Along with Victor Grayson's victory at Colne Valley in the same year, the result was erroneously greeted by socialists as the sign of a dawning socialist electoral popularity. Many in the ILP, dissatisfied with the Labour Party's parliamentary record, began to press for either a more socialist stance from the Labour Party or a secession by the ILP from that body.

In fact an analysis of the voting shows that Curran's share of the vote was actually down as compared to 1906 by five percent and that his win was the result of the division of those forces which had supported Palmer in the previous election. In any case Curran had not campaigned on a socialist platform but, as in 1906, had played down his socialism and emphasised his trade union credentials, not even mentioning socialism in his election address.[46]

On the death of the Liberal member for Newcastle in 1908 another by-election was held. The Newcastle Trades Council and the local LRC were in favour of contesting the election and favoured J. J. Stephenson of the ASE as candidate. Fearing the consequences of a breakdown of the electoral understanding in double member constituencies, the NEC of the Labour Party passed a resolution declaring it not to be in the interests of the Labour movement to contest the seat.[47] In the absence of a Labour candidate and impressed by the success of Grayson and Curran, the Newcastle socialists were determined to find a candidate. E. R. Hartley of the SDF and the ILP stood, backed by the Newcastle Socialist Institute, the SDF and many of the local ILP. Hartley's 2,971 votes give us a measure of the strength of hardcore socialism in Newcastle which was much as it had been thirteen years earlier when Hammill had stood. It puts in context the wisdom of the ILP leadership in working within an alliance with the unions and thus getting a candidate like Walter Hudson elected as a Labour candidate in tacit agreement with the Liberals. Hartley's vote was big enough however to do much towards letting the Unionist candidate win, just as Hammill's intervention in 1895 had done.

In 1907, the DMA and the NMMCA voted to affiliate with the Miners' Federation of Great Britain, the case for keeping out of the MFGB having been weakened by the Liberal government's decision to bring in an Eight Hours Bill. In 1908, however, the MFGB voted to affiliate to the Labour Party and this meant that the North-East miners had also to affiliate and that their MPs had to cease to be Liberal-Labour MPs and sign the Labour Party constitution. This was no problem for J. Taylor, while J. Johnson, who was initially opposed to joining, eventually agreed to do so, but Burt, Fenwick and Wilson refused to disavow the political beliefs of a lifetime and declined to sign the constitution.

The ILP's role in winning over the mining unions to the Labour Party had been considerable and that these major unions in the region were now part of the Labour Party strengthened the position of both that party and the ILP. This achievement must, however, be qualified: any expectation that the membership of the unions would simply fall in line with the leadership's change of political allegiance was to be confounded and Liberalism among North-east miners was to die hard; while the growth of ILP influence among hitherto Liberal and labourist unions was bought at the price of a dilution of socialist purity. The ILP miners represented a variety of political views from militant socialism to a reinterpretation of the previous Radical and Nonconformist. tradition, which sought to find in ethical socialism a development from Liberalism. As one convert to Socialism, William Straker, the Secretary of the NMMCA, put it: 'Speaking for myself, my socialism is the outgrowth of my religion. My religion is that of the humble Nazarene who stood for the Fatherhood of God and the brotherhood of man.' He went on to describe how 'Liberalism sprang from Whigism ... Radicalism sprang from Liberalism ... and now ... from Radicalism springs Socialism'.[48]

The year 1909 marked the high point of ILP success, as indeed it marked the peak of Labour success before 1918. The general elections of 1910 were to provide a considerable setback. Labour went into the January election with eight candidates and six MPs, Johnson at Gateshead now being Labour, and emerged with three MPs. Two ILPers were defeated: Curran at Jarrow, where Godfrey Palmer, Sir Charles's younger son, regained the seat by a narrow margin, and Summerbell at Sunderland, where both he and the Liberal lost their seats to a Unionist and an Independent Tariff Reformer. However important it was for the future, the recruitment of the mining unions to Labour paid no immediate electoral dividend. The unpopularity of the eight-hour day and the continuing Liberalism of rank-and-file miners helped to put House at the bottom of the poll in Bishop Auckland and ensured Johnson's defeat at Gateshead, where miners marched through the town on election day with banners carrying the slogan, 'Down with Johnson and the Eight-Hour Day'.[49]

As far as ILP-sponsored candidates were concerned, the NAC was, like the Labour Party, in a cautious mood after the setbacks of January 1910. A Labour Party delegation reported to the NAC in April that its opinion was that, 'apart from the seats now held very few candidatures ought to be undertaken at the next election.' The ILP might have been seen to have some right to provide the candidate for Sunderland, where Summerbell's death, shortly after the January election, had left the candidature vacant but the Teacher's Union Secretary, Frank Goldstone, was selected by the Trades and Labour Council and his election was Labour's solitary gain in December 1910. The more active of the region's eight or so ILP branches were keen to run an ILP candidate. A meeting of the North East Federation attended by delegates from forty branches was asked to vote on the two constituencies to be contested and Jarrow was unanimously chosen with NW Durham as the next most popular choice.[50] In the event A. G. Cameron of the Carpenters and

Joiners' Union was adopted against the claims of the ILP which pressed such candidates as M. Timm, Tom Peacock and Tom Richardson. There was, thus, no ILP sponsored candidate in the North East in December 1910.

The rewards for Labour and the ILP for winning over the miners' unions to the Labour Party were slow in coming. By 1918 the affiliation of the mining unions had not secured the Labour Party a single extra seat. Two by-elections showed the rank-and-file miners in the heart of the coalfield to be still largely Liberal. In 1913 Alderman House was beaten into third place at Houghton le Spring, a constituency where the majority of voters were miners, and in 1914 G. H. Stuart of the Postmen's Union was, although backed by the DMA, similarly in third place in NW Durham.[51]

By 1914 the ILP had made little obvious progress from its position in 1909 though much had been achieved when set against the circumstances of 1900. Some of its problems were caused by relative success. The party had done much to win the mining unions to the Labour Party and had done so by preaching a brand of ethical socialism which built upon the older radical tradition; this success made such ethical socialism the new 'common sense' of the union leadership; the ILP had permeated a sectionalist labourism but its impact as a separate force for a socialist society was thereby diluted. Equally, whereas before 1910 the ILP had been the sole independent Labour organisation in the Teesside towns and in South Shields faced by Liberal-Labour Trades Councils its very success in helping win a broader base for the Labour Party meant that it was, thereafter, just a part of a much more right-wing Labour movement.

Neither in ideology nor in administrative structure was the ILP the perfect vehicle for the pragmatic parliamentarianist strategy pursued by the national leadership and, with the tacit Progressive alliance in government after 1910, the strains began to tell. Activists, especially in the branches in the riverside towns, became discontented, felt the atavistic urge towards alliance with socialist groups outside the Labour Party or the attractions of the BSP or of Syndicalism. The Middlesbrough ILP complained that Labour MPs 'were supporting the Liberals in Parliament continually, even to the detriment of Labour's interests'. Yet the majority of ILP members were too conscious of their achievements to wish to leave the Labour Party and were determined to convert it from within.

The party's electoral ambitions at the beginning of the Great War were, so far as sponsoring candidates of its own in the region was concerned, modest and continued to be so through to 1918. It had decided to fight Bishop Auckland with local candidate, Ben Spoor, even though the choice of a non-miner for the constituency was risky. Despite the perennial ambitions of the enthusiasts of Darlington and Stockton to run candidates (this time NAC member, Russell Williams, and journalist and political agent, Egerton Wake, respectively) and periodic calls for a candidate for Jarrow, the position remained the same in 1918 and Spoor was the only ILP-sponsored candidate in the North East at the general election.

As elsewhere the impact of the war cut both ways upon the ILP's fortunes. It brought into the party a substantial number of neo-pacifist radicals from the Liberal ranks, including the Northumberland squire, C. P. Trevelyan, but drove a wedge between the party and mainstream trades unionism. The great strength of the ILP had been that, though it contained a middle-class element of journalists, teachers and feminists, it had been a largely working-class organisation, influential in the leading trades unions. The war-time years distanced the party from the unions, even while its membership increased, and this at a time when the industrial side of the Labour movement made an impressive advance. As Duncan Tanner has put it: 'Local Labour parties increasingly came under the influence of expanding trades unions with an enhanced interest in the Labour Party. They encouraged wholehearted support for the war (pushing Socialists out in the process if necessary), and reinforced Labour's *social* roots.'[52]

The ILP's influence in major unions had, paradoxically, been strongest when there were only lukewarmly committed to the Labour Party and still had to contend with the many Liberals in their midst. Once unions became more dedicated to an active role within the Labour Party and threw their financial weight behind it, ILP influence diminished. ILPers within unions were required to put the unions' economic and political policies first, while the gap grew between ILP-sponsored MPs and MPs who were members of the ILP but were sponsored by unions. The ILP sponsored fifty candidates nationally in 1918, four times as many as in 1910 but the trades unions sponsored about 160 candidates and half of them came from the miners, the ASE and the railway unions, the three in which the ILP had been so influential.

The adoption by the Labour Party of its new constitution early in 1918 was a watershed for the ILP. The constitution altered the federal character of the Labour Party and opened its door in all constituencies directly to individual sympathisers who, previously, would have had to join through a socialist society, usually the ILP. Throughout the country the ILP now had to face competition from local Labour Parties.

There was a logical case for the ILP dissolving itself or for becoming a pressure group or think-tank rather than a party within a party. The new constitution committed Labour to socialist aspirations and a dual party structure could only be confusing, as was the distinction between ILP-sponsored MPs and those who simply happened to be *inter alia* members of the party. In practice as the ILP moved leftwards during the 1920s this distinction became more important and MPs who were ILP members tended to back the Parliamentary Labour Party in its disputes with the ILP group. It is noteworthy that, once constituency Labour Parties and women's sections of the Labour Party became available to women, they, rather than the ILP, became the focus of female activities and loyalties. Women like Margaret Gibb and Bella Jolley, and, at the parliamentary level, both Margaret Bondfield, MP for Wallsend 1926–31, and Ellen Wilkinson, MP for Middlesbrough East 1924–31, were by the mid-'twenties critics of the ILP.

Yet, despite the basic weaknesses in the party's position, the decision to soldier on as a separate party seemed until 1924 to be justified. Political parties do not easily wind themselves up and there was a strong feeling that Labour alone was not to be trusted with socialism. During the period of Clifford Allen's leadership,the party was to appear more successful than ever before in terms of membership and elected representatives. Division 2 (Northumberland, Durham, Cleveland and Cumberland) saw its membership go up from just over 1,000 in 1923 to more than 2,000 in 1924 and it went on rising until 1926 when, with 2,330, it had a higher membership than South Wales. After the General Strike , the membership fell back to 1,440 and at the beginning of 1929 it stood at 1,200. The party nationally claimed over 5,000 local councillors out of over 10,000 Labour councillors after the municipal elections of 1924 and certainly, in the North East as elsewhere, it put a great effort into local government elections, though it is impossible to disentangle Labour from ILP and Labour councillors in the region. Out of the forty-five ILP candidates returned in the country in December 1923, there was a formidable detachment from the North East which included B. C. Spoor, C. P. Trevelyan, the Reverend Herbert Dunnico and John Beckett, while there were many ILP members among the other North Eastern Labour MPs such as Ellen Wilkinson, Margaret Bondfield, Robert Smillie, W. Whitely and J. J. Lawson. R. E. Dowse's conclusion that 1922–24 marked the 'Indian Summer' of the ILP is, however, born out by North East developments[53] as is Arthur Marwick's comment on the effects of Labour's great advance in December 1923 that, in making this great jump forward, 'Labour ... dislocated the neck of the ILP'.[54] The disguised weaknesses of its position in the North East were to interact with national developments to bring about this dislocation.

A major problem for the party lay in its relationship with the DMA. The dimensions of the problem can be discerned from the results of the first post-war general election when the only seats that Labour won in the North East were in largely mining constituencies, four in Durham (Bishop Auckland, Houghton-le-Spring, Barnard Castle and Chester-le-Street) and Morpeth in Northumberland. Labour failed to win any of the Newcastle, Middlesbrough or Sunderland seats[55] and generally lost ground in the industrial and seaport towns while it advanced in the coalfield. These results point towards the pattern of inter-war elections in the region. In good years Labour would pick up seats in the towns but its reliable base was in the coalfield as had been that of the Liberal Party some twenty years earlier. This had serious implications for the ILP, despite the fact that one of the MPs elected, B. C. Spoor at Bishop Auckland, was ILP sponsored and two others, J. W. Taylor (Chester-le Street) and R. Richardson (Houghton-le-Spring) were ILP members.

Winning its first county council majority in 1919, Labour was on course to become the political establishment of County Durham but Labour and the DMA had become largely synonymous. The DMA-controlled Labour Party was in time to consolidate its position as the source of power and influence in the county, making full use of the patronage at its disposal. The long-term result for the ILP, which had done much to bring this about, was that it gradually became a dissident minority of more left-wing miners and schoolteachers.

The old Lib-Lab leadership of the North East miners had been such unreconstructed Liberals that, in contrast to Yorkshire, the opposition to them had only had to move marginally leftwards to outflank them. The Durham miners had found in the Labour Party a more fitting vehicle than the Liberal Party for their developed trade union consciousness but as Robert Moore has pointed out; 'This does not necessarily represent a marked difference from the days of Liberal domination: under both Liberal and Labour leadership trade union and political activities were bargaining activities conducted according to the rules of the market'.[56] Many ILPers were to find that the Lib-Lab officials and councillors of their youth had become the Labour union establishment, the aldermen and even MPs of their later years and that such men sat easily alongside ex-ILPers who were now simply Labour.

W. R. Garside found it possible to write a long and detailed history of the DMA from 1919 to 1960 and only mention the ILP on one page.[57] This did little justice to the formative role of the ILP in winning the miners to Labour and to aspects of socialism, most notably state ownership of the mining industry. Garside also ignored the post-war ILP influence in Bishop Auckland, Seaham and Consett, and the ILP's dissenting voice elsewhere for, in the short term, the ILP was able to resist the hegemony of the DMA's establishment in certain areas. We can discern in Seaham and Consett, as at Bishop Auckland, a strong ILP presence based both on ILP branches and some union lodges. The ILP had, in these constituencies, put down roots which were cultural as well as political. and represented some success for the policy of making socialists. The ILP and the Workers' Educational Association had together succeeded with groups of local activists in creating a culture of self improvement and a desire for horizons wider than those of the DMA leadership.

In 1918 one of the three gains that the ILP made in the whole country was at Bishop Auckland[58] which was largely a mining constituency though with a substantial number of railwaymen at Shildon, Ben Spoor had worked for the YMCA in Salonika during the war and he was invalided home after the Armistice. His victory was, according to Arthur Marwick, 'totally unexpected at Head Office because of the poor state of ILP organisation in the constituency. Spoor owed his triumph above all to his reputation as a lay preacher, and to his work as a local councillor.'[59] When in 1919 Jack Lawson, an ILP member who had contested Seaham as the DMA's and Labour Party's candidate in 1918, gave up the Seaham candidature in order to take on Chester le Street after J. W. Taylor's death, the new divisional branch demanded a national figure as their candidate. As Maureen Callcott has written: 'Interestingly, and arguably indicating the extent of the political education and awareness of the "bookish" miners [a phrase of Beatrice Webb], the national figure chosen was Sidney Webb ...'[60] Webb won three elections at Seaham before retiring to allow

Ramsay MacDonald a safe seat in 1929. That MacDonald was able to hold Seaham in the circumstances of 1931 suggests that ILP influence did not extend, by then at any rate, beyond political activists.

Consett was the nucleus of the old NW Durham division where the ILP had been strong before 1914 and continued to be active in the twenties, 'organising regular political, social and educational functions'.[61] Here the party had long wished to sponsor an ILP candidate and in 1922, against DMA opposition, the divisional Labour Party which was full of ILPers and had ILP schoolteacher Tom Fuge as secretary, adopted the Reverend Herbert Dunnico with the support of many miners.[62] During the 1931 crisis Dunnico left the ILP and, after losing Consett in the election, joined MacDonald in the National Labour Party.

In Northumberland there were really only two solidly mining seats, Wansbeck and Morpeth, but the ILP gained considerable influence in both of them. They were guarded for Liberalism until the war by the formidable combination of Fenwick and Burt but in 1918 J. Cairns took Morpeth for Labour, although a Coalition Liberal held on to Wansbeck, defeating the redoubtable Ebby Edwards. Cairns was an ex-Liberal who had followed, rather than led, his union towards Labour and there is an irony in the fact that, while he was standing for Labour at Morpeth, the man who had done so much to spread the ILP message in Northumberland, Matt Simm, was standing as a Coalition National Democratic Party candidate in nearby Wallsend.

On Cairns' death in 1923, he was succeeded by one of the few trades union leaders of the inter-war period to belong to the ILP, the Scottish miner's leader and ex-President of the MFGB, Robert Smillie. He in turn was followed by Ebby Edwards, MP for Morpeth 1929–31. George Warne who won Wansbeck in 1922 was a member of the ILP but basically a solid union and Labour Party man who drifted away from the ILP after becoming a Junior Lord of the Treasury and then a party whip in 1924. His successor, George Shield, was a similar stout member of the burgeoning union and Labour Party establishment. But the ILP was never as effectively squashed in Northumberland as in Durham and continued to be a force especially in Ashington. In Jack Lees, who was MP for Belper in Derbyshire 1929–31, the NMMCA produced one of the intransigents who led the ILP towards disaffiliation. The ILP maintained, however, a strong influence in only a minority of seats in the coalfield after 1918, its fortunes in the region's industrial towns and ports were mixed. Save for the exceptional year of 1931, the coalfield had become the stronghold of the Labour Party and the mining unions but the towns were by no means solidly Labour; only in 1929 did Labour win a majority of the twelve borough seats on Tyneside, Teesside and Wearside, in which year it also won the urbanised county divisions of Wallsend and Jarrow.

The ILP was a strong force in many of these seats but, after 1918, it not only faced opposition from trades unions and trades councils but from Irish catholics. As Irish catholics transferred their allegiance from the Liberal to the

Labour Party, they increasingly gave North East Labour politics, in Sunderland , Jarrow, Gateshead, Middlesbrough and Wallsend in particular, a green rather than a red tinge. When Jeremiah McVeagh, an ex-Irish Nationalist MP, contested Sunderland for Labour in 1924 it was widely held that he had maximised the important local catholic vote. Irish catholic influence was, in general, deeply hostile to the ILP.

Sunderland is an example of a constituency where internecine warfare characterised the local Labour Party and there was open friction between the ILP and other groups with an ILP list of candidates being drawn up for almost every internal election. Archie Potts has concluded that: 'The Sunderland Party lost some active members when the ILP disaffiliated from the Labour Party in 1932, but on balance it probably benefited by the removal of what had been a major source of disruption throughout the 1920s.' [63]

The ILP was more dynamic and effective in Gateshead than anywhere else in the region. Although the constituency was marginal and was won by Labour in only three of the inter-war general elections, the ILP succeeded in making a contribution, not only to Labour politics but to the cultural life of the town. Rather as earlier in Middlesbrough with Marion Coates Hansen, the party owed much to a well-to-do woman, Ruth Dodds, who gave a loan which enabled it to purchase its meeting place,Westfield Hall, edited the local Labour paper *The Gateshead Herald*, and was leading light in the drama group, 'The Progressive Players'. [64] Maureen Callcott describes the Gateshead ILP as a very dedicated, socially mixed group of people who established an exceptionally thriving organisation which lasted through the 1920s and provided the driving force of Labour Party strength in Gateshead. [65] Fred Tait, a Gateshead schoolmaster, was prominent in the ILP and was divisional representative on the NAC in 1932 when he argued strongly in favour of disaffiliation from the Labour party, rather against majority feeling in the division, which was no doubt why he was replaced by Tom Stephenson, a miners' agent. The ILP seems to have been often but not always in control of the Gateshead Labour Party, securing the election of John Beckett in 1924, but seeing the more moderate Sir J. B. Melville and then Major H. Evans succeed him while Ernest Bevin was the unsuccessful Labour candidate in 1931. [66]

The ILP was never very strong in Newcastle and nor was the Labour Party very successful there between the wars. [67] Newcastle Central returned Sir Charles Trevelyan in four successive elections but he was somewhat *sui generis*. Initially an ILP MP, he transferred his candidacy to the constituency Labour Party in 1926 though he remained in the ILP. If the cultural activities of the Gateshead ILP represent one aspect of the party's attempt to go beyond the material in politics and create a socialist art and leisure, Sir Charles at his country seat at Wallington patronised another, more fey cultural strand popular in some ILP circles. Folk dancing and music on the lawn created a sort of arts and craft version of a teetotal and herbivorous Merrie England.

With exceptions such as Gateshead and Darlington, where the ILP maintained its pre-war strength within the Labour Party and had in

A. L. Shepherd (1926–31) a strong ILPer, the party saw an erosion of support after 1921 as Labour activists and MPs had increasingly to choose between loyalty to the Labour Party or to an ever more dissident ILP. The North East party members were, nevertheless, rather moderate or realistic in ILP terms and, although some like Tait and Beckett championed disaffiliation from the Labour Party, most were only too well aware that this move would lead to the political margins.

After 1932, the party was simply one of the leftist factions of British political life, further removed from the trades unions than was the Communist Party and without influence upon the Labour party, even as that party moved to the left in the reaction to the 1931 debacle. The departure of more practical members to the Socialist League hastened this development. Withered and attenuated, it was nevertheless to die hard and to have an attraction for socialists who despaired of the Labour Party but could not stomach the discipline and intellectual somersaults required by Communist Party membership. It remained intellectually creative, found its moments in support for particular causes such as that of Republican Spain and left opposition within the Republican ranks, while during World War II it provided, along with the Commonwealth Party, a focus of opposition to wartime political consensus. John McNair, who was active in the ILP from the heady days of Pete Curran's victory at the Jarrow by-election of 1907 to the time he retired as general secretary of the national ILP in 1965, had a career devoted to the party which almost spans its history. As late as the immediate post-war period some of the North East branches remained active. In Ashington meetings were well attended and lively. Under McNair's leadership the party was a tolerant home for diverse elements of the left and one where intellectual debate was seen as integral to socialism rather than an obstacle to its fulfilment.[68] It was not, however, a political party of any stature.

To many left-wing historians the ILP was a failure,[69] while to Liberals and Social Democrats it was only too successful in helping to fracture the progressive Alliance of the early twentieth century.[70] In the North East the party played a major part in the development of a Labour Party separate from Liberalism and mildly socialist in its aspirations. It has been described as preaching, 'a sentimental socialism often interlaced with christianity',[71] but any political theory that is without sentiment is an arid creed and the ethical socialism and disavowal of class warfare that distinguished it in its period of success enabled it to build upon the Nonconformist and Radical Liberal traditions of the North East.

Notes

1.   H. Pelling, *Origins of the Labour Party* (1965), p.118.
2.   I define the North East as Northumberland and Durham plus Middlesbrough.
3.   Martin Pugh in *The Tories and the People 1880–1935* (1985) has shown how string

the Primrose League was in many North East towns.

4. The small town of Blyth some ten miles along the coast from the mouth of the Tyne was surrounded by pits and had been developed to export coal but it was quite sharply divided between seafaring and mining elements. It was by no means entirely Liberal in its political sympathies. As one old lady told the author in the early 'seventies: 'They're all pit howkies up there and church and Primrose League round here'. As early as 1886 it had its Primrose League habitation with a membership that expanded from 377 to 1,100 over the next seventeen years (see Pugh, *op. cit.*, p.244).

5. In only one of the borough constituencies, Gateshead, did the proportion of female servants fall below ten in a hundred households in 1901. H. Pelling, *Social Geography of British Elections 1885–1910* (1967), p.324.

6. A rare instance of a unionist victory in a mining seat and it was not repeated in Houghton-le-Spring until 1931.

7. A. W. Purdue, 'George Lansbury and the Middlesbrough Election of 1908', *International Review of Social History*, XVIII, 1973.

8. D. Howell, *British Workers and the Independent Labour Party 1888–1906* (1983), chapter 17.

9. *Newcastle Courant*, 15 April, 1887. Quoted in Martin Searles, 'The origins of New Unionism on Tyneside', *North East Labour History Bulletin*, 25, 1991.

10. E. P. Thompson, *William Morris. Romantic to Revolutionary* (1976), pp.440–5.

11. Pelling, *op. cit.*, p.54.

12. Searles, *op. cit.*

13. Pugh, *op. cit.*, pp.127–8. The 100 members of the Elswick habitation in 1891 had grown to 1,500 by 1894 and to 3,400 by 1905.

14. Hardie was, at first, reluctant to back the Conservatives against Morley but a leader in the *Workman's Times* by Joseph Burgess, which accused him of trying to dictate to the movement by ignoring the wishes of the Newcastle ILP, persuaded him. See F. Reid, *Keir Hardie* (1978), p.137.

15. Thomas Burt (Lab) 3,171; Maltman Barry (C) 2,707.

16. D. Howell, *op. cit.*, p.373.

17. *Ibid.*, p.358.

18. Exact figures are difficult to determine because one has to decide whether to include members who had not paid their fees and because after 1918 the North East became part of a larger northern division which included Cumberland.

19. Pugh, *op. cit.*, p.2.

20. Deian Hopkin, 'The Membership of the Independent Labour Party, 1904–10: a spatial and occupational analysis', *International Review of Social History*, 1975.

21. *ILP Report*, 1918.

22. David Clark, 'South Shields Labour Party', in M. Calcott and R. Challinor (eds.), *Working Class Politics in North East England* (1983), p.98.

23. He may, according to Howell, *op. cit.*, p.486, have been called Grievson.

24. *ILP Annual Report 1906*, NAC Papers, British Library of Political and Economic Science.

25. NAC Minutes, 13, 14 and 15 Oct 1908. M 890/1/5.

26. *Jarrow Labour Herald*, 4 May 1906 and 7 Sept 1906.

27. Hopkin, *op. cit.*, p.195.

28. Maureen Callcott has published a number of articles on Labour women in the North East upon which much of the above is based. See: 'Labour Women in

North East England', *North East Labour History*, 17, 1983, and an obituary 'Connie the Rebel: Connie Lewcock (1894–1980)', *North East Labour History*, 18, 1981.

29.　Ian Hunter, 'Labour in Local Government on Tyneside' in M. Calcott and R. Challinor (eds.), *op. cit.*, p.26

30.　Monthly report, June 1884, ILP, NAC Papers, British Library of Political and Economic Science, M890/1/1. (1968).

31.　R. Gregory, *The Miners in British Politics 1906–14* (1968).

32.　*Ibid.*, p.46.

33.　Howell, *op. cit.*, p.51 refers to Edwards as 'the Northumbrian equivalent of W. P. Richardson', but Edwards was no conventional ILPer. He joined the ILP in 1906 but was expelled three years later for being too close to the SDF and selling copies of *Justice*. See R. Page Arnot, *The Miners in Crisis and War* (1961), p.83.

34.　Gregory, *op. cit.*

35.　J. W. Taylor (Lab) 8,085; S. D. Shafto (Con) 4,895; A. B. Tebb (L) 4,606.

36.　Howell, *op. cit.*, p.73.

37.　I am indebted to my post-graduate student Mr F. Lawson for this and other information about the ILP and the ASRS.

38.　1906 Election: W. Hudson (Lab) 18,869; P. Cairns (L) 18,243; Sir W. R. Plummer (Con) 11,942; G. Renwick (Con) 11,223.

39.　In 1894 the Darlington ILP put forward a resolution favouring the change of the party's name to Socialist Party while the following year the Stockton ILP had to be discouraged from running a parliamentary candidate. NAC Minutes 10 Sept 1894 and 7 Feb 1895. M 890/1/1.

40.　For a fuller account see: A. W. Purdue, 'Jarrow Politics, 1885–1914: the challenge to Liberal hegemony', *Northern History*, XVIII, 1982.

41.　*Northern Democrat*, Dec 1907.

42.　A. W. Purdue, 'Arthur Henderson and Liberal, Liberal-Labour and Labour Politics in North East England 1892–1903', *Northern History*, XI, 1975.

43.　NAC Minutes, 2 Oct 1905 and 18 Dec 1905.

44.　See A. W. Purdue, 'George Lansbury and the Middlesbrough Election of 1906', *International Review of Social History*, XVIII, (1973).

45.　General Election, 1906, Sir C. M. Palmer(C) 8,147; P. Curran (Lab) 5,093. By election 1907; P. Curran (Lab) 4,698; P. Rose-Innes (Con) 3,930; S. L. Hughes (L) 3,474; J. O'Hanlon (Mat) 2,122.

46.　See H. Pelling, *Popular Politics and Society in Late Victorian Britain* (1968) and Purdue, 'Jarrow Politics', *op. cit.*

47.　NEC Minutes, 10 Sept 1908.

48.　Report of Special Council meeting of the NMMCA, 24 Dec 1909. Northumberland County Record Office.

49.　*The Times*, 18 Jan 1910.

50.　NAC Minutes, 15 Oct 1910. The order of preference gives some indication of the distribution of ILP strength: Jarrow, NW Durham, Gateshead, Sockton, Tyneside, Wansbeck and Darlington.

51.　See A. W. Purdue, 'The Liberal and Labour Parties in North East Politics 1900–1914: the struggle for supremacy', *op. cit.*

52.　Duncan Tanner, *Political Change and the Labour Party, 1900–1918* (1990), p.426.

53.　Robert E. Dowse, *Left in the Centre: The Independent Labour Party 1893–1940* (1966), p.91.

54. A. Marwick, 'The Independent Labour Party 1918–32', Oxford BPhil. thesis, 1960, p.165.

55. There was a redistribution of seats in 1918 and Newcastle was divided into four divisions and Middlesbrough into two, while Sunderland remained a two member constituency.

56. Robert Moore, *Pitmen, Preachers and Politics* (1974), p.188.

57. W. R. Garside, *The Durham Miners 1919–1960* (1971).

58. B. C. Spoor (Lab) 10,060; G. R. Vicks (Co-Lib) 7,417; D. V. Rutherford (L) 2,411.

59. A. Marwick, *op. cit.*, p.69. Much of this thesis was later published as *Clifford Allen, The Open Conspirator* (1964).

60. M. Callcott, 'The making of a Labour stronghold: electoral politics in County Durham between the two World Wars', in M. Calcott and R. Challinor (eds.), *op. cit.*, p.69.

61. *Ibid.*, p.69.

62. 1922 Election: Rev. H. Dunnico (Lab) 14,469; A. Williams (L) 9,870; S. E. D. Wilson (Con) 6,745.

63. Archie Potts, 'Forty years on. The Labour Party in Sunderland 1900–1945', *North East Labour History Society Bulletin*, 24, 1990, p.15.

64. Connoisseurs of left-wing dramatic societies had a wide choice on Tyneside. They could go to the Peoples' Theatre which had ILP origins but was by the inter-war period simply a rather accomplished and intellectual dramatic society putting on plays like those noted by J. B. Priestley in English Journey (*Peer Gynt, Widowers' Houses* and *The Trojan Women*); they could attend The Progressive Players with its politically committed fare; or, by the late 'thirties, see the more agitprop offerings of the Left Book Club Theatre Guild.

65. M. Callcot, *op. cit.*, p.69.

66. Gateshead was to return to its leftist allegiance with the election of K. Zilliacus as Independent Labour MP in 1945.

67. There were four constituencies in Newcastle and in the seven general elections 1918–35, Labour won Newcastle Central four times, Newcastle West four times, Newcastle East twice and never won Newcastle North.

68. R. Challinor, 'John McNair: A Truly Human Tyneside Socialist', *North East Labour History*, 25, 1991.

69. See R. Miliband, *Parliamentary Socialism* (1971).

70. See, for instance, D. Marquand, *The Progressive Dilemma, From Lloyd George to Kinnock* (1991).

71. R. Challinor, *John S. Clark, Parliamentarian, Poet, Liontamer* (1977), p.15.

2. The ILP in Lancashire and the North West

Jeffrey Hill

If any of Britain's industrial regions were to be described as 'strongholds' of the Labour Party in the years before the First World War, the one with the most convincing claim would be the north west. In 1906 nearly half of the Labour MPs returned in the General Election were from constituencies in Lancashire and its immediate surroundings. Although the proportion dropped slightly in the elections of 1910, Lancashire still represented the largest regional contingent of Labour's pre-War parliamentary force. It has become almost axiomatic to interpret this electoral emergence of Labour as the outcome of a political strategy closely associated with the Independent Labour Party: the 'labour alliance'. In fact, the idea had its origins in the minds of early ILP leaders keen to stress their liaisons with the wider Labour Movement, and equally keen to distance their strategies from those of the allegedly more 'doctrinaire' Social Democratic Federation. In spite of this, however, there seems precious little ILP influence among the first wave of those Lancashire Labour MPs. Only two – Philip Snowden (Blackburn) and J. R. Clynes (Manchester North East) had achieved any prominence in the socialist movement at this stage – and Snowden was the only one not to have been sponsored by a trade union. In fact, the moderate union element was extremely strong in the Labour Party of this region before the First World War. It was typified by David Shackleton (Clitheroe), a man of impeccably Liberal, Nonconformist credentials, who owed his eminence in the Labour Movement to the support he derived from the Lancashire Weavers. In many other parts of the region the Labour organisations that had sprung into being to sponsor a parliamentary candidate were little more than management committees whose purpose was to mobilise the trade union vote. Of socialism there was little sign.

Are we therefore to dismiss the ILP in this region as a movement with scant significance in the party it had helped nationally to bring about? So it might seem if the whole issue is looked at in this way. But there is another approach to an understanding of the ILP. This might be outlined in the question: is it correct to discuss the ILP's development in terms of the labour alliance in the first place? Indeed, are there other political strategies to be kept in mind? The fact is that the party's development in this region was complex and diverse. Where a uni-directional approach might be appropriate for other regions, there were peculiarities in Lancashire which affected the ILP's tactics here in a variety of ways. It is the uniqueness of the north west experience which this essay seeks to bring out.[1]

On the face of it the ILP should certainly have prospered in this region. However the party's aims are characterised, there seems little doubt that chief among its objectives was a desire to expose the injustices of industrial capitalism and to secure a better deal for working people. The markedly proletarian nature of the north west with its heavy concentration of workers in textiles, mining and engineering[2] singled it out as a fruitful area for a movement seeking to instill a consciousness of *class*. This mission, though, encountered a series of pitfalls. The most difficult came in the form of a notoriously fragmented political culture which divided the working class between Liberal and Tory. Politics was to do with status, religion, ethnicity and masculinity: not class.[3] Closely related to this was the problem of the organised Labour Movement, especially the powerful trade unions in cotton and mining. Because of the divided political loyalties of their members, union leaders were suspicious of involving their organisations in activity which might result in alignment with one or the other political parties, lest this might introduce factionalism in the ranks. Until the early years of the twentieth century there was little likelihood of the financial (and moral) weight of these unions being lent to politics. Nor were the ILP's problems always external ones. Within the party itself were a series of personal and ideological tensions which sometimes worked against a coherent approach among the region's branches. Some of these tensions were not unconnected with a feature which affected the ILP in this region more than anywhere else: namely, the prior existence of a socialist movement – the Social Democratic Federation (SDF) – whose roots gave it seniority in certain districts and made ILP penetration difficult.[4] Faced with such hazards it is perhaps not surprising that the ILP's passage in Lancashire was less than smooth.

Although by the end of 1894, just over two years after the launching of the party, there were almost 30 branches reported in the region,[5] the most buoyant socialist activity was to be found at this time in the Manchester area – the birthplace of the ILP in the north west. This was no coincidence. Indeed, the early ILP might be seen as the continuation of an already existing strain of independent working class politics which had started with the SDF in the mid-1880s. Under the direction of an energetic Londoner, John Hunter-Watts, the SDF branches of Bolton, Oldham and, principally, Salford had orchestrated a series of campaigns for municipal action on the unemployed question.[6] By the summer of 1891 this had grown into a movement for labour representation led by a group of local socialists with a base in the trade unions. Bill Horrocks of the Gasworkers, the former miner W. K. Hall, Alf Settle, an engraver, and George Tabbron of the Brassfounders, all took a leading role in bringing the SDF into contact with other labour forces, including the Trades Council.[7] The intransigence of the Manchester Liberal Union in 1891 over the issue of labour representation in municipal affairs prompted a concerted move to establish a party along the lines of the Bradford Labour Union, with whose leaders (especially Bartley of the *Workman's Times*) the Manchester people were in touch.[8] Though personal animosities undermined early plans, and thwarted a proposed parliamentary campaign in Salford South, important precedents were established through this activity. In the first place it served to bring together an *alliance* of labour and socialist forces – SDF, Blatchfordites, Fabians and a group of 'labourites' inspired by the views of Joseph Burgess, editor of the *Workman's Times*. Secondly, and through Burgess, support from the 'new unionist' elements of the local trade unions was secured, though a link with the craft unions which still controlled the Trades Council proved more elusive. Thirdly, a distinctive brand of agitation was inherited from the SDF on unemployment. Each of these developments converged in the conference of May 1892 which set up the ILP in Manchester and Salford.[9] Thus, far from being a rival to the SDF, the ILP had emerged as its natural extension.

Right from its inception, therefore, the ILP exhibited many of the features which were to attend its future development. The inter-related concerns of building socialism through a strategy of electoral independence were prominently displayed in the first two clauses of the Manchester party's constitution of 1892:

1. That the programme of the party shall be 'The nationalisation of the land and other instruments of production';

2. That the party shall devote itself to securing the election of members to all representative bodies for the purpose of realising the programme of the party.[10]

The order of priority was not insignificant, and the subsequent development of the ILP showed that these objectives could as easily provoke discord as they could the harmony which had originally produced them. There were many in the early party whose preference was for 'making socialists' rather than securing election victories. Their influence never entirely disappeared. Such a one was John Trevor, the founder of the Labour Church and former Unitarian minister of Upper Brook Street Chapel. Trevor's mission was to convert people to an appreciation of the ethics of socialism: 'the Emancipation of Labour', he asserted, 'can only be realised so far as men learn both the Economic and Moral Laws of God, and heartily endeavour to obey them.'[11] Similar sentiments were to be found in the writings of Alex Thompson ('Dangle' of the *Clarion*) and the Cambridge graduate Fred Brocklehurst, later elected to the National Administrative Council. But this ethical form of socialism was pre-eminently associated with Robert Blatchford.

Such was Blatchford's influence over the ILP as President in its early days that the party was popularly known in the district as 'Blatchford's Party'.[12] His socialism was clear, simple and emotional. 'The policy of the *Clarion*', he had declared in the paper's opening issue, 'is a policy of humanity'.[13] Casting himself as socialism's 'recruiting sergeant' he sought to make it the ideology of a mass movement. The outstanding success of his *Merrie England*, which sold three quarters of a million copies within a year of its appearance in 1893, engendered a cascade of Clarion clubs in the region, in which the members enjoyed cycling, singing, rambling and other pursuits. Through them a distinctive socialist culture was nurtured. These beginnings seemed to herald a bright future for socialism. They certainly created a powerful legacy in the idea of 'socialist unity'.

Moreover, as David Howell has pointed out,[14] Blatchford's style had an important resonance in this region, with its traditions of popular Toryism. Blatchford was keenly aware that a new political movement in Lancashire would need to draw support from both Liberal and Conservative working men, and not just the former as in most other areas. '*Both* parties are our enemies, and *our object is to defeat both*',[15] he reminded his readers in 1893. A socialism which was seen to draw too deeply on the austere, temperance, chapel mind would strike no chords with the pub-based xenophobia of popular Toryism, a creed with deep roots in the working class districts of many of the region's towns, above all Liverpool. It was this factor which prompted Blatchford's insistence on a policy of electoral independence in both the local and national ILP. Known as 'the Fourth Clause' (because of the clause in the Manchester party's constitution which prevented ILP members from voting in elections for candidates of any other party) this issue provoked much debate and dissension in the ILP nationally in the 1890s. Lancashire socialists were never fully convinced that the party in other areas had detached itself from a Radical tradition, a fear given substance in the Halifax by-election of 1893 when the ILP nominee John Lister took care to emphasise his *labour*, not socialist, pedigree.[16] On the other hand, many numbers of the national ILP, and virtually the whole of its leadership, saw the Liberals as their principal rival for the working-class vote. Keir Hardie, for example, wanted the ILP voter to be free, if necessary, to vote tactically against Liberal candidates. The Fourth Clause effectively disfranchised him, however, and for this reason Hardie opposed Blatchford's strategy. But Hardie's analysis of the options open to voters – 'the choice', he argued at Bolton in 1895, 'lies 'twixt the ILP and the Tory'[17] – made little sense in many parts of Lancashire. Consequently Lancashire ILPers made repeated attempts at the Party's annual conference to have the Fourth Clause adopted, until after a series of setbacks the idea was dropped in the late nineties.

In company with this issue was a continuing emphasis on socialist unity. Blatchford was convinced that two separate socialist movements were 'doomed to be beaten in detail'[18] and during 1893 and 1894 pressed his case strongly in the pages of the *Clarion*, even after his resignation as President and the removal of the paper to Fleet Street. But progress was limited. Blatchford's well known capacity for making enemies affected not only the national ILP but the Manchester party itself. By 1894 he was on very bad terms with his erstwhile ally on socialist unity, Leonard Hall, now President of the local party. The two carried on a vigorous journalistic duel in the *Clarion* which eventually resulted in Hall's renunciation of the Fourth Clause and his

46

withdrawal as ILP parliamentary candidate for North East Manchester.[19] This rather squalid affair did nothing to enhance the cause of socialist unity, especially after Blatchford's proposals for a united socialist party had been rebuffed by the leadership of the SDF.[20]

In any event, the temptation for the historian to be distracted by the magnetic appeal of Blatchford must be resisted. It masks the dualism that had been present in the ILP at its inception, and obscures the fact that the principal emphasis in the Manchester party's strategy at this time was on labour alliance. Under the influence of Hall, who had been the leading light in the formation of the Lancashire and Adjacent Counties Labour Amalgamation,[21] and his Vice President James Heaviside the labour orientation of the ILP was pronounced. Unemployment agitation was revived during the trade depression of 1892, contacts were made with the pit districts of east Manchester during the miners' lockout of 1893 with a campaign for the nationalisatlon of the mines (Burgess produced a special issue of the *Workman's Times* for the colliers), and an example of strict independence was set in the municipal elections of 1893 when the ILP put up 12 socialist candidates.[22]

Possibly the most important feature of this thrust came with the publication in 1893 of the ILP's Municipal Programme. Evolving from earlier SDF schemes it offered a comprehensive plan for social reform and urban renewal. Among the more prominent demands were: the abolition of slum dwellings and the building of healthier homes, cheap transport for workmen, an 8-hour day for Corporation employees, pensions for those employed by the municipality, equal pay for men and women, and free food and clothing for needy schoolchildren. The programme aimed to give local authorities greater powers to improve the community, which would involve the removal of constitutional obstacles such as the Aldermanic Bench and the scrapping of the rating system and the Poor Law.[23] It went much farther than the Liberal municipal scheme of the following year,[24] and had the potential to act as manifesto for a wide range of voters, not just committed socialists. However, to realise the vote-winning potential of this ideological initiative the ILP needed an electoral machine, and until the organisational changes set in motion by party Secretary Joe Nuttall and his successor Thomas Gunning at the turn of the century such a machine did not exist.

By the mid 1890s the result of these developments was a closer liaison between the ILP and the Trades Council in local affairs. not only did the Trades Council share in the work on unemployment relief, but was willing to support seven ILP candidates in the municipal elections of 1894, when two local miners leaders – J. E. Sutton and Jesse Butler – were returned to the City Council for the ILP.[25] At the same time a United Labour Party contested the School Board elections and took votes from the Progressive candidates.[26]

These were encouraging signs for the future development of the labour alliance principle. But, as caution against false optimism, came the results of ILP parliamentary candidatures in various Lancashire constituencies in the 1895 General Election. With the exception of Tattersall at Preston and

R. M. Pankhurst in Gorton, where a deal with the Liberals allowed him to stand alone against the Conservative, the outcome was discouraging. Half of the campaigns produced humiliating polls.[27] The *Clarion* expressed by its silence what many must have felt at the time.

Outside of the Manchester area, as the 1895 campaigns revealed, the ILP had established a presence without anywhere asking a big impact. The somewhat eccentric campaign by Tattersall at Preston, achieving almost 5,000 votes, was really no indication of the relatively modest foothold established by the ILP in that Tory area, as Howell's analysis makes clear.[28] In fact, in the Tory strongholds of the western and central parts of Lancashire, branch activity was sporadic. Little, if any, serious work appears to have been achieved in the mining areas around Wigan and St. Helens.[29] In Liverpool an attempt was made in conjunction with the Fabian Society to establish a Labour Representation Committee based around a group of new unions in which James Sexton was influential. Thirteen Labour candidates – half of them in the ILP's stronghold of Everton – were promoted for the 1895 municipal elections. But disagreements which erupted soon after the inevitable failure led to the LRC'S break up.[30] These developments lent no encouragement to those who imagined the ILP could adapt to popular Toryism.

In reality, though, if the labour alliance strategy was to work at all it was in the cotton districts that its viability would be proved. It was here where the strong trades unionism that might provide the foundations for an independent labour party existed. Though quite vigorous branches operated at Bolton (another former SDF centre), Nelson, Ashton-under-Lyne and Oldham their problem lay in persuading the cotton unions of the need for independent political action. The difficulties are clearly pointed up by events in Oldham. Here J. R. Clynes had done much to extend ILP influence among the newer unionists in the gas and labouring trades as President of the Trades Council. But he ran up against the stumbling block of the Spinners' Union which, in company with the Engineers, effectively ran the Trades Council. In attempting to push the cotton workers towards political action Clynes found himself deposed as President. On resuming his pressure in 1894, this time as Secretary, Clynes simply provoked the Spinners' Union into withdrawing from the Trades Council, draining it of members and finance and leaving him in charge of a rump of unskilled workers.[31] The ILP branch itself encountered lean times in the later nineties, especially when Clynes scaled down his socialist activities to concentrate on union building. It was only revived after appealing to the NAC for help in reorganisation.[32] Relations between the cotton unions and the ILP never did run smoothly in Oldham and, significantly, it did not feature in the LRC campaign of 1906.

The most influential ILP branch in the cotton district was probably that of Nelson, a recently incorporated borough where the Weavers' Union had involved itself in labour politics since the first municipal elections in 1890. As in Manchester the formation of the ILP here owed something to the impetus of Social Democrats. It was they who took the initiative in December 1892, following the defeat of a Trades Council candidate in the municipal elections by a Liberal, to bring together a coalition of socialists, radicals and trades unionists in an organisation known as the Independent Labour Party.[33] The co-operation achieved by this alliance resulted in the return of two labour candidates in the borough council elections of 1893 and a further three in the School Board contest.[34]

It was from the foothold thus gained by the ILP in Nelson, together with the influence being exerted by the SDF in nearby Burnley, that socialism obtained some leverage on cotton union policy. The issue which attracted most socialist attention was the Eight-Hour Day, to which the cotton unions were at this time favourably disposed, largely for economic reasons relating to the state of the cotton market.[35] Indeed, it was largely as a consequence of the pressure brought by weavers in Burnley and Nelson that the United Textile Factory Workers' Association – the parliamentary lobbying agency of the cotton unions – was persuaded in 1894 to ballot members of the various unions on the joint issues of Eight hours and labour representation.[36] The ballot provided some measure of ILP and SDF influence among cotton workers at this time: the centres where support for both issues was strongest were the weaving towns of Burnley, Padiham, Nelson and Colne, which were also the areas of socialist influence. But influence was clearly too limited to ensure that labour representation would be of an independent kind. When the UTFWA decided to implement this part of the ballot it soon became evident that cotton union candidates would stand in traditional party colours.[37]

By the mid 1890s, therefore, the ILP's persona in this region was beginning to take shape. The two political strategies – socialist unity and labour alliance – which were to dominate debate in the party during the next two decades had been fashioned. As yet, however, neither had gained ascendancy. Moreover, the party's geographical coverage established by this time continued, by and large, to be that in which the party campaigned in the years leading up to the First World War. Generally speaking the ILP tended to prosper more in the eastern parts of Lancashire than in the traditional Tory areas to the west and centre. The first two or three years of the ILP operations in Lancashire, therefore, were formative ones. There were no radical departures from these early patterns in subsequent years.

As confirmation of the ILP's propensity for variety there was a significant move in the late nineties to maintain Blatchfordite ideas of socialist unity. In the generally depressed climate for working class politics prevailing in the aftermath of the 1895 General Election the attractiveness of a union of socialist forces was perhaps not surprising. Symptomatic of the period, and discouraging for advocates of the Labour alliance strategy, was the withdrawal of the cotton workers from political activity following disagreements between the Spinners' and Weavers' unions over their joint legislative programme. An indication of the extent of disunity was provided when, in 1896, the UTFWA was disbanded.[38] Even the usually active Nelson Weavers withdrew from municipal politics. This was a time, for both socialist parties, of retreat into the sub-cultural life of branch activities, Labour Churches and Clarion Clubs. Though the ILP claimed an impressive number of branches in the North West at this time,[39] many of them were fairly moribund as far as active politics were concerned. Rarely were more than a quarter of them represented at the national ILP conferences, a sure sign of the real level of vitality. Other problems accentuated this general malaise. The early proliferation of branches had given rise to numerous organisational problems: laxity in the collection of membership dues, neglect of basic administration and the referring of a host of minor matters to the NAC (much to the despair of Ramsay MacDonald). Low finances circumscribed the political activity of many branches, reinforcing the self-absorbing tendencies always inherent in the idea of socialist unity.[40]

Nevertheless, there was strong feeling over this issue in Lancashire at the end of the century. It came to national prominence when the NAC reopened negotiations with the SDF on the question of a fusion of the two parties. Support from Lancashire branches was firm and indicated at the annual conference of 1896, when Fred Brocklehurst of Manchester introduced a motion to change the ILP's name to 'National Socialist Party'.[41] When it became known later that the NAC had rejected the SDF's terms for a fusion there was an instantaneous reaction from Lancashire. Many branches felt that the NAC was cheating the party by insisting on an overwhelming vote in favour before the principle of fusion could proceed. The NAC attempted to justify its switch to a policy of federation with the SDF by asserting that 'In Blackburn, Nelson, Rochdale, Ashton and several other places the local branches of the ILP and SDF already work cordially side by side and for elections and many propaganda purposes are already virtually federated together.'[42] In spite of the truth in this statement local militants interpreted the situation differently, seeing the state of affairs so described as making fusion all the more desirable. Littleborough ILP called for 'one militant socialist party', while the groups at Droylsden and Preston refused to enter the ILP's second ballot since they had already voted decisively in favour of fusion. Bolton West, Everton and Blackburn opposed the NAC, and Stockport announced its intention to withdraw from the party 'as a protest against the undemocratic action of the NAC.'[43] The Lancashire arguments were clarified by Charles Higham of Blackburn at the 1899 national conference in Leeds. He spoke of the 'excellent working arrangement' between the two parties in his own town, an arrangement which, he claimed, illustrated the ridiculous position of the NAC whose members he accused of self-interest in taking the line they did.[44]

This general mood in favour of socialist unity nevertheless concealed marked variations in practice at the local level. Co-operation between the ILP and SDF did not always lead in the same direction. Two branches – both nominally supporters of socialist unity – typify the variations on this theme. They are Blackburn and Rochdale. At Blackburn, the town where the SDF had made its first foray into Lancashire politics back in 1884, ILPers and social democrats established the *Blackburn Labour Journal* in 1897 in an endeavour to capitalise on the Trades Council's growing disillusionment with the local political parties and their neglect of labour questions in municipal affairs.[45] Selling for a penny, the *Labour Journal* was claiming a circulation of over 6,000 by 1900 with its even-handed condemnation of both political parties. In Tory Blackburn it had the audacity to rejoice, in 1899, at the defeat of Cotton Union leader James Mawdsley as Conservative candidate in the Oldham by-election, but in the main directed its attacks at the Liberals. A distinction was made between the wealthy Liberal paymasters of the party, thought to have little regard for social questions, and the Radical rank-and-file who might be willing to transfer their loyalty to the socialists.[46] The courting of this radical residuum emerged as one of the key tactics in the celebrated parliamentary election campaign fought by Philip Snowden in Blackburn in 1900. Against the chauvinism engendered by the 'khaki' nature of the contest, in a town depressed by a slump in the cotton trade, Snowden's election team emphasised social and economic reforms and avoided any revolutionary sloganising.[47] In the absence of a Liberal candidate the socialist party was given the moral support of the liberal *Northern Daily Telegraph* and some of the local Liberal clubs sent out volunteers to help Snowden.[48] The presence of Tom Hurley, a local Catholic trade unionist, as one of Snowden's principal lieutenants served to win over a section of the Irish vote.[49] Though Snowden did not succeed in displacing either of the two Tories his 7,000 votes – proclaimed by the *Labour Journal* as 'a new era in electioneering' – gave strong encouragement to the feeling that, with a more favourable political climate, a socialist labour candidate could be returned in Blackburn. Further proof of the potential of this ticket was provided in local elections during the next few years. Co-operation between the two socialist parties continued to be close and, equally important, the electoral alliance with the Trades Council was consolidated. In 1904, for example, the alliance opposed Tory candidates in all but one of the wards being contested, returning four representatives to the borough council.[50] By this time too the *Labour Journal* had increased its size and circulation, and in contrast with its early polemical, lampooning style now carried weighty articles an issues such as free trade, poverty and even the usually neglected topic foreign affairs.[51] These were the foundations for Snowden's victory in 1906.

In Rochdale the socialists displayed many of the same features. A respectable ILP parliamentary campaign in 1895 by G. N. Barnes paved the way for the establishment of an energetic socialist movement in the nineties. ILP and SDF groups held frequent joint meetings and co-operated in a programme of municipal reform through the pages of the *Rochdale Labour News* – '... a medium whereby all municipal jobbery, extravagance and incapacity will be exposed.'[52] The *Labour News* stated as the aims of the socialists: 'We want to take possession of our Town Council in order to control the affairs of our town for the improvement of the lives of its inhabitants –

destruction of slums and the erection of better houses; improved sanitation and WCs.'[53] The crucial difference, however, between developments in Rochdale and those of Blackburn concerned the contrasting political traditions of the two towns. Unlike Tory Blackburn, Rochdale's working class, and in particular its organised sections, was strongly committed to the Liberal Party. Many members of the Trades Council, though nominally independent in their industrial capacity, were privately Liberal.[54] The socialists had only one supporter on the Trades Council, from the relatively unimportant Bakers' Union.[55] In these circumstances the ILP and SDF carried their fight against the established political parties into the industrial arena by attacking the trades unions as a reactionary movement unable to grapple with the problems of the working class.[56] As may be imagined this tactic was hardly likely to bring electoral success, and for a long time the Rochdale socialists simply did not count as a vote-winning force locally. Severe defeats were regularly experienced in municipal polls and the 1900 General Election saw a very weak socialist campaign by the journalist C. Allen Clarke produce only 900 votes.[57] The next few years, with the socialist group passing under the leadership of the 'left' ILPer S. G. Hobson, saw Rochdale moving clearly away from the labour alliance principle, and after 1906 seeking seriously to develop a form of working-class politics *outside* the Labour party. As David Howell has pointed out, the capacity of this type of politics to win votes was by no means negligible, as was instanced by Hobson's 20% of the poll at Rochdale in 1906.[58]

It would be misleading, having seen the variety of tactics employed in the ILP during these years, to suggest that the party's future course of action was clearly mapped out. At the turn of the century no particular advantage seemed to lie in one form of activity in preference to another. But around 1902–03 the picture did change significantly. Now local socialist politics were influenced much more by *national* events than had been the case previously. The most important of these influences was of course the orientation of trades unions towards labour representation, and in particular the very positive way in which the miners and cotton workers of Lancashire embraced the issue. Important, too, was the establishment of the Labour Representation Committee in 1900 and the way in which (in the light of Liberal failures in 1900) local LRCs quickly proliferated in Lancashire during 1903 and 1904.[59] Though social democrats continued to participate in these local committees the decision of the SDF nationally to withdraw from the LRC in 1901 meant that its members were prevented from engaging in any parliamentary ventures through the LRC after this date.[60] On the other hand, ILP branches which had already been operating within a labour alliance found no such limitations, and electoral successes came easily in contrast with the lean years of the previous decade. Election victories at both local and parliamentary level often produced a Labour bandwaggon which gave the party real influence politically. Nelson might be taken as an example.

The backbone of the labour movement in Nelson was the Weavers' Association, which had a tradition of 'progressive' politics – campaigns for labour representation, the eight-hour day and nationalisation of industry had been a regular feature of its activities. Members of Nelson Weavers were represented at the foundation conference of the LRC in 1900, and in the next year the Weavers followed up by appointing a special sub-committee to organise labour campaigns in municipal elections.[61] Similar developments were taking place at the same time in nearby Colne. The decisive event which forged the formal alliance of ILP and trade unions in these two towns was the Clitheroe by-election of August 1902, in which David Shackleton was returned unopposed as the LRC candidate.[62] The negotiations which resulted in the selection of Shackleton as the Labour candidate reveal quite plainly the eagerness of the ILP to sponsor a labour alliance man, even if this meant moderating the socialist line. Initially the Nelson ILP had wanted Philip Snowden to contest the seat, though such a move would undoubtedly have prompted Liberal intervention in the contest.[63] On realising this Snowden himself backed down in favour of the more moderate Shackleton, telling the Weavers' leader in Colne: 'I think that Mr. Shackleton, as a trade union official and one so thoroughly acquainted with the staple trade and with the labour conditions of the district, has a far better claim and would make a more useful representative.'[64] The SDF, by comparison, was less convinced and refused to support him.[65]

The election of a Labour MP stimulated local party organisation. A Clitheroe constituency LRC, which permitted individual membership, was created to handle the organising of parliamentary elections. In municipal affairs there were LRCs in each of the small industrial towns of the constituency bringing trade union and ILP representatives together. The SDF was not included.[66] In spite of Liberal overtures to set up a Progressive alliance the Labour Party in Nelson felt confident enough to go its own way in ploughing an independent line electorally and ideologically. By 1905 it had 15 councillors and a working majority on the borough council. In the following year a Labour Mayor was elected, the first in Lancashire. Already a significant re-alignment of political forces was taking place as Liberals and Conservatives made moves to cement an anti-socialist alliance: 'it would seem,' reflected the *Nelson Workers' Guide* 'that municipal contests are not to be between Liberal and Conservative, but between Labour and anti-Labour, in other words, between employer of labour and the labourer.'[67] The appeal of the Labour Party lay in its practical approach. It pursued a 'fair contracts' policy, urged the municipalisation of tramways and public baths, and in 1905 secured a reduction in the gas rate. Opponents' claims that Labour councillors would be ignorant spendthrifts proved unfounded. In fact, Labour was a moderate municipal government whose socialist philosophy was always rather muted.[68] But the strides made during these few years were crucial in cementing the position of a Labour Party whose prestige withstood later assaults from syndicalists and communists. The ILP had participated in the construction of a political machine capable of dominating civic life in and around Nelson for years to come.

In certain respects these developments were replicated in Manchester, where by 1914 the Labour Party could mobilise a 15-strong group in the City Council. There is a very strong indication in both places that what was happening amounted to more than simply the re-working of an old political alliance into Progressivism – that in fact the replacement of a major political party was taking place, a process which might also have been dimly evident in Preston, though here the ILP's contribution to the process was much slighter than in the other two places.[69] These transformations, though clearly giving great credibility to the labour alliance idea, were not without their problems for the ILP. These were most obvious in Manchester. Here, the more radical elements of the party regarded the Labour alliance strategy, especially as manifested nationally in the obsequious position adopted by Labour towards the ruling Liberals at Westminster, as unduly constricting. Many 'left' ILPers joined hands with social democrats in direct action campaigns over unemployment, taking to the streets to protest against the Government's failure to produce 'right to work' legislation and getting involved in battles with the police in the course of occupations of unused and derelict land in Manchester and Salford. The solutions which it seemed were needed to remedy unemployment – involving radical new measures in land nationali-sation and public spending – found little sympathy in the prevailing climate of new Liberalism which appeared to be suffocating the Labour Party in the years immediately following its national emergence. It was no coincidence that much of the impetus for this more direct kind of politics came from the old centres of socialist unity and from Manchester in particular, where agitation on unemployment went right back to the 1880s. It was in Manchester that the initiatives for reconstituting socialist unity stemmed, culminating in the setting up in 1911 of the British Socialist Party by social democrats, the 'left' elements of the ILP and various groups of 'unattached socialists' – often to be found in the *Clarion*'s orbit. Although the challenge posed by this move was played down by the *Labour Leader* it seems likely that some of the 41 ILP branches that had sent delegates to the Socialist Unity conference actually did secede from the party, and that several unaligned socialist groups were prepared to throw in their lot with the newly-formed BSP, having previously gravitated more towards the ILP than the SDF.[70] The tensions occasioned by this split certainly shook the ILP in the north west. Some indication of the reverberation can be gleaned from the lengthy and impassioned speech by Egerton P. Wake, of Barrow-in-Furness ILP at the party's 1914 Conference, when the issue of socialist unity was once again under scrutiny. Claiming a 'mandate' to speak for Lancashire, Wake strongly opposed any proposals for unity with the BSP. 'The Lancashire Divisional Conference', he pointed out, 'had considered this matter very carefully, and, with only two dissentients, had decided against these proposals. That decision had been based upon painful experience. During the last four years they had been engaged in Lancashire in purging their movement, and now it was proposed to open the floodgates to let in all the hounds of dissension again ... it would mean that the BSP would come in to their local Labour Parties, and all their electoral work would be paralysed by the resumption of all the old quarrels over questions of dogma that they had had in the past.'[71] With such developments the characteristic variety of the ILP in Lancashire was maintained up to the First World War, the achievements in constructing labour alliances always being countered by initiatives of an alternative socialist kind.

What kind of socialism did the ILP bring to this region? Many previous discussions of the ILP's ideology have stressed its legacy of radicalism.[72] But, as we have already seen, David Howell's work on the Lancastrian party has highlighted the insistence by some factions on making room for the Tory working class – renowned for its hedonistic masculine culture compounded of pub, sport, locality, Church and nation. It was personified in local worthies such as 'th'owd gam cock', W. H. Hornby of Blackburn, and institutionalised in the county's extensive network of Primrose League branches.[73] Constructing a socialism to accommodate this political culture meant dissociating the party from the Liberal influences and traditions so noticeable in the ILP elsewhere, and nowhere more evident than in the ideas and morality of Keir Hardie. Whilst Hardie might serve as the 'archetypal' ILPer as far as other regions are concerned, what he stood for was frequently contested in Lancashire by an alternative style of socialism usually associated with Robert Blatchford. Blatchford was chalk to Hardie's cheese. Blatchford represented the hearty good fellowship of the ILP, and his *Clarion* provided the inspiration for the 'club life', popular with so many branches in the north west. Scarcely an opportunity was lost by the Blatchfordites to castigate the chapel-bred sobersides in the movement. Alex Thompson's disdainful parody of Keir Hardie as 'The man of sorrows, with a crown of thorns on his brow, staggering up Calvary under the weight of his cross', was just one example of this.[74] The personal antipathy felt towards Hardie by Robert Blatchford intensified by Hardie's aspirations to leadership of the ILP[75] – typified these contrasting aspects of the ILP.

Because of Blatchford, and because of the absence of strong nonconformist roots in Tory areas of Lancashire, the ILP came to assume many of the features often to be found within the SDF, a movement with which the ILP worked closely in many areas. Between them, the two organisations provided a natural focus for the many socialist groups in the region which were still nominally uncommitted to a national socialist party, and whose ideological attachments were therefore rather fluid. In this they mirrored Blatchford himself, always something of a freewheeler. Of course, the SDF's earnest devotion to tackling Marxism was lacking in the ILP, but there was usually an equally strong emphasis on club life, on 'living as socialists', uninhibited by any deeply felt temperance or religiously- derived moral convictions. A keen interest in sport and open air recreations was very evident. Clarion clubs were immensely popular in the north west, providing singing, scouting and rambling as well as opportunities to pursue the craze for cycling. In 1896 came the Clarion vans to bring another lively propaganda feature to socialist life.[76] As if to cock a snook at religious conventions, Sunday was the time normally reserved for these activities.

Nevertheless, in spite of all this, it was not a wholly secular socialism. Although few ILP leaders seem to have been religious – an irreverent agnosticism certainly characterised the *Clarion* circle – the party did develop a religious side to its activities. This came in the form of John Trevor's Labour Church. Trevor sought to bring together the fundamental ethics of Christianity and socialism, very much as Hardie did, and to weave them into a seamless robe: 'making freedom and religion synonymous terms to the extent that the two be understood to be indissolubly united'.[77] Labour churches were established on this basis in a number of Lancashire towns in the 1890s, seeking to draw congregations on a non-denominational basis and often with a markedly secular approach to services – string bands and socialist hymn books being much in evidence.[78] By September 1892 the Manchester Labour Church had established five different meeting places in the city, whilst at the Labour Church conference of the following year further movements were represented from Accrington, Barrow, Bolton, Salford and Oldham.[79] By the end of the decade not all of these foundations were active and only two of the Lancashire churches – those of Hyde and Stockport – maintained long histories.[80] There were no new foundations after the turn of the century. In the end the Labour Church proved to be a peripheral feature of ILP propaganda, and Eric Hobsbawm's verdict – 'its chief function was to lubricate the passage of Northern workers from Liberal Radicalism to an Independent Labour Party and having done this it disappeared'[81] – just about sums up the role of the Labour Church. Its main support seemed to come in areas of Liberal and nonconformist traditions rather than towns noted for strong Tory sympathies. But its brief existence does underline the presence of a religious element in the ILP, alongside the dominant strain of secularism.

In terms of political ideas and programmes, the most distinctive feature of the ILP was its adoption of a 'statist' political ideology. In other words, a politics emphasising the need for state or municipal intervention to remedy working people's material insecurity. In all the towns where ILP branches formulated a serious political programme for community action an emphasis on *municipal* schemes of improvement was strong. As we have seen, the Manchester ILP had elaborated just such a comprehensive municipal programme by 1893. This was developed in later years into a blend of ethical socialism and trades union reformism to produce a moderate brand of municipal labourism similar to that put forward by the ILP in its other main centre of activity, Nelson.[82] In Manchester, however, because of the continuing influence of social democratic agitation, this municipal reformism was never limited to council chamber debates. It was always complemented by a street-based form of direct action, sometimes rowdy. The objective of both was usually the same, however: the implementation of a community programme of reforms to make the material environment a more decent one for ordinary people. Though a municipal programme was more usually found in areas where a strategy of labour alliance had been pursued this was not always the case. Rochdale socialists, for example, evinced an equally keen interest in municipalism within the context of socialist unity. Moreover, municipal intervention did not always strike a chord with the interests of local trade unions. Preston provides an interesting case of ILP and trade union divergence, largely over this very issue.[83]

The question of whether this form of interventionist politics appealed more to certain kinds of workers than to others is problematical. Tanner's recent work (drawing in part on ideas from Savage's study of Preston) strongly asserts a connection between Toryism and 'statism', arguing that municipal intervention made sense to workers in areas where the local economy was shaky, with employment irregular and casual. To this may be added the notion that communities with a strong tradition of 'voluntarism' – in the form, for example, of Co-operation – might equally be drawn to municipalism, whereas the politics of intervention would introduce a discordant note in areas of individualism.[84] There is some value in this line of thinking. It may well be that in Blackburn, for example, the ILP's emphasis on a practical socialism helped to win over many Tory loyalists. Nelson, by contrast, had a tradition of co-operative activity, so much so that the Labour Party envisaged its municipal undertakings being grafted on to existing Cooperative Society ventures.[85] On the other hand, we should be wary of an over-rigid approach to this question. Interventionist politics was not exclusive to Tory or 'voluntarist' districts. The most comprehensively formulated programme of municipal reform in the region – that presented to the voters of Burnley by the local SDF branch – was to be found in a town of very strong radical and chapel traditions.[86] As against this the ILP made little headway before the First World War in any of the 'classic' Tory districts of west and central Lancashire, where an unstable local economy and the absence of collective industrial action by the working class might be thought to have produced fertile terrain for municipalism. In the chief centres of ILP activity – Blackburn, Nelson and Manchester – it seems that the party prospered because it was able to take up a variety of social and political mantles and develop out of them a programme based upon the idea of *community*. Though there were obvious associations between the ILP and ideas of 'class' and 'labour', what came over most visibly in the party's municipal programmes was neither of these ideas, but that of community. And this was a notion as present in radical discourse as it was in that of the socialists.[87]

The years before 1914 are the seminal ones in studying the ILP in the north west, for it was during this time that the essential features of the party were established. The same is true of the Labour Party itself. After a dramatic appearance in 1906 Labour's fortunes in the north west declined, its progress effectively halted in the region by the slump of the inter-war years. Lancashire never provided more than one in seven Labour MPs between the Wars, compared to its dominant position before 1914. Lancashire ILP branches maintained a lively invective against the policies of MacDonald and Snowden in the 1920s,[88] but the party owed its influence as a political force to those areas where its roots were struck pre-War.

In all this, one thing remains all too apparent: the ILP had a limited influence in working-class politics. This can be gauged by considering the fact that by 1910 there were 16 constituencies in the north west where some form of independent labour politics had become established, resulting in the formation of a Labour or independent socialist party. In addition, the 8 parliamentary divisions in Manchester, Salford and Liverpool were also covered by centrally-based Labour Parties in those cities. In many of these places 'independent labour politics' meant a non-socialist Labour Party, in effect an electoral organising committee dominated by the locally powerful trade union. The Lancashire coalfield parties at Wigan, St. Helens, Ince, Westhoughton and Newton-le-Willows represented *par excellence* this state of affairs. But similar features were evident in the parties at Oldham, Bolton, Stockport and Gorton.[89] In less than half of the total number of independent labour areas could the ILP be said to have exerted significant influence over the local political situation. Of these Manchester, Nelson, Blackburn, Accrington, Barrow and Liverpool saw the ILP active inside the Labour Party. In three other places – Rochdale, Preston and Ashton-under-Lyne – it opted for a future outside.[90]

This relative distribution of influence in the early Labour Party sums up the role of the ILP. It was certainly not the sole agent in bringing about the electoral breakthrough of the early years of the century. Much of the Labour Party at this time owed its origins to influences other than socialist ones. Indeed, the ILP in the north west was not exclusively a movement committed to the labour alliance principle. Because of factors peculiar, perhaps unique, to the region, the ILP had experimented with strategies which pointed in directions quite different from those in which the national leadership felt the party should go. Many Lancashire members, though probably not a majority, were convinced that socialist unity represented the correct line of development, and they continued to press their case in the movement up to the First World War, if not beyond. They ensured that the contribution of this region to the development of socialism in Britain was a distinctive and dynamic one.

NOTES

1. See David Howell, *British Workers and the Independent Labour Party, 1888–1906* (Manchester UP, Manchester, 1983), especially chapter 9.
2. For the economic and social characteristics of the region see: J. K. Walton, *Lancashire: a social history* (Manchester UP, Manchester, 1987); Patrick Joyce,

Work, Society and Politics: the culture of the factory in later Victorian England (Harvester Press, Brighton, 1980).

3. For the political features of the region see especially P. F. Clarke, *Lancashire and the New Liberalism* (Cambridge UP, Cambridge, 1971); Duncan Tanner, *Political Change and the Labour Party, 1900–1918* (Cambridge UP, Cambridge, 1990, ch.5; Patrick Joyce, *Visions of the People: industrial England and the question of class, 1848–1914* (Cambridge UP, Cambridge 1991); Jeffrey Hill, 'Working Class Politics in Lancashire, 1885–1906: a study in the regional origins of the Labour Party', unpublished PhD thesis, University of Keele, 1971; and Howell, *op. cit.*

4. The development of the SDF in the north west is discussed in J. Hill, 'Social Democracy and the Labour Movement: the Social Democratic Federation in Lancashire', *Bulletin of the North West Labour History Society*, 8, 1982–83, pp.44–55.

5. At the foundation of the National ILP in 1893 there were 19 branches already operating in Lancashire (ILP, *Conference Report*, 1893). A year later the number had risen to 26 (*Workman's Times*, 13 Jan 1894. In 1895 *The Labour Annual* listed 45 branches in Lancashire. By 1896, 87 branches were reported in Lancashire and Cheshire. This had dropped to 60 by the following year, with an estimated 2,600 members. In 1900 the ILP claimed organisations in 25 parliamentary divisions, in addition to branches in Manchester, Salford and Liverpool. (ILP, *Conference Report*, 1896, 1900; *Directory and Branch Returns*, 1897). Delegates representing 40 branches attended the Annual Conference of 1907; in 1912 – after secessions following the formation of the British Socialist Party the previous year – there were only 26 branches represented, though by 1914 the number had risen to 50. (ILP, *Annual Conference Report*, 1907, 1912, 1914).

6. *Justice*, 19 Jan, 12 Feb and 10 Dec 87.

7. *Ibid.*, 14 Sep 1889; *Workman's Times*, 7 and 28 Aug 1891; 9 Jan 1892; *Clarion*, 9 Apr 1892.

8. *Workman's Times*, 21 and 28 Aug, 18 Sept 1891.

9 *Clarion*, 9 Apr 1892.

10. *Workman's Times*, 28 May 1892.

11. *Labour Prophet*, Feb 1892.

12. See A. M. Thompson, article in *Manchester Guardian*, 1 Jan 1944.

13. *Clarion*, 12 Dec 1891.

14. See Howell, *op. cit.*, pp.208–9; 380–2

15. *Clarion*, 12 Dec 1891.

16. See E. P. Thompson, 'Homage to Tom Maguire' in A. Briggs and J. Saville (eds.), *Essays in Labour History* (Macmillan, London, 1967 ed.) pp.276–316.

17. *Bolton ILP Pioneer*, Feb 1895.

18. *Clarion*, 11 Aug 1894.

19. *Ibid.*, 1 Jul, 24 Nov and 1 Dec 1894; *Labour Leader*, 6 July 1895 .

20. See 'Notes from the North' in *Justice*, 9 Feb 1895.

21. *Labour Prophet*, Feb 1894.

22. *Manchester Guardian*, 2 Nov 1893; 2 Nov 1894; E. S. Pankhurst, *The Suffragette Movement* (Longman, London, 1931), pp.95, 129–30.

23. *Workman's Times*, 5 Aug 1893.

24. On Manchester Liberalism see Jeffrey Hill, 'Manchester and Salford Politics and the Early Development of the Independent Labour Party' *International Review of Social History*, XXVI (1981), Part 2, pp.171–201.

25. See Manchester and Salford Trades Council, *Annual Report*, 1894, 1896; *Manchester Guardian*, 2 Nov 1894; *Clarion*, 27 Oct 1894.
26. *Manchester Guardian*, 3 and 20 Nov 1894; Pankhurst, *op. cit.*, p.119.
27. ILP National Administrative Council (NAC), Minute Book, 3 Jul 1895; Pankhurst, *op. cit.*, p.133. ILP candidates in the 1895 General Election received the following votes: Tattersall (Preston), 4,781; Pankhurst (Gorton), 4,261; Brocklehurst (Bolton), 2,694; Barnes (Rochdale), 1,251; Johnston (Manchester NE), 546; Christie (Hyde) 448; Sexton (Ashton UL), 415; Curran (Barrow IF), 414.
28. See Howell, *op. cit.*, pp.212–4
29. On the ILP in the Wigan coalfield see: *Workman's Times*, 16 Sep 1893; NAC Minute Book, 10 Sept 1894.
30. *Labour Chronicle* (Liverpool), Nov–Dec 1895; Liverpool Trades Council, *Annual Report*, 1894–5, 1895–6, 1896–7 (Liverpool Record Office).
31. Oldham Trades Council, *Annual Report*, 1892, 1893 (Webb Trade Union Coll., London School of Economics; *Workman's Times*, 11 Mar 1893; *Colliery Workman's Times*, 2 Dec 1893; J. R. Clynes, *Memoirs* (Hutchinson, London, 1937), vol. 1, p.75.
32. NAC Minute Book, 1 Oct and 12 Dec 1898; *ILP News*, Jan 1898.
33. *Nelson Chronicle*, 23 Dec 92.
34. *Burnley Socialist*, 21 Oct and 24 Nov 1893; Nelson Trades Council, MS Minute Book, 21 Mar 1893 (Offices of Nelson Weavers' Association); *Nelson Chronicle*, 5 Dec 1893.
35. See Hill, thesis, pp.275–6.
36. Amalgamated Weavers' Association, General Council Minute Book, 10 Mar 1894; United Textile Factory Workers' Association (UTFWA), Conference Report, 1894; *Burnley Gazette*, 1 Sept 1894.
37. UTFWA, Report on the Ballot on the Eight-Hour Day and Labour Representation (Conference Report, 1895); Report of a Special Representative Meeting, 19 Jan and 28 Feb 1895; *Burnley Gazette*, 31 Oct 1894.
38. UTFWA, Report of Legislative Council, 1895–6.
39. See note 5, above.
40. *ILP News*, Apr 1897; July 1898; May–July 1899.
41. ILP *Conference Report*, 1896 .
42. *Ibid.*, 1899.
43. Reports in NAC Minute Book, 16 Jun, 25 Jun–16 July; and frequent reports Aug–Sept, Nov–Dec 1898.
44. ILP *Conference Report*, 1899.
45. Blackburn Trades Council, Annual Report, 1897 (Webb TU Coll.) NAC Minute Book, 26 Feb 1897.
46. *Blackburn Labour Journal* (BLJ), Sept 1898; Oct 1900.
47. *Blackburn Times*, 29 Sept 1900.
48. *ILP News*, Oct 1900.
49. *BLJ*, Oct 1900.
50. *Northern Daily Telegraph*, 2 Nov 1904.
51. See *BLJ*, Dec 1902; June–July 1903.
52. *Rochdale Labour News* (RLN), July 1897.
53. *Ibid.*, Nov 1896; Dec 1897.
54. Howell, *op. cit.*, pp.227–8.

55. *RLN*, Nov 1989; Jan 1899.

56. *Ibid.*, July and Dec 1897.

57. *Ibid.*, Nov 1896; Dec 1897; May 1898; Jan and Mar 1899; *Labour Leader*, 15 Sept; 27 Oct 1900.

58. See Howell, *loc. cit.*; *Rochdale Citizen*, Nov 1905; Jan 1906

59. By 1905 there were 59 Lancashire-based trade unions and 20 trades councils affiliated to the Labour Representation Committee. In addition there were 14 local LRCs established. (LRC, *Conference Report*, 1905, p.75).

60. See Hill, 'Social Democracy and the Labour movement', pp.51–2.

61. Nelson Weavers, MS Minute Book, 15 July, 26 Aug, 23 Sept 1901.

62. See Frank Bealey, 'The Northern Weavers, Independent Labour Representation and Clitheroe, 1902', *Manchester School*, 1957, pp.26–60.

63. *Ibid.* The Liberals had pointed out that 'a socialist is not regarded as a Labour man purely, by some Liberals, and whilst they may be willing to forego any claims they may have for a *bona fide* Labour man, they would not feel the same obligation in dealing with a socialist.'

64. *Cotton Factory Times*, 11 July 1902.

65. *Ibid.*, 18 July 1902.

66. *Nelson Chronicle*, 7 Nov 1902; Clitheroe Division Labour Representation Association rules, set out in circular from national LRC, March 1902. (*Infancy of Labour*, 2 vols, 1900–1912, London School of Economics).

67. *Nelson Workers' Guide*, 11 Dec 1903.

68. *Nelson Chronicle*, 18 Sept; 9 Oct 1903; *Colne and Nelson Times*, 6 Oct 1905.

69. See Michael Savage, *The Dynamics of Working Class Politics: the Labour Movement in Preston 1880–1940* (Cambridge UP, Cambridge, 1987), pp.145–56.

70. See N. Reid, 'Manchester and Salford ILP: a more controversial aspect of the pre-1914 era', *Bulletin of the North West Labour History Society*, 5, (1978–9), pp.25–31; D. Morris, 'The Origins of the British Socialist Party', *ibid.*, 8 (1982) pp.29–43.

71. *Justice*, 7, 21, 20 Oct; 4, 18, 25 Nov 1911; *Labour Leader*, 6 Sep; 8 Dec 1911; ILP, *Annual Conference Report*, 1914, p.98ff.

72. See Joyce, *Visions of the People*, pp.77–9: '... it is clear', says Joyce, 'that socialist conceptions of the economy, of class and of society and the individual had a great deal in common with radical Liberalism.' (p.79).

73. See Martin Pugh, *The Tories and the People 1880–1935* (Basil Blackwell, Oxford, 1985) pp.122–7; the Primrose League had a large working class membership in the north west.

74. A. M. Thompson, *Here I Lie, the Memorial of an Old Journalist* (Routledge, London, 1937), p.98.

75. *Clarion*, 11 Feb 1893.

76. *All About the Clarion Vans* (*The Clarion*, London, 1904); Denis Pye, 'Fellowship is Life: Bolton Clarion Cycling Club and the Clarion Movement: 1894–1914', in *Labour's Turning Point in the North West 1890–1914*, (North West Labour History Society, Manchester, 1984), pp.20–30; Chris Waters, *British Socialists and the Politics of Popular Culture 1884–1914* (Manchester UP, Manchester, 1990).

77. John Trevor, *An Independent Labour Party* (Labour Church Tract No. 2, 1892).

78. See D. F. Summers, 'The Labour Church and Allied Movements in the late 19th and early 20th Centuries', unpublished PhD thesis, University of Edinburgh, 1958, esp. p.197.

79. *Labour Prophet*, Aug 1893.
80. *Labour Annual*, 1899, p.80. By 1899 there were only 5 active Labour Churches in the region – at Bolton, Farnworth, Hyde, Rochdale and Manchester and Salford: all districts with a nonconformist tradition.
81. E. J. Hobsbawm, *Primitive Rebels: Studies in Archaic Forms of Social Movement in the 19th and 20th Centuries* (Manchester UP, Manchester, 1959), p.162.
82. See Hill, 'Manchester and Salford Politics and the Early Development of the ILP', p.199.
83. See Savage, *op. cit.*, p.154.
84. See Tanner, *op. cit.*, pp.131, 141; Savage, *op. cit.*, p.20.
85. *Nelson Workers' Guide*, 2 Nov 1903.
86. See Dan Irving, *The Municipality. From A Worker's Point of View* (Twentieth Century Press, London, n.d. c.1910); *The Socialist and North East Lancashire Labour News* (Burnley), 14 Oct 1893.
87. Tanner, *op. cit.*, p.147; Joyce, *Visions of the People*, pp.78–9.
88. See Hill, thesis, pp.357–79.
89. See R. E. Dowse, *Left in the Centre: the Independent Labour Party 1893–1940* (Longmans, London, 1966).
90. See Howell, *op. cit.*, pp.227–8 (Rochdale); Savage, *op. cit.*, pp.152–6 (Preston); S. Carter, 'The ILP in Ashton-under-Lyne, 1893–1900', North West Group for the Study of Labour History, *Bulletin*, 4 (1977–8), pp.63–91.

3. The ILP and the Scottish National Question

Ian S. Wood

'We would achieve more with a Scottish Parliament run by socialists meeting in Edinburgh in a year than we could ever achieve under a Conservative government meeting in Westminster in a hundred years.'[1]

This was said by Gordon Brown MP, on Sunday May 3, 1992, on Glasgow Green. The occasion was the first sizeable Labour gathering in Scotland after a General Election result which had been, at the very least, a setback to the cause of Home Rule.

The location was symbolic. James Maxton, whose biography Brown has written, had often spoken on the Green in very similar terms on the national question, once declaring that a Scottish Parliament could achieve more in five years than a British House of Commons could deliver in 25 or 30 years.[2] At other times Maxton, though denying any spirit of national exclusiveness, came close to support for an independent Scotland:

> Give us our Parliament. Set it up next year. We will start with no traditions. We will start with ideals. We will start with purpose and courage. We will start with the aim and object that there will be 134 men and women pledged to 134 Scottish constituencies, to spend their whole energy, their whole brainpower, their whole courage and their whole soul, in making Scotland into a country in which we can take people from all the nations of the earth and say: "This is our land, this is our Scotland. These are our people ..."'[3]

In 1918, Maxton had been a co-founder of the revived Scottish Home Rule Association and was elected to its national committee, while in the General Elections of 1922 and 1923, like all ILP candidates in Scotland, he pledged himself personally to self-government. In May 1924, he was a sponsor of George Buchanan's Private Member's Bill, which called for a federal form of Scottish Home Rule. Three years later, he supported the much more ambitious legislation launched by the Rev. James Barr, which called for Dominion status and the withdrawal of Scottish MPs from Westminster.[4]

Brown's biography, in fact, devotes little space or real analysis to its subject's Home Rule allegiance and other work on Maxton suggests that it was a faith which had died by the early 1930s.

> That Maxton had come to adopt a neutral position vis-à-vis national struggles by this time was a manifestation of his move towards revolutionary Socialism and internationalism and his total rejection of gradualism and narrow nationalism.[5]

The reality was less clear-cut than this, though by the lifetime of the second Labour Government, the ILP had begun to distance itself from a Home Rule

Association which, after the failure of Barr's bill, began to support nationalist, as opposed to Labour candidates, in by-elections.

Until then, it had been possible and indeed common to combine activism in the ILP with commitment to the Home Rule Association's aims. Maxton was an example of this, as was Christopher Grieve, a local activist and councillor in Montrose who was later to become better known as Hugh MacDiarmid, Scotland's greatest poet of this century.

Grieve had been an ILP member before 1914, rejoining it after the completion of war service. Having obtained newspaper work in Montrose, he was elected to the borough council there in 1922, also founding in the same year, a branch of the SHRA. Twelve months later, he narrowly failed to persuade the council to affiliate to it, his motion being defeated only by the Provost's casting vote.

The Montrose years were important to Grieve's development as a poet, but they also provide proof that conscientious ILP membership was not incompatible with the increasingly militant cultural and political nationalism which he espoused.[6] Grieve's abrasive, polemical style and increasingly bitter rejection of everything English, did not endear him to others who had also entered politics through the ILP, and certainly not to John MacCormick, founder of the Scottish National Party, whose autobiography is dismissive of Grieve's contribution to the national cause.[7]

MacCormick joined the ILP as a student at Glasgow University, partly because he could identify with what seemed to him the clear position on Home Rule which it had inherited from Keir Hardie, Cunningham Graham and the leaders of the original Scottish Labour Party created in 1888. Writing of Barr, Maxton and other ILP leaders of his generation, MacCormick describes the process by which he became sceptical of their true commitment to Home Rule:

> I think that most of them had a special sentimental compartment in their minds and it was there that they cherished as a somewhat distant dream the idea of Scotland governing herself: many of them had begun their active political life as Liberals in the Gladstonian tradition and Home rule was inherited along with other items of the radical faith.
>
> As the years went on and as positions of power and influence opened up to them, they gradually forgot their Scottish sentiment and like so many other Scotsmen of their time, concentrated their energies in a party loyalty which far transcended national considerations.[8]

There is, in fact, good evidence of Maxton's continued interest in debates on questions of nationality and self-government, especially after 1932, during the period of the Irish Free State's trade war with the British government. Maxton identified himself strongly with the Irish case, while stressing that Socialists could not support nationalist struggles which had no class dimension to them. A struggle for National Independence and against Imperialism he declared in the *New Leader*, 'can only be fully justified, if it combines with it a struggle for the overthrow of capitalism as well.'[9]

Although support for political nationalism grew in Scotland and the new Scottish National Party was able to raise its vote at successive elections, it was not until the outbreak of war that Maxton found himself occupying the same ground as an element within the movement. The approach of war had already divided the party over England's right under the 1707 Treaty of Union to conscript Scots. Bodies such as the Scottish Neutrality League and United Scotland produced leaflets and organised anti-war meetings and the National Party succumbed to serious divisions over what its position on the war should be.

In 1941, there was a series of arrests of anti-war nationalists and of young Scots who had either refused to register for military service or declined to undergo Army medical examinations. Maxton spoke in Parliament against these arrests, as well as a Special Branch raid on the home and business premises of R. E. Muirhead, a businessman and former ILP activist who had become a tireless publicist for the cause of independence. The National Party had in fact modified its 1937 Conference resolution refusing to accept any call-up in Scotland for as long as it was denied self-government, and Maxton was able to point this out, as well as to pour ridicule upon the ineptitude with which some of the raids and arrests had been carried out.[10]

There were times, indeed, when the British authorities seemed to be obsessed with the existence in Scotland of stereotypes like the deranged great-niece of the Laird of Mugg who assured Guy Crouchback, in the second volume of Evelyn Waugh's great trilogy of war novels, that:

When the Germans land in Scotland the glens will be full of marching men come to greet them, and the professors themselves at the universities will seize the towns. Mark my words, don't be caught on Scottish soil on that day ...[11]

Maxton's correspondence with Muirhead shows that he took the arrests seriously,[12] particularly that of John Waddell, who was sentenced to 12 months in Barlinnie Prison for refusing an Army medical. Maxton felt this was particularly severe and he worked tenaciously, but without success, to have the case reopened.[13] He committed himself as strongly to the plight of a much better known Scot who was arrested the following year, for refusing either to register for military service or to apply for classification as a conscientious objector.

This was Douglas Young, product of Merchiston Castle, a famous Scottish public school, Oxford graduate, lecturer in Classics at Aberdeen University, poet and Socialist, who had persuaded himself that the defeat of Britain and its allies would allow Scotland to conclude a separate peace. 'The Germans,' Young predicted, 'will look around for aborigines to run Scotland, and it is to be wished that the eventual administration consist of people who have in the past shown themselves to care for the interests of Scotland.'[14]

In the summer of 1942, Young, an amiable eccentric and fine scholar, was sentenced to a year's imprisonment and his supporters approached Maxton to see whether he could raise the case in Parliament. Maxton was sympathetic, but pessimistic about what he could do[15] and Young served most of his sentence, though the Secretary of State for Scotland, Tom Johnston, a socialist with an ILP pedigree as good as, if not better than Maxton's, used prison regulations to maximise the number of books Young could have in his cell in Edinburgh's Saughton prison.

While Young was still in prison, the ILP's Scottish Divisional Council met for its annual conference in February 1943, and one resolution before it called for the party to reaffirm 'its support of the right to self-government for Scotland.' Maxton asked the conference for leave to move this resolution and did so with force and eloquence, invoking his own speeches of 20 years earlier when the first ILP-backed Home Rule bill had been presented to Parliament. He was, however, careful to distance himself from the wartime Anglophobia of a vocal element within Scottish nationalism. He stated that

> I am not prepared at any time to whip up the population of Scotland to fight for their independence from the English association. I believe that Scotland should have self-government, I believe that Scotland will procure self-government. I do not believe that it is going to be done by a rebel fighting nationalist movement.[16]

He also made clear his acceptance of amendments to the effect that self-government would be best created on a federal basis and that only through Socialism would the emancipation of the working class ultimately be achieved. 'I have not the slightest objection to these amendments,' Maxton declared,

> They set forth largely what is my own view, that our interest in Scottish self-government is not the idea of Scotland standing alone against the world, but the conception of a self-governing Scotland putting its maximum quota into an International Socialist Commonwealth.[17]

Referring to the ILP's proven record of support for Indian and Irish Independence, he argued that Scotland's case for self-government was no different in principle, and he ended his speech by urging all nationalists to join the ILP rather than dissipate their energies in the currently fragmented politics of the Home Rule cause.[18]

When recruited to the Speaker's conference on electoral reform in 1944, Maxton kept in touch with nationalist opinion to gauge how far the debate on alternative electoral systems could be linked to the Home Rule case.[19] Nationalists such as Muirhead recognised this and were generous in their tributes, after Maxton's death two years later, to the man who had espoused the cause of Scottish self-government at the outset of his political career and had kept more faith with it than an increasingly Unionist Labour Party.[20]

Maxton's passing had, of course, been preceded by the departure both from Parliament and government itself, of Tom Johnston, another product of the ILP. Unlike Maxton, he opposed the party's disaffiliation from Labour in 1932 and initially committed himself, with Patrick Dollan, to supporting the short-lived Scottish Socialist Party, as a way of maintaining the ILP's educative and propagandist role. Johnston had lost his Parliamentary seat in the previous year's rout of Labour, though some close to him believed this to be a welcome release for a man who disliked London as much as Johnston claimed to do.

His memoirs are eloquent on the bleakness of weekends in London which he and other Scottish MPs had to endure before the introduction of free railway passes.[21] However, he was never as fierce in his antagonism to the city as Dollan, who declared, after one visit in 1927:

> The break-up of the capital is essential to the establishment and maintenance of an industrial order. London is the strongest prop of capitalism in Europe. The militarism, opulence, indolence and extravagance of London are appalling to the provincial Socialist. It neither seems to know nor to care about the wrongs and grievances of the millions living and working for its maintenance. It staggers along like a giant bully satiated with power and ease and confident in its authority to maintain its parasitical dominance for eternity.[22]

This was the language not so much of nationalism as of an anti-metropolitan populism belonging to a tradition dating back to William Cobbett. Johnston, however, could react with particular anger when he felt Scottish sensibilities were treated with almost calculated disdain in the capital. In 1927, for example, Prime Minister Baldwin unveiled a new set of murals in St. Stephen's Hall, one of which showed the Scottish Commissioners in 1707 presenting Articles of Union to Queen Anne. 'This is resented', Johnston wrote, 'because it depicted one of the most humiliating episodes in Scottish history'[23] and, with the support of Scottish MPs, he tabled a motion in Parliament for the Office of Works to have its funding reduced, as a protest.

In that same session, it fell to Johnston to second the Rev. James Barr's bill to give Scotland not merely devolution but full Dominion status and an end to further Westminster representation. The bill failed, and both causes were by then clearly slipping down the scale of Labour's priorities. Johnston later admitted to his own reservations about the bill which had attempted to go much further than the ILP's previous attempt at Scottish Home Rule legislation in 1924. As his biographer has put it, 'reaction in the Scottish Labour movement varied this time from mild irritation to outright relief. Enthusiasm on the issue had ebbed distinctly.'[24]

It would never have been easy for someone with so vivid a sense of Scottish history as the author of *Our Noble Families* and *The History of the Working Class in Scotland* to abandon his allegiance to a cause that had brought him into politics as an integral part of his Socialist belief in the right of all nations to self-government. After entering Parliament in 1922, he was in demand at the great rallies organised by the Home Rule Association, to commemorate Bannockburn and the execution of Wallace. These were huge events in which 'Scots Wha Hae' and 'A Man's a Man for a' That' were sung with the same fervour as the 'Internationale' by crowds of 40,000 and more.

Johnston saw the value of such manifestations of national feeling but could voice doubts too, as in 1923 after participating in a large Wallace Day demonstration in Glasgow.

> Let us hope that the pageantry and the great demonstration last Saturday in Glasgow are indications not of a narrow, sterile wha's like us pride, but a resurgence of that national feeling which seeks to cherish the distinctive quality and genius which is ours by birth and tradition and by social custom and which, if cherished and strengthened, may be to the glory and profit of all mankind.[25]

There was, in other words, no infatuation in Johnston's mind with self-government as a nationalist end in itself. This is abundantly clear from his memoirs, in which he devoted an entire chapter – entitled 'A Nation Once Again' – to the questions of nationalism and self-government.[26] Essentially, it has been argued that he saw Home Rule's potential benefits for Scotland in the same way that he saw decentralised power and active local government: as opportunities for more people to become involved in running their own lives.[27] His Housing Act, which as an under secretary at the Scottish Office he saw through Parliament in 1930, helped to do this by substantially enlarging the slum demolition and re-housing powers of elected local authorities.[28] But, unlike John Wheatley, ILP architect of another great Housing Act, he never allowed his success to distract him from the issue of Scotland's future constitutional relationship to the British state.

A political apprenticeship served in *Forward* and the ILP enabled Johnston, even after he left the party in 1932, to maintain his belief in Home Rule as a Scottish priority. Proof of that lies in his work for the London Scots Self-Government Committee, of which he became president in 1937 and, of course, as Secretary of State for Scotland from 1941 to 1945. Despite the onerous demands of that office, he patiently reviewed all the cases of imprisoned nationalist war resisters and kept in contact with leading nationalists such as MacCormick and Muirhead. The North of Scotland Hydro-Electric Board, which was his greatest legislative achievement of these years, was not just 'a source (among others) of the enduring Scottish sense of government as society's sword and shield against private greed.'[29] It was an autonomously Scottish body with a remit to manage a vital resource in and for Scotland.

It has been suggested that after his experience as Secretary of State, Johnston's developed a preference for efficient administration in Scotland once the commanding heights of Whitehall had been captured in 1945 by moderate collectivists.[30] Certainly, he often argued in the post-war period that Home Rule was irrelevant without the creation of a secure economic and administrative base in Scotland, but in 1949 he was happy to join with John MacCormick, another former ILP activist, in the all-party Scottish Convention which re-launched the debate on self-government and initiated the hugely successful National Covenant.

An essential point of contact for both former and continuing ILP members who wanted to influence the Home Rule debate, remained Roland Eugene

(R. E.) Muirhead. Born in 1868 at Lochwinnoch in Renfrewshire, he served an apprenticeship there in his father's successful skin tanning business before emigrating to South America at the age of 19 to absorb and study different cultures. He worked on ranches in Argentina and Paraguay, the latter country having a particularly powerful influence upon his political development:

> In Paraguay I was impressed by the fact that that country, with less than 100,000 population, was able to control its own affairs in its own way. Looking back, that is when I realised that Scotland was handicapped from lack of self-government.[31]

For a time he also lived in an Owenite colony in the United States, having inherited a family tradition of radicalism which dated back to the Scottish Chartist campaign of the 1840s. He ended his travels in 1891 and returned to Scotland to take over the running of the tannery on enlightened lines, giving workers a share both in the running of the factory and in the profits. Much of the company's substantial returns were invested by Muirhead in radical causes, and he became one of the original directors of *Forward* when it was launched in 1906, with Tom Johnston as editor. Two years later he joined the Lochwinnoch branch of the ILP in which he remained active until the late 1920s.

John MacCormick met him in 1927 in the course of talks which led to the formation of the National Party of Scotland. Muirhead attended these in his capacity as secretary of the revived Scottish Home Rule Association, although within the year he would terminate his membership of both this and the ILP. MacCormick remembered him vividly 20 years later:

> He was as difficult to negotiate with as granite is to carve, but whenever the combined argument of his colleagues pushed him into a new position, he would entrench himself there as immovably as in his former redoubt. He was of the calibre of the old Covenanters who defied the government's dragoons and gladly died for their faith. Like them, he made up in sincerity what he lacked in humour and although he was a wealthy man he always dressed shabbily in a kind of hodden grey, well suited for a conventicle on the moors.[32]

Muirhead's breaking point with both bodies was the failure of Barr's 1927 Home Rule bill in Parliament, despite support from the Scottish ILP. In April of the following year, he was instrumental in forming the Provisional Committee of the National Party of Scotland and was elected its first chairman after he finally resigned from the ILP. It was a reluctant parting of the ways, and he was careful to preserve his party membership cards which may still be seen, along with the copious deposits of papers and correspondence which he bequeathed to the National Library of Scotland.

The ILP's role, and the part it could play in a continuing campaign for Scottish self-government, remained important to Muirhead, especially after its disaffiliation from Labour in 1932. He took encouragement from the party's decision, three years later, to launch a Scottish edition of its paper, *The New Leader*, and communicated his optimism to James Carmichael, secretary to the party's Scottish Divisional Council:

> ... the ILP is coming back to Keir Hardie's view that Scotland is a National Unit. I hope it may not be long until the ILP in practice makes it a National Unit. If the ILP in Scotland had become an Independent National Unit while I was a member, I should not have resigned to join with others in a new body to secure Scottish self-government.[33]

Muirhead himself stood for the National Party in his native county of West Renfrewshire, increasing his vote from 1,931 to 3,609 against Labour and National Government candidates. He was grateful to the ILP's Scottish Divisional Council and the local constituency party for not putting up their own candidates and in fact, made a financial contribution to the ILP's General Election fund.[34]

Between 1935 and the outbreak of war in 1939, Muirhead became increasingly impatient with an ILP structure which he felt effectively neutralised the Home Rule allegiance of the party's Scottish Divisional Council. His reputation as a generous financial supporter of radical causes, as well as his 20-year membership of the party, made it automatic that in May of 1941, his name would be on the ILP's mailing list to raise desperately-needed funds after the destruction of its London offices in a German air raid. Muirhead's reply to F.W. Jowett, the honorary treasurer of the party's National Administrative Council, survives to show how highly qualified was his support for this appeal. He began his response by reiterating the reasons for his resignation in 1928, quoting in full conference resolutions on Home Rule.

> It is a sad reflection on the consistency of the ILP that no lead has been given by the chiefs of the ILP in favour of a Scottish National legislature although accepted by the ILP some 20 years ago.[35]

His only reason for contributing a cheque, he went on to say, was as a thanks offering for Maxton's readiness to put a series of leading questions in Parliament about the arrests of anti-war Scottish nationalists. He finished his letter by returning to the wider issue of Home Rule:

> I have often wondered why the purely democratic claim of Scottish self-government should have been so long cold-shouldered by the body initiated by Keir Hardie. Can any democratic reason be given why the ILP should not have been in the forefront all these years in pressing the claim for Scottish as well as Indian self-government?'[36]

Later in 1941, Muirhead went back to what he claimed was the disparity between the ILP's English leadership's support for Indian self-government and its indifference to Scotland's case. He was responding to a further call upon his funds by Jowett, this time in support of Fenner Brockway's candidature at the Lancaster by-election.[37] It prompted a reply from Brockway himself, ostensibly to Muirhead's May 27 letter to Jowett, although he chose to make broad defence of the ILP's position on questions of nationality and self-government as well as putting Scotland's claims into a perspective of his own.

> I would apply the principle of self-determination all round, but frankly, I don't regard the absence of democratic rights in Scotland as comparable with the absence of such rights in India. I think we must find a political structure for the British Isles which will prevent any domination over Scotland or Wales from London and which will give Scotland and Wales democratic control in all things essentially Scottish and Welsh. At the same time, I think it is clear that there must be a political and economic federation of the three countries. I don't think we have yet worked out sufficiently the solution of this problem and your letter will at least stimulate us to give further attention to it.[38]

The following month, John McNair, a fellow Scot who had become secretary to the ILP's National Administrative Council and who in 1955 wrote a biography of his close friend Maxton, took over from Brockway the task of trying to reassure Muirhead of the party's firmness in its commitment to Home Rule for Scotland. In a letter, he stressed that:

> ... the ILP Parliamentary group support the cause of National self-government for Scotland. Maxton has reminded the NAC that the only party to present to Parliament as a party a Scottish Home Rule bill was the ILP. We are alive to all aspect of the issues involved.[39]

With only three MPs remaining in Parliament and only 0.6 per cent of the total UK vote at the last General Election in 1935, the ILP had become a marginal force in British Labour politics and Muirhead devoted increased efforts to Labour itself on the Home Rule issue. This, however, lies outside the remit of an essay devoted to the relationship between the national question in Scotland and the ILP. Yet, even after John McGovern's decision to join the Labour Party in 1946, Maxton's death the same year and Campbell Stephen's passing in 1947, events which ended the ILP's representation at Westminster, Muirhead kept up his contacts with what was left of it, arguing the Home Rule case and accepting regular invitations to attend as a fraternal delegate the annual conferences of the party's Scottish Divisional Council, as they diminished in number year by year.[40]

He could still be optimistic about what he claimed as late as 1947 was the ILP's return to its old love with respect to Scottish self-government after having meandered in the wilderness over 20 years.[41] This was hardly fair to the party's Scottish Divisional Council, but in February of that year it reiterated its support for the principle of self-government. It was an opportunity for Muirhead to set out in the pages of *Forward* his vision of Scotland. He argued that

> I am one of those old-fashioned people who places considerable value on national life, customs and language. These are all growths of the ages and

71

as such are part of our very being and not to be lightly regarded or set aside. No better means for retaining all that is best in the life of a nation has yet been devised than that of a National Parliament through which national sentiment finds expression and embodiment in the laws of the land.[42]

Forward continued to have Muirhead's financial support despite his own resignation from the ILP, at any rate until 1946 when control of the paper was transferred outside Scotland. From its earliest days when he had been a director, he had worked hard to make sure that it incorporated the case for self-government within its unflagging presentation of a Socialist case. Johnston, in his memoirs, paid tribute to the importance of Muirhead's financial support, but also recalled an unnamed but rather cynical friend who used to say he always knew when the *Forward* was in exceptionally deep water; it would then come out with a specially strong Home Rule issue: that would be preparatory to 'touching' Mr Muirhead for a loan![43]

James Maxton, Thomas Johnston and Roland Muirhead were all products of the ILP although only Maxton remained with it until his death. There is evidence that he had come to feel its time had already passed and John McGovern was of the opinion that the ILP had died before Maxton did.[44] He also quoted Maxton prior to his final illness: 'I think that the ILP will go down, as it's steadily losing its finest stock and has a small unstable element left that has no united policy. I feel that I must go down with it.'[45]

In fact, the loss of talented activists was not a new threat to the party, particularly in Glasgow where in the two inter-war decades even the most vigorous branches had to face unemployment and emigration as a constant drain on their membership. As far back as 1924, the Glasgow ILP Federation's minutes congratulated the Pollokshaws branch on the success of its football team in the previous season, 'but alas, the flower of that victorious team is now over the water and far away, America claiming them.'[46]

Loyal to the lead given by Maxton and McGovern, the Glasgow Federation upheld the 1932 Bradford conference decision that the ILP should disaffiliate from Labour. A haemorrhage of Scottish membership marked the year prior to this act of 'suicide during a fit of insanity'[47] as one account describes it, but 24 out of the 32 Glasgow branches supported disaffiliation, accepting Maxton's view that a liberated ILP never had real prospects of 'creating a united working class movement that shall be serious in its efforts to achieve a Socialist Commonwealth in this country in the immediate future.'[48]

This was already a forlorn hope as core support for the party contracted to only a few Glasgow constituencies from which its impact on the continuing debate on self-government could only be a limited one. Even before the near-terminal crisis of disaffiliation, some leading members of the Scottish ILP, such as John Wheatley, were being drawn inexorably along the road of hoped-for Socialist advance within the confines of the existing British state.

Others who had served their political apprenticeship in the ILP saw no incompatibility between the twin goals of Socialism and self-government.

Edwin Muir, a fine poet and key figure in the Scottish literary revival, was one of them, and in 1935 he wrote of how he could see a Scotland 'ripe for two things: to become a nation and to become a Socialist community.'[49]

Muir was sceptical of Home Rule as an end in itself, arguing that 'a hundred years of Socialism would do more to restore Scotland to health and weld it into a real nation than a thousand years – if that were conceivable – of Nationalist government such as that to which the National Party of Scotland looks forward.'[50] More than half a century later, Scots remain neither Socialist nor self governing, 'a lethargic and divided people quick to resent a trifling insult but incapable of action to remedy their plight.'[51]

The current frustration, not just of the broad labour movement in Scotland, but of all who seek self-government as a democratic alternative to the archaic structures and conventions of the Anglo-British state, has revived memories of the ILP's degree of commitment to Home Rule. During the 1989 Glasgow Central by-election, the Scottish National Party distributed a vivid leaflet entitled 'The New Clydesiders', a title it claimed for its candidate in Central and for Jim Sillars, already elected for Govan in 1988. The leaflet used photographs of Wheatley and Maxton, describing them as:

> Men of integrity and determination who fought the people's fight and went to jail rather than accept defeat. But the old Clydesiders were Home Rulers – good men who failed to beat the Westminster system.[52]

Beating that system and substituting for it a polity commensurate with Scotland's claim to nationhood remains a major challenge to socialists and democrats in our country.

Acknowledgements

I should like to thank the staff of the Manuscripts Room of the National Library of Scotland for the assistance they gave me in my preparation for this chapter. I am also grateful to Mr. Kevin Pringle, research officer of the Scottish National Party, for his promptness in sending me a copy of the party's Glasgow Central by-election leaflet. Thanks are also due to Dr. Ian Donnachie for referring me to some important sources which have proved valuable.

NOTES

1. *Scotsman*, 4 May 1992.
2. G. Brown, *Maxton* (Edinburgh, 1986), p.161.
3. *Ibid.*
4. M. Keating and D. Bleiman, *Labour and Scottish Nationalism* (London, 1979) pp.102–3.
5. W. Knox, *Scottish Labour leaders 1919–1939* (Edinburgh, 1984), p.207.
6. A. Bold, *MacDiarmid* (London, 1988), pp.152–3.

7.   J. MacCormick, *The Flag in the Wind* (London, 1955), pp.13–15.
8.   *Ibid.*, pp.14–19.
9.   *New Leader*, 24 Sept 1932.
10. *Ibid.*, 2 Aug 1941.
11. Evelyn Waugh, *Officers and Gentlemen* (London, 1955), pp.66–7.
12. National Library of Scotland, (subsequently NLS) Acc. 3721, Box 17, File 429. R. E. Muirhead to J. Maxton, 9 May 1941.
13. *Ibid.*, 14 July 1941.
14. NLS, D. Young Mss., D. Young to Muirhead, 1 Aug 1940. See also C. Harvie, *Scotland and Nationalism* (London, 1977), p.53.
15. NLS, Acc. 3721 Box 51, File 213, Muirhead Papers, 14 July 1942.
16. *New Leader*, 13 Feb 1943.
17. *Ibid.*
18. *Ibid.*
19. NLS, Acc. 3721 Box 51, File 429, Muirhead to Maxton, 14 July 1944.
20. *Ibid.*, 20 Dec 1949.
21. T. Johnston, *Memories*, pp.62–6.
22. *New Leader*, 4 Feb 1927.
23. *Ibid.*, 15 July 1927.
24. G. Walker, *Thomas Johnston* (Manchester, 1988), pp.79–80.
25. *Forward*, 1 Sept 1923.
26. Johnston, *op. cit.*, pp.62–6.
27. Walker, *op. cit.*, p.44.
28. *Ibid.*, pp.99–100.
29. N. Archerson, *Independent on Sunday*, 9 June 1991.
30. C. Harvie, *Scotsman*, 16 May 1941.
31. Knox, *op. cit.*, p.217.
32. MacCormick, *op. cit.*, p.24.
33. NLS, Acc. 3721 Box 19, File 519, Muirhead to James Carmichael, 21 Nov 1935.
34. *Ibid.*, Carmichael to Muirhead, 31 Oct, 22 Nov 1935.
35. *Ibid.*, Muirhead to F. W. Jowett, 27 May 1941.
36. *Ibid.*
37. *Ibid.*, Muirhead to Jowett, 13 Oct 1941.
38. *Ibid.*, F. Brockway to Muirhead, 22 Oct 1941.
39. *Ibid.*, J. McNair to Muirhead, 12 Nov 1941.
40. *Ibid.*, Muirhead correspondence, 13 Jan 1951, 6 Oct 1953, 8 Feb 1954, 3 Dec 1957.
41. NLS, Acc. 3721 Box 631 File 35 Muirhead to *Forward*, 10 Feb 1947.
42. *Ibid.*
43. Johnston, *op. cit.* p.33, also Knox, p.218.
44. J. McGovern, *Neither Fear Nor Favour* (London, 1960), pp.167–8.
45. *Ibid.*
46. ILP Glasgow Federation, Annual Aggregate Meeting, minutes 4 Apr 1924.
47. R. K. Middlemass, *The Clydesiders* (London, 1965), p.259.
48. J. Scanlon, *The Decline and Fall of the Labour Party*, p.11, Preface by Maxton.
49. E. Muir, *Scottish Journey* (Edinburgh, 1980, first published 1935), pp.233–4.
50. *Ibid.*
51. *Ibid.*, p.xxxi, Introduction by T. C. Smout.
52. The New Clydesiders, Election Communication from Alex Neil, SNP candidate for Glasgow Central, June 1989.

4. Breaking Moulds: The Leicester ILP and Popular Politics

Bill Lancaster

'The ILP grew from bottom up', observed Joseph Clayton in 1926 and in recent years this statement has become an axiom of Labour History. Local studies and grander surveys of the party all emphasise diversity and particularity. Nevertheless we can identify important factors and key variables that often form the ingredients necessary to the emergence of a local party. In some areas strong traditional institutions of Labour such as trade unions, trades councils and co-operation in both its retail and production forms were important. Local working-class culture also played a vital role. In this instance we need to draw a wide compass which includes religiosity, ranging from radical nonconformity to the radical High Anglicanism of the new slum ritual congregations that emerged in the 1880s. Organised unbelief in its secularist garbs was also often present sharing some psychological similarities with orthodox religion and at the same time nurturing the old radical artisan traditions that stretched back to the world of Robert Owen and beyond. Away from formal cultural institutions we encounter the informal, always difficult to quantify but nevertheless highly important. The persistence of St Monday, the independent milieu of the working-class pub, popular pastimes, new communal identities based on neighbourhood all served to shield workers from the hegemonic mission of Liberalism.

Formal political organisation, especially a strong Liberal Association with a radical hue, often had a part to play. Frustrated expectations of political office could, as Pelling has argued, channel working-class leaders into independent labour politics.[1] In other areas, however, the opposite was the case. The frontier township of West Ham in the 1890s consisted of a shifting population of itinerant dockers, gas workers and building employees in a marshy environment noted for its absence of a middle class and a weak Liberal presence. Yet the West Ham of the 1890s elected England's first socialist MP and socialist town council.[2] West Ham serves as a salutary reminder to those who argue for more generalisation in the field of working-class politics. All too often the above variables could work against independent Labour politics. The co-operative movement with its new slogan of 'Labour and Wait' offered for many an alternative path to the Commonwealth.[3]

Strong trade unions and trades councils dominated by a working class Liberal old guard often stifled nascent party branches. Nonconformity provided more formidable adversaries of the party than activists. Secularism, similarly, could produce a staunch hostility to socialism based on the old language of radical individualism or in some instances provide recruits to the ILP's socialist rivals.[4]

The discussion above draws away from the construction of a typology of an ILP branch and moves towards an emphasis on local particularity. But is this not to reduce the study of the early socialist movement to a formless kaleidoscope of contingency? This chapter aims to explore this problem by examining the emergence of the ILP in Leicester and it will conclude by comparing the Leicester experience with that of other Midland towns such as Coventry, Northampton and Nottingham.

Leicester does not fit readily into the mental map of the ILP. One's imagination, when thinking of the party, is naturally drawn to the factory towns of the Pennines and some coalmining districts, particularly in Scotland. Yet Leicester could boast the fourth largest branch of the ILP, an unusually large number of councillors and guardians, a highly successful local ILP weekly that survived until 1928, a close association with Ramsay MacDonald the town's first Labour MP and a structure of party organisation that was to become the national model.[5]

Leicester's image is no doubt further clouded by the town's economic prosperity for much of the twentieth century. With its modern mix of light engineering and clothing and an unusually high proportion of working wives, Leicester enjoyed the second highest level of family income in Western Europe during the 1960s. Nineteenth-century Leicester, however, had a far less fortunate experience.

During the 1840s the town was virtually dependent upon the woollen hosiery trade. This industry had suffered a terrible decline since the early 1830s. The poverty of its workforce gave rise to the stark popular image of the 'lean hungry stockinger' and a major Royal Commission on their economic plight. Not surprisingly Leicester was a major centre of Chartist activity, sometimes led by Thomas Cooper, and numbered among its young supporters A. J. Mundella and Thomas Cook, the future travel agent.[6] The 1850s witnessed the arrival of the ready-made shoe industry, a development that was to end widespread local poverty, increase rapidly the population size and shape the political trajectory of Leicester during the following half century. I have discussed elsewhere the realignment of Leicester Liberalism during the 1850s: what we need to note here is the strong radical element in local politics and the persistence of a radical working-class identity within local liberal politics.[7]

The working-middle class alliance in local politics was underpinned by the economic prosperity generated by the footwear industry. Beginning in 1850 this trade was to enjoy four decades of unprecedented expansion. Unlike other boot and shoe districts the Leicester trade employed the latest technology and specialised in fashion items. Despite the widespread utilisation of American machinery and the intensification of the division of labour the industry was based on the workshop system. It was not until 1891 that the factory became the dominant unit of production. The triumph of the factory in the Leicester footwear industry is one of the paradoxes of Labour History: the factory was introduced on the insistence of the workers who perceived the system as the most conducive to unionisation and the best defence against the cut price tactics of dishonourable workshops. Thus in 1891 over 24,000 workers moved from workshops into factories.[8]

Up until the late 1880s, workers in the footwear industry enjoyed the best of both worlds. Rising demand led to relatively high wages and industrial concentration. Shoemakers flocked from other older manufacturing districts bringing with them the craft's notable radical artisan tradition. What they found on arrival was a mixture of the new and the familiar. Leicester was rapidly becoming Europe's largest centre for footwear production, yet the organisation of the industry, despite the input of new technology, was still based on workshop production. These units were to be found everywhere, in spare rooms in dwelling houses, in back gardens and with larger ones springing up overnight on spare land. The labour process was also familiar. The craft had been subdivided into four main areas since early in the century and the new American machinery was often peddle powered, tending to increase production rather than fundamentally alter the technique of manufacture. The itinerant artisan, accustomed to piece work in a largely unsupervised environment, fitted easy into this milieu. St Monday was still honoured by these disciples of St. Crispin, while excursions during the day to pubs, races and fairs were common. Leicester's footwear manufacturers were concentrating into larger concerns but continued with the traditional production process. It was after all familiar and highly flexible. Besides, why tie up capital in factories and time in developing management structures when labour was abundant and demand was high? Thus the artisan shoemakers enjoyed their golden age between the 1850s and mid 1880s, an experience that was to be of profound political importance.

Industrial relations in footwear if not always friendly were usually harmonious up until the 1880s.[9] Disputes generally arose over the introduction of new styles which were increasingly the creature of popular fashion. Such changes often required adjustment to piecework rates which could give rise to fractious behaviour from both sides. But more often than not workers and manufacturers were primarily concerned with defending their common interests. The defence of uniform local piece rates protected both workers and manufacturers from renegade capitalists trying to steal an advantage, whilst the main enemy of both were the country sweatshops in the surrounding villages. This commonality of interest was to have two important ramifications for local politics.

The first was the unusually high degree of unionisation amongst Leicester shoemakers. The National Union of Boot and Shoe Operatives (NUBSO), formed in 1874, had over one third of its membership in Leicester where its headquarters were based. The majority of union officials came from the town and Leicester issues generally dominated the society's affairs. The second was the close relationship between the union and the Leicester Liberal Association. The Association was undoubtedly dominated by footwear manufacturers, with Sir Edward Wood, Chairman of Freeman, Hardy and Willis increasingly at the helm of local liberalism as the century neared its close.[10] The Association nevertheless enjoyed a considerable working-class presence throughout the period. Thomas Smith, NUBSO's first general secretary, became the full- time secretary of the Liberal Association in 1878 and his two immediate successors, Sedgewick and Inskip, sat with him as Liberal councillors in the town hall.[11] Not surprisingly this strong working-class input into Leicester Liberalism endowed he party with a strong radical hue. The republican P. A. Taylor was one of the two Liberal MPs until 1886 and Henry Broadhurst represented the town after 1894.

The above discussion fits neatly into the classic model of Lib-Labism. Yet Broadhurst's election in 1894 was the beginning of the end of Leicester's working-middle class alliance. He was, surprisingly, opposed at the polls by Joseph Burgess standing for the ILP. Burgess gained over 4,000 votes after campaigning for less than a week and this result almost allowed a Conservative victory.[12] More worrying for Leicester Liberalism was the demise of William Inskip's power in NUBSO when the union conference in 1894 clipped the wings of his political ambition by refusing to allow him to stand as the Liberal candidate for Northampton.[13] In less than a decade the Liberal alliance was seriously weakened by the rise of a young generation of socialists in NUBSO. But what were the changes behind this development, why socialism and why the ILP?

Socialism did not emerge in Leicester out of the ranks of shoemakers. Its lineage rather begins amongst hosiery workers in an industry that had many links with, but was increasingly being overshadowed by footwear. Leicester hosiery enjoyed a revival after 1850.[14] The 'lean hungry stockinger' gave way to a new generation of workers, largely based in workshops and increasingly utilising new machinery in the ancillary parts of the Labour process. The industrial revolution in hosiery began in the 1860s in the Nottingham cotton hosiery trade with the adoption of the 'Cotton's' patent powered knitting frame which led to factory, production. Because of patents protection the 'Cotton's' machine could not be utilised by the Leicester woollen trade until the early 1880s. The introduction of power frame knitting in the early 1880s was relatively painless. The old hand-frame knitters had been in decline for over a decade and the new machines became the preserve of young men well versed in mechanised production thanks to their experience on ancillary machines.[15] These workers, however, were not wage slave proletarians. Their background was that of the workshop milieu and even in the early factories they continued to rent machinery as had been the norm in the industry for over a century. Moreover, the high capital costs of machinery and building necessitated twenty-four hour working in order to recoup investment. Legislation had made women's night work illegal which guaranteed male control of the new and more important technology. The 'Cottons patents' operators turned themselves into a factory-based labour aristocracy, whilst below them the majority of the workforce consisted of women utilising cheaper less sophisticated technology.

Despite rising demand for wool hosiery, based on the growing fad for woollen underwear, the second half of the 1880s were difficult years for the Leicester Amalgamated Hosiery Union, (LAHU). Two processes served to undermine the union's position. The first was the trend in many factories to introduce fully mechanised production which later in the decade involved a new generation of lighter power frames. Many factory owners sought to turn the male 'Cotton's' operatives into overlookers of a number of new machines. The union's policy of one man one machine heralded a confrontation with employers. It also strained relationships within the union, particularly between women who formed the majority of union members, and the all male leadership, the representatives of the 'Cotton's' men.[16] Disputes over operating the new plant often resulted in firms leaving Leicester in order to avail themselves of more compliant labour in the country areas.

The exodus of a major portion of the Leicester hosiery industry to nearby towns and villages is a classic example of centre-periphery economics.[17] It also served to politicise the union leadership. Economics was never very far from politics in Leicester. The working-middle class alliance of Leicester Liberalism had been forged by John Biggs the hosiery capitalist at the mid century and hosiers had dominated local politics until the 1880s when they began to be overshadowed by footwear manufacturers in the Liberal Association. Thus Labour disputes in hosiery often contained a political dimension. But should this be any surprise? Hosiery was the town's oldest major industry and its worker's radical pedigree stretched back through mid century republicanism to Chartism, Owenism and the era of the corresponding societies. Moreover, this radical tradition was not broken by post-Chartist developments. It survived as an important element in local radical Liberalism and it continued a separate existence in local secularism.[18]

The Leicester Secular Society has recently been well served by historians and the complex development of Britain's largest provincial branch of infidelity need not detain us here. What we need to note, however, are the following points. Despite middle-class patronage the Society was always predominantly artisan/working class in composition. Secularism added an element of audacity to local politics whether it be religious disputations or more substantial matters such as the anti-vaccination campaign conducted by secularists in the 1870s.[19] The steady stream of lectures from national and international radicals and revolutionaries kept local members in the forefront of major developments. In particular the Bradlaugh-Hyndman debate of 1884 on socialism was eagerly debated in Leicester and the local Secular Hall became a major venue for socialist lecturers. It comes as no surprise, therefore, to find Leicester's first socialist organisation, a branch of the Socialist League, being formed in the Secular Society in 1885.[20] Predictably the membership was dominated by secularist hosiery workers, led by Tom Barclay the LAHU's first secretary. Branch 13 of the Socialist League soon ran into conflict with the middle-class individualists who dominated the society and moved on to the Spiritualist Hall in Silver Street before settling in the LAHU offices in Horsefair Street.[21]

Much of the Socialist League's activities in Leicester were closely linked to hosiery industrial relations, particularly the union's attempt to recruit country workers. But there was more to this process than the grim 'class struggle at the point of production'. Barclay and his great friend and LAHU executive member George Robson came from the strong working class autodidact tradition. Lovers of art, literature and culture in general, as well as radical discourse, these two were also avid consumers of extension and correspondence courses. Barclay, a son of Irish itinerant rag and bone collectors, was also steeped in the tradition of Irish radicalism. Their fellow leaguer and LAHU officer, J. Warner, was a descendent of the bearer of the Chartist Banner at the Battle of Mowmaker Hill. True to his family's tradition of direct action Warner turned to Anarchism on the demise of the League. Branch 13 also attracted the support of some young middle-class secularists. James Billson, a friend of G. B. Shaw, and Maximilian Bunting, both from local manufacturing families, were members along with Archibald Gorrie, the main benefactor of the League in Leicester. The middle-class League members shared a love of culture with the artisans which affected other areas of local life. The Leicester Socialist League inhabited a world that was anything but provincial. They could attend lectures by Dr. Aveling in the main room of the new Secular Hall, surrounded by sculpture and walls clad with William Morris tiles. They could retire afterwards to the new vegetarian restaurant and select refreshments from a menu illustrated by Walter Crane. The more adventurous would accompany Barclay on visits to Edward Carpenter's home in the Peak District. Engels once remarked that English craftsmen were the best educated in Europe in the 1840s. He was, of course, referring to the great tradition of artisan self education; in many ways that tradition was very much alive in the Leicester of the 1880s.[22]

Branch 13 was one of the most enduring in the Socialist League. However, by the late 1880s middle-class support was in decline, scared off by anarchism and revolutionary language, and membership failed to increase beyond a hardcore of twenty or so activists. Nevertheless the League did much groundwork in establishing a socialist presence in Leicester. The Chartist tradition of street-corner oratory was revived and the League's policy of socialist education was beginning to attract a few young trade unionists from the footwear industry. But perhaps the League's major bequest to the local labour movement was the establishment of the Leicester Labour Club. This club in the early twentieth century was to become both a popular drinking club and the home of the local labour movement, a classic institution of an homogeneous working class. Yet its origins were of a quintessential artisan nature. On the 18th March 1888 James Holmes, the general secretary of the LAHU, together with Barclay, Robson, Warner and eighteen others met in a house in King Street for the purpose of a political dinner in celebration of the Paris commune. This traditional ceremony was followed by a lively discussion which resolved to establish a socialist club. Subscriptions were taken and the club opened as the Labour Club.[23] The League's final bequest to the Labour movement was the establishment by Barclay in the early 1890s of the Leicester Independent Labour Press which produced the *Pioneer* from the early 1890s.[24]

The artisan facade of popular politics in Leicester in the 1880s was largely the product of the persistence of workshop production which served to nurture old radical traditions. Yet by the late 1880s this style of politics was being undermined by rapid economic and social development. Hosiery was now factory based, footwear was entering a period of rapid structural change and new neighbourhoods of red bricked terraces were rapidly expanding in the west of the town. Of most importance, however, was a development that was taking place in most of Britain's town centres. New shoe shops owned by American companies were quickly opened up, often on short leases, in major shopping areas. The claim that Britain nearly lost its footwear industry in the early 1890s is no exaggeration. The highly mechanised Massachusetts industry was, after much struggle, factory based and producing shoes on an assembly line system. Moreover, the Americans produced popular fashion goods which were the bedrock of the Leicester trade. Needless to say British manufacturers could not compete with the newcomers.[25] Nevertheless the solution to the British problem was ready at hand. Throughout the industrialised world footwear was increasingly being produced by machines manufactured by the United Shoe Machinery Company of America. This concern held a worldwide monopoly on virtually all modern footwear machinery, a monopoly closely protected by patents. The company also pursued a unique distribution system. Machines were leased, not sold, and payment was based on the number of items produced. The majority of local manufacturers had been using a variety of these machines for some years, many were adaptable to workshop production and the workers did not see them as a threat so long as the traditional division of labour and organisation of production remained intact. The logic of machine production was a fully-mechanised manufacturing process. The obstacle to this objective was the inability to develop a machine to perform the lasting tasks. Lasters were the most numerous and best organised section of the workforce. For example, virtually every elected officer of NUBSO came from this section. They also possessed a fair element of skill; manipulating and shaping the upper to the last was a difficult process and some workers underwent a form of apprenticeship.[26] The development of a lasting machine in 1889 revolutionised the Massachusetts industry. Workshops were replaced by factories, the old division of labour was obsolete and production was carried out on an assembly line by semi-skilled operatives. Finally, to seize their advantage, American manufacturers developed their own retail outlets in foreign markets.

The only response available to the Leicester trade was to follow the American system. The machine company had extensive showrooms in Leicester; with the new technology and thanks to the leasing system, local manufacturers could revolutionise the industry with the minimum of capital investment. The only major obstacle was the workforce. The factory system had been the main form of organisation in Leicester since 1891, a year or so before the invasion of American products. Attempts to rationalise production, however, invariably met with stiff opposition as workers sought to preserve the *status quo*. Lasting machines were introduced into some factories in 1891 but a typical response according to the trade press was:

> In Leicester if they run a machine for five minutes at full speed, they seem to think it necessary to stop it and see that no breakage has occurred. Then they walk about the shop and borrow an oil can or spanners wherewith to do some totally unnecessary thing. This occupies anything from five minutes to an hour, and then the machine is run again for a few minutes, and if the operator is questioned he says 'machines are no good; I could do the work quicker and better by hand'. And so he could, for he takes care not to let a machine beat a shop mate working by hand on the same job and in short does all he can to induce manufacturers to abandon mechanised devices and go back to hand labour and not to earn as much money as possible per week, but as much as possible per job. In other words to keep the cost of production as high as possible.[27]

When American imports took a significant share of the market in late 1893 the obduracy to mechanisation could not be tolerated. The local manufacturers began to act in unison to co-ordinate the coming struggle through the Leicester Boot Manufacturers' Association. The employers were assisted by advisers from the American Machine Company who promised high productivity if they were allowed access to factories and given control of shop floor organisation. This vista of proletarianisation and a declining home market led to a rapid deterioration in industrial relations. The era of disputes being settled by trade union leaders and manufacturers who shared the Liberal benches in the town council was rapidly disappearing. The first casualties of this worsening climate were Liberal trade unionists. These men, led by NUBSO's General Secretary William Inskip, cut their political teeth in the halcyon days of the 1860s and 1870s. They were bound to Liberalism by the language of manliness, self help and individualism. Above all they shared a sense of producers' or occupational consciousness with the employers. For these men the days of face to face relations with the master in a workshop was still a vivid memory. The language of class and socialism ran counter to the lessons of their personal experiences and their vision of the world for which they had laboured for so long.

Their young members did not share this vision. They were the products of the Board Schools and the large, impersonal workshops of the 1880s. The bosses were distant figures, residing in the grand houses up the London Road.

Yet they were still imbued with the artisans sense of natural justice that was rooted in a communally agreed piece-work system of wage payment. The employers were perceived to be breaking this consensus and the elected leadership of their unions were silent in response. The younger workers, particularly the lasters, developed a number of strategies in their attempt to cope with the new industrial situation. The first was to wrest power from the old guard. The initial step to this goal was control of the Leicester No 1 Branch, whose 11,200 members formed almost a third of the national membership. Led by the young laster T. F. Richards this task proved to be relatively simple. Richards' oratory, inflected with socialism from his association with Barclay, was highly popular with young workers, whilst older members haunted by the spectre of the strong youth, paid by the day and paced by the Americans in operating the lasting machine, were anxious for any alternative to the impotency of the old guard. A second strategy was the potent – but with hindsight utopian – scheme of co-operative production. Labour historians generally have overlooked the renaissance of producers' co-operation in the late nineteenth century. In many ways this is an important oversight. The idea of producers' co-operatives was at its peak in the 1890s and the centre of gravity of this revival was the east midlands, particularly amongst shoemakers.[28] In Leicester, in the early 1890s, the co-operative commonwealth was more than an utopian fantasy. Striking workers from the local CWS footwear factory had established the Equity producers' co-operative in 1887 and by the early 1890s were employing several hundred workers.[29] A group of workers who were members of the Millenarian Church of Christ and pioneers of the local ILP established the Anchor producers' co-operative in the 'Garden City' of Humberstone in 1893.[30] Co-operative production held the promise of freezing the existing labour process and utilising machines on the workers own terms. Furthermore, despite hostility from the CWS there were many friendly retail societies willing to market their products.

Co-operative production dominated the affairs of NUBSO in the early 1890s and provided a substantial base of support for the young radicals.[31] Indeed even after the Richards group became committed socialists, co-operative production remained their main priority up until 1895. Thus the militancy of Leicester shoemakers on the eve of the formation of the local ILP needs to be kept in perspective. A relatively small group of young lasters, led by Richards, were able to gain the ascendancy of local union politics primarily by their advocacy of co-operative production rather than socialism.

When Keir Hardie arrived in Leicester on 2 June 1894 to address a meeting at the local ice rink he was surprised by the size and enthusiasm of his audience. The meeting had been organised by the SDF of which Richards was a member although no local branch existed. The purpose of the gathering was to discuss the fracture in Leicester politics caused by the candidacy of Henry Broadhurst at the forthcoming parliamentary by-election. Broadhurst's reputation as the nation's premier working class representative was under a cloud caused by the scandal surrounding his involvement with the Brunner chemical works.[32] The affair had added piquancy in Leicester because of Broadhurst's close involvement with William Inskip on the TUC Parliamentary Committee. In particular the Leicester Trades Council, dominated by NUBSO, was seriously debating its traditional alliance with the local Liberal Association. We need to bear in mind that in this period, in many towns, the Trades Council was the major working-class political institution that frequently nominated or backed candidates in elections ranging from School Boards to General Elections. The Leicester Liberal Association was acutely aware of the Trades Council's power and nurtured close relations with the Council, even hosting an annual 'Labour Dinner' for Council officers.[33] However, the gathering storm in the footwear industry and discontent in hosiery over the haemorrhage of trade to the countryside served to weaken the old alliance with Liberalism which was increasingly perceived as the bosses party. The Trades Council's decision to back Broadhurst only if he stood as Trades Council candidate and not as a Liberal signalled the ending of the traditional *status quo*. Broadhurst went ahead with his candidacy, the Liberal Association nominating him as a Liberal-Labour candidate which further enraged the local labour movement.

Keir Hardie's visit was more than a major labour personality stepping into a local controversy. Hardie was deeply aware of the potential importance of Leicester to his new party. NUBSO was one of the largest trade unions in the country and its role as powerbroker in the TUC promised a major contribution to Hardie's vision of the ILP as the unifying force between socialism and the organised Labour movement. Hardie made a point of praising NUBSO's local organisation and the importance of trade unions to working people. This was in stark contrast to recent visitors from the SDF who had lectured the Leicester socialists on the futility and conservatism of trade-union activity.[34] Hardie concluded his stay with a visit to the Labour Club. Warning the members that 'Liquor and Labour don't mix' and the dangers of turning the club into a 'lounge for loafers',[35] Hardie oozed respectability, a quality that was a strong hallmark of the Richard's group. Hardie's stay in Leicester had important outcomes that were to profoundly alter the contours of Leicester's Socialist and Labour movement. In terms of formal politics a branch of the ILP was immediately established and Burgess represented the party at the by-election. In other areas of popular politics the arrival of the ILP was of great importance.

The first noticeable shift witnessed the growing formalisation of popular politics. In 1894 an ILP-Trades Council manoeuvre resulted in the removal of Barclay as editor of the *Pioneer*. A similar development removed the growing anarchist group, led by Warner and other ex-Socialist League members, from the Labour Club. This routing of the easy going, beery socialism of the Barclay group also had an impact on women. The socialism of the 1880s inhabited a world of informal gatherings in the Secular Hall, the Spiritualist

Hall, ice rinks and country excursions. These venues were gender free and women could find space to express their political aspirations. Kate Barclay and Clare Warner were notable figures in this period, often taking the platform at meetings. These two sisters of the two most prominent Socialist Leaguers have left little in the way of historical record save for mentions in Barclay's autobiography and a few snippets in the local Labour press.[36] Nevertheless it is possible to detect eddies which suggests that women were beginning to have an impact on local socialism in the later 1880s and early 1890s. For example, an article by Mrs. Saunderson in the penultimate issue of the *Pioneer* to be edited by Barclay was full of references to Bebel and Carpenter and made an appeal for a feminist dimension to local socialism. Significantly she concluded that the chances of such a perspective developing were being hampered by, she claimed, the ILP's tendency to cut itself off from all forms of influence that did not have a direct bearing on the 'Labour Question'. The establishment of the male members only 'Labour Club' as the meeting place of the ILP adds much weight to Mrs. Saunderson's charge.[37]

It would, however, be unfair to portray Leicester socialism as a movement that followed the path of bureaucratisation and formalism. Stephen Yeo in an important article has argued that such a process was a distinctive feature of British socialism which accelerated after the mid 1890s.[38] Despite the tightening control of the local institutions of socialism by the Trades Council -ILP group Leicester socialism continued to display many features that were rooted in local radicalism. For example the ILP's campaign in local government elections which commenced in 1895 reflected both the defeat of the shoemakers at the great lock-out of that year and the replacement of co-operation as the route to the Commonwealth with the even older notion of land reform. Rising levels of unemployment after the lock-out and the de-skilling of the workforce produced by assembly line manufacturing breathed new life into the 'land question'. A vision of artisans turned into healthy agriculturalists dominated local debate on the question of rising poverty and connected with Morris's utopianism and the atavistic nerves of the old radical tradition.[39]

Also after 1895 the culture of socialism became richer and more widening. Clarion cycling groups and choirs, socialist picnics, a socialist church all indicate the emergence of ILP socialism as both a political and cultural movement.[40] By the early 1900s the Leicester ILP could boast strong roots in the formal labour movement, the party now dominated the town's considerable trade-union organisation and at the same time reflected the richness of local working culture. Amos Sherriff a lapsed Salvationist turned socialist was the local purveyor of the *Clarion* cycle and leader of the *Clarion* readers' group as well as an ILP Guardian. J. T. Taylor a leader of the millenarian Church of Christ and a leading figure at the Anchor workers' co-operative and the Humberstone Garden City was also ILP treasurer and councillor. George Banton a carpenter and notable non-conformist lay preacher was chairman of the Trades Council and an ILP councillor; while

85

T. F. Richards in many respects the founder of the party in Leicester was a councillor and one of the most powerful figures in NUBSO. Finally F. J. Gould, the full-time secretary of the Leicester Secular Society, severed his links with 'radical individualism', joined the party, became a councillor and a notable campaigner on education, particularly on the question of religious education in Board Schools.[41]

Besides this rich diversity another dimension on the personnel of the ILP needs to be underlined, their age. None were born before 1860 and most were in their thirties. This youthfulness of the party was to have important implications for the future of Leicester Liberalism. Banton and Chaplin, for example, had both been secretaries of working class Liberal wards before their conversion to socialism.[42] Their defection was soon followed by the collapse of Liberal ward organisation in working-class areas and within a decade the working-class Liberal councillors was a moribund species in Leicester. All the evidence suggests that between 1895 and 1906 Liberalism in Leicester lost a generation of support to socialism, a loss from which the party was never to recover. Moreover, the youthfulness of Leicester's population, thanks to recent large scale in-migration, amplified this important process.

Little wonder that Ramsay MacDonald chose Leicester as his political base. The Leicester ILP, Trades Council and local trade union branches had been advocates for the formation of the LRC. Also the presence of many working-class institutions from clubs to the local socialist press provided a firm platform for parliamentary campaigning. On the other hand MacDonald had strong attractions for Leicester socialists. Apart from his background in the SDF and the Bristol Socialist Society his connections with Secularism through his journalism added to his local appeal. And, of course, as principal author of the LRC, the Leicester socialists perceived MacDonald as a candidate commensurate with their status as a major centre of the ILP.[43]

MacDonald's first parliamentary campaign in 1900 was in many ways a damp squib for Labour. The election was dominated by the Boer War, with the local regiment under siege at Ladysmith, acrimonious divisions within Liberalism in Leicester caused by the war, and some ill-feelings over MacDonald's pacifism. Labour were unable to improve on Burgess's 1894 vote but the flack from the South African issue gave the Conservatives their first parliamentary victory in over 40 years. Leicester Liberalism was forced to undertake a serious investigation of its electoral setback. After an internal struggle the old radical wing of the Liberal Association under the leadership of Sir Edward Wood, defeated the local Liberal Imperialists.[44] Wood, however, realised that it would take more than party unity to restore the fortunes of the Association. Central to this task was the healing of relations with the local labour movement. Wood was in no doubt that the ILP and the LRC were now permanent institutions and that co-operation rather than competition was the key to future political success. This strategy was greatly eased by the close personal relationship that developed between Wood and MacDonald. So close was this relationship to become that MacDonald was even able to persuade Wood to become a major investor in the *Pioneer*.[45]

It is of no surprise from a Leicester perspective that MacDonald and Gladstone concluded their electoral pact well away from national scrutiny in the local isolation hospital. Both Liberal and Labour campaigners in local elections were already using the rhetoric of 'progressivism' and forming local ward electoral 'arrangements' to defeat the Conservatives in local elections. This cosy world of compact was largely based on the workers in the two major industries acceptance of the victory of the employers and the machine. The effects of this victory, however, was an incremental increase in unemployment as more factories converted to assembly line production. This process accelerated during the recession of 1904–5 and ultimately destroyed the local Lib-Lab pact.

Poverty became the dominant issue in Leicester in the two years prior to the 1906 general election. Once-proud shoemakers and their families with no hope of employment in the restructured industry were being forced into the 'test yard' and the workhouse. 'Relief without Pauperisation' became the burning issue during this period and Labour increasingly campaigned for an expansion of municipal employment to ease the problem.[46] This idea of intervening in the local labour market was anathema to local liberals and this division drove a wedge between the two parties. Local government elections became extremely bitter, Labour became firmly identified as the only party willing to tackle poverty and the Liberals were again perceived as the party of the bosses firmly wedded to the sanctity of market forces. Yet poverty was no longer the preserve of the 'residue' and the prospect of the 'test yard' loomed large in the minds of many skilled workers.

The following table clearly shows the electoral effect of Labour's campaign on poverty:

Table 1   Labour candidates returned 1902–07

	Board of Guardians	*Town Council*
1902	2	2
1903		4
1904	11	7
1905		11
1906		11
1907	16	

Liberal organisation in working-class wards collapsed during this period and as early as 1904 there is clear evidence of a Liberal-Tory pact in local elections.[47] Many Liberals were naturally bitter at this turn of events and frequently referred to the Labour Party as the ILP. Thus the birthplace of the 'progressive alliance' was, in terms of local politics, its earliest failure. This point is underlined by the growing tensions over unemployment demonstrations during the winter of 1904–5 and the subsequent unemployment march to London in 1905. Yet despite these tensions the parliamentary pact held in Leicester and MacDonald and Broadhurst were elected as members for Leicester in 1906. Pressure from the national leadership, the influence of Wood, the cross party appeal of MacDonald and the bitter memory of damaging in-fighting all served to guarantee a low key, innocuous election process.

By 1906 the ILP pioneers could look back with pride to major achievements gained in just twelve years. A firm sustainable base of support had been built, particularly in the working-class wards in the west end alongside the Narborough Road. Much of this was based on the NUBSO system of organising and retaining members employed at home and in small shops. The ILP network of 'street captains' which Henderson and MacDonald incorporated into their model for local organisation was a continuation of the shoemakers system.[48] A culture of labour was also established, with their own newspaper, clubs and social activities. Independent working class representation was by 1906 a fact of life in local politics recognised not least by the Liberals. A doyen of the party was their national representative and the damaging divisions within socialist politics that marred so many local movements had been avoided.

Yet for all of the period under review Leicester remained the beacon of the new party in a region of indifference. How can we explain this phenomena? The paucity of research on other towns and cities in the region works against accurate, meaningful comparison and some of what follows needs to be viewed as speculative and hopefully stimulation for future research. But first we need to state a somewhat obvious point. Despite the growth in trade and interlocking, yet competitive, national economies, most areas in Britain continued to be dominated by local economic forces and their individual histories. What happened in one town was never experienced the same way in another. Let us begin with the obvious comparison of nearby Northampton, Leicester's sister footwear town which also enjoyed a radical tradition. Northampton could boast a secularist past which included the notorious election of Charles Bradlaugh to parliament. Bradlaugh, however, represented the rumbustious tub-thumping strand of secularism in contract to Leicester's support of Holyoake with all the latter's emphasis on co-operation, organisation and education, a comparison materially expressed in the grandeur of the Leicester Secular Hall in contrast to the paucity of of secular premises in Northampton. This taste for noisy iconoclasm continued with Northampton becoming one of the few provincial strongholds of the SDF.[49]

This difference in political tone needs to be placed alongside the structure of the footwear industry in the two towns. Northampton specialised in men's boots and military footwear and it did not experience the frequent fluctuations of the fashion-based Leicester trade. Units of production remained small and military specifications mitigated against rapid mechanisation. Moreover, Northampton was a weak centre of trade unionism. Only one in twenty shoemakers were members of NUBSO in comparison to one trade unionist every 2.4 workers in the Leicester trade. Northampton could muster only 600 NUBSO members in 1888 against 6,323 in Leicester.[50] The location of NUBSO's headquarters in Leicester and the domination of the union by Leicester men was also deeply resented in Northampton. A cursory look at union conference reports from the mid 1890s gives an initial impression that James Gribble, the leader of NUBSO in Northampton, was in the SDF to spite his arch-rival Richards of Leicester. There may be a modicum of truth in this impression but note needs to be made of the deep differences in popular political culture between the two places.

Coventry provides a different, yet, nevertheless interesting comparison. The alliance between Liberalism and workers had been smashed in the 1870s when the town's silk industry became one of the first casualties of the Cobden free trade treaty. Economic decline in the 1870s and early 1880s resulted in a falling population and political torpor.[51] The renaissance of Coventry's industrial base in the 1880s, thanks to the bicycle industry was largely fuelled by migrant labour. Yet these workers came to a new industry, to be employed in a new labour process largely without precedent. Semi-skilled 'metal bashing' did not attract skilled engineering workers and an organised labour movement was virtually absent. This lack of a popular political tradition and the dearth of labour institutions, together with a booming economy and rising living standards, pushed the ILP to the political margin. Nevertheless the party did manage to get one councillor elected and prompted the council along the path of housing reform.

A similar picture emerges in Nottingham. The local lace industry suffered from free trade and many workers favoured the Tories and tariff reform. Local miners, thanks to good working conditions remained loyal to Liberalism and new industries such as tobacco,bicycles and Boots the Chemist ensured a prosperous, diversifying economy. Nottingham did, of course, possess a labour tradition including trades unions, co-operatives and a strong secular movement. John Burns had campaigned for Parliament in 1885 assisted by Joseph Burgess, the ILP pioneer but Nottingham remained largely indifferent to the socialist revival.[52]

This short comparative excursion may leave the impression that the botany of the ILP in the region is as complex as that of the slipper orchid! Only in Leicester do we find the right soil, sub strata, drainage and climate. This, however, is not a misleading metaphor. The period under review, described by Clapham as the age of 'Machines and National Rivalries', did witness the cracking of Britain's political mould.[53] But the impact of the forces analysed by Clapham was extremely variegated. Massachusetts manufacturers were not in the market for British army boots, Midland entrepreneurs were as good as any in the world in the mass production of bicycles, and the local coal industry remained impervious to the international battles of carboniferous capitalism. Political traditions and modes of working-class organisation were equally prone to particularity. This is not to deny that the ILP was a national party, with national personalities, its own press and a common agenda. But surely the patchiness of the ILP map and indeed that of the Labour Party up until 1914 warns us against glib talk of 'national political culture' and alerts us to the richness and diversity of Britain's unevenly developed working class? Only in Leicester did several cracks meet and the mould fall apart.

NOTES

1. H. Pelling, *Origins of the Labour Party* (1965), chapter 10, *passim*.
2. F. Reid, *Keir Hardie, The Making of a Socialist* (1978), chapter 6.
3. S. Yeo (ed.), *New Perspectives in Co-operation* (1989).
4. E. Royle, *Radicals, Secularists and Republicans, Popular Freethought in Britain, 1860–1915* (1980) offers the best survey of Secularism in Britain.
5. B. Lancaster, *Radicalism, Co-operation and Socialism, Leicester Working Class Politics 1860–1906* (1987) gives a full account of the party in Leicester.
6. A. T. Patterson *Radical Leicester A History of Leicester 1780–1850* (1954) is a highly readable survey of Leicester's early 19th Century history. See also J. F. C. Harrison, 'Chartism in Leicester' in A. Briggs (ed.), *Chartist Studies* (1959).
7. Lancaster, *op. cit.*, chapter 6.
8. *Ibid*, chapter 8.
9. *Ibid*. See also A. Fox, *A History of the National Union of Boot and Shoe Operatives, 1870–1957* (1958), chapter 8.
10. Lancaster, *op. cit.*, p.99.
11. *Ibid.*, p.46.
12. J. Burgess, *Will Lloyd George supplant Ramsay MacDonald* (1926), p.63.
13. NUBSO Conference Report, 1894.
14. F. A. Wells, *The British Hosiery and Knitwear Industry: Its History and Organisation* (1972) is the major survey on the industry.
15. Lancaster, *op. cit.*, chapter I.
16. Webb Collection, Section A, vol 34.
17. Lancaster, *op. cit.*, pp.18–20. See also A. L. Friedman, *Industry and Labour, Class Struggle at Work and Monopoly Capitalism* (1977) for a discussion on centre periphery economics.
18. Lancaster, *op. cit.*, chapter 4.
19. *Ibid.*, pp.82–83.
20. *Ibid.*, pp.87–88.
21. *Ibid.*, p.89.
22. A vivid portrayal of these socialist pioneers is to be found in Tom Barclay's autobiography *Memoirs and Medleys, The Autobiography of a Bottle Washer* (1934).
23. *Commonwealth*, 24 Mar 1888.
24. For a discussion of the *Pioneer* see Lancaster, *op. cit.*, pp.112–3.
25. *Ibid.*, chapter 2. See also the essay by J. T. Day 'The Boot and Shoe Trade', in H. Cox (ed), *British Industries under Free Trade* (1902).

26. Lancaster, *op. cit.*, chapter 2.
27. *Shoe and Leather Record*, 19 Feb 1892.
28. B. Lancaster, 'Towards the Co-operative Commonwealth?', *Midland History*, 1988.
29. *Ibid.*, See also E. O. Greening, *A Pioneer Co-Partnership* (1923).
30. Lancaster, *op. cit.* See also A. Mann, *Democracy in Industry* (1914).
31. NUBSO Conference Report, 1894.
32. Lancaster, *Radicalism, Co-operation and Socialism*, pp.123–4.
33. *Ibid.*, p.99.
34. *Ibid.*, p.117.
35. *Labour Leader*, 2 June 1894.
36. Lancaster, *op. cit.*, pp.110, 127.
37. *Pioneer*, 3 Jan 1895; 'Rules of the Leicester Labour Club', 1896, p.15.
38. S. Yeo, 'A New Life: The Religion of Socialism in Britain 1883-1886', *History Workshop Journal*, 4, 1977.
39. Lancaster, *op. cit.*, pp.166–8.
40. *Ibid.*, chapter 9.
41. *Ibid.*
42. Leicester Liberal Association, *Annual Report, 1892*.
43. Lancaster, *op. cit.*, pp.150–162.
44. *Ibid.*, pp.158–161.
45. *Ibid.*
46. *Ibid.*, pp.163–170.
47. *Ibid.*
48. A. Henderson and J. R. MacDonald, *Notes on Organisation and the Law of Registration and Elections* (1904).
49. On Northampton see K. Brooker 'The Northampton Shoemakers reaction to Industrialisation: Some thoughts', *Northamptonshire Past and Present*, 6, 3, 1980; and the same author's 'James Gribble and the Rannds Strike of 1905, *ibid.*, 6, 5. 1980. On the SDF in Northampton and provincial Britain see P. A. Watmough, 'The Membership of the Social Democratic Federation 1885–1902', *Bulletin of the Society for the Study of Labour History*, 34, 1977
50. Lancaster, *op. cit.*, p.115.
51. See the essays by D. W. Thoms and T. Donnelly, and B. Lancaster in B. Lancaster and T. Mason (eds.), *Life and Labour in a 20th Century City. The Experience of Coventry* (1986).
52. For Nottingham see P. Wyncoll, *The Nottingham Labour Movement* (1988); R. A. Church, *Economic and Social Change in a Midland Town: Victorian Nottingham* (1966).
53. J. H. Clapham, *An Economic History of Great Britain* (1963 ed.).

SECTION II

LOCAL STUDY — BRADFORD

1. Late Victorian and Edwardian Bradford

Tony Jowitt

Bradford became at once one of the most provincial and yet one of the most cosmopolitan of English provincial cities. Its provincialism was largely due to its geographical situation. It is really in a back-water. The railway main lines went to Leeds, ten miles away, and not to Bradford, with the result that Leeds, though it has never had the world-wide reputation of Bradford, is a larger city and of much greater local importance. It was Leeds and not Bradford that became the great marketing centre of West and Mid-Yorkshire. Leeds has a University and law courts; Bradford has not ... A city that has mixed trades will probably have some of its corners rubbed off; it must work with other places, but Bradford with its one trade, was all corners, hard provincial angles ... And then there was this curious leaven of intelligent aliens, chiefly German-Jews and mostly affluent ... That small colony of foreign or mixed Bradfordians produced some men of great distinction, including a famous composer, two renowned painters and a well known poet.

There was, then, this odd mixture in pre-war Bradford. A dash of the Rhine and the Oder found into our grim runnel – t' mucky beck. Bradford was determinedly Yorkshire and provincial, yet some of it suburbs reached as far as Frankfurt or Leipzig.[1]

J. B. Priestley's description of the Bradford of his youth depicted a community of contrasts, of stolid Yorkshire folk and cosmopolitan merchants, of the narrow concerns of individual chapels and the world-wide concern of the worsted textile industry which spread its business tentacles to every corner of the globe. In particular he described the last flourish of a powerful provincial culture which had been such a strong feature of nineteenth century Britain.

What came to an end during the First War – at least in my experience – was a kind of regional self-sufficiency, not defying London but genuinely indifferent to it. My father, for example, never read a London newspaper. What happened "down south", outside politics was no concern of his.[2]

Bradford displayed a powerful, independent local life style, best exemplified in the field of culture and politics and a rich local diversity in a period before metropolitan control embraced it. And yet it is clear that the situation in Bradford was something of an Indian Summer, the last flowering of nineteenth century provincial life which had made Bradford one of the important cities of Victorian England. In that late-Victorian and Edwardian period it was to reach its apogee due to its powerful political culture and in particular because it was the heartland and the great early centre of the Independent Labour Party (ILP), its vibrant and dynamic cultural life, the most admired educational system in the United Kingdom and finally because it still remained the wool textile capital of the world. This chapter will examine the history of Bradford in the last decade of the nineteenth century and the first decade of the twentieth in an attempt to understand why it became the heartland of the ILP and a centre of progressive ideas and politics.

Bradford was a classic nineteenth century industrial city, expanding from little more than a large village at the beginning of the century to the worsted textile capital of the world by 1851. During that period it was the fastest growing industrial community in the British Isles and although its growth slackened after 1850 it continued to expand; the population throughout the century growing from 13,264 in 1801 to 103,778 in 1851 and by 1911 it stood at 288,458.[3] After 1881 the growth of the city was largely due to the extension of the municipal boundaries and the incorporation of the surrounding districts.

After 1870 there was a dramatic fall in the local birth rate from well above the national average to well below it, which seemed to signal a decision on the part of textile workers to escape from the low wage/large family spiral which was an ongoing problem in textile communities. These communities were associated with low wages, high levels of male unemployment and under-employment, high levels of female and adolescent labour and a high birth rate. In the late Victorian and Edwardian period however textile workers seem to have started to consciously limit family size in order to break out of this situation and to break the dependence on family wages in the textile industry. Significantly research amongst those involved with the Bradford ILP has shown that small families predominated.

Table 1   Decennial population increases in Bradford 1801–1911[4]

1801–11	1811–21	1821–31	1831–41	1841–51	1851–61
21%	64.1%	65.8%	53%	55.3%	2.8%

1861–71	1871–81	1881–91	1891–1901	1901–11
37%	23.9%	11.3%	5.6%	2.7%

At the end of the century Bradford had the highest proportion of one-child families in the country and was closely followed by the neighbouring community of Halifax. In common with other large urban areas, Bradford was also clearly experiencing the beginnings of the movement out of the city wards to suburban or semi-suburban areas. This movement was fuelled by the shortening of working hours and the development of an efficient, cheap, urban transportation system; horse buses and steam trams from 1882, electric trams from 1898 and the trolley bus from 1911.[5] Bradford, however, was to remain until well into the twentieth century a socially mixed community with a mixture of social classes in virtually every ward in the city.

The massive population explosion of the first half of the century has been associated with the growth, mechanisation and concentration of the worsted textile industry on the town, for apart from the ironwork to the south at Bierley, Bowling, Low Moor and Shelf, and some coal mining and stone quarrying, textiles was virtually the only source of employment. Throughout the century textiles remained the dominant source of employment; in 1881 approximately a third of the male labour force and two-thirds of the female labour force were directly engaged in textiles. [6] However the worsted textile industry had a clear sexual and age imbalance. In the early stages of production in the first half of the century the mills were primarily staffed by young people. John Wood's spinning mill, the biggest in Bradford in 1833, had 521 workers of whom only 18 were aged over 21.[7] Although the Factory Acts and the development of education somewhat curtailed the youthfulness of the textile labour force it still retained the proportions of adolescent workers. In 1873 at Daniel Illingworth's Whetley mills 650 out of the 943 workers employed there were aged seventeen or under.[8] The Bradford trade apart from a few areas such as night machine combing, dying and sorting was dominated by female workers.

Table 2   Composition of textile labour force in Bradford 1911 (%)[9]

	males under 18	males 18+	females under 18	females 18+
Combing/ Carding	3.1	60.9	2.4	33.6
Spinning	20.2	9.4	31.7	38.7
Weaving	5.6	14.3	10.9	69.2
Dyeing	10.1	82.9	1.2	5.8

The Bradford worsted trade more than the neighbouring woollen and cotton industries was predominantly made up of adolescent and female workers in the biggest sectors of spinning and weaving.

Up to the 1870s the Bradford trade experienced massive and sustained growth but from the mid 1870s, with the onset of the Great Depression, it experienced a series of set backs which were to have a profound effect not only on the trade but on the labour relations within the mills and the community and eventually on the political composition of the city. Indeed it is from the 1870s that the long slow decline of the local textile industry commences.

The first problem that confronted Bradford trade was a change in fashion. Up to the 1870s Bradford manufactured women's dress goods from a mixture of fibres which produced a hard lustrous material. At that point there arose a demand for a softer, more free-flowing type of material, associated with all-wool worsteds, a trade largely ceded to French producers. Coupled with this change in fashion was the growth of textile industries elsewhere in Europe and the USA, which were defended from British competition by the erection of protectionist tariffs. From the 1870s tariff walls against British worsteds went up around the world, culminating in the infamous McKinley tariff of the early 1890s, the spark for the Manningham Mills strike, and the less well known but worse Dingley tariff of the late 1890s which decimated the Bradford trade with the USA. Bradford manufacturers were therefore confronted with a series of problems – closed or difficult markets for their goods, increased imports into the home market by foreign producers and a lessening demand for its staple product. These changes occurred during the period of the so-called 'Great Depression' which was a period hostile to innovation and re-equipping.[10] The problems faced by the Bradford trade led to major modifications in its structure and organisation and in the composition of the workforce which were to have dramatic economic, political and social effects.

The Bradford trade modified its product, changed its markets and introduced changes in the form and nature of production. Faced by changes in fashion and a harsher competitive situation the Bradford manufacturers did not change to the French system and produce all-wool worsteds as this would have entailed re-equipping and dramatic changes to the labour force. Rather they retained their existing systems and turned to the production of men's suitings, overcoats, mackintoshes, flannels and furnishing fabrics. In addition they directed more attention to their domestic market and areas which were free of tariffs, in particular the Empire. The most dramatic change, however, was the wholesale development of semi-manufactures. As other countries developed their own worsted industries Bradford turned to supplying them with spun yarn and, when and where spinning capacity developed abroad, with combed wool (tops). The export figures for the worsted industry between 1880 and 1904 show that the total amount of piece goods exported increased by 4%, yarns by 40% and tops and noils by 533%, a clear indication of a movement back down the production cycle and sectionalism and fragmentation within the trade.[11] This increased sectionalism, most marked in the combing and dyeing sectors where commission working was widespread, produced a much harsher and competitive industry.

The changes associated with the textile industry in this period brought in their wake significant changes in the relationship between employers and their workforces. Before 1850 Bradford had been almost synonymous with deep social divisions expressed most clearly in a powerful, militant and sometime violent Chartist movement. In the third quarter of the nineteenth century Bradford had been closely associated with the development of a paternalistic ethic in an attempt to heal relations between classes in the newly industrialised and urbanised Bradford. The outstanding example of employer paternalism was Saltaire, where Titus Salt attempted to

> Marry the technology and economic structure of the nineteenth century to the ordered authority and intimate relationship of a pre-industrial rural society.[12]

This exercise was copied on a more limited scale by the dyeing magnate H. W. Ripley in Ripleyville. Other manufacturers, although not attempting such grandiose schemes, encouraged the development of a conciliatory atmosphere through the organisation of works trips and the provision of a series of workplace social and recreational facilities in such things as works canteens, brass bands, cricket clubs and libraries.

In the late nineteenth century this attempt to inculcate harmonious workplace and community relations was breaking down under two forces. The first was the movement out of a direct role in the industry by the leading families and employers. The desire for a different type of lifestyle was startlingly clear. The majority of millowners' sons were educated at public schools and Oxford and Cambridge and aspired not to a career in the mill but in the armed services, the professions, politics or the life of a gentleman of leisure. So Henry Mitchell, son of Sir Henry Mitchell, the foremost spokesman of the trade in the period, was educated at Bradford Grammar School and Trinity College, Cambridge and went into the army. Hugh Ripley, son of H. W. Ripley was educated at Cheltenham for the army; Reginald Thompson, son of Matthew Thompson, was educated at Uppingham and Trinity College, Cambridge and lived the life of a gentleman of leisure; Percy Holden Illingworth, son of the prodigious entrepreneurial forbears in Henry Illingworth and Mary Holden was educated at Jesus College, Cambridge, was well known as a rugby player and big game hunter and later became an influential politician. There was clearly an aspiring after a higher social position than that which the mill could bestow, which saw the transference of both money and personnel from Bradford to landed estates throughout the whole of the United Kingdom. The largest purchase of all was Samuel Cunliffe Lister's buying of two North Yorkshire estates for close to three quarters of a million pounds, but this was only the largest of a number of such moves which included the fosters of Black Dyke Mills purchase of Hornby Castle, Angus Holden's purchase of the Nun Appleton Estate, Francis Willey's of Blyth Hall in Nottinghamshire and Sir James Roberts' purchase of a Scottish estate of 7,000 acres. The movement out of the town led not only to a lessening of interest in the firm and workforce but also to the replacement of direct involvement by an attitude which was more concerned with the amount of money that could be squeezed from the firm for conspicuous consumption elsewhere.

The second reason for the breakdown of paternalistic relations stemmed from the movement out of trade and the economic conditions of the late nineteenth century, which witnessed a period of declining profits which in turn led to a squeezing of the labour force in order to keep up profits. There were thus attempts to replace male by cheaper female labour, to increase the numbers of adolescent and young workers, particularly half-timers, and to speed up machinery, as the *Bradford Observer* noted:

One weaver will now mind in two looms as much as 11,000 to 12,000 ends for practically less wages than were once paid for minding two looms with a matter of 800 ends each.[13]

There was also an increase in the number of machines per worker; in mohair spinning one frame per operative was replaced by one operative looking after six machines.

There is little doubt that there was a sharpening of the relations between employers and workers which gave an impetus to the development of trade unionism amongst textile workers. During the period there was an increase in the number of textile trade unionists, most strikingly amongst the dyers who by 1914 were close to 100 per cent unionisation, but there were successes amongst semi-skilled workers like the Combers.[14] However trade unionism was notoriously difficult to achieve amongst young workers in the trade who left it on reaching the point of payment of adult wages, because of the multiplicity of the piece and wage rates, because of the incidence of short time working and because of employer hostility. As Ben Turner, later to become President of the largest textile union in the 1920s said of Bradford: 'The most heart breaking district for trade union organisation that I ever came across.'[15]

Rivalry amongst the textile trade unions was endemic. Status was extremely important and sectionalism prevented attempts to create general improvements. The Warpers' Association was specifically set up because they believed 'their craft was of high importance and that they were of superior character to some of the other mill operatives'. These attitudes were carried over into the community, for as Ben Turner said:

> The weaver was looked down upon by the overlooker ... a woollen spinner despised the average man in ordinary grades of labour ... the woolsorter had his special chair in his special snug at his customary public house and a wool comber or a labouring factory worker had to be above the ordinary if he was allowed in that place.[16]

In particular, many trade unionists were clearly hostile to women workers. The Yorkshire Warp Twisters made the exclusion of women from their trade the central tenet of their strategy and fought successful strikes in 1899 and 1902 to prevent the introduction of female Warp Twisters. Particular hostility was directed at working women, which was in sharp contrast to Lancashire where women workers were much more heavily unionised. By 1914 it was said of the trade union position, that it was

> ... still in its infancy ... none of the pressing problems that affect it have been satisfactorily handled. Craft prejudice, narrowness of outlook, suspicion and benefit-hunting' are rampant. Indeed compared with any other industry or occupation this branch of the textile trade of England is lamentably backward.[17]

Although sectionalism and sexism amongst textile trade unionists were major barriers to progress the greatest problems lay in the state of the trade and the employer offensive on labour costs. In the twenty-five years before the First World War unemployment and irregular working became commonplace. Woolcombing provided the most striking example of the appalling conditions of work. Woolcombers commonly worked a 64-hour week, some working from 5.15pm till 6am without a break, often in temperatures over 100°F. Further their work was casual as they were taken on each evening, and were expected to turn up each evening even when it was known there was no work available.[18]

The textile industry at the end of the nineteenth century was one which was marked by poor working conditions, low wages and where conditions were deteriorating. This decline in the staple industry, which in 1911 still provided the biggest source of employment, employing some 27,393 males and 34,232 female workers was not matched by gains in other areas of employment. In the late Victorian economy generally there occurred a development of new industries and new types of work, particularly in fields such as transport, retailing and lower middle class jobs such as clerical work, teaching and local government. Bradford manifested aspects of this employment change but at a much lower level than was experienced nationally. Thus there was an increase in engineering which in 1881 employed 4.4% of male workers, rising to 9.4% in 1911. There was a similar rise in transport employment from 5% to 10.9%. Even smaller changes were experienced in white-collar employment.[19] Bradford therefore entered the twentieth century with only minimal changes in its employment structure, it remained overwhelmingly a manufacturing city and one which was overwhelmingly dependent on worsted textiles.

During the heyday of the Bradford trade the textile industry was made up of a large number of small firms but dominated by a much smaller number of large enterprises. Those firms were synonymous with the development of the trade – Titus Salt, Samuel Cunliffe Lister, Isaac Holden, the Illingworths, the Priestmans, the Mitchell brothers, H. W. Ripley, the Wauds and the Priestleys. After the 1870s very few large industrial empires were created in the town: only two firms could be said to have emerged in this period to rival those already mentioned, the firms of James Hill and Francis Willey. The decline of the textile oligarchy, the men who had created so much of the Victorian City, was also to be seen in municipal affairs. In 1880 the town council could boast a fair sprinkling of the leading figures of the town amongst its ranks, including G. M. Waud, Matthew Thompson, John Priestman, Frederick Priestman and Edward Priestman, Angus Holden, Briggs Priestley and Alfred Illingworth. By the early twentieth century the only important families still represented on the Council were the Godwins, the Priestleys and the Priestmans. In their place on the Council were a much greater number of shopkeepers and small business men with a sprinkling of manual workers whose entry had come through the rise of the Independent Labour Party.

There was a clear fall in the socio-economic status of the Corporation and at the same time with the extension of the city boundaries the introduction of people like farmers and shopkeepers. And although large employers of labour like H. B. Priestman remained important on the council, increasingly important figures were drawn not from the staple textile industry but from areas like building, which had three important figures on the councils of the

Table 3   Occupations of Council Members[20]

1880		1911	
Textiles	32	Textiles	24
Other Business	15	Other Business	24
Professionals	3	Professionals	12
Gentlemen	7	Gentlemen	5
		Drink	2
		Shopkeepers	9
		T.U. Officials	2
		Farmers	2
		Manual Workers	3

later period – Alderman Gadie, David Milner and Albert Dickinson – and other areas of business such as Edward Fattorini the Jeweller, and Enoch Priestley the butter factor and seeming 'lord of Wibsey'.[21]

In the same way that the council saw a fall in the status of its members, a similar process of decline can be seen with regard to religion, particularly Nonconformity and in particular the decline of the great city centre chapels like Horton Lane Congregational Chapel, that great symbol of Nonconformist ascendancy in mid-nineteenth century Bradford. In the 1850s it had been recognised as Bradford's 'Cathedral of Nonconformity' providing many of the early mayors and aldermen for the city, including Robert Milligan, Titus Salt, Henry Forbes, Samuel Smith and Henry Brown. By 1900 it was rapidly becoming run down, as most of its middle class flock moved to the suburbs and some even further to the dormitory towns of Ilkley and Harrogate. As the *Bradford Weekly Telegraph* commented:

> What is to become of Horton Lane Congregational Chapel – the building which has been described as Bradford's Nonconformist Cathedral. Things are in a parlous state – no congregation to speak of, no Sunday School worth mentioning, no pastor.[22]

Although Eastbrook Wesleyan Chapel could induce large numbers to take part in its evangelical missionary work, generally there was an increasing fear about the future amongst many dissenters. As one local correspondent to the local press said:

> Congregationalism is not the only free church which has fallen from its high estate in Bradford as you put it. I could take you any Sunday to Wesleyan and other Methodist Chapels where there is a beggarly array of empty benches at every service. Every device has been tried to draw the public – even in some cases sensational advertising. For the present the people seem to have lost faith in the churches. They feel they have no need for their ministrations.

Attempts to popularise religious attendance in services such as the Pleasant Sunday Afternoon Services and Men Only Meetings had done little to stem the decline in attendances.[23]

During the nineteenth century Bradford had been one of the great citadels of Nonconformity. The 1851 Religious Census had shown that in Bradford the great bulk of the urban working class attended neither chapel or church, but of those who did attend religious worship, over 60% belonged to the different Nonconformist sects.[24] Bradford was therefore the third most Nonconformist urban area in England. This connection between Bradford and Nonconformity was further cemented in the 1860s and 1870s when Bradford was in the forefront of the Dissenters campaign to disestablish the Anglican Church.[25] But although in this period Nonconformity showed its political power it was itself beginning to be faced by a decline of its strength within the town. In 1851 the two most militant of the dissenting sects, the Congregationalists and the Baptists, had made up 21% of those attending church or chapel. In 1881 in the *Bradford Observer* census this proportion had fallen to 16.4%.[26] It is clear that after 1881 they continued in this slow decline and the great city centre chapels of Horton Lane Congregational Chapel, Kirkgate Wesleyan Chapel and Westgate Baptist Chapel saw their congregations dwindling and in the long run possibly more important the movement out of their area of the large millowners and the middle class generally. Many also as they rose in the social scale, transferred their allegiance to the Anglican Church, thereby placing greater strain on those who remained, for as Isaac Holden, the Wesleyan Methodist, said as early as 1871:

> One of the evils of a favoured religious sect is that its prestige and privilege entice away the wealthy from us so that the few who remain have too heavy a burden to carry to be able to assist the more wealthy establishments.[27]

The Primitive Methodists found a similar sluggishness, for, as the 1913 Annual Synod of the Bradford and Halifax district reported:

> We recognise that workers were never more busy in the work of the church; they were never more devoted; but we are making no inroad; we win no trophy. Working in the midst of an immense population we seem hardly to do more than hold our own.[28]

The Methodists who had shown the largest growth of all the religious bodies in the first half of the nineteenth century continued to expand after 1850 but at a much reduced rate and after 1880 they were faced by similar problems to the other Nonconformist denominations.

The two denominations that did significantly improve their position after the middle of the century were the Anglicans and the Roman Catholics. The Anglicans had been severely embarrassed by their numbers in the 1851 census, when it was seen that less than 25% of those attending actually adhered to what was supposedly the national religion. They made a major effort to improve the situation through the work of the Church Building Society and the monetary support of Francis Sharp Powell of Horton Hall, Charles Hardy from Low Moor Ironworks and also John Hollings, Lister and the Rands. Between 1850 and 1875 the Anglicans built 22 churches in Bradford, largely in the inner city area, thereby making its position more respectable at the 1881 Census, but in the long run creating a major problem for the twentieth century Anglican Church of inner city churches denuded of their parish by population movement. But the major growth denomination was the Roman Catholic Church, which increased its churches between 1851 and 1881 from one to seven, and the number of worshippers from 4,028 to 9,926, the latter figure representing 15.1% of all worshippers. Further, the Catholics were the only denomination that attracted the working classes, the great bulk of their supporters being Irish immigrants or their offspring. Indeed, it could be argued that by the late nineteenth century, Bradford rather than being a stronghold of Nonconformity was becoming a centre of Roman Catholicism. This success was reflected in its building programme, for unlike the Nonconformists and Anglicans, the Catholics have never had the problem of decaying city centre places of worship.

The problems facing the religious denominations were clearly reflected in the letter columns of the Bradford press. The range of things blamed was myriad, ranging from the bizarre to the ridiculous, from the old perennial of drink to the new craze of cycling. One of the main elements that was seized upon was the new forms of entertainment of Edwardian England. Most prominent amongst these new forms was the cinema; when opening the Elite picture house in August 1913 the Lord Mayor said that twenty-six picture houses were already operating in the city and plans had been passed for a further ten.[29] The cycling craze was particularly strong in the 1890s; the walk craze of 1903, and roller skating rinks being opened; all of these contributed to a new pattern of leisure activity. But the the greatest spectator sport of all, and a constant source of complaint amongst clergymen and editorial writers alike, was football. As the *Bradford Weekly Telegraph*, commenting on the Eastbrook Wesleyan Mission, said, 'Mr Nield made the brotherhood boom and Mr Muir has increased it, but football is the biggest brotherhood that Bradford has.'[30] This craze had its own heady success in 1911 when Bradford City carried off the F.A. Cup at the Crystal Palace. [31]

A further group saw social conditions as lying at the heart of the church attendance problem and some like the Rev. Rhondda Williams at Greenfield Congregational Chapel gained something of a reputation not for his advocacy of the 'New Theology' but for the stress that he placed on the social role that Christians ought to fulfil. It must be said that this element was in a minority and the majority remained wedded to laissez faire liberalism, and invariably placed the blame on drink. Temperance advocates were particularly concerned with the major expansion of clubs in the city for it was found in 1910 that there were 159 clubs: 34 Conservative clubs, 17 Liberal, 39 Labour, 12 Trades, 7 Oddfellows, 7 Irish and 44 purely social.[32] Others seized upon the morals of the working classes. As the Rev. Hodgson of Kirkgate Wesleyan Chapel stated, 'Christ would see in Bradford, crime, superstition and the hopeless helplessness of poverty and sinfulness. He would see in short, a horrible devil's cauldron.'[33] Indeed the fact that the ministers, particularly the Nonconformists, largely ignored social conditions and remained wedded to the non-interventionist Liberal party was to be an important element in the formation of the Independent Labour Party and the Labour Church in Bradford.

Social conditions in late nineteenth century Bradford were appalling. When she came to the town in 1893, Margaret McMillan found the poor children 'worse than anything that was described or painted'.[34] The death rate in 1884 was very little different from that of the 1840s when the town can only be described as an open sewer. By the late nineteenth century there was a wide variation in social conditions throughout the city which produced a wide variation in mortality and health statistics. Thus in 1888 the infantile mortality rate fluctuated from 130 per 1000 in affluent Heaton and 116 per 1000 in semi-rural Bolton to 219 per 1000 in Bradford West and 266 per 1000 in Exchange Ward.[35] A similar set of figures is revealed for the years 1908–12 when the figure for Bolton Ward had fallen to 83 deaths per 1000 live births, but in Bradford West it was 165 per 1000 and in Exchange Ward 245 per 1000.[36] Within smaller areas conditions were even worse. In the Longlands area off Westgate there was a population density of 300 persons per acre with death rates in 1895 and 1896 of 62 per 1000 and 69 per 1000 compared with figures for the whole of the city of around 20 per 1000.[37] In this area were concentrated some of the worst back to backs in the city, and altogether in 1884 there were over 26,000 houses of this type in Bradford. In August 1910 the Local Government Board said there were 28,000 back to backs in Bradford, which they thought meant over 100,000 persons or 39% of the population lived in such houses and that almost two-thirds of the population of Bradford lived in a house without a bath.[38]

In the mid nineteenth century Bradford had been dominated by the Liberal Party, built upon the alliance between the middle classes and the skilled working classes – the so-called labour aristocracy of overlookers, woolsorters, warp dressers, dyers, lithographers, carpenters, stone masons and others who looked to collaboration with the middle classes in a movement hostile to the urban bourgeoisie. Although unstable, and always liable to split apart under the strain of too vociferous dissenting demands, the Liberal Party in Bradford remained the single most important political grouping up to the 1880s.

From 1880 the pre-eminent position of the Liberal Party came under serious attack, so that by 1914 there was a three-party system in operation in the city. Although with hindsight it is very easy to see the most important factor as the formation and development of the Independent Labour Party, leading to the present day two-party system, more easily forgotten but just as important was the rise of the urban Conservative Party. Before 1880 Conservative successes were invariably the result of Liberal disunity but after that time it was increasingly clear that a different situation was emerging. By 1895 the Tories were strong enough to win all three Bradford parliamentary seats at the General Election, and to repeat that success at the 1900 Khaki general election when the Liberals were split over the Boer War.

Table 4 Parliamentary Election Results 1880–1914

C	Conservative
I	Independent
ILP	Independent Labour Party
L	Liberal
LU	Liberal Unionist
SDF	Social Democratic Federation
Soc	Socialist

1880

W. E. Forster (L)	14245
A. Illingworth (L)	12922
H. W. Ripley (C)	9018

1885

Central Division

W. E. Forster (L)	5275
G. M. Waud (C)	3732

Eastern Division

A. Holden (L)	4713
J. Taylor (C)	4367

Western Division

A. Illingworth (L)	4688
H. B. Reed (C)	3408

1886 by-election

Central Division

Shaw-Lefevre (L)	4407
B. Hoare (C)	3627

1886

Central Division

Shaw-Lefevre (L)	4410
G. M. Norwood (LU)	3957

Eastern Division

H. B. Reed (C)	4519
A. Holden (L)	4223

Western Division

A. Illingworth (L)	3975
A. Stirling (LU)	2623

1892

Central Division

Shaw-Lefevre (L)	4710
Marquis of Lorne (C)	4245

Eastern Division

W. S. Caine (L)	5575
H. B. Reed (C)	5373

Western Division

A. Illingworth (L)	3306
E. Flower (C)	3053
B. Tillett (ILP)	2749

1895

Central Division

J. L. Wanklyn (C)	4024
Shaw-Lefevre (L)	3983

Eastern Division

H. B. Reed (C)	5843
W. S. Caine (L)	5139

Western Division

E. Flower (C)	3936
J. C. Horsfall (L)	3471
B. Tillett (ILP)	2264

1896 by-election

Eastern Division

R. H. Greville (C)	4921
A. Billson (L)	4526
Kier Hardie (ILP)	1953

1900

Central Division

J. L. Wanklyn (C)	4634
A. Anderton (L)	4007

Eastern Division

R. H. Greville (C)	6121
W. E. B. Priestley (L)	5514
J. Sheldon (I)	111

Western Division

E. Flower (C)	4990
F. W. Jowett (ILP)	4949

1906

Central Division

Scott-Robertson (L)	4954
V. Gibbs (C)	3614

Eastern Division

W. E. B. Priestley (L)	7709
V. Caillard (C)	4277
E. R. Hartley (SDF)	3090

Western Division

F. W. Jowett (ILP)	4957
E. Flower (C)	4147
W. Claridge (L)	3580

1910 January

Central Division

Scott-Robertson (L)	5249
Howick (C)	3608

Eastern Division

W. E. B. Priestley (L)	7709
Browne (C)	5014
E. R. Hartley (Soc)	1740

Western Division

F. W. Jowett (ILP)	8880
E. Flower (C)	4461

1910 December

Central Division

Scott-Robertson (L)	4677
G. H. Pauling (C)	3381

Eastern Division

W. F. B. Priestley (L)	7778
R. Mortimer (C)	4734

Western Division

F. W. Jowett (ILP)	7729
E. Flower (C)	4339

The Liberal Party after the 1880s was being squeezed increasingly from both sides. If it made concessions to its working class supporters it could and did lose its moderates, and if it failed to make those concessions then it failed to attract working class support. In addition to their difficult position in the middle of the political spectrum the Liberals were faced with changes in electoral procedure which damaged the Party's prospects, for from 1885 Bradford was changed from a single double member constituency into three separate constituencies each returning a single member. Also the Liberals were faced in the mid 1880s with a major split over the question of Home Rule for Ireland. Locally this split on Home Rule was probably made worse by the death in 1886 of W. E. Forster, for his death released many moderate voters from a personal commitment to the Liberal Party. So the mid 1880s saw a partial break up of the party and a transference by many moderate Liberals of political allegiance to the Conservative party or to the Liberal Unionists, although the latter fairly rapidly became an adjunct of the Conservatives.

At the 1886 General Election the Conservatives concentrated all their energies on the Eastern Division, leaving the Liberal Unionists to oppose the Liberals in the two other divisions. This strategy was successful: the Conservatives captured East Bradford and this in turn sparked off a Conservative revival reflected in the growth of necessary ancillary organisations such as the clubs which were later to be such an important part of the success of the early ILP. In 1880 the Conservatives had only 6 clubs in Bradford but by 1895 this had risen to 25, whereas Liberal clubs in the same period only increased from 15 to 21.[39] The tide was clearly turning towards the Tories and increasingly the wealth of the town was to be found there, not in the Liberal Party. Men such as Samuel Cunliffe Lister, J. H. Mitchell, Francis Willey, the Ripleys and the brewing family of the Hammonds, provided the funds which financed this growth and as the debate about protectionism versus free trade continued, more and more businessmen turned towards conservatism, as exemplified in 1903 when Bradford played an important role in Chamberlain's Tariff Reform campaign. Conservative success at the Parliamentary level followed with the capture of all seats in 1895 and 1900, and on the municipal level the Conservatives gained control of the School Board in 1894, and captured seats on the Board of Guardians and controlled the City Council in the last few years of the Nineteenth Century.

At the same time the Liberals also had to contend with a threat from the left. In Bradford there was a mix of social classes in all the constituencies, and in the majority of the wards, which meant that the Liberals always had middle class candidates to accommodate. Unlike mining communities where the solid strength of the working classes made the Liberals face reality and sponsor working class candidates, in Bradford the Liberals sponsored exclusively middle class candidates. Pressure for working men to stand grew in the Liberal Party in the late 1880s, but it made little impression on the Liberal oligarchy, for the whole tenor of the late nineteenth century Bradford Liberalism remained wedded to the monopolistic situation of the mid-nineteenth century. As E. P. Thompson has said:

> The prevalent tone ... is one of surfeited, self-satisfied Liberalism. Local papers were busy celebrating the improvements in standards of life since the hungry forties, and recalling for the hundredth time the wisdom of the repeal of the Corn Laws.[40]

The weakness of the trade unions in Bradford coupled with the need to accommodate middle class candidates meant that working men were not able to stand for the Liberal Party and articulate working class demands. There was therefore in this period an increasing tension between the Liberal oligarchy and the working class leaders. And the necessity for the working class to have their own representatives was strikingly brought home during the Manningham Mills strike and the furore about the right to hold meetings. The *Yorkshire Factory Times* commented:

The operatives have from the first been fought not only by their employers at Manningham but by the whole of the monied class of Bradford. From the highest dignitary down to the lowest corporate official 'law and order' has been against them.[41]

And it was out of defeat and the failure to gain improvements through industrial action, and the fact that the organs of local power, supposedly under democratic control, were blatantly used to thwart their economic objectives, that the Independent Labour Party developed.[42] The emergence and early history of the Bradford ILP is analysed in detail in the following chapters.

After 1900 there was a resurgence of Liberal fortunes, although they were never to return to their position of pre-eminence in the nineteenth century. The Liberal revival in Bradford was due primarily to the triggering into action of the Nonconformist conscience in relation to the Conservative 1902 Education act, and Chamberlain's campaign for tariff reform. Both aimed at the very heartland of Liberal Beliefs – free trade and a cheap food policy, and religious freedom and the role of religion in the educational system.

Throughout the nineteenth century education had been bedevilled by the question of religion and its role within any educational system. The 1902 Act destroyed the School Boards and put education under the County Borough, and was aimed to safeguard the voluntary schools run by the Anglicans and Roman Catholics, which were running into financial problems, and also the Grammar Schools which were facing the rapidly improving rate supported higher grade schools. The Act enraged local Liberals and even bought Alfred Illingworth out of retirement to stump the platforms again. As the *Bradford Daily Telegraph* wrote: 'In Bradford we have something like a return to old times when the voice of the people was emphatic and all but unanimous against reaction in any form.'[43]

The more militant dissenters refused to accept the Act, and led by Alfred Illingworth and the massed ranks of Nonconformist ministers withheld a portion of their rates. It was like the heroic days of the Church Rates agitation of the late 1830s all over again. The movement of passive resistance had strong support in Bradford and showed that Nonconformity was still an important force in the city, for in the first batch of passive resisters taken to court were the three Baptist ministers and a Congregational minister. The local newspaper commented: 'It was a bizarre scene: solid, respectable citizens indicted by their fellow magistrates and allowing bailiffs to confiscate their possessions which some of them, like Alfred Illingworth sent their servants to repurchase at the local saleroom.'[44]

The movement, however, faltered, although Bradford did provide a significant number of passive resisters, in the face of more moderate Liberals like W. E. B. Priestley who argued for the acceptance of the Act and for the Liberals to work within its provisions. He clearly recognised the composition of the Education Committee would be determined by the composition of the Council and here the Liberals had a majority.[45]

From the passage of the 1870 Elementary Education Act Bradford had been in the forefront of the political debate surrounding the whole question of education. The Act itself had split the Liberal Party locally at the 1874 election when W. E. Forster, the sitting Liberal member, had to stand against his own party because of the violent hostility to him on his Education Act by the militant dissenters. Although relations within the Liberal Party were healed by the late 1880s education still remained a bone of contention between the parties. This was due to the fact that the 1870 Act created a dual system of education, a School Board system and a voluntary system, and these two systems became associated with the respective political parties. All the School Board elections after the first one were fought on party political lines, which meant that through careful electoral management the Liberal/Radicals were able, apart from 1892–4, to retain control of the School Board. On the Boards they set about creating a coherent city wide system of elementary education and from the base position in 1870 they had, by 1902, 50 Board schools in the town compared with 41 voluntary schools (34 Anglican schools and 7 Roman Catholic schools). The supremacy of the Board schools was more clearly reflected in the number of pupils, for there were 32,886 pupils in Board schools compared with 15,354 in the Voluntary schools. [46] By following an expansionary policy, and therefore a high education rate policy, they put a great deal of pressure on the Voluntary schools whose parents had both to pay the School Board rates and provide donations to support their own denominational establishments. A pressure which by 1902 meant that the Anglican schools had a debt of £12,000 and the Roman Catholics one of over £5,000.[47] An even greater threat to the position of the voluntary denominational schools and the fee paying schools of Bradford Grammar School, The Girls' Grammar School and Thornton Grammar School, lay in Bradford's policy of establishing higher grade schools. The School Board had interpreted the 1870 Act in a very liberal way by introducing what were known as Higher Grade Schools, of which there were 6, by 1902. They were not secondary schools in the obvious sense that pupils went there when they had finished their primary education, but rather primary schools which continued through to a later leaving age than was the case with the ordinary primary schools. In Bradford they became renowned for providing a ladder through which pupils could climb to higher education and were justly famous for the quality of their education, particularly in the scientific field. What made them even worse in the eyes of their opponents was the fact that children of poor parents could obtain free scholarships in order to attend these schools; thus by 1914, 69.7% of the places in the municipal secondary schools were free places compared with 31.6% at the grammar school and only 12.2% at the Girls Grammar school. The 1902 Act was also intended to deal with this but in the fact the secondary system continued to develop in Bradford. The Inspectors' Report of 1909 said that the proportion of pupils in secondary schools was 'Very much higher than is usually to be found in the country'. In 1911 Bradford had 1,997 secondary scholars compared with 1,208 in the much larger city of Birmingham. [48]

The other area in educational policy with which Bradford became associated was educational welfare, for under the pressure of the ILP Bradford was in the forefront of introducing the measures to ensure that children stood a chance to benefit from education. The most important of these were the appointment of a Medical Superintendent of Schools, Dr. James Kerr, in 1893; the foundation of the Dental Clinic in 1910 with a full-time school dentist; the introduction of the first school nurse in 1908; the opening of the School Clinic in Manor Row in 1908; the opening of the Open-Air School at Ruck Wood, Thackley in 1908, followed by other open air or camp schools at Daisy Hill, Bolling Hall and Grange Road before 1914; the provision of facilities for physically handicapped children and also for what were termed 'feeble-minded'; and lastly, of course, the provision of school meals.[49] As Margaret McMillan said in 1910:

> There is but one city in England today which, as far as I know, has made any serious preparation as yet for undertaking in the near future this new work so important for the race. That town is Bradford. Not that Bradford has anything approaching today an ideal system of elementary education for her children. Alas no! But she has the elements at least of a new system and she has been gathering them now for years.[50]

Having said all that, however, there was in the city one glaring abuse which continually besmirched Bradford's name as a progressive educational city: the 'half time' system of education. In 1891 Bradford had 7,018 half timers on the school rolls and though the number declined up to its abandonment in 1921, it remained as an indictment of the ILP's inability to overcome the arguments of its supporters amongst the working classes and trade unions.

Since 1800 Bradford has been synonymous with immigration and the development of local ethnic communities. During the nineteenth century two very dissimilar groups settled in Bradford and had a powerful impact on its development. In the middle of the century it was a magnet for thousands of Irish immigrants fleeing the demise of the Irish textile industry, over-population and subdivision of land in the west, and finally the Great Famine of the 1840s. The majority of the Irish in Bradford came from Sligo and Mayo and the Irish born represented close to 10% of Bradford's population in 1851. Despised for their affiliation to Roman Catholicism, for their different language and customs, they were herded into ghetto areas in White Abbey, Wapping, New Leeds and the bottoms of Manchester and Wakefield Roads where they created their own institutions and cultural forms. These were associated with the church and Irish nationalism in particular. They remained in many respects a distinct and separate entity in Bradford. Largely confined to the worst areas of the inner city their role within the Labour movement only really blossomed after the partial independence of Ireland after 1920 and their large scale movement into the local Labour Party.[51]

The other major ethnic community in the late nineteenth century was almost completely different from the Irish. The continental merchants, always referred to as German merchants although they came from all over Europe, were generally rich, well educated and cosmopolitan in attitude and behaviour. From the 1830s they had come to organise the world-wide merchanting of Bradford goods and although their numbers were not great their influence on Bradford far outweighed their numbers. This influence was most marked in the economic and cultural spheres. There is little doubt that they provided an immense impetus to the local textile trade, providing merchanting outlets throughout the world, and their significance was reflected in the construction and development of the warehouses which were to dominate the centre of the city through to the urban redevelopment programme in the 1960s. As important was their cultural impact, both through important individuals such as the composer Delius, the artists Sichel and Rothenstein and the writer Umberto Wolfe and their sponsorship of cultural events. They provided a powerful stimulus to both local cultural formations and also brought to it important national and international figures. Finally their impact on local philanthropy should not be forgotten. It was the German Dr. Bronner who set up the Eye and Ear Hospital, which was largely subsidised by Jacob Behrens. It was the first German Mayor of the town Charles Semon who donated the Semon Convalescent Home in Ilkley and least forgotten should be Jacob and Florence Moser who amongst a huge range of philanthropic initiatives set up and ran the only child nursery for working women (the Nest), financially supported whole wards at the Infirmary and set up a series of pension schemes. Sadly the German community vanished from sight during the First World War, for as Priestley recognised when he returned on his *English Journey* to Bradford in the 1930s they had provided a rich diversity, and enriched the host community by their very differences.[52]

Bradford in the 1890s was a vibrant, dynamic community, particularly after the formation of the Independent Labour Party. Important figures such as George Bernard Shaw were frequent visitors and the hope within the community inspired people like Margaret McMillan to settle in the town and to work for the betterment of its citizens. Not least were new ideas and new visions impinging on women. Many of the most respected and influential figures in the early ILP were women, such as Margaret McMillan, Katherine St. John Conway and Caroline Martyn and they inspired not just male activists but also countless women to aspire to a wider and more fulfilling role within the community, attested by not only their involvement in the ILP at all levels but also in a militant local Suffragette movement.

In any short essay which attempts to encapsulate the life of a community in a particular period there are areas of life which will remain uncovered, either through the writer's ignorance or shortage of space and to that this chapter is no exception. Little or no attention has been drawn to the growing importance of municipal intervention in areas such as housing which saw the development before 1914 of council housing in the Longlands and Faxfleet areas; to the plethora of public houses in the city and the vast variety of recreational and leisure activities conducted in them; to family relationships and changing attitudes to children. Whilst these merit more detailed attention I hope to have delineated the main themes which characterised Bradford of the period. Above all it was a dynamic, lively, exciting community. The writing of local history always lays before its exponents the pitfall of 'boosterism', of accentuating and over-emphasising the importance of the particular area being examined, but even having regard to this, it is clear that Bradford in the twenty-five years before the First World War was a very special place. As J. B. Priestley was later to write:

> The Bradford of those years was no ordinary city ... In those pre-1914 days Bradford was considered the most progressive place in the United Kingdom. The Independent Labour Party was born in Bradford. Our Subscription Concerts were famous; in addition we had our permanent symphony orchestra and two magnificent choral societies; and we had two theatres, besides the music halls and concert party pavilions; a flourishing arts club and three daily papers ... I am prepared to bet that Bradford produced more well-known people – musicians, scientists, writers, performers and the like – than any place anything like its size in the whole Kingdom.[53]

NOTES

1. J. B. Priestley, *English Journey* (London, 1943), pp.158–160.
2. J. B. Priestley, *Margin Released: A Writer's Reminiscences and Reflections* (London, 1962), p.30.
3. *Parliamentary Papers*, Census of England and Wales, 1851, 1881, 1911.
4. D. G. Ross, *Bradford Politics 1880–1906*, PhD thesis, University of Bradford 1977, Table 1, p.3.
5. For the development of an urban transportation system in Bradford in this period see D. Croft, *Bradford Tramways* (Oakwood Press, 1976).
6. *Parliamentary Papers*, Census of England and Wales, 1881.
7. Answers of John Wood, jun., Bradford in Answers of Mill Owners to Queries, c.1, p.121 – Factory Inquiry Commission, Supplementary Report, *Employment of Children in Factories*, Part II, reprinted in Irish University Press (Dublin), *Industrial Revolution, Children's Employment*, vol.5, c.1, p.121
8. E. H. Illingworth (ed.), *The Holden–Illingworth Letters* (Bradford, 1927), p.489.
9. *Parliamentary Papers*, Census of England & Wales 1911, Vol x. Occupations and Industries, Part II, p.664.
10. A full analysis of the problems facing the Bradford textile trade in the last quarter of the Nineteenth Century is given in E. M. Sigsworth, *Black Dyke Mills* (Liverpool, 1958), pp.72–134, and in G. Firth, 'The Bradford Trade in the Nineteenth Century', in D. G. Wright and J. A. Jowitt, *Victorian Bradford* (Bradford, 1982).
11. E. M. Sigsworth, *op. cit.*, pp.79, 83 and 103, and for its impact on the labour force see J. A. Jowitt, 'The retardation of Trade Unionism in the Yorkshire Worsted

Industry' in J. A. Jowitt and A. J. McIvor, *Employers and Labour in the English Textile Industries, 1850–1939* (London, 1988).

12. J. Reynolds, *Saltaire: An Introduction to the Village of Sir Titus Salt* (City of Bradford Metropolitan Art Galleries and Museums, 1976), p.28. For a detailed examination of mid-nineteenth century West Yorkshire paternalism see J. Reynolds, *The Great Paternalist* (London, 1983) and J. A. Jowitt, *Model Industrial Communities in Mid-Nineteenth Century Yorkshire* (Bradford, 1986).

13. *Bradford Observer*, 31 Dec 1888.

14. For trade unionism in the West Yorkshire textile trades see K. Laybourn, 'The Attitude of Yorkshire Trade Unions to Economic and Social Problems of the Great Depression 1873–1896', PhD thesis University of Lancaster, 1973, and J. A. Jowitt, 'The retardation of Trade Unionism in the Yorkshire Worsted Industry' in J. A. Jowitt and A. J. McIvor, *op. cit.*

15. B. Turner, *Short History of the General Union of Textile Workers* (Heckmondwike, 1920), p.124.

16. B. Turner, *About Myself* (London, 1930), p.130.

17. G. D. H. Cole and W. Mellor, 'Sectionalism and Craft Prejudice, Yorkshire's Need for the Greater Unionism', *Daily Herald*, 14 Apr 1914, cited in J. Bornat, 'An Examination of the General Union of Textile Workers 1883–1922', PhD thesis University of Essex, 1981.

18. For the woolcombers see *The Times*, 28 July 1899 and R. H. Sherrard, *White Slaves of England* (London, 1897). It should be noted that long hours of work were not confined to the textile industry. Shop workers worked more than 70 hours per week and tramwaymen even longer.

19. D. G. Ross, *op. cit.*, Table 4, p.7 and pp.15–16.

20. For the composition of Bradford Town Council in 1880, see D. G. Ross, *op. cit.*, Appendix C and for the 1911 City Council see the *Bradford Weekly Telegraph*, 20 Oct 1911.

21. *B.W.T.*, 20 Oct 1911.

22. *B.W.T.*, 14 Aug 1908.

23. *B.W.T.*, 21 Feb 1908.

24. For the 1851 Religious Census and its findings in Bradford see K. S. Inglis, 'Patterns of Religious Worship in 1851', *Journal of Ecclesiastical History*, vol XI, 1960, pp.74–86 and J. A. Jowitt, 'The Pattern of Religion' in D. G. Wright and J. A. Jowitt, *op. cit.*

25. For the relationship between the Liberal Party, Nonconformists and the parliamentary elections of the third quarter of the nineteenth century see D. G. Wright, 'Politics and Opinion in Nineteenth Century Bradford 1832–80', PhD thesis, University of Leeds 1966, D. G. Wright, 'The Bradford Election of 1847' in J. A. Jowitt and R. K. S. Taylor, *Nineteenth Century Bradford Elections* (Bradford Centre Occasional Papers No.1, 1979).

26. *B.O.*, 17 Dec 1881.

27. Isaac Holden to Rev. J. B. Grant, 25 May 1871 – in the *Holden Illingworth Letters*, (Bradford, 1927), p.466.

28. *B.W.T.*, 9 May 1913.

29. *B.W.T.*, 8 Aug 1913.

30. *B.W.T.*, 23 Feb 1912.

31. *B.W.T.*, 28 Apr 1911.

32. *B.W.T.*, 25 Mar 1910.

33. *B.W.T.*, 11 Feb 1910.
34. D. Cresswell, *Margaret McMillan: A Memoir*, (London, 1948), p.95.
35. Borough of Bradford, *Report on the Health of Bradford for the year 1888*, (Bradford), p.11.
36. City of Bradford, *Report on the Public Health of the City for 1912*, (Bradford), p.17.
37. *B.O.*, 14 Oct 1898.
38. *Bradford Trade and Labour Council Yearbook*, 1914, (Bradford), p.55.
39. K. Laybourn, 'Bradford Politics 1880–1900', unpublished, p.12.
40. E. P. Thompson, 'Homage to Tom Maguire', in A. Briggs and J. Saville, *Essays in Labour History*, (London, 1960).
41. *Yorkshire Factory Times*, 1 May 1891.
42. See subsequent chapters in this Section.
43. *Bradford Daily Telegraph*, Sept 1902.
44. D. G. Ross, *op. cit.*, pp.304–5.
45. *B.D.T.*, 14 Mar 1903.
46. *Education in Bradford since 1870* (Bradford Corporation, 1970), p.53.
47. *Yorkshire Daily Observer*, 23 May 1903.
48. For the development of Higher Grade Schools in Bradford see A. B. Ellis, 'Higher Grade Schools in Bradford before the 1902 Education Act', MEd. thesis, University of Leeds, 1965. For the report of the Inspectorate see *Bradford Weekly Telegraph*, 12 Mar 1909.
49. For the educational welfare provision in Bradford see *Education in Bradford since 1870* – chapter on the Development of Special Services.
50. *B.W.T.*, 1 July 1910.
51. The history of the Irish Community in Bradford is still awaiting an historian, but for the community in the mid-nineteenth century see C. Richardson, 'The Irish in Victorian Bradford', *Bradford Antiquary*, II, pp.294–316 and C. Richardson, Irish Settlement in mid-nineteenth Century Bradford, *Yorkshire Bulletin of Economic and Social Research*, Vol 20, no.1, May 1968, pp.40–57.
52. Information about the German community is again limited but some basic information can be found in A. R. Rollin, 'The Jewish Contribution to the British Textile Industry: Builders of Bradford', *Transactions of the Jewish Historical Society of England*, XVII, pp.45–51
53. F. Brockway, *Socialism over Sixty Years, the Life of Jowett of Bradford 1864–1944* (London, 1946), preface by J. B. Priestley, p.8.

2. The Manningham Mills Strike, December 1890 to April 1891

Keith Laybourn

The Manningham Mills strike, which lasted for nineteen weeks between 17 December 1890 and 27 April 1891, was one of the most divisive issues in Bradford's history. In recent years it has assumed a major role in the various interpretations of the emergence of the Independent Labour Party. E. P. Thompson, in his essay 'Homage to Tom Maguire' has placed the strike within the context of the economic and social developments in the West Riding and revealed how vital the defeat at Manningham was to the political ambitions of the working classes.[1] Contemporaries were also aware of the political importance of the event. In October 1892, Fred Jowett, the first ILP MP for Bradford in 1906, contesting the Manningham Ward at the municipal election of the Bradford Trades Council and the embryonic ILP stated that

> In the Lister strike, the people of Bradford saw plainly, as they had never seen before, that whether their rulers are Liberal or Tory they are capitalists first and politicians afterwards.[2]

Yet despite its obvious political importance, insufficient attention has been paid to the exact nature of the dispute. This chapter attempts to redress the balance. It develops two main themes. First, it stresses the importance of the strike in bringing together a group of trade unionists who subsequently formed the Bradford Labour Union, soon to become the Bradford Independent Labour Party. Secondly, it seeks to reveal how the Manningham Mills strike deflected trade unions away from the Liberal Party and towards the Independent Labour Party, an essential corollary to the emergence of a viable working-class political party.

The dispute had begun on 17 December, a week after the directors of Lister's Manningham Mills informed the operatives of their intentions of reducing wages by up to 25 per cent, in anticipation of the adverse impact of the McKinley Tariff which had been introduced by the United States Congress. The operatives resisted the reduction, Samuel Cunliffe Lister and his directors insisted that the reduction would be introduced and eventually, after more than four months, the obduracy of Lister prevailed.

1. The contestants

Samuel Cunliffe Lister, the founder and major shareholder of Manningham Mills in 1890, was one of the most uncompromising of those who had established Bradford's textile supremacy during the mid-nineteenth century.

He had started his business at Manningham in 1837, had developed and patented a large number of silk textile machines during the 1850s and 1860s, and had made himself a vast personal fortune out of his endeavours. When his mill burnt down in 1871, he built the present Manningham Mills and, during the difficult economic situation of the 1870s and 1880s managed to extend business quickly, tripling his labour force to over 5,000 by 1889.[3] In the same year Manningham Mills became a joint-stock company, with Lister as the largest shareholder. Indeed, during the mid 1880s Lister had gradually transferred his interest to land and had bought the Swinton Park and Jervaulx Abbey estates for £800,000.[4]

Lister's financial success had been a reward for his perseverance and business acumen. However, his blunt business style did not not endear him to his workforce which, despite being unorganised, was frequently involved in short disputes. The *Yorkshire Factory Times*, the weekly newspaper of the Yorkshire textile trade unionists, reflected that

> ... it is becoming apparent that from the multiplicity of labour disputes the mammoth establishment at Manningham is taking a lead, and the past year has not in the number of wages and labour disputes, known or unknown to the public, become less productive than its predecessors.[5]

Lister's refusal to negotiate with his workforce was a root cause of much of this disturbance. During the Manningham Mills strike, he adamantly refused to allow his directors to make concessions to the operatives and, during its course, incensed the strikers by constant reference to the high wages he paid. Undiplomatically, Lister threatened to move his business to Addingham, near Ilkley.

In the face of such obstinacy it is hardly surprising that the Manningham operatives were eventually defeated. As in the majority of textile firms in Yorkshire, the Manningham Mills textile workers had no trade union organisation, and the fact that the strike lasted nineteen weeks was almost entirely due to the help provided by the West Riding Power-Loom Weavers' Association which organised woollen and worsted weavers. A Society of Silk, Seal and Plush Finishers had been formed in 1890 and had successfully fought a strike in February 1890, backed by the Weavers' Association. But such success was shortlived, and by the end of 1890 the society had collapsed. This was despite the fact that trade unionism had been given an additional fillip by a successful strike at Manningham in October. On that occasion, the plush and velvet weavers had struck for a wage advance and the management had immediately conceded.[6] In view of the demand for wage reductions two months later, this capitulation by the management would appear to have been a tactical retreat designed to avoid industrial conflict until after the McKinley Tariff was introduced. In the meantime, the firm was able to produce goods for the American market, and introduce measures to avoid financial repercussions unhindered by labour difficulties. With the first rumours of the raising of the American tariff Lister & Co. Ltd had sent an agent to the United

States to arrange for the stockpiling of cloth in American warehouses before the introduction of the tariff.[7] In order to supply this requirement the directors put all the departments on overtime. The months of October and November were crucial, for the McKinley Tariff had been passed, although not yet introduced. The Tariff came into force in December 1890 and towards the end of November the mood of the directors began to change. Two managing directors, Reixach and Watson, had visited the United States and on their return were interviewed by the *Bradford Observer*. Asked whether the American tariff would affect the Bradford trade they replied: 'There are, no doubt, strong grounds for anticipating this.'[8] Their pessimism was well founded and there were to be consequential problems for the operatives.

2. The outbreak of the dispute

The first indication of the impending dispute occurred on Tuesday, 9 December 1890 when a notice was circulated informing the 1,100 workers in the velvet department that their wages would be reduced from 24 December. On the following day Mr. Reixach explained the reduction in terms of the likely impact of the McKinley Tariff and added that Lister & Co. would be unable to compete with other manufacturers if they continued to pay 'artificially high wages'.[9]

There was the predictable hostile reaction from the velvet weavers who, lacking their own organisation, called upon the Weavers' Association to help. On 10 December, a meeting of the velvet weavers was held at the Primitive Methodist Schoolroom at Manningham. Allan Gee and W. H. Drew, the representatives of the Weavers' Association, were present. Both Gee, in Huddersfield, and Drew, in Bradford, subsequently rose to prominence in their local trades councils and their local Independent Labour Party branches. Drew in fact became the Secretary of Bradford Trades Council in the late 1890s, remaining in that post until his departure to Canada in 1907.[10] These later lions of the West Riding Labour movement were critical of the operatives for allowing trade unionism to disappear. They doubted whether the wage reduction could be resisted. However, the operatives were resolved to resist the wage reductions and Drew and Gee undertook to organise a Workpeople's Standing Committee to negotiate with the Manningham directors. In the meantime the operatives were persuaded to stay at work until negotiations could be held.[11] The Standing Committee met the directors on 15 December but found them unwilling to alter their proposed wage reductions.[12] This was communicated to a meeting of the operatives that evening and, after another unsuccessful meeting with the directors on the following day, the strike commenced.[13]

From the start the major issue was the question of wage levels. At one of the early meetings, called by the Standing Committee, a velvet weaver stated that Lister's wages were low compared with other similar establishments in

Yorkshire. At Saltaire the same rate of pay was offered, whilst at Allerton velvet weavers were paid a 1d. (0.4p) per yard more. Other examples of the low wages paid by Lister were also presented, Drew also referred to the firm's intention of reducing the wages of the winders and pickers to a mere pittance. Prior to the strike, two girls could dress and pick a warp in a day, for which 5s 1d. (25p) would be paid or 2s 6½d (13p) per girl. With the intended reductions it was maintained that their daily earnings would fall to 3s 5d. (17p), or 1s 8d. (8p) per girl.[14]

The operatives were further aggrieved by the fact that the profits of Manningham Mills had been £138,000 in the previous year and that this had enabled the firm to announce a dividend of 10 per cent. Ben Turner, a leading member of the Weavers' Association, suggested that the firm might care to reduce its total profit by 5 per cent, some £7,000, in order to achieve the type of saving in costs which reductions of up to 25 per cent of wages were designed to achieve. It was felt that since the firm had made substantial profits in the past it should also be prepared to withstand losses in the future.[15]

The flames of the dispute were fanned by the public exhortations of past grievances. The operatives were suspicious of the lack of a reciprocal nature of the wage movements at Manningham and Gee observed: 'There had never been a 20 per cent advance but there had been reductions a plenty.'[16] At other meetings, it was stressed that the firm had reduced wages by 30 per cent during the 1880s and that this had never been returned in the boom years.[17] The employment structure within the firm added to this feeling of injustice. Tensions had been created by the fact that female labour was replacing skilled male labour which was being driven out of the industry. To this uncertainty of employment was added the additional complication of strained working conditions. Overlookers and under-managers in the firm earned their wages through driving the workers to increase output.[18] This increased tension between the 'superiors' and the operatives, a situation which was worsened by the action of the Manningham management in driving the workers. One Manningham worker remarked upon this situation:

> ... the opinion of the work people with whom I am acquainted is that there are too many gentlemen to maintain who wear collars and cuffs; also petty undermanagers strutting about with pencils and notebook who might be better employed.[19]

Wages, status and the feeling of injustice are, of course, the staple issues of any strike. However, what distinguished this from the others is that it obtained a much wider audience than the majority and that, in its wake, arose issues of liberty and free speech, economics and politics which were to divide society in the West Riding of Yorkshire.

The cause of the operatives was immediately taken up by the working classes and trade unionists in Yorkshire. The Weavers' Association, which was mainly responsible for the organisation of the strike, circulated 25,000 copies of a *Manifesto* appealing for support from trade unions, co-operative societies and the public. In this document, the Workpeople's Standing Committee (Strike Committee) outlined the implications of the dispute for the working classes.

> In the face of these low wages we are of opinion that we should be doing not only an injustice to ourselves but to the whole of the textile industry in the West Riding of Yorkshire by accepting the proposed reduction. Our battle may be your battle in the immediate future. We trust, therefore, that in our present state of need and disorganisation you will liberally support us.[20]

This appeal raised £11,000, much of it coming from the trade unions. The Yorkshire Miners' Association contributed generously and the mining districts always provided a good collection. Indeed, when James Murray, a miner from Barnsley, attended a strike meeting he informed the strikers that if all the workpeople of Manningham Mills would come out then the miners would make a sterling effort to support them.[21] The Bradford Typographical Society, one of the wealthiest in Bradford, provided £10 and other societies contributed smaller amounts.

Yet this support was not simply financial; one of the main features of the strike was the way in which it united politically diverse elements of the trade union movement. The Yorkshire Miners' Association, the Bradford Power-Loom Overlookers, and the various other 'Liberal' trade unions were represented at some of the strike meetings. Particularly prominent were R. Wilson of the Overlookers' Society and Edward Hatton of the Bradford Society of Woolsorters. Politically moderate trade unions affiliated to the Labour Electoral Association (a Liberal organisation designed to get working men returned to local or national office as Liberals) were represented by Samuel Shaftoe, of the Skep and Basket Makers' Society and the Machine Woolcombers Society, and by John Sewell of the Bradford branch of the Amalgamated Society of Tailors. At this time Shaftoe and Sewell were also secretary and treasurer, respectively, of the Bradford Trades Council. But it was the more radical trade unionists who dominated the platform at the meetings of the strikers. At these meetings, Gee, Drew, Ben Turner, and Greaseley of the Weavers' Association combined with Taylor, J. L. Mahon, W. Cockayne and Tom Maguire of the Gasworkers and General Labourer's Trade Union and the Leeds Socialist League. They were supported by socialist members of the more skilled organisations, such as James Bartley and Edward Roche of the Bradford Typographical Association and Fred Jowett of the Bradford Power-Loom Overlookers' Society. The hitherto politically moderate Amalgamated Society of Engineers provided another two radicals in George Cooke and George Cowgill. Socialists from outside the immediate area were also called into the dispute, including Isabella and Bessie Ford, May Abraham, Violet King, Ben Tillett and Tom Mann. The list of trade union and labour leaders involved in helping the Manningham operatives reads like a hagiography of labour leaders.

The strike temporarily united the diverse elements of the Bradford Trades Council. The years between 1888 and 1893 had seen a widening of the gulf between Socialists and Liberals on the Trades Council, during which the former gradually assumed control of the latter. The struggle was personified in the conflict between James Bartley and Samuel Shaftoe. The rift occurred in 1889 when Bartley wrote a letter to the *Bradford Observer* in which he announced that

> I categorically stated that Mr. Shaftoe was not in favour of an eight-hour bill thereby stamping him an adherent of the older trade unionism while I as an advocate of an eight-hour bill represent the principle of state interference.[22]

The gulf widened during the next two years and the Council threatened to split. But the strike temporarily conflated into one body trade unionists of various persuasions. As a result Shaftoe and Bartley stood upon the same platform. At its monthly meeting on 6 January 1891 the Trades Council resolved

> That this Council expresses its heartfelt sympathy with the Manningham operatives in their struggle with capital, and pledges itself to use all the influence in its powers to obtain pecuniary assistance from its various trade societies.

The following month it reaffirmed this commitment at its monthly meeting and to the press.[23]

Occasionally there was middle-class support for the strikers. Lady Dilke sent her support, moral and financial, and the Bradford middle class support was represented by the Radical Liberals. The most notable representative of this group was W. P. Byles, editor of the *Bradford Observer*, and subsequently MP for Shipley from 1892 to 1895. His newspaper was favourable to the workers and, with his wife, he often campaigned with the Weavers' Association. Unfortunately, the Radical Lib-Lab Liberals were few in number and limited in their support. The majority of Liberals did not appear to have supported their views and when Byles contested the Liberal candidature for Shipley he found himself opposed by the 'money bags' of Bradford and only gained nomination after a hard fought election in which he threatened to contest the election with or without the support of the local Liberal Party organisation whose conduct, he felt, had broken the sacred rules of political cricket.[24] Although his influence amongst the Liberals was limited, Byles was important to the strikers for as a shareholder in the Manningham firm he could raise issues at the shareholders' meetings, particularly the view that dividends ought to be reduced. Shaftoe, for one, was impressed by the attitude of the Byles's and at a public meeting, on 9 February 1891, he stated that

> He thought Mr. Byles had a few days before given some excellent advice in connection with a limited liability company which paid 10 per cent dividend. He reminded them that a little less dividend should be paid and the balance be given to the workers.[25]

Other members of the middle class were less forthcoming and silently gave their support to Lister.

Samuel Cunliffe Lister was born into a County and Conservative family and became a leading Conservative in Bradford. As a member of the Carlton Club he commanded the respect of the West Riding Conservatives and they rallied to his defence. But Bradford was, as yet, a Liberal stronghold and it was not at all certain that he would gain Liberal support. But within days of the dispute beginning that support became obvious .

On the whole it would appear that Lister gained that support as the champion of capitalism. He was, after all, fighting socialism and trade unionism, the avowed enemies of capitalism. In a letter to the *Bradford Observer*, he asked strikers not to be misled by the union, nor by its leaders who were paid agitators. The letter also declared that Allan Gee was sub-editor of the *Yorkshire Factory Times*, a trade union newspaper, and that W. H. Drew and Ben Turner were its paid reporters, and that 'They are all well-paid men who ought not to pose as the weavers' leaders.'[26]

The strike leaders had no illusions of middle class support. Drew declared that they knew

> ... perfectly well that to a great extent the sympathies of the wealthier Bradford citizens were not with the workpeople in the struggle to obtain what they believed to be their rights. Their were of course a few exceptions, and to these people every honour was due.[27]

Although this statement was made at the beginning of the strike, before the issue of free speech arose, the pattern of opposition and support had changed little throughout, and the *Yorkshire Factory Times* was later able to declare that

> The operatives have from the first been fought not only by their own employers at Manningham but by the whole of the monied class in Bradford.[28]

Thus the Manningham dispute became a conflict between the middle and working classes of Bradford and, indeed, the West Riding of Yorkshire.

3. Negotiations

In conducting the strike the main problem of the two sides was to find common ground for negotiations. This proved increasingly difficult as both parties indicated their intention of making the strike a test case for future industrial relations in the textile trade. The intransigence of the management was quickly apparent and, towards the end of the strike, a letter in the *Bradford Observer* informed the public that

> I can confidently assert that if the dispute had occurred at any other firm in the district, it would have been settled months ago; but it is appears that Lister's, have determined to keep them there though all the business of the firm, and the money of the shareholders, be scattered to the wind. My

knowledge of Mr. Lister through a period of forty years has led me to the conclusion that so long as he is allowed to lead all is well, but when once anyone becomes antagonistic to his ideas they must submit, when they prove their position equally as strong as his at all points.[29]

With such lack of tact it was hardly surprising that negotiations failed. Instead, the two sides made claim and counter-claim about the level of wages paid at Manningham. Mr. Reixach put the management's case in a letter to the *Bradford Observer* on 20 December, maintaining that male plush weavers earned an average of 21s 6d. (£1.07). These were favourably compared with the 13s 10d. (69p) average earned by female weavers in the fancy dress goods department at Manningham.[30] The gist of the letter was that silk and plush operatives and weavers were well paid and that a 20 per cent wage reduction would still allow most weavers to earn more than £1 per week.

This claim was rejected by the weavers who stressed that Reixach's estimates related to earnings over a short period during which time a great deal of overtime had been worked. It was felt that the average earnings would have been much lower if the period had been extended, in which case unemployment would have significantly reduced earnings. A survey of earnings in the woollen and worsted industry, conducted by E. P. Arnold-Forster, suggested that unemployment and broken time caused a loss of earnings averaging between four and five weeks during the early 1890s.[31] It would appear that the silk trade was similarly afflicted and one male weaver who kept a record of his earnings over twelve years found that they varied between 5s 9d. (29p) and £2 per week, and averaged 16s 5d. (82p) over twelve years. Other accounts also suggest that the earnings of weavers were lower than Reixach's estimates.[32]

Lister exacerbated the argument when, subsequently, he sent a letter to the *Bradford Observer*. Apart from accusing the strikers of wanting payment for broken time he also accused them of frittering away their good earnings:

> That they have earned in the past not only good wages but very good wages, is certain, or the Manningham ladies, the plushers as they are called, could not dress in the way they do. Silk and flowers, hats and feathers, no lady in the town can be fairer. No one likes better to see them comfortably and befittingly dressed than I do; but there is a reason to all things. What is the result of all this? What I never cease to present and teach – utter need for thrift. The women spend their money on dress and the men on drink; so that the begging box goes round – it matters not what the wages are.[33]

This was a direct attack upon the morals of the Manningham operatives and it brought an immediate response from both the *Yorkshire Factory Times* and the *Bradford Observer*. Both considered the demand for thrift to be uncalled for from a man who had thought little of spending £200,000 on buying an estate at Swinton.[34] Lister was typically outspoken and his subsequent letters to the press only served to complicate the negotiations.

The first serious attempt to bring the two sides together occurred during the first two weeks of January 1891, when a group of nonconformist ministers and prominent trade unionists met at Horton Lane Methodist Chapel. Amongst those present were the Rev. Dr. K. C. Anderson, of Horton Lane Congregational Chapel, Rev. C. W. Sharp, of Horton Lane Methodist Chapel, Paul Bland, of the Gasworkers and General Labourers, W. Sugden and Edwin Halford. The two clergymen had approached the directors for proposals which they could pass on to the Strike Committee. They came back with two recommendations – that the men should return to work and that the dispute should be settled on the basis of an arbitration award based upon the wages paid to weavers of six Bradford worsted mills. This was presented to the Strike Committee on 12 January and rejected.[35] Much against the mood of the meeting Drew forced through a counterproposal which was that weavers would accept the average wages paid to the silk plush weavers of Saltaire. This the management rejected on the grounds that the firm of Titus Salt & Co. was closing down its silk department and intending to move to the United States, a statement which the Rev. Dr. Anderson found to be totally without foundation. The directors refused to be drawn on the issue, even when the offer was made for a second time on 14 January 1890. On the following day, Drew presented an alternative of taking the average of the wages paid to weavers in six firms producing the same class of goods as Manningham Mills. This proposal was also rejected.[36] The first part of the negotiations had thus been taken up with the management wanting comparisons with the lower-paid worsted weavers whilst the Strike Committee wanted comparisons with the more highly-paid silk and plush weavers. Even though the overtures of the nonconformist ministers had been rejected it is interesting to note that the Rev. Dr. Anderson continued to work for a resolution of the dispute and the Trades Council records, in March 1891,

> That this Council do accept the invitation of the Rev. Dr. K. C. Anderson DD to be present at Horton Lane Chapel on Sunday Evening next. When he will preach on a sermon on Industrial Freedom and the significance of the Widespread Labour difficulties.[37]

The second attempt to resolve the strike was undertaken by E. W. Hammond, the Mayor of Bradford. He approached the directors for proposals. They gave him precisely those which they had communicated through the Nonconformist ministers. He presented them to the Strike Committee and they were summarily rejected.[38] However, the directors took up the initiative and made two further offers to the Strike Committee. The first came from Lister in a letter to the *Bradford Observer* in which he wrote:

> Now, what I propose (and feel certain that the directors will agree to) is that the Mayor shall appoint an accountant – anyone he pleases – to examine Lister & Co's books, and that the strikers shall receive 15 per cent more than the dress goods weavers. In case of any dispute, the Mayor ... shall be the sole arbitrator, and that his decision will be final.[39]

This proposal was rejected by the Strike Committee on 18 January and the Manningham directors came up with the alternative proposal of paying 15 per cent above the average wages paid in the silk department at Manningham. This was also rejected by the velvet weavers who felt that an average of 14s plus 25 per cent was not as good as the wages that had been guaranteed by the directors in their earlier letters to the press. Negotiations lapsed and it was two weeks before the Mayor brought the two sides together again. At a meeting on 2 February the two sides merely reaffirmed their positions, the directors offering 15 per cent above the wages paid to the fancy silk (Japanese) weavers. No progress had been made and, indeed, Lister added a new distraction. He emphasised that the main competition to his firm came from Germany and that the Manningham silk and plush weavers were being paid twice as much as their counterparts at Crefeld.[40]

Lister's statement was, of course, difficult to disprove although it is doubtful whether the Crefeld weavers would accept wages as low as 7s. or 8s. (35 or 40p), assuming that the average wages of the Manningham operatives were only 16s (80p). M. de Grieff came to the aid of the weavers on this question when he wrote a letter to the *Bradford Observer* informing the Bradford public that the Crefeld velvet, silk and plush weavers were often earning 22s. (£1.10p) per week and the more skilful men earned 26s. to 28s. (£1.30p to £1.40p) for a 56 to 60-hour week.[41] Although Lister rejected these statements by suggesting that these wages referred only to male labour, de Grieff countered by indicating that nearly all the Crefeld weavers were male. There was no cheap female labour employed to reduce costs. Lister's argument was thus effectively undermined.

Although a number of other attempts were made to bring the two sides together, more than a month progressed before a third round of negotiations began. On 20 March, W. P. Byles, editor of the *Bradford Observer*, and the Workpeople's Standing Committee drew up three proposals. There were

1. that they would accept the average wages paid in the pile goods trade at Saltaire;

2. that they would accept Lister's offer of 15 per cent on top of the best wages paid to woollen and worsted weavers in Bradford;

3. that they would accept the average wages paid in the same trade by six firms in the region.[42]

The directors were only prepared to consider the second offer. Their only objection to it was their claim that Lister had never made the offer and that they had in fact offered 15 per cent above the average wages paid in the Japanese fancy silk department at Manningham Mills. In a letter to the *Bradford Observer*, Lister confirmed that his only offer had been a comparison with the 'Japanese' weavers, and that had been the only basis upon which he would negotiate.[43]

Understandably, Drew and the Strike Committee were annoyed at the firm's denial that they had ever made the third, or 'Bradford', proposal. Not only had Lister clearly made such an offer as the letter quoted earlier indicates, but so had the directors. The various offers became confused and it appears that when Lister made his proposal it was naturally assumed that the 15 per cent above the dress good rates referred to a comparison with six Bradford worsted firms. Admittedly there were differences between the dress goods, principally made of mixed and woollen cloth, and worsted goods. For one thing, the latter was a better paid trade and there was a higher percentage of labour in the trade. But the difference was only a few shillings and the operatives might be forgiven for misinterpreting Lister's offer.

By the end of March and the beginning of April 1891, the Manningham mill directors were scenting victory and, consequently, rejected an offer or arbitration made by the Strike Committee on 8 April 1891.[44] While the strikers were seeking common ground the directors were retreating from settlement proposals they had already made. In this situation the organisation of strikers was of vital importance.

4. Organisation

The weakness of the Manningham strikers became obvious as the number of strikers increased. James Murray and the mining representatives at organisational meetings had called for greater unity amongst the Manningham operatives, hoping that they would all be out on strike.[45] The Yorkshire Miners' Association promised to continue a weekly levy of 186 branches until the strike ended.[46] Yet the Strike Committee was not in favour of this, doubting its own ability to support all the Manningham operatives. But the number of strikers did increase, the chances of success diminished, and the Strike Committee became increasingly conscious of the need to obtain a quick settlement.

At the beginning only 1,100 operatives came out and only the velvet department of the mill was closed. Subsequently, they were joined by the overlookers, the velvet, cotton and silk dyers, and eventually by 1,700 workers from the spinning department. By the beginning of March nearly 5,000 workers were out on strike or had been locked out. This increase imposed financial burdens on the Strike Committee, and Drew estimated that £1,000 would be required to continue the strike. The Strike Committee asked the spinners not to come out but they rejected the plea and joined the strike on 2 March 1891.[47] This action may well have been decisive for it added considerably to the burden imposed upon the strike funds and the spinners were the first to return to work at the end of the dispute.

The one encouraging feature of this widening of the dispute was that the overlookers joined with the strike hands. At the beginning of the strike they had been blamed for many of the disputes at Manningham Mills but within weeks their attitude to the strikers had changed. The overlookers now refused to train blackleg labour and 24 of them had been dismissed by the firm without a week's pay in lieu of notice, and the rest of them came out in sympathy. As a result of this change of direction Drew became more optimistic, noting that in most disputes 'the masters had succeeded in putting one class of workers against another, but in the present instance the overlookers were with the hands'.[48]

To make the strike more effective, regular meetings were held in the Jubilee Hall, Manningham, and the Star Music Hall, Bradford. Every Thursday, and occasionally on Mondays, a procession would pass through the town to remind the public of the strike. In order to prevent the use of blackleg labour, the strike hands also picketed the entrance of the mills. Although it was at a very moderate level, this picketing led to the eventual widening of the significance of the dispute. There had been disturbances in and around the mills in early January and a number of arrests were made. But nothing came of them and it was not until the end of February that the arrest of two mill hands threatened to bring public disorder. Both cases were dismissed and shortly afterwards a meeting was held to celebrate their release. This was held on 22 February and was supposed to be attended by Tom Mann, Ben Tillett and Ben Pickard. The advertisement was a ruse to attract a larger crowd and none of these national figures attended.[49] Nevertheless, the ploy was successful and more than 10,000 people attended meetings at St. George's Hall, the Star Music Hall, and an overflow meeting in Forster Square. Most of the principal trade unions in Yorkshire reaffirmed their support for the strikers and that occasion was, up to then, the largest of the strike meetings held in Bradford. It attracted the attention of the Bradford public and the Bradford authorities.[50]

5. The free speech debate

Several days after this meeting, Mr. Withers, the Chief Constable of Bradford, acted to prevent the Strike Committee using licensed premises and brought pressure to bear upon the proprietors of the Star Music Hall. Rightly or wrongly, this action was seen as an attempt to stifle free speech and was to play a vital part in guaranteeing working-class support for the future Independent Labour Party.

The Strike Committee was not allowed to use the Star Music Hall on 25 February.[51] As a result of this action, Drew interviewed the Chief Constable, asking his reasons for depriving the strikers of a platform. Withers purported to have two reasons: in the first place, he objected to the disorderly conduct that had attended the meeting at St. George's Hall and Forster Square; in the second, he objected to the anti-religious sentiments and the frequent criticisms made of Bradford's Chief Magistrate that had been expressed at the strikers' meetings. Withers was determined that the scenes at these meetings would not be repeated and asked Drew to sign an undertaking that future meetings would be conducted in an orderly manner. Without this undertaking the Chief Constable was reluctant to allow the Strike Committee to hold meetings; but Drew refused to sign believing that no large body of people could be better behaved.[52]

Various members of the Bradford Watch Committee stressed that the Chief Constable had acted without their approval. On 2 March, Alderman John Hall denied that the Watch Committee had given the Chief Constable the right to interfere with public meetings.[53] Councillor John Sheldon also made similar statements at St. George's Hall on 28 February. Regardless of these refutations, the Watch Committee came under strong criticism. Ward committees of the Liberal Association attacked the restrictions of 'free speech' and the Radical Liberals now allied themselves firmly with the strikers. Their leader was W. P. Byles who stated at one meeting that

> Had it been a strike meeting he would not have been present preferring not to take sides publicly in the dispute at Manningham. Until the last few days he never thought it would ever be his lot to stand before a Bradford audience to plead for the sacred principles of freedom of speech.[54]

The intervention of the Chief Constable did little to dissuade the Strike Committee from its intention of holding meetings, and it continued to hold outdoor meetings, and meetings at St. George's Hall and the Valley Parade Ice Rink. The controversy over 'free speech' added greatly to the attendance and it was not uncommon for 10,000 or even 20,000 persons to attend meetings.

The crescendo was reached on Sunday 12 April when the Bradford Trades Council had secured Ben Tillett for a meeting at St. George's Hall. Drew had met the Chief Constable, the Mayor and the Town Clerk on the preceding Tuesday to obtain permission to hold an overflow meeting in Dockers' Square (now Norfolk Gardens), an area between the Town Hall and St. George's Hall. Permission was not granted and the strikers were offered an alternative, the municipal fairground, which was some distance away.[55] This was not achieved without violence, during which the Chief Constable and 60 policemen emerged from the Town Hall and taunted the crowd. The meeting was eventually removed to Peckover Walks.[56] At the new venue the audience was addressed by Councillor Saunders, a Labour Councillor from Walsall, Turner, Jowett, Paylor and, later, Ben Tillett. Later in the day a second attempt was made to hold a meeting in Dockers' Square and Councillor Saunders was arrested, tempers were frayed, the police refused to charge Saunders, and he refused to leave the police station.[57] Apart from these aspects of the proceedings, the meeting at St. George's Hall went off successfully and the 5,000 persons present cheered Ben Tillett and his attack upon the Bradford authorities.

Events came to a climax on the following day, Monday 13 April. Socialists, communists and anarchists from Leeds and Sheffield came to Bradford, asserted the right of public meeting and circulated pamphlets such as the *Communist Appeal to Criminals*. Their intention was to create disorders and they thus became involved in disturbances and stone-throwing. But the authorities were prepared and, apart from calling in extra police, brought in 106 rank and file soldiers of the Durham Light Infantry. The Mayor read the

Riot Act and the streets were cleared by the police, and later by the soldiers charging into the crowds with 'fixed bayonets'. Surprisingly, only 10 arrests were made despite the fact that disturbances continued throughout the day and into the late evening.[58] Later accounts emphasised the feeling of revolution that pervaded Bradford on that day. W. R. Donald, President of the Bradford Typographical Society at that time, later recalled spending the evening at an inn in Ivegate, a street near the Town Hall, and hearing the screams of women and children as the troops pursued the crowds up Ivegate with fixed bayonets. It reminded him of scenes from the French Revolution.[59]

Donald was, perhaps, overdramatic but there is no doubt that these events left an enormous impression upon all social and political groups in the town. The *Bradford Observer* insisted that the disturbances on 13 April had been caused by outsiders and that very few Manningham operatives had been present.[60] Having cleared the operatives of responsibility, it was necessary to identify the guilty party. In most eyes it was the Watch Committee and the Chief Constable who were responsible for the disorder. Drew reminded them that the Watch Committee had allowed a meeting to take place in Dockers' Square on the previous Saturday, the day before the first meeting, and that the Strike Committee therefore felt that the Watch committee was discriminatory in its policy over the use of the Square.[61] Many thought that the police and the Manningham directors were conspiring together, and Ben Tillett wrote that one would 'suspect that the police were the agents of Lister and his co-ordinators, in making it difficult to maintain order and good tempers among the men and women interested in their struggle'.[62] The Central Division of the Liberal Party also considered that the strikers had been unfairly treated. At a meeting in the Mechanics' Institute the resolution was passed:

> That this meeting of the Liberal Central Division protests against the unjust action of the Watch Committee in refusing to permit the holding of a meeting on Sunday last in Dockers' Square, and regrets that by their action the authorities have instituted an invidious distinction, numerous meetings having been held there without objection or interference.[63]

A group of radicals meeting at Laycock's Temperance Hotel, East Parade, decided to play upon this new found support by holding another mass meeting on the following Saturday. The Watch Committee was prepared for this and had 290 soldiers, 200 Bradford police, and 198 police from other Yorkshire forces, in readiness for disturbances. Although the meeting drew crowds estimated at between 60,000 and 90,000 the soldiers and police were not required and the day passed peaceably. The meeting was divided between five platforms and was addressed by prominent Bradford trade unionists. For the first time widespread sympathy was expressed for the strikers.

The industrial confrontation was widened, but this hid the fact that the strike was on the point of collapse. Four days after the meeting, on 22 April, the spinners returned to work. Five days later, the rest of the strikers acknowledged defeat and also returned to work. With this collapse coming so soon after a number of large demonstrations in favour of free speech, the majority of those indirectly connected with the strike were stunned. Yet defeat was not entirely unexpected by the participants and Drew had warned of the difficulties involved in supporting a large number of striking operatives. In the week before the collapse there had also been correspondence to the editor of the *Bradford Observer* which had reflected upon the poverty prevailing in the Manningham district. One correspondent suggested that 'it is the opinion of several trade unionists known to me that Mr. Drew and the leaders would act wisely by at once putting an end to the strike and suffering of the locked out operatives.[64] But the decision to end the strike still came as a shock, and added to the acrimonious atmosphere which gave initial impetus to the demand for working-class political independence.

6. The path to political independence

Announcing the end of the strike the *Yorkshire Factory Times* made the prophetic statement that 'Labour has so associated itself that even defeat must be victory'.[65] This expression of opinion may be one reason why E. P. Thompson suggested that the only immediate hope for an Independent Labour Party lay in the defeat of the workers.[66] It is certainly a notion which requires examination. It would appear that this dispute did bring together trade unionists of various persuasions and unite them on one platform. It also provided an issue which was to link trade unionists with socialists in the formation of the Independent Labour Party.

Committed socialists such as Ben Turner and W. H. Drew, later joined by Charlie Glyde and George Cowgill, united with Liberals and others in their condemnation of the Watch Committee. This criticism served to undermine the confidence that working men had in the impartiality of the local authorities and gave them a determination to seek municipal, parliamentary and school board representation for themselves. The annoyance and frustration which had arisen over the Manningham dispute was best expressed in the words of Charlie Glyde at one of the Peckover Walks' meetings in April 1891, when he stated that

> We have had two parties in the past; the can't and the won'ts, and it's time that we had a party that will.[67]

The 'party that will' was formed one month later at a meeting at the Firth's Temperance Hotel, formerly Laycock's Temperance Hotel, in East Parade. Its formation was very closely associated with the strike and its embryonic development occurred on the strike platform at Peckover Walks. Charlie Glyde, George Minty, James Bartley and W. H. Drew formulated possible methods of making the working men an effective political entity and by the end of the strike rumours were circulating that the labour movement intended to contest all three parliamentary seats in Bradford. Even the normally restrained *Bradford Observer* was shocked at this prospect and remarked that

A startling statement is being circulated by some of the leaders of the labour movement in Bradford to the effect that at the next general election the Labour Party is to run independent labour candidates in each of the three divisions.[68]

A few days later it reported on a meeting of the labour representatives at Firth's Temperance Hotel, East Parade, Bradford. The meeting was held four days after the return of the Manningham operatives; those present were still bitter at the defeat and determined to establish their political independence. Drew and Bartley felt that only genuine working-class representatives would be acceptable in future local and parliamentary elections, and they suggested that Ben Tillett ought to contest Bradford East in the next general election (in fact he contested Bradford West). The meeting also revealed a split between the members of the Labour Electoral Association, still committed to working through the Liberal Party, and the Independent Labour Party. Samuel Shaftoe was both a Liberal, being a member of the Bradford Liberal 600, and a member of the Labour Electoral Association. In supporting the LEA, Shaftoe was prepared to accept the candidates of other parties where no Labour representative or working man was contesting an election. The early Bradford Labour Union/ILP activists were reluctant to do so, preferring its members not to vote if there was no suitable working-class candidate. This split was evident at this meeting when Shaftoe suggested that the meeting was unrepresentative of the Bradford Labour movement and therefore not capable of offering Ben Tillett a parliamentary candidature in Bradford East. Bartley, Drew and Roche ruled the criticism to be out of order.[69]

The split between the two sides, both ideologically and tactically, extended and served to divide the trade unions and trades councils in Bradford and Yorkshire. The Bradford Trades Council split on this issue, and allied topics, and in 1892 and 1893 the ILP became the dominant political group on the Council. The majority of the newer trade councils in Yorkshire were also dominated by the ILP. But of the older bodies only Bradford was dominated by the ILP before the formation of the Labour Union, the candidature of Tillett, and the challenge of the ILPers on the Trades Council which allowed the national organisation to be brought to Bradford. It was the Manningham Mills strike which had provoked the response.

There were also other immediate results arising from the strike. In his autobiography, Ben Turner stated that the strike produced many propagandists for both trade unionism and socialism.[70] The appeal of trade unionism increased and the feeling of the time was expressed in a poem by Ben Turner:

> Come weaver lasses bright and fair,
> And make your Union stronger,
> Come make your wages better yet,
> Your warps from growing longer.

> The varying price lists which now rule
> Are neither just nor proper.
> With unionism you can thrive
> Without it – come a cropper.[71]

Many working men and weaving lasses took note of these sentiments and within nine months of the strike the *Yorkshire Factory Times* was proclaiming that the defeat had added 10,000 trade unionists to the Yorkshire trade union movement; railwaymen, dyers, enginemen, and tram drivers as well as textile operatives. Evidence to the Royal Commission on Labour in 1892 indicated that the membership of the West Riding Power-Loom Weavers' Association had increased by nearly 2,000 within nine months of the strike,[72] and a branch of the Weavers' Association had been formed in Bradford in August 1891.[73] Other societies also expanded and did equally well.

Many unions gave themselves completely to the new political organisation. The Weavers' Association had its entire executive in the ILP, and even the Amalgamated Society of Engineers, once the bastion of craft unionism and Gladstonian Liberalism, provided many members of the Bradford and West Riding of Yorkshire branches of the ILP. In 1895 during a debate in the columns of the *Bradford Labour Echo*, the organ of the Bradford Labour Church from 1894 and the Bradford ILP from 1897, Drew, Bartley and others reflected that they had seen trade unionism and the ILP as synonymous terms and that that was how the original members of the ILP had viewed their embryonic organisation in May 1891.[74] The Manningham Mills strike established a link between political independence and trade unionism which was to be the hallmark of Bradford Labour organisation, and which was to carry it through the crisis of confidence it experienced in the mid 1890s.

Apart from acting as an impetus to trade union organisation, and a catalyst for the political ambitions of trade unions, the Manningham Mills strike also provided a useful 'whipping boy' for past failures. For several years afterwards it was maintained that the strike would have been successful if there had been some prior organisation. In a large labour demonstration in May 1891 Miss May Abraham referred to the Manningham Mills dispute and underlined that the missing ingredient for success had been an effective trade union organisation.[75] By the same token defeat was a stimulus to such organisation and to political aspirations amongst the working classes.

7. Conclusion

The Manningham Mills strike made a profound impact upon Bradford society. It magnified the lacuna which existed between capital and labour, and justified Robert Blatchford's prophetic statement in his book *Merrie England* that 'To be a trade unionist and fight for your class during a strike and to be a Tory or a Liberal and fight against your class at an election is folly'. Above all the strike destroyed the deferential attitude of the working class to politics, and encouraged their hegemonious aspirations. Many years later the strike was fondly remembered by Fred Jowett and other trade unionists who had participated.[76] He reminded his readers of his own role in the early years of the ILP and one should remember, that as a result of the Manningham experience, Jowett had foreshadowed the end of the traditional two-party system and the possibility of a socialist millennium when he informed the Liberals and the Conservatives, at an election speech in 1892, that

> You have run this machine too long, we see the prejudicial results of your management – starvation, misery, crime, and a state of general unwashedness, body and soul, and we mean to take the matter in hand and to try to make a better thing of it ourselves ....[77]

The political climate was right for change; Manningham provided the opportunity.

NOTES

1. E. P. Thompson 'Homage to Tom Maguire', J. Saville & A. Briggs, *Essays in Labour History*, Vol.1 (London, Macmillan, 1960). This is similarly developed by J. Reynolds and K. Laybourn, 'The Emergence of the Independent Labour Party in Bradford', *International Review of Social History*, xx, Pt.3 (1975), pp. 313–46; C. Pearce, *The Manningham Mills Strike in Bradford December 1890–April 1891* (University of Hull Occasional Papers in Economic and Social History, No. 7, 1975); and K. Laybourn and J. Reynolds, *Liberalism and the Rise of Labour 1890–1918* (London, Croom Helm, 1984), pp.40–2.
2. *The Labour Journal*, 7 Oct 1892.
3. C. A. Manning Press, *Yorkshire Leaders: Social and Political*, Vol. II (Leeds, 1895), pp.37–8.
4. *Bradford Observer*, 7 Mar 1887.
5. *Yorkshire Factory Times*, 12 Sept 1890.
6. *Ibid.*, 31 Jan, 7 Feb 1890.
7. *Bradford Observer*, 7 Mar 1887.
8. *Ibid.*, 7 Nov 1890.
9. *Ibid.*, 10 Dec 1890.
10. See the biographical sketches in *Dictionary of Labour Biography*, edited by J. Bellamy and J. Saville, Vol.3 (1976) and Vol. 4 (1977).
11. *Bradford Observer*, 12 Dec 1890.
12. *Ibid.*, 16 Dec 1890.
13. *Yorkshire Factory Times*, 20 Dec 1890.
14. *Bradford Observer*, 16 Dec 1890.
15. There is some confusion over the total amount of the reductions, but £7,000 was the figure which most trade union leaders estimated, thus suggesting that the wages of the department totalled £35,000 a year, i.e. about £35 per operative per year.
16. *Bradford Observer*, 12 Jan 1891.

17. *Ibid.*
18. *Yorkshire Factory Times*, 14 Feb 1890.
19. *Ibid.*, 21 Feb 1890.
20. *Bradford Observer*, 17 Dec 1890.
21. *Ibid.*, 23 Jan, 23 Feb 1891. The Bradford branch of the National Brassworkers' Society gave £1 10s (£1.50), Bradford Shuttlemakers gave £2 and the Bradford Woolsorters' Society gave £1 7s 10d. (£1.39).
22. *Ibid.*, 26 Aug 1889.
23. *Ibid.*, 23 Feb 1891.
24. In the first vote his candidature was rejected but it was made clear by the Shipley Working Men's Cub that the working men, in this predominantly working-class town, would vote for Byles.
25. *Bradford Observer*, 10 Feb 1891.
26. *Ibid.*, 27 Jan 1891.
27. *Ibid.*, 2 Jan 1891.
28. *Yorkshire Factory Times*, 1 May 1891.
29. *Bradford Observer*, 15 Apr 1891.
30. *Ibid.*, 20 Dec 1890.
31. *Ibid.*, 3 Feb 1892. 3
32. *Ibid.*, 20 Dec 1890, 14 Jan 1891.
33. *Ibid.*, 26 Dec 1890 .
34. *Ibid.*, 27 Dec 1890. Also *Yorkshire Factory Times*, 2 Jan 1891.
35. *Bradford Observer*, 13 Jan 1891.
36. *Ibid.*, 16 and 17 Jan 1891.
37. Bradford Trades Council, Minutes, 3 March 1891.
38. *Bradford Observer*, 19 Jan 1891.
39. *Ibid.*, 17 Jan 1891.
40. *Ibid.*, 3 Feb 1891.
41. *Ibid.*, 16 Feb 1891.
42. *Ibid.*, 21 March 1891.
43. *Ibid.*, 23 March 1891.
44. *Ibid.*, 9 Apr 1891.
45. *Ibid.*, 23 Feb 1891.
46. *Ibid.*, 24 Feb 1891.
47. *Ibid.*, 3 March 1891.
48. *Ibid.*, 12 Jan 1891.
49. Ben Turner objected to this ploy; see his *Short History of the General Union of Textile Workers* (Heckmondwike, 1920), pp.134–7.
50. Even the Home Office asked to be informed of events, *Bradford Observer*, 17 Apr 1891.
51. *Bradford Observer*, 26 Feb 1891; *Yorkshire Factory Times*, 27 Feb 1891.
52. *Bradford Observer*, 27 Feb 1891.
53. *Ibid.*, 2 Mar 1891.
54. *Ibid.*, 2 Mar 1891.
55. *Ibid.*, 8 Apr 1891.
56. Ben Turner, *Short History of the General Union of Textile Workers*, pp.129–38.
57. *Bradford Observer*, 13 and 14 Apr 1891.
58. *Ibid.*, 14 Apr 1891.
59. *Yorkshire Factory Times*, 16 Sept 1904.

60. *Bradford Observer*, 14 and 15 Apr 1891.
61. *Ibid.*, 17 Apr 1891.
62. *Yorkshire Factory Times*, 24 Apr 1891.
63. *Bradford Observer*, 17 Apr 1891.
64. *Ibid.*, 17 Apr 1891, a letter from 'Nuneaton'.
65. *Yorkshire Factory Times*, 1 May 1891.
66. E. P. Thompson, 'Homage to Tom Maguire', in *Essays in Labour History*, Vol. 1 (1960), edited by J. Saville and A. Briggs.
67. *Bradford Observer Budget*, Apr 1891.
68. The Independent Labour Party was formed in Bradford on 21 May 1891. The preliminary meeting was held at the end of Apr 1891.
69. *Ibid.*, 1 May 1891.
70. Ben Turner, *About Myself* (London, 1930), pp.68–9.
71. Ben Turner, *Heavy Woollen District Textile Workers' Union* (1917), p.61.
72. *Yorkshire Factory Times*, 1 Jan 1892. By 1892 the approximate number of members was 5,000, *Parliamentary Papers, Royal Commission on Labour, XXXV, 1892* Group C, Volume I, 38 evidence of Allan Gee and W. Downing, QQ4786–5154.
73. Ben Turner, *Short History*.
74. *Bradford Labour Echo*, 1 June 1895.
75. *Bradford Observer*, 24 Aug 1891.
76. *The Labour Magazine*, Vol. V, Oct 1926. Article by Ben Turner entitled 'Looking Backwards: the Formation of the ILP', pp.260–1.
77. *The Labour Journal*, 7 Oct 1892.

3. The Bradford ILP and Trade Unionism c.1890–1914

Keith Laybourn

In 1895 James Bartley reaffirmed the political independence of the ILP:

> By common consent of the members, the I.L.P. has adopted as it method open and uncompromising hostility to both Liberals and Tories. The main reason for which it exists is to fight Liberals, Tories, and all comers for the State and municipal direction and control of the industries of the nation. Every document officially issued in its name, every journal, national and local, advocating its theories, every speech delivered by its prominent men and women bears evidence that deep, bitter, and relentless antagonism to Liberals and Tories is the very essence of the movement.[1]

He advised the ILP's 'weak-kneed' critics that they would find 'themselves in congenial company in the Labour Electoral Association, but that they are a source of weakness and, consequently, danger.' Bartley was thus asserting that, even at its nadir, the Bradford ILP was unwilling to compromise its political independence. Eighteen years later, on the eve of the 1913 municipal elections, E. R. Hartley, speaking for a far more confident Bradford Labour movement, was strident in his advocacy of independence: 'Let there be no mistake, we shall sweep out both Blue Tories and Yellow Tories without ruth or remorse.'[2] Neither at its nadir nor at its zenith was the Bradford Labour movement prepared to be coerced into forging a compromise with the other political parties. It was this kind of independent spirit and determination, instilled into the ILP by socialist stalwarts over many years and galvanised by Bradford's traumatic industrial and employment problems, which helped to ensure that Bradford remained one of the centres of ILP activity before the First World War.

From an unpromising beginning in the 1880s the Bradford socialists prepared the ground for the rapid development of the Bradford ILP during the 1890s. Between 1891 and 1914, the rise of the Bradford ILP was meteoric. The Bradford Labour Union was formed in May 1891, and had acquired more than 2,000 members, 19 clubs, and two councillors, by early 1893. A Labour Church was formed at the end of 1892, a Labour Institute was opened in 1893, and, in recognition of the rising importance of the Bradford Labour Union, the inaugural meeting of the National ILP was held at Bradford in January 1893.[3] Twenty-one years later, in April 1914, Bradford was also the setting for the ILP's 'Coming of Age Conference'. By then the Bradford ILP had established its right to share political power with the Liberals and the Tories, and had destroyed the two-party system which had previously prevailed. Its financial membership had risen to over 1,400, after having fallen to about

1,000 in the late 1890s. It acquired its first MP in 1906, and held the balance of power in municipal politics between November 1906 and the First World War. It is hardly surprising that Bradford's local ILP leaders felt proud of their achievements and the euphoria of success was reflected in J. H. Palin's boastful comment that 'The history of Bradford will be very largely the history of the ILP.'[4] It wasn't, but the sentiment articulated the intent of the burgeoning Bradford Labour movement.

The purpose of this chapter is to explain why the ILP emerged in Bradford in such a dramatic manner and to account for the failure of the existing political parties to contain Labour's challenge. These two themes are central to the current debate being waged over the rise of Labour and the decline of Liberalism. One group of historians believe that the rise of Labour was inevitable, although they often disagree on the reasons for Labour's inexorable growth.[5] A second group have noted the remarkable resilience of Liberalism; surviving on its traditional links with Nonconformity in Wales, revitalised by 'New' Liberalism in Lancashire, and sustained by a combination of the 'Old' and the 'New' Liberalism in the North East of England.[6] For a variety of reasons, the Liberal party is considered to have been in good shape on the eve of the First World War and it was only accident of war which led to its subsequent political demise. This article supports the views of the first group and suggests that the political Labour movement was well established in Bradford in the 1890s, that the Bradford working-class voters had shifted their allegiance from the Liberal party to the ILP well before 1914, and that Bradford's 'Old' Liberals had effectively destroyed 'New' Liberal activity by 1903. In contrast to what P. F. Clarke has suggested in his book *Lancashire and the New Liberalism*, there is little evidence of a Liberal revival in Bradford. Indeed, the Bradford ILP made rapid gains in local and parliamentary elections, largely at the expense of the Liberal party. The main reason for this was not so much the growth of anti-Liberalism or the growth of a thriving ethical and cultural socialist movement in Bradford, though both were present, but the overwhelming support which the Bradford ILP garnered from the local trade union movement. It was the growth of class politics, engendered by the industrial and social conditions of Bradford in the 1880s and 1890s, which principally explains the transfer of trade-union support from the Liberal party to the ILP and the unwillingness of Labour leaders to compromise with Liberalism.

The economic and social climate of Bradford in the 1880s was not propitious for the development of a powerful labour movement. The Bradford woollen and worsted textile industry was experiencing serious economic depression from 1875 to 1914, with only the occasional and fleeting moment of industrial recovery.[7]

Until the late 1880s there was little likelihood that a viable political party of the working classes would emerge in Bradford. The depression in trade had increased unemployment and diminished the industrial muscle of even the most well-established trade unions. The Bradford Trades Council had practically collapsed in the early 1880s and local trade unionism was still firmly linked with an overbearing and paternalistic Liberal organisation. These developments consigned early efforts to obtain an independent Labour party into oblivion.

Yet there were several lines of development which converged in the 1880s to re-awaken the demand for political independence amongst some members of the Bradford working classes. The first was the formation of socialist groups in Bradford. E. P. Thompson has argued that the two-party system was broken in Yorkshire because 'working men and women took a conscious decision to form a socialist party. The fertilisation of the masses with socialist ideas was not spontaneous but was the result of the work, over many years, of a group of exceptionally gifted propagandists and trade unionists.'[8] In Bradford, the formation of a branch of William Morris's Socialist League brought together a number of these men who were to form the backbone of the ILP for the next generation, including Fred Jowett, Edwin Halford, George Minty, Paul Bland and James Bartley. It was a small group of about a dozen men who kept alive the spirit of protest which was developing amongst trade unionists in the 1880s.[9] Although most of its members were new to socialism, a few brought with them experience derived from earlier secularist and republican activities. Edward Royle has indicated that Bradford was one of the centres of freethought in the late nineteenth century. The Bradford Secularists had acquired their first hall as early as 1864, and by 1878 there were branches of both the British Secular Union and the National Secular Society in Bradford.[10]

There were also attempts to form a Republican club by the early 1870s, though no lasting organisation was formed until the mid 1880s. Both James Bartley and C. 'Leonard' Robinson were active republicans in the early 1870s and, in later years, Bartley recalled that

> In 1872, however, there was not so much Socialism in Bradford. I remember a few young forward spirits who met occasionally, in an informal way, in "The Black Bull", an old hostelry situated in a close off the top of Ivegate,.... One of their number was a disciple of Louis Blanc [who lectured in Bradford in 1860] and he always carried about with him a little blue paper-backed book, of which the Frenchman was the author, dealing with the organisation of Labour. This gentleman made a proposal that a Socialist Society should be formed, but nothing came of it. That was the first suggestion to organise Socialism in Bradford of which I have knowledge.[11]

Leonard Robinson went back further, 'had imbibed Chartist principles as a boy and was an admirer of Ernest Jones, and founder of a Republican club in Bradford in 1870.'[12] He was perhaps the only prominent member of the Bradford Socialist League who could claim a direct, and continuous, link with Chartism. The vast majority of Bradford's Chartists, and their descendants, did not find a home in the Bradford ILP. George White died, alone, in the Sheffield workhouse in 1868. Peter Bussey, the famous physical-force Chartist, left for America in 1840 and on his return became an innkeeper in Horsforth, playing no further part in political agitation.[13] Isaac Jefferson, Bradford's 'Wat Tyler', was paraded at Radical meetings in the 1860s, and his son, Cornelius, was active with the Bradford Political Union in 1865.[14] David Lightowler after his release from prison, retained his commitment to manhood suffrage and proclaimed his secularism widely but still joined forces with Bradford's middle-class Radicals. Thompson has rightly maintained that the link between Chartism and the ILP was broken and that many Chartists had come to terms with Liberal Radicalism.[15] This was the case in Bradford, and the socialists of the 1880s had to relearn 'Chartist values anew'.[16]

The secularist strand of socialist activities was led by J. W. Gott, who had helped to form the British Secular League and became editor of *Truth Seeker*, one of the secularist movement's most prestigious journals. Gott was a revolutionary socialist, and few of the Bradford secularists he organised could have ever felt at home in the more reformist ILP. Indeed, probably few ever joined and only F. Gazeley, a secularist lecturer, appears to have been the only prominent secularist member of the ILP, acting for many years as President of the East Ward Club.[17]

The new generation of socialists who prepared the way for the emergence of the ILP were influenced largely by William Morris's lecture to a Bradford audience in February 1884. Although Morris was sceptical about his impact, his audience included Fred Jowett, and others, who went on to form the Bradford branch of the Socialist League in 1886.[18] It was Jowett who first warned Liberals and Conservatives, in 1887, that 'A Labour Party cannot in justice to their interests identify themselves with either party.'[19] The desire for an independent political party of the working class was evidenced, and renewed, in a direct, if selective, line from the views expressed by William Morris.

Secondly, there was a trade revival in the late 1880s which led to a remarkable expansion in local trade union membership. The 3,500 or so Bradford trade unionists of 1885 had increased to more than 13,500 by 1893, the vast majority of whom were affiliated to the Bradford Trades Council.[20] It was an expansion which coincided with the increasing estrangement of trade unionists from the Bradford Liberal Association.

In the early 1880s, when the Bradford Trades Council had been ineffective in an industrial sense, it had also been politically insignificant, largely ignored by the Bradford Liberal Association. Even Samuel Shaftoe, President and then Secretary of the Trades Council almost continuously from 1872 to January 1893, and an ardent Liberal, was unable to motivate a more benevolent spirit within the Liberal Association, which continued to reject the Trades Council's demand for representatives on public bodies.[21] In such a climate, it is hardly surprising that some trade unionists, such as Jowett, were already beginning to question their untruthful relationship with the Bradford Liberal Association. But until the 1890s this Liberal intransigence remained a relatively minor consideration amongst those who joined socialist organisations. Thereafter, it appears to have been used by the ILP as evidence of the true colours of the Liberal party on the occasions when it was seeking political compromise with the ILP.

A third development, less vital than the other two but of some importance before the First World War, was the interest in the social conditions of the working classes shown by a small group of ministers of religion. Admittedly, the salvation of the individual soul was more important to the majority of ministers and their congregations than the creation of 'heaven on earth'. Nevertheless, a tenuous link was forged between religion and the Labour movement in 1885 when the Rev. Dr. K. C. Anderson, the new pastor of Horton Lane Congregational Church, shocked his congregation, which included many wealthy businessmen, by stating that the 'socialist indictment against modern society is a true bill; we cannot answer the charge.'[22] For the next eight years, Anderson attempted to improve the lot of the working classes through the work of his congregation, and personally attempted to intervene in the Manningham Mills strike.[23] Anderson influenced the Rev. T. Rhondda Williams, who became pastor of Greenfield Congregational Chapel. Williams described his mentor as 'a man of keen, logical mind and with a trenchant style, whose plough drove through the field of orthodoxy'.[24] When Anderson left Bradford in 1893, it was Williams who assumed his mantle. He helped set up the Social Reform Union in October 1893. It was a small organisation of about 100 members formed to help religion face up to Bradford's social problems, but it included some of Bradford's leading religious figures such as the Rev. Dr. Duff and Professor Armitage of the Yorkshire United Independent College, Rev. R. Roberts of Frizinghall Chapel, and George Speight and W. H. Scales, its treasurer and secretary, respectively.[25] However, only two of the leading members of the organisation – Rev. E. Ceredeg Jones, a Unitarian, and Arthur Priestman, a Quaker – were drawn from outside Congregationalism.[26]

Rhondda Williams was a friend of Rev. R. J. Campbell and was an advocate of the 'New Theology', well before Campbell formed his League of Progressive Religion and Social Thought.[27] Williams maintained that 'The truth is that any minister who refuses the advocacy of social reforms and confines himself to the work of individual salvation is shirking the crucial problems of modern life.'[28] The Social Reform Union was designed to take up the social problems of modern life and it established a Vigilance Committee to deal with policing, a Children's Aid Committee and an Industrial Questions Committee. It joined with the ILP, the Fabian Society, and the Trades Council, to for the Bradford Unemployed Emergency Committee towards the end of 1893. This committee conducted a survey of unemployment in Bradford and suggested methods of tackling the problem.[29] Indeed, it was through the Social Reform Union that Arthur Priestman, a Quaker, one of Bradford's leading industrialists and brother of H. B. Priestman, Bradford's Liberal leader from 1900, found his way into the Bradford ILP of which he became president in 1906.[30] Rev. Roberts also followed this routeway to the ILP, though with less permanence. Roberts, pastor of Frizinghall Chapel and, later of Brownroyd Congregational Chapel, sat alongside Margaret McMillan as an ILP representative on the Bradford School Board between 1897 and 1902. It is also significant that the Brownroyd Congregational Adult Class bought one share in the Labour Institute Ltd. in March 1897.[31] Roberts also helped to form the Bradford Ethical Society in 1898, the principal objective of which was the moralisation of society.[32] Such Congregational crusading, inside and outside the ILP, inspired an analogous movement amongst Anglicans, the Rev. W. B. Graham being, for a short time, active in Bradford socialism and a founder member of the Church Socialist League.[33] Graham explained his position in the following manner: 'To me, as many others, Socialism seems a logical outcome of our Lord's teaching as applied to the modern democratic state'.[34]

It is too easy to dismiss the influence of Nonconformity on the Bradford ILP, as E. P. Thompson has done, or, on the other hand, to exaggerate its importance.[35] The fact is that Nonconformity, and Congregationalism rather than Methodism, did exert a fitful influence upon the Bradford Labour movement. At various times, Fred Jowett had attended Horton Lane Congregational Chapel, Anderson's chapel. W. H. Drew, the strike leader during the Manningham Mills dispute, had been a Congregationalist. Many leading Congregationalist ministers either joined the ILP or spoke on its platforms. The religious influence was evident in both the membership and the ethical approach adopted by many members of the ILP, some of whom found themselves immersed in the work of the Bradford and Eccleshill labour churches and the plethora of Socialist Sunday schools which emerged after 1899. Yet religion in Bradford never assumed the importance of the Labour movement that was evident in Colne Valley.[36] It never represented more than a small fraction of the total support for the ILP, though its influence was more pervasive than its numbers might indicate. Similarly, such support within organised religion was often limited and isolated. T. Rhondda Williams admitted that 'When I had been two years in Bradford I spoke on the platform of the Yorkshire Congregational Union and was considered, I think, a young man of some promise. Soon after this my heresies began to get about, and not for sixteen years was I again asked to speak at the Yorkshire Union.'[37] One must also be aware that a large number of Congregationalists, such as Walter Sugden and W. P. Byles, of the *Bradford Observer*, were more interested in establishing a new progressive alliance between Liberalism and Labour than in building up the fortunes of an independent Labour party. Also, at one extreme of Congregationalism were many businessmen, such as James Hill, who were totally opposed to the ILP and fervently committed to 'old-time' Liberalism.[38] Not too much should be made of the religious fringe of the Bradford Labour movement, but it cannot be dismissed.

By the late 1880s the Bradford Labour movement was set on course for rapid development. An active minority of socialist agitators, playing upon the frustrations of a rapidly expanding trade union membership, began to undermine Liberal dominance amongst working men. Socialists were being sent to the Trades Council as delegates and were even active in the formation of the Bradford branch of the Labour Electoral Association, formed in 1887 to encourage the Liberals to put forward working-class candidates for local and parliamentary honours.[39] Yet these advocates of socialism and independence were small in number. What made them a tenable force was the Liberal Association's constant neglect of working-class voters, Shaftoe's compromising attitude over political and industrial affairs, and the inability of the Bradford Labour Electoral Association to deliver the political goods it demanded. But what eventually transformed the Trades Council from its Liberal political stance towards socialism and independence were two related events – the Manningham Mills strike and the formation, in its wake, of the Bradford Labour Union.

Much has been written about the Manningham Mills strike. E. P. Thompson considers it to have been the pivotal moment in the education of the working classes in Bradford and the West Riding, transforming their attitude on political questions.[40] It certainly helped to polarise opinion, the *Bradford Observer* reporting that 'The struggle took on the character of a general dispute between capital and labour since it was well known that a large number of prominent Bradford employers agreed to the action which Mr. Lister had taken.'[41] The *Yorkshire Factory Times* announced the end of the strike with the prophetic statement that 'Labour has so associated itself that even defeat must be victory.'[42] Indeed, throughout the dispute trade unionists of all persuasions were temporarily conflated into one united body. Shaftoe stood alongside Drew in the common defence of the Manningham weavers. The dispute, described in the previous chapter, led to the formation of the Bradford Labour Union.

The Bradford Labour Union was conceived in the frustrations of working men attending meetings following these events. The need for political action was manifestly obvious for working men could no longer trust either Liberals or Tories to look after their interests. Even Shaftoe declaimed: 'The Labour Party intended to have labour representation in the Town Council and to take the whip out of the hands of those who have been flogging them in the past fortnight.'[43] Charlie Glyde summed up the frustration: 'We have had two parties in the past, the can'ts and the won'ts and its time that we had a party that will.'[44]

The 'party that will', the Bradford Labour Union, was formed about six weeks later on 28 May 1891. Its intentions were defined as being 'to promote the interests of the working men in whatever way may from time time be thought advisable and further the cause of direct Labour Representation on Local Bodies and in Parliament.'[45] Within a year it was exerting a divisive influence when it requested the Bradford Trades Council to support Ben

Tillett for the West Bradford parliamentary contest in the general election of 1892. The Trades Council minutes of 14 June are brief and simply record its support for Tillett. The *Bradford Observer* was more forthcoming:

> The proceedings of Tuesday's meeting of the Trades Council were very lively. The Labour Union members were determined to get a general vote in favour of Tillett .... They have had a majority on the Trades Council for some time ... they managed to get the vote but only after heated discussion.[46]

The motion of support for Tillett was in fact won by 47 votes to 33, a clear reflection that the political balance of the Trades Council had changed. Furthermore, Tillett's good third in the parliamentary contest, registering more than 2,700 votes, reflected the strong support he had gained from trade unionists in Bradford West.[47]

The socialists on the Trades Council compounded their victories in January 1893 with the removal of Shaftoe as secretary, replacing him with George Cowgill, the former president of the Trades Council and a member of the Bradford Labour Union. Yet Shaftoe's defeat, by 48 votes to 38, reveals the narrowness of the socialist dominance and the strength of feeling which still persisted for the Liberal party. Indeed, some societies left the Trades Council in protest at the Tillett resolution and the removal of Shaftoe. Shaftoe was more resigned and took his defeat to be the 'usual reward for a lifetime spent in the cause of labour'.[48]

These were heady days for the Bradford Labour Union. On 8 January 1893, only a few days after the removal of Shaftoe, the Labour Church was opened at Peckover Street. On 13 and 14 January, the first national ILP Conference was held at Bradford.[49] The membership of the Bradford Labour Union was also expanding rapidly, and the Union was working closely with the Trades Council in order to win trade union wage rates for all workers. This 'Fair Contracts' campaign, begun by the Trades Council in 1889, was fought for by Labour Union/ILP candidates at every municipal, School Board, and Board of Guardian, election during the 1890s. But the Trades Council was hesitant about accepting the domination of one political party in its affairs, now that it was free of Liberal control. Its membership covered the entire political spectrum, and many were not socialists, even in the widest sense of the word.

This became obvious in 1895 when the Trades Council dropped its apolitical stance and accepted the Dyers' resolution, introduced by Joseph Hayhurst, 'That no person be accepted by the Council as a candidate for an elective body who is not pledged to support the collective ownership of the means of production, distribution and exchange.'[50] Many members of the Trades Council were critical of this decision since it kept Liberal and Tory trade unionists from office and thus created tensions between a large minority of the Trades Council membership and the ILP. During the late 1890s, when the growth of the Bradford ILP was temporarily halted, it was plainly obvious that many trade unionists did not vote for ILP candidates. The result was that many members of the Bradford ILP gravitated towards adopting a broader electoral policy to encompass all shaded of trade-union opinion. The formation of the Workers' Municipal Federation – as a more formal organisation than the Municipal Election Committee which had been formed in 1900 – was evidence of this desire.[51] The WMF's objectives were couched in the general terms initially adopted by the Bradford Labour Union in 1891: 'To secure the return of Labour representatives on the City Council, Board of Guardians and the now defunct School Board'.[52] Thus it sought to avoid truculent political conflict within the Bradford Labour movement by offering a general objective to which all could agree, regardless of political differences.

Notwithstanding the fact that the ILP decided not to join the WMF, the formation of the new organisation anticipated a movement towards political unity within the Bradford labour movement. Even without formal membership, the ILP found its views well represented on the WMF through the many trade union and Trades Council representatives, such as W. H. Drew, George Licence, A. T. Sutton, Tom Brown and James Bartley, all of whom were leading figures in the ILP.[53] Of the first sixteen members of the Executive Committee, at least five were prominent figures in the Bradford ILP.[54] It was this informal presence which helped to smooth out relations between the WMF and the ILP, and which paved the way for more formal consultations between the two bodies. In 1904, the WMF resolved to endorse the ILP nominees contesting municipal elections and, in 1905, the Executive Committee of the WMF decided to 'receive a deputation from the I.L.P. with a view to avoid clashing in contest of seats.'[55] By 1907 relations were so good that it was resolved 'That the Federation agrees to run their candidates jointly with the I.L.P. and That a Committee be appointed to do this work.'[56] Thereafter the Joint Committee of the ILP and the WMF made the local political arrangements for the Bradford Labour movement until 1919, when the WMF absorbed into and became the basis of, the Bradford Labour Party.[57]

The WMF was designed to unite trade unionists in obtaining the best arrangements they could from any political party but in reality it operated with the ILP and against the Liberals and Tories. It was partly encouraged in this policy by the continued intolerance of the Bradford Liberal Association, which had been unwilling to withdraw its candidates and allow A. N. Harris, president of the WMF, a straight run with the Conservatives at the 1902 municipal election in Listerhills ward.[58] This experience imbued the WMF with a sense of its own independence which meant that subsequent Liberal overtures were rejected.[59] After the events of 1902 Liberal vicissitudes had no place in the discussions and debates of the WMF, and the organisation looked to its own strength and to the ILP for political gains.

The WMF was, indeed, a remarkably successful political organisation in its own right until 1910, when the distinctions between the WMF and the ILP candidates ceased to have any significance.[60] By 1905 the WMF could claim five representatives on the City Council, half of the Labour group at that time. With the ILP it was able to hold the balance of power on the City Council between 1906 and the First World War.

The strength and confidence of the Bradford ILP derived from its capture of the local trade union movement. The Socialist–Labour group of 1906 is particularly revealing for, despite the departure of Jowett to Parliament, seven of the remaining nine members were trade unionists.[61] Even the exceptions, E. R. Hartley and Arthur Priestman, advocated trade-union measures at election times. Indeed, there were many members of the Bradford ILP who would have subscribed to the vociferous comment of Councillor C. L. Robinson that

> ... an I.L.P. man cannot be a true Labour men unless he favours the principle of trade unionism, and that the position of a trade unionist is very anomalous one when he be not an I.L.P. man, or at any rate perfectly independent – that it, prepared to steer clear of Liberal and Tory alike. Yes, I certainly think that the "trade unionist" and "I.L.P.er" ought to be absolutely synonymous terms.[62]

Not surprisingly, then, the vital trade union interests appeared on the municipal programme year after year. Most notable was the demand for the introduction of a 'fair contracts' resolution on all local administrative bodies. Such a resolution was agreed by the Council, the Guardians and the School Board during the 1890s.[63] But there was constant evasion of the measure and the Bradford ILP attempted to introduce a penalty clause against those who failed to pay trade union wage rates.[64] This was pressed on the City Council at the turn of the century but always proved difficult to enforce.[65]

Trade-union objectives therefore underpinned the municipal and local election policies of the ILP. Election leaflets were studded with trade-union demands, and the Bradford ILP was firmly rooted in the local trade union movement. Yet the policies of the Bradford ILP threatened more than they achieved when measured in terms of the impact upon the lives of the majority of the working class.

In many respects, the ILP policies lacked a coherent strategy. They were mainly a set of responses, or palliatives, to social problems. J. B. Priestley reflected that 'In the prewar days Bradford was considered the most progressive place in the United Kingdom', but there was little that was innovative in the policies of the ILP or the City Council to justify such an accolade.[66] The majority of the Bradford ILP's social and economic achievements were confined to speeding up the process of municipalisation in Bradford, often in the wake of other cities. Bradford was not the first town to have a municipal tramway nor was she the first to have a municipal gas and water supply. The two major achievements of the Bradford ILP were municipal housing and municipal school feeding, both of which were supported by parliamentary legislation. But the first was a protracted and difficult issue to resolve, limited in its real impact, and it was only in the latter that the ILP could claim to be a pace-setter. Only municipal school feeding was to push Bradford to the forefront of municipal reform.

Between 1904 and 1907 the issue of municipal school feeding proved to be one of the most controversial of all subjects in the evolution of municipal welfare. At the national level, as B. B. Gilbert has suggested, it was a fertile source of violent controversy over the state's interference with parental responsibility.[67] At the local level, the same contention emerged fuelled by the trenchant opposition to Bradford Liberalism. In Bradford, the school-feeding debate resolved itself into a conflict between the Liberal party, with its emphasis upon the provision of charity and poor relief, and the ILP with its demand for municipal provision of school meals. What was remarkable in Bradford, however, was the bitterness and intensity of the conflict, followed by the sudden and complete capitulation of the Liberal opposition to municipal school feeding. In December 1904, Bradford's Liberal councillors rejected a previous resolution to introduce school feeding.[68] By October, 1907, Jonathan Priestley, headmaster of Green Lane School, was serving school meals at White Abbey Dining Room, one of the five dining rooms simultaneously opened by the Bradford Education Authority.[69] This transformation was the product of a combination of factors which conflated during 1906 and early 1907.

The failure of the charities to cope with the poverty and destitution of the working classes and the ineptitude of the Board of Guardians in dealing with the problem of child feeding, as evidenced in local surveys, suggested that municipal intervention was necessary. One survey, conducted by Dr. Crowley the Medical Superintendent of the Bradford Education Authority, suggested that at least 6,000 children were under-fed and that 15,000 had 'nourishment below the normal' in the Bradford schools.[70] As W. Leach, editor of *Forward*, the ILP journal, complained, 'Here then, in all its nakedness, is laid bare the results of Bradford Liberalism's school feeding policy.'[71] It was a lesson taken to heart by H. B. Priestman, the local Liberal leader and the father-in-law of Dr. Crowley. Within weeks the Liberal Party had changed its position and was supporting municipal school feeding. But such a change had been nurtured by a variety of other developments throughout 1906 and 1907.

Despite their victory in two of Bradford's three parliamentary seats in the general election of 1906, the Liberals were losing ground in the local elections. In November they lost overall control of the City Council and, in March 1907, were swept from power in the Board of Guardian elections.[72] With the passing of the Education (Provision of Meals) Bill in December 1906, and the timely death of Alfred Illingworth, Bradford Liberalism's political supremo, in January 1907, the scene was set for a change of direction.[73]

If municipal school feeding was the apogee of the Bradford ILP's local successes then its nadir was undoubtedly its inability to force action on unemployment, the constant problem facing working-class families. Partly as a result of foreign tariffs, Bradford experienced high levels of unemployment between 1891 and 1895, and again between the winter months of 1902 and 1909. With up to a quarter of Bradford's population affected by unemployment in these periods it was to be expected that the ILP would be assertive in its demand for action. The eight-hour day, land reforms, land colonisation and municipal workshops were fiercely debated as possible solutions to unemployment. The ILP was even drawn into surveying the extent of unemployment in Bradford during 1893 and 1894, as a member of the Bradford Unemployed Emergency Committee.[74] But in the end, despite all its efforts, the ILP was unable to do much to alleviate the condition of the unemployed.

The death knell for local initiative on unemployment was to a large extent sounded by the failure of the Girlington land grabbing scheme of 1906. Towards the end of July, 'Under the leadership of Mr. C. A. Glyde, about a dozen men have exercised their Imperial prerogative and taken possession in the name of the unemployed, of a small piece of vacant land belonging to the Midland Railway Company at Girlington.'[75] They built a house made out of sods, affectionately known as 'Klondyke Villa', and planted vegetables. The colony attracted much local interest in its early days but disputes developed amongst the men and, towards the end of October, the colony closed amidst argument. Along with a similar episode in Leeds, the 'Girlington Klondyke' excited interest but offered no permanent outlet to even the small number of unemployed it involved, and a subsequent effort to form a land colony, which incorporated the support of the Bradford City Guild of Help, fared no better.[76]

Yet even if it was not possible to instigate a major social and economic revolution, the Bradford ILP was able to gain some satisfaction from its work. It did raise the pace of events. It provided experience for socialists who were still in the business of educating the working classes to the need for an independent working-class party. Above all, the Bradford ILP was able to secure an increasing working-class vote by its aggressive, if comparatively fruitless, pursuit of class interests. From 1906 the Bradford ILP continued to make major inroads into the support of the other two political parties. But it was the Liberals who were the main losers of Labour's continued growth.

P. F. Clarke has argued that Edwardian Liberalism in Lancashire was not merely surviving on the strength of local Nonconformity and a free-trade tradition but was rapidly extending its support from 1906, and especially after 1910 due to the move from community to class politics. He maintains that this growth of class politics was of benefit to the Liberal party since its organisation became increasingly national in focus, with career politicians replacing local Liberal 'big-wigs' and Liberal intellectuals encouraging Lloyd George, and others, to introduce a synthesis of Liberal and Socialist policies which would attract working-class support. This 'New' Liberalism, a reforming ideology which placed its emphasis upon state intervention extending liberty in a positive way by equalizing opportunities, replaced the

'Old' Liberalism with its emphasis upon simply removing the impediments to individual freedom. The 'New Liberalism', with its offer of social reforms, served to retain and recapture much working-class support which would have otherwise gone to a burgeoning Labour party. Had it not been for the problems of the First World War the Liberal party would have continued as the leading progressive party in British politics.[77]

Clarke's views have been examined by many historians. Dr. Kenneth Morgan has rejected the suggestion that Welsh Liberalism followed the course depicted by Clarke, for in Wales it was 'Old' Liberalism which remained rampant until 1914.[78] M. D. Pugh has argued that Yorkshire presents a mixed picture of 'New' Liberals being returned in constituencies with 'Old' Liberal support, the main reason being that 'there was less sense of change than in Lancashire because there was less need for change.'[79] In Bradford, however, there was much need for change but little evidence of it and the Liberals were, therefore, unable to arrest the growth of the ILP after 1906.

In the 1880s the Liberals had been omnipotent in Bradford politics returning all but one of the nine elected MPs.[80] The 'Liberal Eight' dominated the School Board, Liberals ran the Board of Guardians unchallenged, and the Liberal Party was the largest party on the Town Council between 1880 and 1898. Yet the Liberal fortunes began to fade with the formation of the Bradford Labour Union in 1891, and with the rise of Bradford Conservatism. Though three Liberal MPs were returned in the 1892 general election the Conservatives swept the board in 1895 and continued to represent all Bradford constituencies until 1906.

From the start Bradford Liberals were fearful of the Labour challenge, castigating it as a plot to strengthen Bradford Conservatism by dividing the progressive vote.[81] They were dismayed when the Labour Union initially announced its intention to contest two parliamentary seats, and annoyed that Ben Tillett should contest West Bradford against Alfred Illingworth in 1892, despite the Liberal offer of a straight run against the Conservatives in the Eastern Division.[82]

The Bradford Labour Union/ILP had made its intention clear: it was going to be an independent political organisation, not a mere appendage to the Liberal party. On the whole, it was able to maintain this stance throughout the first twenty-three years of its existence. It was helped in this pursuit by the insensitivity of the Liberal Association which had flouted the demand for working-class representation before and, to some extent, after the decisive shift in trade-union support brought about by the Manningham Mills strike. This insouciant behaviour is largely explicable by the fact that Bradford Liberalism was dominated by a few important Dissenting and Nonconformist industrial families, most notably the Illingworths.[83] Personally wealthy, the 'money-bags' of Bradford Liberalism, a Baptist, and Bradford's most influential MP following the death of W. E. Forster in 1886, Alfred Illingworth was the embodiment of 'Old Liberalism' in Bradford. Opposed to many economic and social reforms, Illingworth was an uncompromising opponent of organised labour.[84] The Newcastle Programme of social reforms was worth nothing in Bradford when faced with Illingworth's opposition. One ILP writer remarked of the Bradford Liberal Association that

> It selects candidates, and decides how far these candidates shall go in their advocacy of reforms. To this section the Newcastle Programme count for nothing unless it be considered of use in gaining votes at election times. Its proposed reforms are never advocated by official Liberals, and any man who takes a very prominent part in keeping its items before the public is cold-shouldered ...[85]

The Liberal Association's defence was that Home Rule came first. This was sufficient to attract the Irish vote, but it did not suffice for an increasing number of working-class voters who became convinced that change was not going to come through the Liberal party. The result was that Liberalism had a declining appeal for the politically-conscious working man, Katherine Conway maintaining that 'In London, he listens to the persuasive reasoning of the Progressives – in the provinces, face to face with Liberals of the Illingworth, Kitson and Pease type, he is doggedly independent.'[86]

Illingworth's malevolence towards Labour can be seen in the case of the East Bradford by-election of November 1896. After Tillett's two parliamentary defeats at West Bradford, in 1892 and 1895, the problems of the Liberals appeared to leave open the possibility that James Keir Hardie would be able to stand in a straight contest with the Conservatives. But in the end the Liberals brought forward a candidate, the progressive vote was divided, and the Conservative candidate was returned. Shortly after the by-election the *Labour Leader* reflected that

> Liberalism in Bradford had been doomed to failure for years it took no account of Labour. The people of Bradford were expected to return to Parliament the manufacturers of Bradford, and to take their political orders from them. Illingworthism was a gospel without sympathy, comradeship, or hope for the Bradford worker, and an attempt to identify it with Liberalism has had its consequence in Keir Hardieism.[87]

Although this was an exaggeration, for much working-class support had moved to the Labour Union/ILP as a result of the Manningham Mills strike, the continuous drip of Liberal support to Labour was partly conditioned by 'Illingworthism'.

Although 'Illingworthism' was the dominant force in Bradford Liberalism during the 1890s there was evidence of initiatives by 'New' Liberals. The ILP held the balance of power between the Liberals and the Conservatives on the Council from 1893 to 1898. The Liberals were able to dominate Council affairs but were conscious of the need to defuse the Labour challenge. In 1894, J. W. Jarratt, an advanced Liberal, helped to formulate a progressive municipal programme for the Bradford Liberal Association, which included a commitment to introduce an eight-hour day and a forty-eight hour week for

Corporation workers, municipal control of nightsoil clearance and tramways, and the introduction of Fair Contracts.[88] Jarratt maintained that if the Liberal party adopted a progressive policy 'they could cut the ground from under the feet of the Independent Labour Party'.[89] When this policy failed to achieve the desired result the Liberals made overtures to the ILP, and there was a meeting between leading Liberals and ILPers in April 1897 orchestrated by W. P. Byles.[90] The opprobrious reaction within ILP circles led to the end of the initiative, though the *Bradford Observer* was proud to report that the Joint Committee of the Trades Council and ILP after having put three test questions to all candidates in 1898 had recommended 'working men to support Liberal candidates in all wards in which no Labour candidate had appeared.'[91] In 1899 the *Bradford Labour Echo* speculated that the feud between the 'Radical Socialists' in the Liberal party and 'old-time Liberalism' could only end 'in the disappearance of old Liberalism'.[92] There was much optimism within Liberal ranks when W. E. B. Priestley's secret mission to Herbert Gladstone led to Jarratt standing down for West Bradford, thus permitting Fred Jowett a straight fight with the Conservative candidate in the 1900 general election.[93] But in the end 'Old' Liberalism prevailed.

The ILP was reluctant to enter into a political arrangement with Bradford Liberalism and opted, instead, to build up its trade-union support. This decision left the 'New' Liberals high and dry.[94] They could not obtain the alliance they sought with the ILP and, as a result of their actions, they had temporarily lost the Bradford Liberal Association the financial support of Alfred Illingworth. The result was that the impact of 'New' Liberalism waned quickly. The end of the attempted Liberal rapprochement with the ILP was signalled by the decision of Rev. R. Roberts to leave the ILP in December 1902 because he objected to the continued isolationist policies of the ILP. His crime, in Labour eyes, was that he had spoken in favour of the Liberal candidate in Tong Ward and against Charlie Glyde the Labour candidate.[95] This defection was followed by Keir Hardie's statement, at the May Day demonstration in 1903, that there was to be no compromise: 'Liberalism and Toryism had divided the workers. Independence had come to unite them.'[96] This was seen as an irrevocable declaration of war against Bradford Liberalism, and Illingworth soon returned to the Liberal camp. As the local Labour press reflected: 'Alfred Illingworth remained in the sulks until his anti-Labour friends secured the upper hand again, after which he walked back into the party leading Mr. Claridge, his candidate, by the hand.'[97] In July 1903 W. Claridge was officially endorsed as the Liberal candidate for West Bradford, and the Liberal honeymoon with Labour was over.[98]

The end of the Liberal attempt to work with the ILP was further signified by the departure of Byles from Bradford in 1903. William Pollard Byles was the leading exponent of 'New' Liberalism throughout the 1890s and frequently expressed his views through the *Bradford Observer*, of which he was a shareholder and sometime editor. His political career during the 1890s is a salutary reminder of the difficulties experienced by Liberals of his ilk. Always a spokesman for the working man, whether in bringing Socialist speakers to Bradford or in speaking up for the Manningham operatives, Byles rose to political prominence through his efforts to become Liberal candidate for Shipley in 1891 and 1892, in the face of staunch opposition from the 'Old' Liberals in the Shipley Two Hundred.[99] The animus created by this contest, Byles's candidature, and his subsequent return as MP for Shipley, served to estrange him from the majority of Bradford's 'Old' Liberals. Defeated at the 1895 general election, Byles searched for a new seat and attempted to presume himself upon the East Bradford electorate as a suitable Lib-Lab candidate in the 1896 parliamentary by-election. Byles's suit was unsuccessful, but his exchange of letters with Hardie reflects the extent of his commitment to 'new' Liberalism. Byles wrote:

> When you say I vacillate between two opinions & do not choose between Liberalism and Labour, you absolutely misunderstand my position. I will explain: you & I hold practically the same opinions. These opinions have led you to disbelieve in the Lib. party as an engine for the reforms you seek, and therefore to leave it & form a separate party. The same opinions have not led me to the same conclusion. Bad and reactionary as many Liberals are, I believe that salvation must come thro the Liberal party wh. still contains more friends of Labour than can be found outside it, and the destruction of which (if it were possible wh. it isn't) would set back the Labour clock a generation.[100]

By the end of the 1890s, having sold his shares in the *Bradford Observer* and having asked Charles Dilke to interpose on his behalf with Hardie, Byles was the ILP candidate for Leeds.[101] His commitment was, in fact, rather vague and he soon returned to the Liberal fold. With little prospect of pursuing a political career in Bradford he decided to move to Manchester and Salford. The political commentator who wrote of Byles's departure might well have been writing the obituary of 'New' Liberalism in Bradford when he reflected that

> He has affluence, he has leisure, and he has ambition. That other desideratum, "troops of friends" is denied him, or at least if he has sufficient to be called troops, his enemies are in battalions. Owing to untoward circumstances Mr. Byles's political life was so circumscribed here in Bradford that it became intolerable. To find greater breathing space, and ampler air, he has had at the age of 64 to expatriate himself, to leave all his friends and associations, to go to live in Manchester. It is a hard fate but it is necessary if Mr. Byles should fulfil the political role to which he is irresistibly drawn.[102]

The commentator also launched a fusillade of personal abuse at Byles, though such action was well in keeping with the *Bradford Daily Telegraph*, a paper which had been established by 'Old' Liberals, such as Alfred Illingworth and James Hill, in order to counter the advanced Liberal opinions being expressed in the *Bradford Observer*.

The secret Gladstone-MacDonald pact of 1903 had no influence in Bradford politics, coming as it did after the failure of local Liberal attempts to work with the ILP. Fred Jowett was, therefore, opposed by Liberal and Tory alike in the West Bradford parliamentary election in 1906. After 1906 there is little evidence of the Liberals attempting to make a pact with the ILP or of them trying to outbid the ILP on social reforms. More obviously, the Bradford Liberals appear to have decided that the only way to resist the Labour challenge was to organise a municipal pact with the Conservatives. There is evidence that the pact operated from November 1906 to November 1913 and that 16 of Bradford's 21 wards were involved.[104] The significant point is that the Conservatives did better from this arrangement than the Liberals.

There is also little evidence of career politicians emerging, as Clarke suggests, to replace the old millocracy politics or of a new reforming ideology becoming dominant in Bradford politics. At the municipal level the main change amongst Liberal representatives was one of social and economic status rather than of religion and outlook. At the parliamentary level, the main thrust of Clarke's argument, neither of the two Liberal MPs returned in the 1906 and 1910 general elections were of the new mould which Clarke has outlined. W. E. B. Priestley was the son of Briggs Priestley, one of Bradford's leading industrialists, a Baptist, and Liberal MP for Pudsey between 1895 and 1900. W. E. B. Priestley obtained much of his political support for 'Old' Liberal reasons. An advanced Liberal, partly responsible for Jowett being given a straight run against the Conservatives in the 1900 general election, Priestley was, for a time, a member of T. Rhondda Williams's Greenfield Congregational Chapel, but left because Williams stood on Jowett's platform in the 1906 general election.[105] Sir George Scott Robertson might be regarded as a career politician, having no local or religious ties but he was certainly not an advanced Liberal.[106] Neither Liberal MP fits Clarke's ideal of the reforming career politician untrammelled by a background which guaranteed some local personal influence. Both Liberal MPs undoubtedly picked up a substantial working-class vote in their campaigns, but that was by virtue of the ILP's decision to concentrate its efforts on West Bradford, and their performances exaggerate the position of Bradford Liberalism in the light of what was occurring in the local elections.

Bradford politics was undergoing fundamental changes between the 1880s and 1914. Some right-wing Liberals were drifting into the Conservative party, as the Bradford Liberal Association made minor political concessions to Labour, and many working-class voters were identifying with the ILP as the Liberal party failed to go far enough in meeting their expectations. In local, if not always in parliamentary, politics the Bradford Liberal Association was no longer the overpowering political force which it had been in the 1880s. It was bedevilled with problems which it could not resolve, and by 1909 and 1910 the Labour group was receiving a larger municipal vote than the Liberals. In 1913 the Labour group gained 43.1 per cent of the municipal vote, compared with the 27.2 per cent gathered by the Liberals and the 29.7 per cent gained by the

Table 1   Political Composition of Bradford Council, 1885–1914[103]

Year	Liberals	Conservatives	Independents	Labour Lib-Lab	Soc-Lab ILP	WMF	Total
1885	43	16					59
1886	43	16					59
1887	43	16					59
1888	45	14					59
1889	44	14	2				60
1890	42	17	1				60
1891	35	23	1	1			60*
1892	31	27		1	2		61*
1893	29	26		1	4		60*
1894	29	27			4		60
1895	28	26			6		60
1896	28	27	1		4		60
1897	28	26	1		5		60
1898	26	29			5		60
1899	27	44	8*		5		84
1900	28	42	8		6		84
1901	42	31	3		8		84
1902	45***	29	2		6	2	84
1903	49***	26	2		5	2	84
1904	45	28	1		4	6	84
1905	42	31	1		5	5	84
1906	38	34	1		5	6	84
1907	30	40	1			13	84
1908	32	42	2			10	84
1909	33	41	2			8	84
1910	35	39	2			8	84
1911	36	34	1			13	84
1912	35	31	1			17	84
1913	29	34	1			20	84

In 1891 the Mayor was neither a councillor nor an alderman.

* Samuel Shaftoe was returned in 1891 as a Trades Council representative. He was in fact a Liberal and was normally included in the Liberal list, though not by the Trades Council. He is indicated as a Lib-Lab in this list.

** The Independents indicated in 1899 and 1900 were said to be mainly members of the Liberal clubs.

† The Liberal figures include an aldermanic vacancy created by the death of John Hardaker, which was not filled immediately.

‡ The Liberal total includes the vacancy created by the death of Joseph Rhodes, which was not filled immediately.

The 1892 list includes C. L. Robinson, the first ILP representatives on the Bradford Council, who was returned unopposed at a by-election in August 1892.

Table 2   Liberal-Conservative Pact

Year	Liberal straight fights with Labour		Conservative straight fights with Labour		Total	
	Contested	Won	Contested	Won	Contested	Won
1906	3	2	4	4	7	6
1907	4	2	1	1	5	3
1908	4	4	4	3	8	7
1909	5	5	4	4	9	9
1910	3	1	2	2	5	3
1911	3	1	4	4	7	5
1912	1	0	1	1	2	1
1913	3	2	5	4	8	6
Totals	26	17	25	23	51	40

Conservatives.[107] Had it not been for the municipal pact with the Conservatives, Liberal fortunes might have been even less impressive. As it was, the Liberal party was only able to hold two-thirds of the wards it contested in a straight fight with Labour, despite Conservative support. The ILP/Labour group was a vital, vibrant, and growing organisation by the early twentieth century and, in Bradford at least, there is little evidence to suggest that the Liberal party was able to check its growth. The Bradford Liberal Association palpably failed to offer 'New' Liberal policies to the electorate and sought to staunch Labour's growth by allying with the conservatives in municipal elections. This ploy did not work.

The Bradford ILP's most significant achievement was to wrest control of the working-class vote between the 1880s and 1914. Propelled forward by the intransigence of local Liberalism and fuelled by the political support which emanated from the major industrial and class conflict associated with the Manningham Mills strike, the Bradford ILP became, as its founders had anticipated, almost synonymous with trade unionism. Yet, as Thompson has suggested, it required a hard-core of socialists to give the Bradford ILP the direction which permitted it to get its message over to the electorate. It just happened that many of the leading socialists were also trade unionists who were able to convince their colleagues of the economic and political limitations of Liberalism. Without the vital trade-union support Bradford socialists would have been 'spitting into the wind', failing to make a significant impact upon Bradford politics and society.

The Bradford ILP achieved much in its early years, encroaching upon the Liberal dominance of the working-class vote and providing the springboard for later parliamentary and municipal successes. After 1906, the ILP's gains were particularly impressive and there is little evidence that 'New' Liberalism was ever the potent and enervating force on the Bradford Labour movement that it might have been on the Lancashire Labour movement. Indeed, in Bradford, it was only in the late 1890s that 'New' Liberal attitudes intruded into politics. But by 1903 their influence had been checked by the resurgence of traditional Liberalism, which was determinedly unresponsive to the demands of Labour.

If the Liberals were failing to respond to the challenge of working-class demands, the ILP was offering itself willingly to the Bradford working classes. Yet it was often upbraided by some of its members, such as Charlie Glyde and E. R. Hartley, who felt that the ILP should be more forthright in its advocacy of socialist measures. Their views were, however, anathema to the average member of the Bradford ILP who wanted to see the immediate tangible benefits of their work in terms of fair contracts clauses and the municipalisation of local services. Although such measures only brought limited benefits to a few thousand of the Bradford working classes before 1914, they attracted significant working-class support for the ILP. Admittedly, the trade-union movement framework of the ILP's policies was extremely restrictive and clearly incapable of offering coherent policies to solve some of the major social issues of the day. But, in the end, the Bradford ILP saw its main task as being to capture working-class support. It had to offer the moderate policies which would establish its working-class credentials. Had the Bradford ILP been too advanced in the proposals it made it would not have attracted the support it did, and it would have left the working-class vote firmly in the hands of the Liberal party. It was modest in its demands, won widespread working-class support, and by the First World War Liberalism was a besieged force in Bradford politics, threatened by an almost equally powerful Labour party. The Bradford ILP was no longer 'one of the little breezes blowing across Bradford' which Alfred Illingworth had detected in 1891.[108] It had made serious inroads into the Liberal vote and the following poem written during the 1906 general election, was a sharp reminder of Liberal neglect and Labour advance.

> A plausible weaver named Claridge,
> Once sought for West Bradford in marriage,
> But was left in the lurch,
> She would not go to Church,
> In Alfred Illingworth's carriage.[109]

The Bradford Labour party emerged successfully because, unlike the Bradford Liberal Association, it was prepared to act as the vehicle for the aspirations of the working classes; aspiration which it also helped to shape.[110]

The First World War created a crisis within the Bradford ILP, partly because the movement was deeply divided on the war issue, but also because of the formation of the Bradford Central Labour Party in September 1918. The impact of the war is examined in detail in the next chapter.

Throughout the 1920s the ILP maintained some control over municipal and parliamentary politics but increasingly found the Labour Party attracting support away from its activities. In the end the Bradford party never reclaimed its pre-1914 pre-eminence in Bradford labour politics. Nevertheless, its leaders still commanded respect and were returned as Bradford's MPs; Willie Leach was returned as the ILP/Labour Party MP for Bradford Central between 1922 and 1924 and between 1929 and 1931 and was later returned as the Labour MP for Bradford Central between 1935 and 1945; Fred Jowett represented Bradford East from 1922 to 1924 and again between 1929 and 1931. The Bradford ILP recovered to more than 1,600 members in the early 1920s and reached 2,377 members by early 1927. Indeed, in 1926, an editorial in the *Bradford Pioneer* of 10 September 1926, written by Frank Betts, the father of Barbara Castle, noted the renewed enthusiasm and activity within the ILP. And in 1927 Jowett Hall was purchased by the Bradford ILP, and was used for drama productions and lectures for some years to come.

Yet from then onwards the Bradford ILP, along with the national organisation, began to decline. The middle class leadership of Clifford Allen, which had revived the party in the 1920s, gave way to the more working class leadership and sentiments of John Wheatley and Jimmy Maxton. The conflict between the two groups was disastrous and the party lost money, support and sympathy as many members moved their sympathies and commitment to the Labour Party. There were many issues of style and presentation which divided the two factions but the ILP's position did not become precarious until the collapse of Ramsay MacDonald's second Labour government in August 1931 and the emergence of his National Government.

The major problem was that, under Jimmy Maxton's leadership, the ILP wished to maintain some freedom of action for its MPs in Parliament. After the general election of September 1931 reduced the Labour Party to almost one-sixth of its former size, the Labour Party was more concerned than ever to ensure that its 50-odd surviving MPs should follow the party whip. This led to difficult relationships between the two organisations in 1931 and 1932. The issue also divided the ILP. Maxton, with the support of Fred Jowett, wished to reject the Labour whip, and ultimately moved for secession. A second group wanted the ILP to join the Communist Party of Great Britain. A third group, led by Dr John Salter and Willie Leach, wanted the ILP to work with the Labour Party and to remain within it.

Against expectations, the 1932 Easter Conference of the ILP decided, by a narrow margin, that it would remain within the Labour Party. Yet the campaign to leave continued and it was decided to call a Special Meeting of the ILP in Bradford at the end of July 1932. Willie Leach envisioned the ILP moving 'into the wilderness with less than half of the membership'. The issue was fought out in the Bradford ILP, where the vote went for disaffiliation by 112 votes to 86. As a result the *Bradford Pioneer* published an Open Letter imploring the delegates attending the Conference not to vote for disaffiliation: 'The ILP was born in Bradford. Have you come to bury it?'[111]. They had.

Maxton, Brockway, Jowett and the 'Suicide Squad' won the day despite the efforts of Leach and the *Bradford Pioneer*: the ILP voted to disaffiliate from the Labour Party. A rather sad editorial noted that:

> The Independent Labour Party now joins the numerous small groups engaged in useless and obscure warfare against the organised Labour army. Along with the Communist Party, the Socialist Party of Great Britain and other eccentric groups quite unknown to the general public, the total sterility of a once great and influential party seems assured.[112]

This view was prophetic for the ILP collapsed rapidly. Only one of the 32 members of the Labour Group on Bradford City Council was prepared to leave the Labour Party; the Bradford ILP lost more than half of its 750 surviving members (five years earlier it had more than 2,300 members) and there were attempts within the Bradford ILP to call another meeting to get the decision reversed. All was to no avail and both the Bradford ILP and the National ILP faded into obscurity. Its support survived in small pockets in Bradford, but declined quickly when even Fred Jowett, the most popular Labour figure in Bradford, was unable to recapture Bradford East for the ILP in the 1935 general election. It struggled on, largely powerless until the 1960s, although the remnants of the movement and its real heart had by that time moved to Leeds.[113]

NOTES

1. *Bradford Labour Echo*, 28 Sept 1895.
2. *Yorkshire Observer*, 3 Nov 1913.
3. H. Pelling, *The Origins of the Labour Party 1880–1900* (Oxford, OUP, 1965 edition), pp.115–23.
4. *Yorkshire Observer Budget*, 13 April 1914.
5. Pelling, *op. cit.*; R. McKibbin, *The Evolution of the Labour Party, 1910–1924* (Oxford, OUP, 1974); D. Clark, *Colne Valley: Radicalism to Socialism* (London, Longman, 1981); J. Hill, 'Manchester and Salford Politics and the Early Development of the Independent Labour Party', *International Review of Social History*, XXIV (1981), part 1; J. Reynolds and K. Laybourn, 'The Emergence of the Independent Labour Party in Bradford', *International Review of Social History*, XX (1975), part 3; K. Laybourn and J. Reynolds, *Liberalism and the Rise of Labour* (London, Croom Helm, 1984); K. Laybourn, *The Rise of Labour* (London, Edward Arnold, 1988); T. Woodhouse, 'The working class', in D. Fraser (ed), *A History of Modern Leeds* (Manchester, MUP, 1980).
6. K. O. Morgan, 'The New Liberalism and the Challenge of the Labour Party:

The Welsh Experience 1885–1929', *Welsh History Review*, 6 (1973); P. F. Clarke, *Lancashire and the New Liberalism* (London, CUP, 1971); A. W. Purdue, 'The Liberal and Labour Party in North-East Politics', *International Review of Social History*, XXVI (1981), part 1.

7. See Tony Jowitt's previous chapter for an analysis of the problems confronting the staple textile industry.

8. E. P. Thompson, 'Homage to Tom Maguire', A. Briggs and J. Saville (eds), *Essays in Labour History* (London, Macmillan, 1960), p.279.

9. F. Brockway, *Socialism over Sixty Years: The Life of Jowett of Bradford* (London, George Allen & Unwin, 1946), chapter one.

10. Edward Royle, *Radicals, Secularists and Republicans* (Manchester, MUP, 1980), p.62.

11. James Bartley, 'Early Days in Bradford', Bradford and District Trades and Labour, *Year Book 1912*, p.67.

12. J. Bellamy and J. Saville (eds), *Dictionary of Labour Biography III* (London, Macmillan, 1977), biography of C. L. Robinson.

13. A. J. Peacock, *Bradford Chartism 1838–1840* (York, Borthwick Inst., 1969).

14. D. G. Wright, 'Politics and Opinion in Nineteenth Century Bradford, 1832–1880', unpublished PhD, University of Leeds, 1966.

15. Thompson, *op.cit.*, p.288.

16. *Ibid.*

17. *Bradford Labour Echo*, 13 June, 12 Sept 1896, 13 Mar 1897, 14 May 1898.

18. P. Henderson (ed), *The Letters of William Morris to his family and friends*, (London, 1950), letter dated 25 Feb 1884; F. W. Jowett, *What made me a Socialist* (London, ILP, 1925), pp.5–7.

19. *Bradford Observer*, 8 Feb 1887.

20. Reynolds and Laybourn, *op. cit.*, p.321.

21. *Ibid.*, pp.325–7.

22. Ross, *op. cit.*, biographical sketches.

23. K. Laybourn, 'The Manningham Mills Strike: Its importance in Bradford History', *Bradford Antiquary*, New Series, Part XLVI, 1976; C. Pearce, *The Manningham Mills Strike, December 1890–April 1891*, University of Hull Occasional Papers in Economic and Social History, 1975.

24. T. Rhondda Williams, *Memoirs of Rev. T. Rhondda Williams: From Orthodoxy to Modernism*, collection of cuttings from the *Bradford Daily Telegraph and Argus*, which does not appear to be published in book form although it is indicated as being so. A copy can be found in Bradford Library.

25. *Bradford Observer*, 31 Oct 1894; *Bradford Post Office Directory 1894* (Bradford, 1894), pp.19–27.

26. *Bradford Observer*, 31 Oct 1894.

27. Williams, *op. cit.*

28. *Ibid.*

29. *Manifesto of the Bradford Unemployed Emergency Committee 1894* (Bradford, 1894).

30. Arthur Priestman joined the ILP about 1895 and, with W. Leach, helped finance many of its activities. *Bradford Labour Echo*, 23 Nov 1895; *Bradford Daily Telegraph*, 4 Oct 1912.

31. PRO, BT 31/34575 – 8/50812, folder marked Labour Institute Ltd., 34575/5. Register of Share, 9 Mar 1896.

32. Bradford and District Trades and Labour Council, *Year Book 1901*, (for 1900),

(Bradford, 1901), p.80.

33. *Forward*, 23 Nov 1905, 17 Nov 1906, 22 June 1907.
34. *Ibid.*, 25 Nov 1905.
35. Thompson, *op. cit.*, p.289.
36. Clark, *op. cit.*, pp.145–50 .
37. Williams, *op. cit.*
38. *Forward*, 4 Mar 1905.
39. Reynolds and Laybourn, *op. cit.*, p.322.
40. Thompson, *op.cit.*, pp.302–7.
41. *Loc. cit.*, 28 Apr 1891.
42. *Loc. cit.*, 1 May 1891.
43. *Bradford Observer*, 27 Apr 1891.
44. *Ibid.*, 20 Apr 1891.
45. *Yorkshire Factory Times*, 29 May 1891.
46. *Loc. cit.*, 18 June 1892.
47. Reynolds and Laybourn, *op. cit.*, 18 June 1891.
48. *Bradford Observer*, 5 Jan 1891.
49. Pelling, *op. cit.*, pp.115–23.
50. *Bradford Labour Echo*, 22 June 1895. Interview with C. L. Robinson.
51. Workers' Municipal Federation, Minute Book, 1902–16, part of the Bradford Trades Council collection deposited with the West Yorkshire Archive Service (Bradford), 15 Canal Road, Bradford.
52. *Ibid.*, the Constitution appears at the beginning of the Minute Book.
53. W. H. Drew was the first secretary of the WMF, secretary of the Bradford Trades Council at the same time, and a prominent member of the ILP. G. Licence was secretary of the WMF between 1905 and 1909. A. T. Sutton became a member of the Executive Committee of the WMF in 1905, at the same time when he was also secretary of the Bradford ILP, and became president of the WMF in 1913. Tom Brown was on the Executive Committee of the WMF in 1902 and between 1906 and 1908. He acted as Fred Jowett's election agent during the general election contest in West Bradford. James Bartley was on the first Executive Committee from July 1902.
54. W. H. Drew, Tom Brown, James Bartley, J. H. Palin and G. East.
55. WMF, Minutes, 17 July 1905.
56. *Ibid.*, 4 Mar 1907.
57. Bradford and District Trades Council, Minutes, 14 Sept 1918, 14 Jan 1919.
58. WMF, Minutes, 3 Oct 1902.
59. *Ibid.*, Minutes for 1904.
60. By 1910 the WMF and the ILP had agreed to pay the expenses of candidates on a ward, rather than an individual, basis.
61. J. Hayhurst, A. Pickles, A. Heaton, G. Minty, J. H. Palin, C. Glyde and T. Warner were all trade unionists.
62. *Bradford Labour Echo*, 15 June 1895.
63. The Bradford Town Council first introduced the measure in 1894. *Bradford Labour Echo*, 26 Mar 1898.
64. Bradford and District Trades and Labour Council, *Year Book, 1905* (Bradford, 1905), p.11.
65. *Ibid.*, and *Year Book, 1904* (Bradford, 1904), pp.39–41; *Year Book, 1905* (Bradford, 1905), pp.93–101.

66. Brockway, *op. cit.*, p.63.
67. B. B. Gilbert, *The Evolution of National Insurance in Great Britain: The Origins of the Welfare State* (London, 1966), p.103.
68. *Yorkshire Daily Observer*, 13 Dec 1904; *Forward*, 17 Dec 1904.
69. Brockway, *op. cit.*, p.63.
70. *Forward*, 15 Dec 1906.
71. *Ibid.*
72. *Ibid.*, 10 Nov 1906; *Bradford Daily Telegraph*, 26 Mar 1907; *Yorkshire Daily Observer*, 27 Mar 1907.
73. Brockway, *op. cit.*, p.63.
74. Manifesto, *op. cit.*
75. *Forward*, 28 July 1906.
76. R. Wharton, *The Girlington 'Klondyke'* (Leeds, 1978); *Forward*, 25 Aug, 1 Sept, 29 Sept 1906.
77. Clarke, *op. cit.*, p.7.
78. Morgan, *op. cit.*
79. Martin D. Pugh, 'Yorkshire and the New Liberalism', *Journal of Modern History*, Vol. 50, No. 3, September 1978, pp. D 1139–D 1155.
80. A. Illingworth was returned on three occasions. W. E. Forster and Shaw-Lefevre on two occasions each, and Angus Holden was returned once. Only H. B. Reed was returned for the Conservatives, at the Eastern Division parliamentary election in 1886.
81. *Bradford Observer* for June and July contains numerous references to the mischievous nature of the ILP decision to contest Bradford West.
82. W. S. Caine offered to stand down from East Bradford in favour of Ben Tillett at the 1892 general election.
83. Daniel Illingworth had built up a woollen manufacturing firm at Whetley Mills in the early nineteenth century. It was developed further by his sons, Henry (1829–1895) and Alfred (1827–1907). The Illingworths were Baptists and intermarried with the Holdens, a powerful and wealthy industrial family of the Wesleyan persuasion. Alfred Illingworth married a daughter of Isaac Holden, MP for Knaresborough 1865–1868 and the Hon President of the Bradford Liberal Association. For further details see W. D. Ross, *op. cit.*, biographical details.
84. The large manufacturing families of the Bradford and Shipley area, such as the Illingworths, Salts, and Ripleys, were all fervent opponents of trade unionism.
85. *Bradford Labour Echo*, 17 Apr 1897.
86. R. Moore, *The Emergence of the Labour Party 1880–1924* (Sevenoaks, 1978), p.61.
87. *Labour Leader*, 21 Nov 1896.
88. *Bradford Observer*, 11 Oct 1894.
89. *Ibid.*
90. *Bradford Labour Echo*, 17 Apr, 1 May 1897. Meetings to take place at the Gladstone Liberal Club and the house of Rev. R. Roberts.
91. *Loc. cit.*, 2 Nov 1898.
92. *Loc. cit.*, 4 Feb 1899.
93. Viscount Gladstone papers, British Museum Add. MS. LXXVI, 46060, f.248.
94. *Bradford Observer*, 13 Dec 1898.
95. *I.L.P. News*, Dec 1902.
96. *Bradford Daily Telegraph*, 4 May 1903.

97. *Forward*, 30 Dec 1905.
98. Ross, *op. cit.*, p.314.
99. *Bradford Observer*, 22 Feb 1892.
100. Francis Johnson collection, 1896/84, letter from W. P. Byles to James Keir Hardie, dated 21 Nov 1896.
101. *Ibid.*, 1899/49, letter from Charles W. Dilke to James Keir Hardie, dated 21 Nov 1896.
102. *Bradford Daily Telegraph*, 31 Mar 1903.
103. Compiled from the issues of the *Bradford Observer* and the *Bradford Daily Telegraph* from 1895 to 1913, including the results of the municipal elections, aldermanic elections, and aldermanic by-elections.
104. Bradford Moor was contested by the Liberals on five occasions and twice by the Conservatives; Heaton was contested by the Liberals and the Conservatives on three occasions each; Great Horton was contested four times by the Liberals and once by the Conservatives; North Bierley (East), Tong, and Allerton wards each saw three Liberal and two Conservative contests; Manningham was contested by the Liberals on four occasions; East Bowling was contested twice by the Conservatives and once by the Liberals; East Ward, Little Horton, and Listerhills were all contested twice by the Conservatives; Eccleshill, Idle, Bolton, North, and West Bowling wards were all contested once by the Conservatives, as part of the pact to keep out Labour.
105. Williams, *op. cit.*
106. Ross, *op. cit.*, particularly the biographical section.
107. Jowitt, *op. cit.*, p.17.
108. *Bradford Observer*, 9 Dec 1891.
109. *Forward*, 13 Jan 1906.
110. K. Laybourn, ' "The Defence of Bottom Dog": The Independent Labour Party in Local Politics', in D. G. Wright and J. A. Jowitt (eds), *Victorian Bradford* (Bradford, Bradford Metropolitan Council, 1982), pp.223–44.
111. *Bradford Pioneer*, 29 July 1932.
112. *Ibid.*, 5 Aug 1932.
113. See B. Winter's chapter 'The ILP: a Century for Socialism', for the present position.

4. War and Socialism: the Experience of the Bradford ILP 1914–18

Tony Jowitt and Keith Laybourn

Recent research on the First World War has emphasised that it was a crucial period of change in British political history. Arthur Marwick has written that during the war 'The Liberal Party was greatly damaged, the Labour Party was greatly strengthened', and Trevor Wilson, one of the leading proponents of the new orthodoxy which highlights the First World War as the prime cause of the decline of the Liberal Party has made a similar point:

> The war not only inflicted such a disaster on the Liberals but provided Labour with the impetus to seize the opportunity. The impact of the war on the nation's economy so increased the importance of the trade unions and so stimulated their political consciousness, that it correspondingly enhanced the position of the Labour Party, which had all along derived much of its limited importance from its association with organised labour.[1]

At the same time as historians have acknowledged a general growth in the strength of the Labour Party they have also recognised that there were divisions within Labour ranks, with trade unions generally supporting the active prosecution of the war by the British government whilst the Independent Labour Party remained largely opposed to it. However, much of the evidence for this internal conflict within the Labour Party has been drawn from national records and the actions of national leaders. This sharp divide between the ILP and the trade union movement had their pro-war and anti-war factions. It is equally obvious that many of those prominent members of the Bradford ILP who were considered to be in the 'anti-war camp' in fact exhibited widely varying opinions about the war. The purpose of this article is, therefore, to elucidate the divisions which emerged within the Bradford ILP and to examine the role of the war in weakening the link between the ILP and the trade union movement, which had been so much a feature of the history of the Bradford ILP between the 1890s and 1914.[2]

Between 1893 and 1932 Bradford had a close and continuing association with the ILP. The inaugural conference of the ILP in 1893 was held in Bradford, as were the Coming of Age Conference in 1914 and the special disaffiliation Conference in 1932, when the ILP severed its connections with the Labour Party. Up to the onset of the war in 1914 the Bradford branch was probably the strongest in the country, and by 1914 it wielded a powerful influence on local politics. With an excess of local pride, J. H. Palin said in his welcoming address to the 1914 Conference:

Bradford has no really historic traditions: in Domesday Book it was described as waste, and nine hundred years of capitalist administration has not improved it. Indeed the only improvement effected in Bradford since its establishment has been caused by the work of the Independent Labour Party. As a matter of fact the history of Bradford would be very largely the history of the Independent Labour Party.[3]

Palin went on to describe the rise of the ILP, with its 1600 paying members, 'which probably neither of the orthodox political parties could boast'. At the previous municipal elections the Party had polled 43.1 percent of the votes cast, had 20 members on the City Council, three members on the Board of Guardians, one member of parliament and:

... they would see that the ILP was not only the political party of the future, but that, so far as Bradford was concerned, it was the political party of the present ... and there was no danger of the Bradford branch going wrong and if they would follow its lead the party would go on, and would eventually become the dominant party in British politics.

As Table 1 shows the Party was capturing an increasing proportion of the municipal vote from 1903 onwards and was polling as well if not better than the other two political parties from 1909 onwards.

Although best known for its connection with social and economic issues, such as the introduction of school feeding and advocacy of municipal workshops, the Party was also concerned with the wider issues of the relationships between individuals and the state and between states. This concern was reflected in the immediate pre-war years by the increasing alarm shown over the growth of militarism and the threatening international situation. Both the Bradford ILP and the Bradford Trades Council responded by supporting international socialist resolutions opposed to the war. In 1912 the Bradford Trades Council resolved to express its approval:

... of the proposal for a general stoppage of work in all countries about to engage in war, and further we urge upon all workers the necessity for making preparations for a simultaneous stoppage of work in those countries, where war is threatened.[5]

Further, throughout 1912, 1913 and 1914 there were articles in the *Bradford Pioneer*, the local ILP newspaper, about the Armaments Trust, secret diplomacy and the need for the party to foster unity across international boundaries. The outstanding feature of the vast majority of these articles was a wordy rhetoric about peace and internationalism rather than the development of any practical policies to confront war. The most frequent writer in the *Bradford Pioneer* on the Peace issue was the Reverend R. Roberts, a Congregational Minister who had had a somewhat stormy relationship with the ILP over the previous twenty years.[6] Roberts reflected one important strand within the ILP, a strand whose primary concern was with individual and

Table 1   The Growth of the Labour-Socialist
Vote in Bradford Between 1891–1913[4]

Year	Liberal %	Tory %	Labour %
1891	47.4	47.3	5.3
1892	41.0	42.3	16.7
1893	38.1	39.5	22.4
1894	40.3	37.3	22.4
1895	44.5	43.7	11.8
1896	44.7	46.1	9.2
1897	39.5	45.7	14.8
1898	41.1	41.9	17.0
1899	43.2	44.0	12.8
1900	36.0	45.2	18.8
1901	41.2	42.1	16.7
1902	36.0	47.2	16.8
1903	46.5	44.7	8.8
1904	42.8	42.0	15.2
1905	34.6	43.4	22.0
1906	26.3	47.0	26.7
1907	35.9	33.6	30.5
1908	31.8	38.2	30.0
1909	30.2	39.0	30.8
1910	31.5	33.3	35.2
1911	33.6	35.4	31.0
1912	32.2	36.1	31.7
1913	29.7	27.2	43.1

national ethicalism, continually stressing overall moral, rather than economic issues. Dominating their opposition was the fervent belief that war was immoral and that the ILP must lead a propaganda fight against militarism. As Roberts wrote in early 1914:

Alone amongst the parties in Great Britain the Labour Party is pledged against militarism ... We must take up the Fiery Cross and carry it to the remotest hamlet in the country, call every man and woman to the colours. 'Down with militarism'. That is our cry – as it is also the cry of our comrades all over Europe. Blazon it on the banners. Write it on the pavements. Sing it in the streets.[7]

The outbreak of war in 1914 came with startling suddenness. As late as 1 August 1914 Continental socialist leaders were still not convinced that war was even a likely possibility. As Haupt suggests, they were the captives of their own myths about their ability to prevent war and unaware of the depths of national chauvinism.[8] They were caught short by the events, pushed on to the defensive and literally became disorientated spectators, waiting to be submerged by the gathering wave of nationalism.

In Bradford, in the midst of the period of national ultimatums, the ILP called a mass meeting on 2nd August which deplored the threatened war but did not advocate immediate working-class action to prevent it. In his speech to this meeting, Fred Jowett, ILP MP for Bradford West, referred to war as a crime against humanity but made no demands for strikes or mass demonstrations to oppose the outbreak of war. Rather he closed his speech with a note of resignation: 'Let us who are socialists keep our minds calm, our hearts free from hate, and one purpose always before us – to bring peace as soon as possible on a basis that will endure.'[9]

Such a unanimity of purpose evaporated with the declaration of war. Very quickly, both the ethical and the trade union elements of the Bradford ILP divided into the anti-war and pro-war factions and similar divisions were apparent within the Bradford ILP. In the first instance, there were pacifists who were opposed to war *per se*. Secondly, those who felt the need to protect Britain and to defend Belgium whilst vigorously opposing the secret treaties which led to war and supporting a call for peace. Thirdly, those who felt that the need for prosecution of the war was essential to the defence of the country and temporarily transcended socialist objectives. Fourthly, and closely allied to this third group, were those who felt that Prussianism was a real danger to the world and had to be defeated come what may.

Contrary to the general impression given by the local Tory and Liberal press, there were very few members of the ILP who adopted an outright pacifist stand. At the national level the main advocates of pacifism were Bruce Glasier, Clifford Allen, Arthur Salter and Fenner Brockway, with Philip Snowden on the edge of this group though he was never a fully committed pacifist.[10] There was a professional, middle-class, temper to this group which was composed largely of writers, journalists, academics and doctors. They took a pure pacifist line that all war was wrong, and some of them supplemented their hostility to war by forming the No-Conscription Fellowship and working with the Union of Democratic Control.[11] Although there was some welling of support for this group when they managed to gain some measure of control at the National conference of the ILP in 1917, it was never a significant force in the politics of the Bradford ILP. Pacifism attracted only a few middle-class members of the ILP, most prominently the Quaker Arthur Priestman and William Leach.[12]

The leading ILP pacifist in Bradford was William Leach, an employer who had joined the party in the 1890s. For more than fifty years he remained one of the leading political figures in the local ILP and Labour movement, being returned as a city councillor before the First World War and as ILP and Labour MP for Bradford Central constituency between 1922 and 1924, 1929 and 1931, and 1935 and 1945. His importance to the local Labour movement was immeasurably increased by the fact that he was also a prolific writer on socialist issues. He was a frequent contributor to the *Bradford Labour Echo*, the Bradford ILP paper of the late 1890s, and became editor of another such paper, *Forward*, between 1904 and 1909. It was through *Forward* that he mounted the publicity campaign which ultimately helped to win municipal school feeding. During the First World War his major contribution was to act as editor of the *Bradford Pioneer*, taking over from the increasingly pro-war Joseph Burgess.[13] From this point the paper moved decisively towards an anti-war stance. In October 1915, Leach articulated the paper's policy:

We hate all war, especially the present one. This is a pacifist or peace journal conducted among other purposes, with the object of stating as well as we can, the ILP position on the hideous tragedy now being enacted in Europe ... Human life is the most sacred thing we know, and its preservation, its development, its best welfare, must therefore be our religion on this earth.[14]

There was a change of atmosphere within the local ILP. Instead of confidence about the continued growth of the Party and the movement, the Pacifists saw themselves as a beleaguered minority led by Leach. However, they made up for their small numbers with an increasing fervour for pacifism. The *Bradford Pioneer* reported extensively on the work of the No-Conscription Fellowship and the Union of Democratic Control, and provided full coverage to the speeches of the many opponents of the War who lectured at the ILP's New Picture House in Morley Street. It referred to Bertrand Russell, an ex-Liberal, as 'a recent and very valuable acquisition to the ILP.'[15] When E. D. Morel lectured at the Picture House he was described as 'that distinguished jail bird ... now a member of the ILP and of the Bradford Branch.'[16]

At the end of the War, William Leach stood for Bradford Central, where he was comprehensively defeated by the Coalition Conservative candidate, who obtained almost 4,800 votes more than he did, although he did have the comfort of being more than 3,300 votes ahead of Sir James Hill, the sitting Liberal candidate.[17] Reflecting upon his defeat, he strongly reiterated his commitment to pacifism:

I have never felt so pugnaciously right in my life. I still disbelieve in war. As long as I am in public life I will not support bloodshed for any cause, whether that cause appears right or does not. It looks as if this victory fervour has swept us out. But it will pass. Liberalism is defunct, Socialism is deferred, and the Coalition will be deflated.[18]

But such pacifist sentiments were not shared by the majority of the leadership of the Bradford ILP, nor many of the contributors to the *Bradford Pioneer*, for the dominant strand within the anti-war section of the Bradford ILP was not pacifism.

The majority of the anti-war section of the Party appear to have followed the lead of Fred Jowett who was never an outright pacifist, but accepted the need for National Defence. Jowett, who had been returned as Bradford's first ILP MP in 1906, was the dominant figure in the Bradford Labour ranks during the First World War. Throughout the War he tried to articulate a viewpoint of what caused the War and how wars could be eradicated in the future. As he argued in his Chairman's speech to the 1915 ILP Conference at Norwich 'Now is the time to speak and ensure that never again shall the witches' cauldron of secret diplomacy brew the war broth of Hell for mankind.'[19] In an important article in the *Bradford Pioneer* in June 1916 he explained that:

> I believe that the war would never have arisen if the government had carried out an open and honest foreign policy and disclosed to the people who had most to lose the relations between themselves and foreign governments with whom they were acting in collusion.[20]

His constant theme throughout the war was that it had been caused by the secret treaties which had been arranged, though frequently denied, by the British Government. 'His fad', as the *Standard* said of Jowett, 'is the democratic control of foreign affairs.'[21] In connection with this Jowett also demanded that the Government should specify its war aims and should be forced towards the negotiating table.

To Jowett, then, the War was caused by the secret treaties arranged by the British Government and should be settled as quickly as possible. But on numerous occasions he declared that he was in favour of a British victory over 'Prussianism' and that he could not agree to the settlement of the War without 'the restoration of Belgium to complete sovereignty'.[22] He constantly maintained that a nation had a right to defend itself and frequently paid homage to those who had given their lives in the War.[23] In many respects Jowett's policy closely resembled the views expressed by Keir Hardie in his famous article 'We must see the War Through, but denounce Secret Diplomacy".[24] Although Jowett's position on the war, as with the stance adopted by Hardie, often appeared ambiguous and at odds with the ILP's declared opposition to the War, he was categorical in his wish to see the War speedily concluded in favour of the allies. On his attitude towards the anti-war resolution passed by the 1916 ILP Conference, of which he was chairman, he reminded one critic that:

> The ILP resolution to which you refer only expressed the view that Socialist Parties as organised bodies should support no war. It did not attempt to lay down such a policy for individuals. If it did I should be opposed to it in principle.[25]

Such a distinction between the actions of individuals within a party and the policy of a party was confusing to many critics of the ILP and permitted Jowett to both support and oppose the war in different guises. Here was a classic case of having one's cake and eating it. But in many respects, his position was clearly understood by many members of the Bradford ILP and offered some common ground between the warring factions within the local party.

The fact is that a substantial proportion of the membership of the Bradford ILP was committed to the war effort either on the negative grounds of the need for National Defence or on the most positive grounds that Prussianism needed to be destroyed. Both shades of opinion, though by no means exclusive to the pro-war position, were evident in Bradford. By the middle of August 1914 the Reverend R. Roberts had totally changed his stance and accepted the necessity of war:

> ... the hour of reckoning has come. This legend of 'blood and iron' has to be shattered. Either it must be smashed or civilisation must go under. Its victory would be the enthronement of the War God in the centre of European civilisation and the crushing of Socialism for generations.[26]

For these groups conversion to the acceptance of war was total and as they had argued in a totally committed way previously about the immorality of war they now argued for an absolute commitment to the active prosecution of the war and the total necessity for an Allied victory. Again Roberts wrote:

> Through 40 years of public life, I have preached peace ... I have never believed humanity would so far break down as to make it necessary to pay the extreme price of waging a war to preserve the peace. Yet for my sins, I have lived to see that ... We are threatened with the ruin of civilised society. The success of Prussia in the awful tussle for life means that humanity will sink in smoking ruin. In the first what is our duty as a British people? We must fight the battle to a triumphant finish. At whatever cost of life and treasure we must fight (I cannot tell the pain it cost me to write that sentence. I never thought I should live to do it).... Better to die than to be Prussianised. Better to be wiped off the face of the earth than to exist squealing and squirming under the Prussian jack boots.[27]

It is quite clear that a substantial group of trade union members of the ILP supported the war effort. Their views were clearly presented by Jessie Cockerline, the regular trade union correspondent for the *Bradford Pioneer* who in an article 'My Country – Right or Wrong', wrote:

> War is upon us and whatever we may think about the management or mismanagement, the civilisation or lack of civilisation which makes war possible, we must put it away for the present and realise to the full that the angel of death reigns as goddess, and her best servitors will prevail. We must realise, and act upon the knowledge, that it is far better to be amongst the victorious than amongst the vanquished and for this reason alone the cry must be "My Country Right or Wrong'.[28]

There were other examples of a similar acceptance amongst the trade unionists in the Party; J. H. Palin and Councillor A. W. Brown being to the fore.

Palin is perhaps the most interesting of these ILP trade unionists who supported the war effort. A prominent member of the Amalgamated Society of Railway Servants, having been the chairman of the ASRS at the time when

169

the union was involved in the Taff Vale dispute, and a leading public figure in Bradford, as an ILP councillor and alderman up to and during the War, Palin was easily the most important pro-war Socialist who remained within the Bradford ILP. Until early 1917 he was the trade union correspondent of the *Bradford Pioneer*, having taken over from Jessie Cockerline, and prominently displayed his support for the War. At first, in 1914 and 1915, his views were tolerated in the confusion of opinion over the War within the ILP ranks, but he became an increasing embarrassment to Leach and the anti-war *Bradford Pioneer*, and was obviously out of step with resolutions passed by the Bradford ILP. This difference of opinion was sharply indicated at the 1916 ILP Conference when, despite being mandated to support a resolution committing all Socialist parties of all nations to refuse to support every war entered into by any government, Palin cut across the comparative equanimity of the meeting and bluntly stated that:

> We do not want the Germans here. Assume that the workers of this country had carried out this resolution at the beginning of the war, and the Socialists of other countries had not, and had rallied or been forced to join the army, where at the moment would Great Britain have been? At any rate, it seems to me that more time is required to get a considered opinion to start afresh after the war.[29]

Although he was reprimanded by T. W. Stamford, President of the Bradford ILP, Palin remained unrepentant and subsequently went to France to help with war transportation.[30] Yet the fact is that despite the preponderance of anti-war sentiments within the Bradford ILP there was a substantial proportion of the membership which supported the Palin line.

When the *Bradford Daily Telegraph* attacked the ILP's resistance to the war effort and their inability to 'raise a single finger to help the country to prosecute the war successfully' Jowett replied that 'In proportion to its membership the ILP has more adherents serving in the army and navy by far than either of the two other political parties.'[31] Censuses of the Bradford ILP membership confirm this impression. A census in February 1916 indicated that of 461 young men in the local party membership of 1473, 113 were in the trenches, four had been killed, one was missing, nine had been wounded, three were prisoners of war, 118 were in training in England, six were in the Navy and 207 were attested under the Derby scheme as necessary home workers.[32] A similar survey in 1918 found that of the 492 members liable for service, 351 were serving in the forces whilst 48 were conscientious objectors or were on national work.[33]

Such fragmentation of opinion was also evident in the Bradford Trades Council, which had been closely connected with the activities of the Bradford ILP since the early 1890s. The pro-war and anti-war factions were fairly equally divided until 1916, when the latter group gained the upper hand with the introduction of military conscription.

The 'Anglo-German War', or 'European War', caught the Trades Council in a quandary. On the one hand, in November 1912, it had passed a resolution calling for a general stoppage in the event of an outbreak of war.[34] On the other hand it was evident from the outset that many members of the Trades Council were smitten by patriotic sentiments when the First World War began. As a result of this imbroglio the Trades Council permitted itself to drift with events. Its commitments to international peace and the International Socialist Bureau were forgotten. It generally followed the Labour Party Policy of working with the Government and the authorities to encourage recruitment, although there were occasional decorous statements from its officials and delegates about the need to secure a peace as quickly as possible. In general, the Trades Council spent the early years of the War dealing with the practical realities of living under war conditions. In 1914 and 1915 the main activity of the Council was to check upon famine prices and food stuff shortages. This activity later gave way to Anti-Rent Raising campaigns, the raising of money through the Lord Mayor's Relief Fund, and to its involvement in the activities of the Joint Food Vigilance Committee, alongside the ILP, the British Socialist Party and the Workers' Municipal Federation. Perhaps the Council's most emotive campaign of the practical type was its attempt to force the Government to accept responsibility for providing pensions to war widows and weekly relief and benefits to soldiers and sailors injured in the fighting. All these campaigns reflect the day to day functioning of the Trades Council.[35] But the Trades Council was also a litmus-paper to the changing mood of the Bradford working class to the War. From the start of the War there was a sizeable minority of delegates to the Trades Council who opposed war. The leaders of this group were George Licence, Charlie Glyde and J. W. Ormandroyd. The anti-war sentiments of Fred Jowett, expressed in the *Year Book* for 1914, also tugged the heartstrings of many delegates, although he was equivocal about the War in subsequent statements.[36] On the other hand the silent majority gave their tacit approval to the War, and activists, such as Alderman J. H. Palin, went to fight in France alongside several hundred Bradford ILPers and several hundred Bradford trade unionists.[37] By 1916 and 1917, however, the attitude of the Council was beginning to change.

The threat of military and industrial conscription, raised in 1915, was pivotal in changing the attitude of the Trades Council, although several other issues conflated to compound the shift in thinking. In June 1915, the Trades Council passed a resolution opposing conscription:

... believing conscription in any form to be a violation of the principle of civic freedom hitherto prized as one of the chief heritages of British liberty, and that its adoption would constitute a grave menace to the progress of the nation; it believes that a recourse to a compulsory system is uncalled for in view of the enormous roll of enlistments since the war began and further; it is impossible to reconcile a national service in industry with private profit-making, and further protests against those employers who are dismissing

171

men because they are of military age. It therefore urges Parliament to offer their utmost opposition to any proposal to impose upon the British people a yoke which is one of the chief concerns of Prussian militarism.[38]

The concern expressed here was just as much about the Munitions Act of 1915, which had suspended Trade Union rights and prevented vital workers from moving from job to job without a certificate of approval from the employer, as it was about military conscription. But it was the threat of military conscription which provoked the major response. The Trades Council delegates began to drift away from supporting the TUC Parliamentary Committee's circular calling for trade union help in army recruitment and, in a series of votes and a ballot in 1915 and 1916, indicated its withdrawal from army recruitment campaigns. A vote of delegates towards the end of 1915 produced an equal number of votes for and against the recruiting campaign.[39] A circular to affiliated trade unions in December 1915, requesting the opinions of societies to the recruiting campaign was voted on by just over a third of the societies and produced a result of 19 societies for and 11 against, though those for represented only 6,757 members compared to the 11,157 against. Many small societies did not vote on the issue and three abstained.[40] Although the vote was inconclusive the introduction of conscription in 1916 led to the Trades Council's withdrawal from direct involvement in helping army recruitment.

The anti-war section within the Trades Council drew strongly from the opposition to conscription, although the opposition to conscription did not in itself signify opposition to the War. The Trades Council pressured the Yorkshire Federation of Trades Councils to hold a No-Conscription Conference at the Textile Hall, Bradford in December 1915 and, in January 1916, it sent delegates to an ILP No-Conscription Conference at Leeds.[41] As the 1916 Annual Report indicates, there were still 'differences of opinion on the War', but it is also clear that the anti-war position was burgeoning in the Council's meetings.

William Leach, editor of the *Bradford Pioneer*, was permitted to present the views of the Union of Democratic Control to the Trades Council, and in September 1915 the Council affiliated to the movement.[42] By 1916 it was possible to organise a Peace Conference under Trades Council auspices. That Conference decisively condemned the Labour MPs for joining the Government and pushed strongly for peace negotiations.[43] The Trades Council also sent delegates to the Leeds Conference of June 1917, at which the Workers' and Soldiers' Council was formed in the hope of forcing forward the demand for international peace negotiations.[44]

By 1917 the Trades Council was increasingly being dominated by, what Palin dubbed, 'militant pacifists'.[45] The 'peace movement' was prevalent within the Trades Council, though there was still a sizeable commitment to the war effort by some of the affiliated unions. Many of those who became committed to the Peace Campaign of 1917 were not so much pacifists, or opponents of the War, so much as opponents of the Government's military conscription policy. The imprisonment as a conscientious objector of Revis Barber, the son of Walter Barber who was secretary of the Trades Council, did much to win trade union support for the 'peace movement'.[46] Thus, by 1917 and 1918, Bradford became one of the centres of the Anti-War movement and the Trades Council had become one of its chief supporters. Although there was a substantial minority of trade unionists who supported the War this was by no means as prevalent a mood within the Bradford trade union movement as it would appear to have been within the national trade union movement. If the Bradford ILP was divided on the issue of the War so was the Bradford Trades Council and the Bradford trade union movement at large.

The emphasis placed upon the 'Peace' movement by the hostile Tory and Liberal press in Bradford has served to conceal the fact that there were substantial differences of opinion within the ILP and the Trades Council over the war issue. The press broadcast the view that Bradford was a hot bed of pacifism and anti-war feelings and that the Trades Council was at the centre of such activities. Prominent ex-Bradford ILP members added to the illusion by offering an informed tarring of all members of the ILP and the Trades Council with the same brush. The leading ex-ILP critics of the Bradford ILP were Joseph Burgess and Edward R. Hartley. Joseph Burgess had had a long association with the ILP. It was his paper, *The Workman's Times*, which had called together delegates from Labour societies to meet at the Bradford Conference in 1893. As an editor of Labour newspapers, and as a supporter of the activities of the Socialist Sunday School movement, he had established for himself great respect within the Labour movement.[47] He worked in Lancashire and London for many years but came to live in Bradford before the First World War, was editor of the *Bradford Pioneer* until the summer of 1915 and was elected President of the Bradford ILP in 1915. A critic of the war at its outset, proclaiming that 'We have no quarrel with Germany ... Stand firm workers, in reaction to the seduction of those who will appeal to you in the name of patriotism', he had quickly changed his position by the summer of 1915. He joined the Socialist National Defence Committee in June 1915 and was threatening to stand as parliamentary candidate for the National Socialist Party for Blackburn at the next general election, although he never did so.[49] The pages of the *Bradford Pioneer* are full of the letters of Burgess and the comments of the Bradford ILP in what one headline referred to as 'The Burgess Comedy'.[50] The Bradford ILP was very sensitive to the antics of a man who had so recently been at the centre of its activities. It was equally sensitive to, and disparaging of, the attacks levelled against it by E. R. Hartley.

Hartley, a butcher by trade, had been a member of the ILP from the mid 1890s and a member of the Social Democratic Federation, later to become the British Socialist Party, since 1902. He had represented the Bradford ILP on the City Council and had stood as the 'Socialist' candidate in the Bradford East parliamentary elections of 1906 and 1910.[51] It was his activities with the

SDF in connection with the Dewsbury parliamentary by-election of 1913 which threw him into conflict with both the ILP and the Labour Representation Committee. Yet he still maintained some support in the Bradford Moor ward of the City where his activities as a councillor, lecturer and singer had won him considerable local respect. At the beginning of the War he very quickly adopted a pro-war stance, anticipated the introduction of military conscription, and became the organising representative of the pro-war British Workers' League in the Bradford area.[52] His main pro-war activity in Bradford began in July 1917, when the 'Peace Campaign' was beginning to reach its zenith and in the wake of the Leeds Conference of June 1917. Both the Bradford ILP and the Bradford Trades Council were represented at this Conference, as was befitting a centre of peace agitation.[53] In response the British Workers' League held its inaugural meeting at Whetley Lane, Bradford and Hartley was the main speaker. The *Bradford Pioneer* sent a reporter to the meeting and suggested that about three-quarters of the 1,000 people present were opposed to the 'anti-ILP tone' of the meeting.[54] The British Workers' League continued to berate the Bradford ILP throughout 1917 and 1918. A. Howarth of the League said that 'Bradford had disgraced itself more than any other town in the country.'[55] Victor Fisher, secretary of the BWL, said to a Bradford audience that 'Sinister pacifism is more rampant in your midst than in any other part of the United Kingdom with the exception perhaps of the Clyde and South Wales.'[56] But such strictures against the Bradford ILP and the Bradford 'pacifists' were of limited impact, especially after the death of Hartley in early 1918.[57]

One of the major questions facing historians is why did the ILP and trade unions begin to go their separate ways after the First World War? This question is particularly important in the case of Bradford, which as Reynolds and Laybourn have argued, maintained its preponderance within the national ILP movement due to the early establishment of a link between the Bradford Labour Union/ILP and the Trades Council.[58] In Bradford the war served to fragment both the ILP and the Trades Council, and fractured the Bradford Labour Movement with the preponderant role played within it by the ILP. It is clear that trade union members of the ILP began to go their own way and that the War had been a major cause of the rupture. Men such as J. H. Palin and Michael Conway, pre-war ILP stalwarts, turned their attention to the newly-formed Labour Party. In addition the ILP took in a significant number of anti-war ex-Liberals during the War who once more by their very presence brought about an increasing divorce with the working classes. Some of the '1917' and '1918' Liberals had more in common with the middle class pacifist strand of the Bradford ILP's thinking than with the average working-class trade union member of the Party.[59] This dichotomy was undoubtedly hardened with the return of many young male members of the ILP from the War.

The First World War had profound consequences for the Bradford ILP and served to disturb the long-established relationship between the ILP and the trade union movement, though perhaps not in the blunt manner which has often been suggested by historians. The War had an unsettling effect on the alliance rather than an immediate catastrophic impact. It would appear that other factors played upon the loosening effect of the War. In particular, the debate over the new Labour Party Constitution of 1918 which was to give power to the trade union movement at the expense of socialist societies such as the ILP served to put a gap between local trade unionists and the local ILP. R. McKibbin has amply demonstrated the tensions which resulted from the ILP's opposition to the 1918 Constitution and has indicated the way in which the Constitution paved the way for the formation of new labour parties throughout the country to which local trades councils became affiliated.[60] The creation of the Bradford Labour Party in April 1919 certainly did much to undermine the position of the Bradford ILP.

The ILP had run labour politics in Bradford since the 1890s. In the 1890s it had dominated the political activities of the Labour movement in connection with the Trades Council. From 1902 onwards it had shared the control of Bradford Labour politics with the Trades Council and the Workers' Municipal Federation, a body which had been formed in order to bring non-Socialist trade unionists more directly into Labour politics.[61] From 1907 onwards the Joint Committee of the ILP and WMF made local political arrangements for the Bradford Labour movement.[62] But in 1918 the basis of the alliance was altered. Bradford was to be re-organised into four parliamentary divisions, instead of three, under the Representation of the People's Act, and a local Labour Conference was held in November 1917 to discuss the changes.[63] At this Conference representatives of the ILP, trade unions and co-operative societies agreed to contest all the seats at the next election and formed a committee of 12 representatives to discuss the selection of candidates. However also out of this committee, and its deliberations throughout 1918, sprang the decision to hold a Conference on the Formation of a Central Labour Party for Bradford in September 1918.[64] A further committee of 11 representatives was set up to draft a constitution and the Bradford Labour Party officially came into existence on the 5th April 1919, formally uniting the ILP, Trades Council and the WMF into one Labour organisation for the first time.[65] It was a move which was to prove the undoing of the Bradford ILP whose importance within local politics began to diminish in the 1920s as the Bradford Labour Party increasingly became the focus of Labour politics.

The Bradford ILP never fully recovered from the traumas imposed by the War and the developments within the wider Labour movement during and after the War. It was already conscious that its prominence within the national ILP organisation was under threat well before the end of the War. It launched the 'Bradford ILP Forward Movement' in 1918, pointing to the countrywide growth of the ILP and the tremendous step forward which had been made in Leicester and Scotland.[66] By implication, Bradford was lagging behind in these encouraging developments and was mindful of the need to protect its 'great reputation' and 'unique position' in the Party. But events overtook it, allegiances changed and the divorce of the ILP from working-class opinion in Bradford finally occurred when the ILP disaffiliated from the Labour Party in 1932. The decision as taken at Jowett Hall in Bradford might have been expected to produce a large-scale defection from the local Labour Party, but this did not happen: only one of the 29 Labour councillors and eight aldermen on Bradford City Council opted to remain in the ILP and Bradford ILP candidates obtained only derisory support in municipal elections during the late 1930s.[67]

Clearly in 1914 the Bradford Labour movement was dominated by the ILP. It is equally obvious that the War started the process that was to lead to the Bradford ILP's sorry state in the 1930s. But the loss of ILP support was more subtle than the conventional view that it resulted from an impasse between socialist opposition to the War and trade union patriotism. The War deeply divided both the Bradford ILP and the Bradford trade union movement and other factors, more to do with the developments within the Labour Party than to tensions within ILP support, helped to define the new relations within the Labour movement after the War. However it is overwhelmingly clear that trade union, and thus working-class, support switched from the ILP to the Labour Party between 1914 and 1920. The end product, as R. McKibbin stressed almost a decade ago, is that 'class loyalty drove out socialist doctrine' within the Labour Party. The anguish which both the national and Bradford ILP organisations faced over whether or not to continue as separate organisations from the Labour Party are indicative that the ILP had recognised the fundamental switch of allegiances that had occurred. The War provided an important, if not necessarily vital, part in explaining why the trade union movement and the ILP began to veer apart. Such a separation of the ILP and trade unionism ultimately proved terminal to the Bradford ILP which had always relied heavily on trade union support. The Labour Party, not the ILP, was to be seen as the liberating force for the working class in the future and the ILP was left to dwell upon the role of Socialists inside, and outside, the Labour Party .

NOTES

1. A. Marwick, *Britain in the Century of Total War* (London, 1970 ed.) p.84; T. Wilson, *The Downfall of the Liberal Party* (London, 1968 ed.) p.29.
2. J. Reynolds and K. Laybourn, 'The Emergence of the Independent Labour Party in Bradford', *International Review of Social History*, XX part 3, 1975, pp.313–346.
3. *Yorkshire Observer Budget*, 13 April 1914, though different papers provide marginally different accounts of Palin's speech.
4. Bradford Trades and Labour Council, *Year Book*, 1912, pp.47–51 and supple-

mentary information from the *Year Books* for 1913 and 1914.

5. Bradford Trades and Labour Council, Minutes, 7 Nov 1912.

6. He had joined the ILP in the mid 1890s and had been returned as an ILP member of the Bradford School Board, alongside Margaret McMillan, in 1897. He left the ILP in 1903 due to its unwillingness to co-operate with the Liberals but drifted back into its ranks before the First World War.

7. *Bradford Pioneer*, 9 Jan 1914.

8. G. Haupt, *Socialism and the Great War: The Collapse of the Second International* (London, 1972), particularly chapter 10, pp.195–215.

9. *Bradford Pioneer*, 7 Aug 1914.

10. Colin Cross, *Philip Snowden* (London, 1966) p.129.

11. Fenner Brockway was particularly prominent in this respect, and Snowden was on the Executive of the Union of Democratic Control alongside Liberal pacifists such as E. D. Morel, also on the Executive, and Bertrand Russell, who was on the General Council of the UDC. Not all ILP members of the UDC were necessarily pacifist, for F. Jowett was also on the Executive. For the Executive and General Council of the Union of Democratic Control see the *Bradford Pioneer*, 8 Nov1915. It is interesting how many of the Liberal members of this organisation formed the '1917' and '1918' Liberals who moved over to the ILP and the Labour Party.

12. Arthur Priestman was a leading Bradford businessman from a prominent industrial family. For details of his career consult the *Bradford Labour Echo*, 23 Nov 1895 and *Bradford Daily Telegraph*, 4 Oct 1912. He died in 1918 and a brief obituary appears in the *Bradford Pioneer*, 25 Jan 1918. See also K. Laybourn 'The Defence of Bottom Dog: The Independent Labour Party in Local Politics', in D. G. Wright and J. A. Jowitt, *Victorian Bradford* (Bradford, 1982), pp.234–235.

13. J. Burgess was editor of the *Bradford Pioneer* until June 1915 when Leach took over. See *Bradford Pioneer*, 29 Dec 1916.

14. *Bradford Pioneer*, 22 Oct 1915.

15. *Ibid.*, 26 Oct 1917.

16. *Ibid.*, 19 Apr 1918.

17. *Bradford Daily Telegraph*, 30 Dec 1918.

18. *Ibid.*

19. *Bradford Pioneer*, 9 Apr 1915.

20. *Ibid.*, 2 June 1916.

21. Cited in F. Brockway, *Socialism over Sixty Years: The Life of Jowett of Bradford 1864–1944* (London, 1946), p.152.

22. *Bradford Pioneer*, 2 June 1916.

23. *Ibid.*, 2 June 1916 and 13 Apr 1916.

24. Republished, from the *Merthyr Pioneer*, in the *Bradford Pioneer*, 21 Apr 1916.

25. *Bradford Pioneer*, 2 June 1916.

26. *Ibid.*, 14 Aug 1914.

27. *Ibid.*, 16 Oct 1914.

28. *Ibid.*, 14 Aug 1914.

29. *Ibid.*, 28 Apr 1916.

30. Bradford Trades and Labour Council, Minutes, 8 Feb 1917. He took up his duties in France on 12th Feb 1917.

31. *Bradford Pioneer*, 21 May 1915.

32. *Ibid.*, 25 Feb1916.

33. *Ibid.*, 1 Mar 1918.

34. Bradford Trades and Labour Council, Minutes, 7 Nov 1912.
35. *Ibid.*, Minutes, 12 Jan, 13 Feb, 8 Nov 1915, and generally throughout the Minutes between 1914 and 1918.
36. Bradford Trades and Labour Council, *Year Book, 1914* (Bradford, 1915).
37. See note 30. Also, Dr. H. Munro, a prominent member of the Bradford ILP before the War, took the first Volunteer Motor Ambulance Corps to the front and a Dr. Munro Fund was formed in order to provide financial help for this unit. *Bradford Pioneer*, 8 Jan and 5 Mar 1915.
38. Bradford Trades and Labour Council, Minutes, 17 June 1915.
39. *Ibid.*, Minutes, Letter of 5 Nov 1915.
40. *Ibid.*, Minutes, Letter and circular 10 Dec 1915.
41. *Ibid.*, Minutes, 8 Nov, 9 Dec 1915; 3 Jan 1916.
42. *Ibid.*, Minutes, 9 Sept 1915.
43. *Ibid.*, Minutes, 7 Dec 1916 and leaflet regarding the Peace Negotiations Conference in the December 1916 minutes. There is a further report on the Conference, which was held on 30 Dec 1916, in the minutes and correspondence for 9 Jan 1917.
44. *Ibid.* Minutes for May and June 1917.
45. M. Ashraf, *Bradford Trades Council 1872–1972* (Bradford, 1972), p.94.
46. Bradford Trades and Labour Council, Minutes, 29 Nov 1917.
47. Burgess is dealt with extensively in H. Pelling, *Origins of the Labour Party* (London, 1954), and in numerous other histories of the ILP and the Labour Party. He produced his autobiography *A Potential Poet* (Burgess, Ilford) in 1927.
48. Bradford Pioneer, 7 Aug 1914; 30 July and 29 Dec 1916.
49. Colin Cross, *Philip Snowden* (London, 1966), p.166
50. *Bradford Pioneer*, 20 July 1917.
51. K. Laybourn and J. Saville, 'Edward Hartley 1855–1918' in J. Bellamy and J. Saville, *Dictionary of Labour Biography*, Vol. III, pp.97–99.
52. *Bradford Pioneer*, 20 July 1917.
53. *Ibid.*, throughout May and June 1917.
54. *Ibid.*, 27 July 1917.
55. *Bradford Weekly Telegraph*, 9 Nov 1917.
56. *Bradford Pioneer*, 13 July 1917.
57. *Ibid.*, 25 Jan 1918.
58. J. Reynolds and K. Laybourn, 'The Emergence of the Independent Labour Party in Bradford', *International Review of Social History*, XX (1975), Part 3, pp.313–346.
59. See B. Barker, 'Anatomy of Reform: The Social and Political Ideas of the Labour Leadership in Yorkshire', *International Review of Social History*, XVIII (1973).
60. R. McKibbin, *The Evolution of the Labour Party 1910–1924* (London, 1974), particularly pp.91–106.
61. Workers' Municipal Federation Minute Books, 1902–1916, in the Bradford Trades and Labour Council collection of the West Yorkshire Archive Service, Bradford.
62. *Ibid.*, Minutes, 4 Mar 1907.
63. Bradford Trades and Labour Council, Minutes, 15 Nov 1917.
64. *Ibid.*, Minutes, 14 Sept 1918.
65. *Bradford Pioneer*, 11 Apr 1919.
66. *Ibid.*, 29 Mar 1918.
67. M. Le Lohe, 'A Study of Local Elections in Bradford County Borough 1937–67', PhD Thesis, University of Leeds, 1972, p.141

SECTION III

ISSUES AND SUBJECTS

1. 'A Call to Arms': the Struggle for Socialist Unity in Britain, 1883–1914

Martin Crick

Socialist unity became an issue on the left of British politics within twelve months of the formation of the Social-Democratic Federation, the country's pioneering Socialist organisation. The autocratic leadership of Henry Mayers Hyndman provoked William Morris, Eleanor Marx Aveling and others into forming a new party, the Socialist League. These two co-existed alongside the Fabian Society through the 1880s until the failure of the League led Morris and others to reconsider their strategy. Thus, in 1892, Morris's Hammersmith Socialist Society approached the two effective Socialist organisations in London, the Fabians and the SDF, with a view to forming a Socialist Federation. They issued a joint manifesto which declared that 'all who can fairly be called Socialists are agreed in their main principles of thought and action'. This projected alliance was short lived however. The Fabians were deterred by a statement of revolutionary principles far more explicit than they had expected whilst the SDF wanted members of the other bodies to join them as the only disciplined Socialist party. But a more fundamental weakness of these unity negotiations was that they had ignored the existence of the Independent Labour Party, formed in January 1893 and already a potent force in the North of England.

The ILP had emerged from the industrial unrest at the turn of the decade, an unrest which had not resulted in any accession of strength to the Socialist forces. A number of independent Socialists and Labour leaders had come to the conclusion that before the working class could be mobilised into a mass Socialist party it would be necessary to organise them for independent Labour politics. This viewpoint was reinforced by the increasing failure of the Liberal Party to respond to working-class demands. The exemplar of this demand for an independent Labour political strategy was James Keir Hardie and he found a ready response in Scotland and in the West Riding of Yorkshire. The new 'Labour Unions' which emerged in the early 1890s were formed not on the basis of political principle but to safeguard the interests of one particular section of the community. Their platform could have been accommodated within progressive Liberalism, but the unbending attitudes of local Liberal caucuses and the Socialist attachments of some of the local leaders led them to form a new political party in January 1893.

The ILP's role in the formation of the Labour Party has been well documented. It is a commonplace of labour historiography that its strategy of an alliance between the Socialists and the trade unions was the only option open to the Labour movement. This is a flawed analysis, largely brought about by the ILP's own propagandists, for until well into the first decade of the twentieth century there were two distinct lines of advance open to the British Socialist movement. The ILP leadership favoured a progressive alliance with the trade unions, in order to capture parliamentary seats. Many of the rank and file, however, placed the emphasis upon 'making Socialists'. They were greatly influenced by Robert Blatchford's *Clarion* newspaper, which believed it was possible to convert people to Socialism in sufficient numbers to create a mass Socialist party. This was also essentially the rationale of the Social-Democratic Federation. Socialist unity therefore became both a strategy and a clarion call, a rallying point for all those who questioned the Labour alliance policy. The debate between the protagonists of the Labour alliance and the supporters of Socialist unity dominated the Socialist milieu, in one way or another, until the outbreak of the First World War.

The SDF had been hostile to the idea of an independent Labour party from the outset. Harry Quelch argued that any Labour party would be simply a 'fortuitous concourse of heterogeneous political atoms ... a bear garden.'[1] The SDF's secretary, Harry Lee, condemned the ILP's founding conference: the ILP had been formed on a negative basis with no definite principles; Socialism was not even mentioned in the title of the party. 'We know that the attempt will fail', said Lee.[2] The Federation saw the new organisation as little more than an appendage of the Liberal Party, doomed to follow previous Labour Electoral Associations and the like into oblivion. Yet the attitudes and pronouncements of the SDF leadership did not reflect what was happening at the grassroots, particularly in Lancashire. Here SDF branches played an influential role in the formation of the ILP in several areas, notably Salford, Manchester, Nelson and Blackburn. In Manchester the SDF remained closely allied to the ILP, at times 'so close as to make any distinctions between them almost impossible.'[3] The six SDF delegates at the ILP's founding conference were all from Lancashire. It is hardly surprising therefore that the first attempts at a national amalgamation of the two parties came from Lancashire.

The ILP and the SDF tended to flourish in separate geographical areas. Whereas the SDF was strong in London the ILP could make little headway there. Conversely one third of ILP strength was centred in Yorkshire, where the SDF failed to boast a single branch in the mid 1890s. Lancashire was the major exception to this trend, providing the SDF with its major provincial base but also allowing the ILP to sink strong roots. It exhibited two features characteristic of the movement at this time. Dual membership of the two bodies was common but there were many Socialists who remained unattached. They were often avid readers of the *Clarion*, adherents of what Stephen Yeo has referred to as 'The Religion of Socialism'. In 1894 Robert Blatchford wrote excitedly that 'Five years ago there were not 500 Socialists in Manchester. Now there must be 30,000.'[4] If only these 'unattached' could be enrolled into the Movement then Socialist unity seemed a distinct possibility. Encouraged by the phenomenal sales of his penny pamphlet *Merrie England* Blatchford launched a Socialist unity campaign in July 1894, based on the premise that all Socialists agreed on root principles and should therefore 'recognise each other's right to liberty in all matters of detail, banding ourselves together under the broad principle of Socialism.'[5] The response disappointed him. The leadership of the SDF could not agree that it shared the same basic principles as the ILP, which they saw as 'a sort of half-way house' for those who might have otherwise joined a real Socialist party.[6] Keir Hardie was equally emphatic in rejecting the idea: 'As an organisation for uniting all the forces into a solid fighting phalanx the I.L.P. fits the bill .... Two years hence, and every section of the workers will be united, marching to victory under the banner of the I.L.P.'[7] Some ILP branches in Lancashire voted in favour but the party in Yorkshire was almost uniformly hostile. By the beginning of 1895 the campaign appeared to have subsided.

The failure of this attempt to unite the Socialist forces can be explained easily enough. As the pioneering Socialist organisation the SDF was jealous of its position. Whilst members in Lancashire and elsewhere were prepared to assist the growth of independent Labour politics as a step on the way to Socialism they saw no need for another Socialist organisation. Indeed many doubted the Socialist credentials of the ILP and questioned its ethical/ religious base. The Federation appeared to be flourishing, reporting 40 new branches in 1895 including six in the hitherto barren area of Yorkshire. There seemed little reason to flirt with what was at best a quasi-Socialist party. For its part the ILP was euphoric at its apparently rapid progress, with its sights set on the coming general election after four exceptionally good by-election results. Hardie, pursuing his campaign for trade union support, saw Socialist unity as a hindrance and the SDF's Marxism as a positive drawback. The pre-eminent position of the Yorkshire region in ILP councils meant that unity with the SDF was never seriously considered at that time. Yet it was the ILP that initiated the next attempt at rapprochement.

1895 was in many ways a crucial year for the British Socialist movement. All 29 ILP candidates were defeated at the general election and the party's confidence was severely shaken, its membership falling from 35,000 to 20,000 in the following year. Two somewhat contradictory results ensued. The leadership became more convinced than ever of the need for pragmatic politics, of the need to form a progressive alliance to capture parliamentary seats, and this could only be achieved by pushing the ultimate Socialist goal further into the future. The blunting of the Socialist influence at the Trade Union Congress of 1895 reinforced this belief. ILP leaders now viewed the establishment of Socialism on a much longer timescale which, as David Howell has pointed out, rendered them 'subject to conservative influences'.[8] Many of the rank and file, on the other hand, began to question the whole direction of this policy. They reverted to the emphasis upon 'making Socialists' and revived the campaign to unite the ILP and the SDF.

For the moment the advocates of one Socialist party were in the ascendancy in the ILP, many of them anxious to assert the membership's voice in the face of what they saw as a move towards centralisation and bureaucracy within the party. Hardie, sensitive to the changed mood, prepared to compromise and suggested an annual conference of all Socialist organisations, trade unions and co-operative bodies. The Easter conference of 1896 instructed the NAC to issue invitations to just such a conference. Initial SDF reaction was hostile. It felt that unity was only on the agenda because of the ILP's internal problems, whilst the Federation itself was doing well. Events soon disposed the SDF to change its position. Its financial solvency was short lived, due to expenditure on the Southampton by-election; its own members began to push for unity, as letters to *Justice* testify; its own internal debate over the party's attitude towards trade unions was swinging in favour of the pro-union tendency. The early months of 1897 saw a remarkable transformation in SDF attitudes.

Quelch remarked of the ILP that 'At present, in principle and aim, it is almost at one with the S.D.F.', and he congratulated it upon its 'distinct tendency to a more definite Socialist position and programme.'[9] Five SDF delegates attended an informal conference of the two parties on 29 July, where it was agreed to set up a joint committee of arrangement pending a decision on points of difference such as the new name of the party. A further committee was appointed for the purpose of arbitration on electoral disputes. Finally the executives of the two bodies agreed that a referendum of the joint membership be held. In what was, admittedly, a low poll the members voted 5,158 to 886 in favour of fusion. Yet that decision was never implemented and the campaign for Socialist unity was halted in its tracks by the refusal of the ILP conference to ratify the decision.

The reasons for the breakdown are complex, but clearly the ILP leadership was largely to blame. Immediately after the vote Hardie waded into the attack in the *ILP News*:

> It may be that there is something in the methods of propaganda, if not the principle of the S.D.F., that not only render it somewhat antipathetic to our members, but out of touch and harmony with the feelings and ideals of the mass of the people It might be therefore, that the introduction of its spirit and methods of attack would check rather than help forward our movement.[10]

His vision of Socialism was radically different to that of the SDF. He objected to the Federation's emphasis on the economic side of Socialism. For Hardie 'It was brotherhood, fraternity, love thy neighbour as thyself, peace on earth, goodwill towards men, and glory to God in the highest.'[11] Prior to the Conference, emphasising the small number of members voting, Hardie and Glasier campaigned vigorously for an alternative strategy, that of federation. At the Conference Hardie accused the SDF of seeking to absorb the ILP, but it was Bruce Glasier, with a masterly piece of rhetoric, who swayed delegates to the NAC's position. The kernel of his case was that

> the ways of the S.D.F. are not our ways. If I may say so, the ways of the S.D.F. are more doctrinaire, more Calvinistic, more aggressively sectarian than the I.L.P. The S.D.F. has failed to touch the hearts of the people. Its

strange disregard of the religious, moral and aesthetic sentiments of the people is an overwhelming defect.[12]

This savage attack was an almost classical statement of later Labour orthodoxy with regards to the Marxist tradition, yet it bore little resemblance to the truth. If the SDF had 'failed to touch the hearts of the people' then so had the ILP! The Federation had, in fact, no position on religion or morality, which it regarded as a matter of individual choice. The Federation's Calvinism, if such existed, was more than matched by the religious enthusiasms of Snowden and Hardie, whilst it relative success in London and Lancashire proved the lie to any charges of sectarianism. Nonetheless the combined weight of Hardie and Glasier persuaded Conference to ballot the members on the options of fusion or federation, with the proviso that a three-fourths majority was required if fusion was to take place. Moreover the question was loaded, the members being asked to vote either for federation or for 'dissolution of the I.L.P. and fusion with the S.D.F.', once more suggesting the idea of absorption.

Participation in the ballot was again low, 2,397 votes being cast for federation and 1,695 for fusion. Not surprisingly Hardie accepted this and ILP policy now became that of federation. Quelch was furious. 'Can it be', he asked,

> that some of the leaders of the I.L.P. calculated upon the presumed disinclination of the S.D.F. to amalgamate and were terribly disappointed to find that the S.D.F. were quite ready to act in a conciliatory and statesman-like spirit.[13]

Some ILPers were also angry. 'It seems to me a most ridiculous proceeding', wrote one, 'to submit a question to a vote of the members, and then, when it is found that the vote does not coincide with the "secret wishes of the chiefs", to override it altogether'.[14] Why had the ILP leadership acted in this way?

After the 1895 general election Hardie's prestige and influence had waned, whilst that of Blatchford had increased. The whole style and tone of his *Clarion* newspaper was in sharp contrast to the more sober and unadventurous *Labour Leader*, and Blatchford repeatedly urged Socialist unity. Thus Hardie's somewhat vague resolution in favour of unity at the informal conference of 1897 can be interpreted as a sop to the Blatchford supporters within the ILP. Meanwhile changes on the ILP Council were strengthening his position. 'New Unionists' Tom Mann and Pete Curran had left to devote their energies to union organisation and had been replaced by a new type of Council member, full-time propagandists and journalists such as Snowden, Glasier and Ramsay MacDonald. They posed no real challenge to Hardie's authority. After the ILP's 1896 Conference the federal structure of the party had been abolished to nullify the fact that Socialist unity forces had gained control of a number of the county federations. As a consequence of these developments Hardie now felt more secure. In a speech to the Thornhill Lees ILP he argued that he had changed his mind because 'he was afraid there might be internal strife if the two bodies came together',[15] but in truth he had opposed the idea all along. As Henry Pelling has commented,

> Following Hardie's lead ... the I.L.P. Council regarded the whole question ... in the light of the much more important problem of how to secure the assistance of the trade unions and co-operative societies in a joint movement for independent labour representation. Fusion with the S.D.F., it was thought, would prejudice the solution of this problem.[16]

The argument about absorption was a red herring; after all, the ILP had three times as many members as the SDF and no details of the fusion process had been worked out. Of more significance was the quite phenomenal influence exercised by the ILP in West Yorkshire on the party nationally. Over one quarter of the paying members came from the West Riding and half of these from Bradford and Halifax. Here opposition to fusion was strong, for there was a negligible SDF presence. Both Bradford and Halifax ILP branches had strong links with the trade union movement and had already started down the road Hardie was advocating. Thus, as early as 1896 the Bradford *Labour Echo* had argued that

> The time has not come for the thorough fusion of forces which the creation of such a party would demand .... The formation of such a party before the time was ripe for it would bring nothing but mischief.[17]

And there the matter rested. The SDF would not consider federation, feeling that was for those who, 'being divided on points of principle, desire to combine for purposes on which they agree.' The ILP undoubtedly lost members as a result of the affair. The Morley branch seceded, the Dewsbury branches of the ILP and SDF fused, and the Bristol SDF and ILP amalgamated to form a Socialist Council. But the protests soon died away. The breakdown of Socialist unity talks in the 1890s meant that the possibility of a British Socialist movement which integrated the moral concerns of the ILP with the scientific Marxism of the SDF had been lost.

As the nineteenth century drew to a close the self-evident decline of the Socialist movement from its peak in the mid-1890s provoked what Harry Snell called a reversal to 'aimless enthusiasm'.[18] There was, says Stephen Yeo, 'A felt sense of failure, of being out of touch and unable to embrace the majority of the working class.'[19] This made the SDF much more favourably inclined to the idea of a Socialist and Trade Union alliance, and its executive decided to participate in the conference of February 1900 which led to the formation of the Labour Representation Committee. Thus Keir Hardie's ambition was realised and, seemingly, the cause of Socialist unity had also been advanced, with both the SDF and the ILP affiliated to the new body. In relation to their numbers the Socialist parties wielded considerable influence, having five out of twelve seats on the Executive. Yet less than eighteen months after the founding conference the SDF voted to secede. This decision was taken because 'We were being committed to the support of men and measures with which we did not agree'.[20] In fact the ILP and the SDF had clashed from the very beginning over the former's failure to back an SDF resolution committing the LRC to a Socialist objective. Hyndman and the majority of SDF leaders later came to regret the decision to withdraw, but criticism of the party must be tempered by an awareness of the context in which the decision was made. In 1901 options were still open, or so it seemed to many Socialists. Trade unions had not rallied to the LRC in any great numbers. Of its two MPs, Keir Hardie and Richard Bell of the Railway Servants, Bell was a Liberal on all questions except those related to his union. He lent little credence to the LRC's claim to independence. The failure to adopt a Socialist basis meant that the Labour Representation Committee seemed indistinguishable from earlier attempts at Labour electoral associations. Internal developments within the SDF also pushed the party towards secession. An 'impossibilist' revolt threatened the unity of the party and the achievements of the LRC, it was felt, did not justify remaining in membership at the cost of internal rupture within the SDF.

The SDF responded to its departure from the LRC by returning Socialist unity to the agenda. They now actively argued for this as an alternative to the Labour alliance, with the enthusiastic backing of the *Clarion*. David Howell has argued that the united Socialist option had, by this time, been effectively ruled out by the emergence of the Labour Representation Committee. 'The logic of national events ... combined with local developments ... to erode the United Socialist alternative, even an environment where it had developed a significant presence.'[21] Similarly Stephen Yeo suggests that by the turn of the century Socialist unity had become less likely because the fervour and commitment of the 1890s, the air of optimism fuelled by a belief in imminent change, had dissipated in the face of the resilience of British capitalism and the retrenchment of the Liberal Party. This led the ILP cabal of Hardie, Snowden, Glasier and MacDonald to take effective control of the party and to steer it on the path of a broad Labour alliance at the expense of Socialist commitment. The events of the first decade of the century however suggest that Socialist unity was still a viable option.

The SDF had developed a substantial local base in Lancashire. In Burnley they presented a serious ideological alternative to Liberalism; in Nelson they had been instrumental in the formation of the ILP branch and played an important role in forming the basis of the Nelson Labour Party; in Blackburn a triangular alliance with the ILP and the Trades Council had, by 1900, outstripped the Liberals as the chief opponent of a very powerful brand of local Toryism. Other than in Burnley an open-minded and pragmatic form of social-democracy seemed to characterise the SDF. Yet this tells only half the story, for the Lancashire branches were also amongst the strongest advocates of Socialist unity. The history of the Socialist movement in this period is often posited in terms of Labour alliance or Socialist unity, but the two were not mutually exclusive. In one sense they were interdependent because it was obviously logical for the Socialists to be a united force if they were effectively to seek cooperation from the trade unions. A second motivating factor was simply the relative strengths of the local bodies; unity was often imperative for survival where either the ILP or the SDF was considerably weaker than the other, and in towns such as Burnley and Blackburn it was the SDF that dominated. Furthermore joint membership was common, many Socialists ignoring national controversies in favour of an enthusiastic and wide-ranging espousal of Socialist principles. Such an approach was certainly stimulated by Robert Blatchford's *Clarion*, which was very influential in Lancashire.

A third explanation for the popularity of Socialist unity in Lancashire can be found in the extended time scale of the Labour alliance policy. The postponement of the social revolution to a more distant future, the concentration upon the gaining of positions on municipal and trade union bodies followed by the grind of committee work, frustrated many activists. As one disappointed member commented, Socialist politics at the turn of the century seemed 'hum-drum and commonplace compared to the good old days of fourteen years ago.'[22] Socialist unity was seen as a return to the crusading days, a revival of the idea of Socialism as a separate culture, a total way of life. Here the pervasive influence of Blatchford and *Clarion* Socialism in Lancashire Labour politics was important. Blatchford's emphasis on hostility to both major parties was essential in an area which differed from national trends because of its strong working-class Toryism. His criticism of the leaderships of both the SDF and the ILP, of the bureaucracies which he accused of strangling the movement, touched a chord in Lancashire, where the rank and file of both parties worked side by side. Thus Socialist unity and Labour alliance were mutually reinforcing aspects of the same policy. The alliance was pragmatic politics, to extend Socialist influence within the Labour movement and to achieve social reforms. Nonetheless the long-term aim remained to convert individuals to Socialism, and Socialist unity can be seen as an impatient response to that time scale.

The history of the SDF in Lancashire gives the lie to the notion that the party was intransigent and dogmatic. What characterised the party there was its flexibility. 'A search through local Socialist literature for indications of SDF dogmatism and isolation from the main currents of working-class life would be an unrewarding experience', says David Howell.[23] Thus in Rochdale, for example, the SDF and ILP mounted an effective alliance to combat the Liberals, an alliance which developed significant links with trade unionists. Their municipal successes encouraged them to contest the 1900 general election with Allan Clarke as their candidate. A poorly organised campaign, lacking funds, gathered only 901 votes but it was sufficient to deprive the Liberals of the seat. The Rochdale Socialists drew the moral that Socialist as opposed to Labour success was possible, and it is worth noting that in Rochdale the ILP branch had 300 members, which made it one of the largest in the county. Socialist unity was not an idea foisted on to weak ILP branches by the SDF. After the national unity negotiations broke down in 1897 Charles Higham of the Blackburn ILP pointed out that in Blackburn, Nelson, Rochdale, Ashton and several other places, the local branches of the I.L.P. and S.D.F. already work cordially side by side and for elections and many propaganda purposes are already virtually federated together.[24]

The Lancashire branches of the SDF had been influential in persuading the national body to affiliate to the LRC. Secession from that organisation therefore caused dismay in the county and a temporary slump in SDF activity. The comments of Howell and Yeo as to the demise of the Socialist unity option are pertinent in relation to this period. But in Lancashire and elsewhere the manifest failure of the LRC to develop a distinctive Labour, let alone Socialist, standpoint led to a search for alternatives and a revival of the unity campaign. Paradoxically it was the Dewsbury by-election of 1902, in the ILP heartland of West Yorkshire, that gave renewed momentum to the cause.

Dewsbury, a Liberal stronghold, boasted one of the few healthy SDF branches in West Yorkshire. Indeed it had completely ousted the ILP from the town, although the parliamentary constituency still contained flourishing ILP branches at Thornhill Lees and Batley. Resentment at the failure of the Liberals to consider Labour representation or to listen to Labour concerns had led the ILP to stand a candidate at the 1895 general election. Edward Robertshaw Hartley performed creditably, polling over 1,000 votes. Thereafter a Liberal counter-attack weakened the ILP s influence on the Trades Council, led many ILPers to question the Labour alliance strategy, and allowed the Social-Democratic Federation to gain support. At the time of the 1900 general election a Labour candidate for Dewsbury was mooted but failed to materialise. In September 1901, however, the Liberal MP Mark Oldroyd announced his resignation on the grounds of ill-health. The resulting by-election caused both national and local controversy.

The SDF's decision to nominate Harry Quelch as Socialist candidate for Dewsbury was seen by the ILP and the LRC as yet another example of the SDF's unreliability. They accused the Federation of pre-empting the issue before a decision had been reached on standing a Labour candidate. What particularly worried the ILP leadership was the effect that Quelch might have on the emergent Labour Representation Committee. In fact the local ILP had been negotiating with the Liberals for a Lib-Lab candidate, anathema to the SDF and the reason for their decision to go it alone. The Liberal Party however, true to form, rejected ILP overtures and chose a Newcastle shipowner, Walter Runciman, as their nominee. This blatant disregard of Labour claims to representation obviously shocked the local Trades Council and ILP, who belatedly fell back upon an alternative candidate, Edward Robertshaw Hartley. Temporarily there was the possibility of two Labour candidates in Dewsbury and the LRC asked Quelch to withdraw. He refused and the NAC of the ILP, realising the potential ignominy of the situation, decided not to contest the seat. They instructed their members to take no further part in the election. Relations between the SDF and the ILP had never been at a lower ebb.

189

Whilst events at Dewsbury demonstrated the problems confronting the SDF after its disaffiliation from the LRC it also showed the increasing tensions within the ILP as a result of the Labour alliance policy. Many Socialists were worried at a rumoured trend towards ILP/Liberal understandings in an attempt to get members into parliament. Thus, to the chagrin of the ILP leaders, support for Quelch flooded in. Particularly galling was the public declaration of support by Edward Hartley, who complained that 'The great work of the official section of the I.L.P. at the present seems not so much to push Socialism as to try and intrigue some half-a-dozen persons into Parliament.'[25] He couldn't understand the hostility of Glasier and Hardie towards the SDF and obviously shared the view that there had been some behind the scenes manoeuvring to intrigue a Lib-Lab into the seat. 'This must end', he said,or 'my connection must cease with a movement which for the sake of getting men into positions will forget all its past and all its principles.'[26] The *Clarion* too threw its weight behind Quelch and Socialist unity once more became a battlecry for all those dissatisfied with the Labour alliance.

In spite of the refusal of the LRC and ILP, either nationally or locally, to back the Socialist candidate, Quelch performed very respectably indeed. Starved of funds, handicapped by the internecine warfare which had preceded his campaign, boycotted by leading Labour figures, he succeeded in wooing many local ILPers and Labour men back to the fold. In the heaviest poll ever recorded for a Dewsbury election the SDF candidate polled 1,597 votes, 517 votes more than Hartley in 1895, and reduced the Liberal majority by more than 1,000. He had done better than any of his critics had forecast and demonstrated that an overtly Socialist candidate could command considerable support both in Dewsbury and, as Victor Grayson later showed, elsewhere in the country. In many ways the election encapsulated the problems of the Labour and Socialist movement nationally. As Philip Snowden was forced to comment, 'The movement nationally seems just now in something of a crisis,'[27] for only two years after its formation many Socialists had become disillusioned with the progress of the LRC. They were suspicious of the aims of their trade union colleagues, fearful that the Socialist ideal was being relegated further and further into the background. The refusal of both the LRC and the ILP to back Quelch confirmed their doubts. Many Socialists viewed with distaste the bickerings of party leaders and yearned for a united Socialist movement, irrespective of party label. This standpoint was forcibly expressed by A. M. Thompson of the *Clarion*, who viewed Quelch's performance as

> a crushing blow to the conflicting "Leaders" and a triumphant vindication of Socialist Unity ... The rank and file of Dewsbury have shown the way; Socialists of all denominations have shut their eyes to the scowlings and nudgings of rival party officials and stood shoulder to shoulder for Socialism.[28]

Thus the *Clarion* renewed its appeal for Socialist unity, a call readily echoed by the SDF. In Bradford, Edward Robertshaw Hartley joined the SDF, reformed the Bradford branch of the Federation, and hoped to promote Socialist unity in the stronghold of the ILP as a prelude to unity nationally. In the middle years of the decade Socialism experienced a reinvigorating upsurge in its fortunes.

If there was enthusiasm for the ideal of Socialist unity after Dewsbury then it was certainly not apparent amongst the leaders of the ILP. Indeed, the election had, if anything, intensified their intransigence towards the SDF. Unity, said Keir Hardie, would reduce the entire movement 'to the impotence of the present S.D.F.',[29] whilst the *ILP News* violently attacked the SDF as a nonentity 'out to revive its ebbing existence by engrafting itself upon the I.L.P.'[30] An appeal in the *Clarion* for unity was dismissed and when the Newcastle ILP initiated a referendum of branches on the question of fusion there was a two to one majority against. Undoubtedly the SDF's departure from the LRC was the prime cause of this hostility. Such a negative response produced a temporary reaction within SDF ranks but the Federation's 1903 Conference suggested that the party should appeal over the heads of the ILP leadership to the rank and file members. This suggestion was deferred but it indicated a trend in SDF thinking which had been sparked by the events at Dewsbury and which would grow stronger as the ILP became ever more entangled with the perceived failings of the Labour Party. Meanwhile the ILP Conference of that year defined its policy; it regarded the LRC as 'a practical and sufficient means of Socialist and Labour unity'. This was to remain, in essence, ILP policy in the coming years, and Hardie remarked in the *Labour Leader* that 'as a live question fusion no longer exists.'[31]

Between 1904 and 1911 the SDF Conference made an almost ritual re-affirmation of its desire for Socialist unity. In an effort to widen its base the 1904 Conference allowed local Socialist Societies to affiliate to the SDF. The Amsterdam resolution of 1904 instructing Socialist parties within each country to amalgamate, and the example of the French parties in doing so, provided a further impetus to SDF efforts. In the localities branches of the two parties often co-operated fruitfully. Nationally, however, the stumbling block remained affiliation to the Labour Party. SDF overtures in 1907, 1909, and 1910 were met with predictable rebuffs, the ILP suggesting affiliation to the Labour Party as a prerequisite for Socialist unity. With SDF conferences voting overwhelmingly against rejoining the Labour Party unity seemed as far distant as ever. Pious resolutions at annual conferences self-evidently did not further the cause, and the Coventry Conference of the Federation finally took positive steps. Responding to the growing feeling that the ILP leadership was out of touch with its membership SDF delegates carried a Rochdale resolution calling on the Executive to issue invitations 'to every S.D.F. branch, I.L.P. branch, local Fabian Societies, who believe in industrial and political action',[32] to attend a conference in Manchester at the end of September. Support was received from a wide range of organisations – local Socialist Representation Committees, Socialist Societies, the Clarion Scouts, the Church Socialist League. Before dealing with the events of 1911, however, we must pause to study the SDF's motives in pursuing its campaign for unity.

There was undoubtedly a considerable body of support within the SDF for Socialist unity. The idea of 'one Socialist party' was an altruistic notion, an ideal to be aimed at. All Socialists had common principles and it seemed wrong that they should be divided, engaged in internecine warfare, when there was a glorious goal to be attained. But more practical reasons lay at the heart of the matter, particularly where the leadership was concerned. Hyndman and the others could see few returns on thirty years of active propaganda and Socialist unity seemed to offer a way out of the impasse. Furthermore the party was plagued by doctrinal disputes. It had split in 1884 and again in 1903–4, during the so-called 'impossibilist' revolt, but dissidents remained within the party. They objected to its domination by Hyndman and the 'old guard', whilst the relationship of the SDF to both the trade unions and the Labour Party remained a source of controversy. Other contentious issues included Hyndman's alleged anti-Semitism and the party's attitude towards religion, always a potential electoral liability. More explosive still were the subjects of female suffrage and the 'woman question' generally.

However, two areas of division overshadowed all others. Many members were dissatisfied with what they saw as the SDF's limited, narrow, economically deterministic view of Socialism and viewed with dismay the official dismissal of strikes ad industrial struggles as diversions from, if not actively damaging to, the working-class cause. The great industrial upsurge of the early twentieth century introduced new ideas into the Labour movement, those of Industrial Unionism and Syndicalism, yet the SDF seemed impervious both to the strike wave and to the philosophy of direct action. Members of the SDF closely involved with the industrial movement could not accept this and challenged the leadership. They sought both explanations for the SDF's lack of progress and for alternative routes to Socialism. The final major area of contention was that of international relations and foreign policy. Hyndman and his supporters continually warned of a German threat to Britain and argued that in certain circumstances declarations of internationalism were pious and irresponsible. Socialists could be forced into the position of championing national and democratic rights against imperialist aggression, they argued, and with Germany seen as embarking upon an increasingly aggressive policy they demanded the expansion of Britain's navy. This provoked an outcry in the party, accusations of xenophobia and 'jingoism', and eventually a humiliating rebuff for the Executive at the 1911 Conference.

Such controversies within the SDF had important consequences for Socialist unity. The leadership hoped to use the unity campaign as a diversion from the party's internal problems, as a unifying force. It was motivated too by electoral setbacks in 1910 and a financial crisis which threatened the continued publication of *Justice*. The dissidents, however, encouraged by their success, hoped to gain new strength from the unity conference and mount a further challenge to the Hyndmanites. Meanwhile external factors also encouraged the party to look towards Socialist unity, whilst influencing other sections of the movement in the same direction.

The political context in which Socialists operated was radically altered with the landslide election of the Liberal Government in January 1906, and the arrival of 29 Labour MPs in the Commons. The subsequent change of name from the Labour Representation Committee to the Labour Party fuelled expectations of growth amongst Labour and Socialists alike. For the next three years all sections of the movement shared in a Socialist revival. The SDF, for example, claimed 100 new branches between 1906 and 1908, and its 21 seats on municipal bodies rose to 124 by 1907. The Labour Churches were reinvigorated, the circulation of the *Clarion* soared. Nothing demonstrated more clearly this renewed vitality in the British Socialist movement than the election of Victor Grayson as MP for the Colne Valley constituency in 1907. He stood on an explicitly Socialist platform, endorsed neither by the Labour Party nor the ILP Council. Many Socialists drew the conclusion that a mass Socialist party could achieve electoral success, for in Bradford Edward Hartley had polled over 3,000 votes in the 1906 general election, again without official backing, Dan Irving in Accrington had done better still, and respectable votes were achieved elsewhere. The ILP meanwhile was under pressure.

There was an essential duality within the ILP in these years as their Socialist commitment clashed with their trade union alliance. The goal of converting their trade union allies was increasingly postponed to a far distant future, particularly after the affiliation of the miners to the Labour Party, and the overwhelming majority of the Liberal Party in parliament meant a hesitant and often supine approach on the part of the Labour MPs. Rank and file dissatisfaction increased, and the failure of the Parliamentary Labour Party over the unemployment issue was a prime cause of discontent. The dual impulses of the ILP began to separate under the pressure of its political role. One ILPer accused the party of losing 'its political and Socialist identity in a frantic effort to gloat over superficial successes.'[33] Others, the Huddersfield ILP being a particular example, objected to the increasingly oligarchic control of the party by the NAC. According to H. Russell Smart, the ILP was now 'a mere machine for registering the decrees of three or four able men.'[34] Members began to choose, consciously, between the ultimate Socialist vision and the trade union alliance.

Between 1909 and 1911 46 ILP branches collapsed. Dissidents campaigned to return the party to Socialist principles; they drew closer to the SDF, sharing its platforms and co-operating in the three by-election campaigns of 1908. At the 1909 ILP Conference there was a consistent vote of one-third or more against official policy. The revolt went a stage further in 1910 when four members of the NAC signed the so-called 'Green Manifesto', *Let Us Reform the Labour Party*, accusing the leadership of a 'suicidal revisionist policy ... bartering the soul of a great cause for the off chance of an occasional bare bone.'[35] MacDonald however outmanoeuvred the malcontents and not one was re-elected to the NAC. Dissatisfied ILPers would have to look elsewhere and it seemed to the SDF a golden opportunity to appeal to them over the heads of their leaders. Other trends also offered hope. As Tsuzuki has noted,

'The growth of local Socialist Societies, independent of the SDF and ILP, and often under the influence of Blatchford's *Clarion*, was a feature of the first decade of the twentieth century.'[36] Apparently those much maligned 'unattached Socialists' were bestirring themselves. In London a Provisional Committee for the Promotion of Common Action among Socialists was formed by members of the SDF, ILP, and Clarion groups. The formation of the United Socialist Propaganda League in 1911, to spread the word in rural areas seemed to confirm this development. Thus the SDF's campaign for Socialist unity gathered momentum. And then came the bombshell! Victor Grayson, having lost the Colne Valley seat in 1910, launched his own appeal in the *Clarion* for the formation of a British Socialist Party.

After his election in Colne Valley Victor Grayson had become a significant focus for the critics of ILP policy. Opinion on the left of the party seemed to be hardening in favour of Socialist unity, a fact emphasised by Grayson himself when he co-authored *The Problem of Parliament* with G. R. S. Taylor and expressly dedicated it to the formation of a Socialist party. When Grayson joined the staff of the *Clarion* in February 1909 he used the paper to agitate for a united party built out of the ranks of the ILP, SDF, and Clarion organisations. As a preliminary step he advocated the formation of Socialist Representation Committees. The first of these was established in Manchester, understandably enough, for it was there that Grayson had first risen to prominence as a Socialist propagandist. Manchester was favourable terrain for such an initiative, having a strong tradition of SDF/ILP co-operation and its ILP branches a reputation for independent thought and action. Grayson, after his defeat at Colne Valley in January 1910, issued a unity appeal which backed the Manchester SRC.

> There are thousands of unattached Socialists that must be yearning for a party that knows its mind and has courage and culture to express it. There are branches that are chafing against the tightly held rein. Let them come together under a common banner and rejuvenate our good cause.[37]

Throughout 1911 the Grayson campaign intensified. SRCs were formed at Birmingham and Liverpool, SDF and ILP branches amalgamated to form Socialist Societies at Oldham, Bury and Ashton. Leonard Hall and H. Russell Smart defected from the ILP. There were, however, significant differences between his campaign and that of the SDF. Whereas the SDF wanted already organised groupings to send delegates to the Manchester Conference, there to discuss the grounds for amalgamation, Grayson appealed to individuals to send in their names for the formation of a completely new party. A mere expansion of already existing parties was not what was needed, he argued. 'For our new wine we must have new bottles.'[38] This did not please the SDF, who saw this as merely increasing the number of rival organisations and making unity that much more difficult. Yet Grayson's fledgling body appeared to have every chance of success. Letters had flooded in to the *Clarion*, embryo branches were already in existence, Clarion Cycling Clubs and Socialist

Churches had agreed to enter the new party. Even before the Conference branches in Birmingham and Sheffield reported 300 and 100 members respectively. Worried SDF leaders urged their members not to fill in the *Clarion* forms but to wait until the Conference itself.

Grayson's response to this was to state categorically that it was the condition of the SDF as much as anything else that made the formation of the British Socialist Party essential. Their plan, he wrote, 'will amount to little more than an enlargement of the S.D.P. [SDF]'[39] There were differences of outlook too. Robert Blatchford appealed to his readers not to confound the principles of Socialism with other principles but to let each man be free to express his views on all points outside the mere plain principles of Socialism. The British Socialist Party was to be a wide, all-embracing party, being 'for direct action in the industrial field as well as for political action on elected bodies.'[40] Leonard Hall also placed the emphasis on direct action, a clear challenge to SDF traditional political orthodoxy and suggestive of problems ahead. Yet these differences were smoothed over before the weekend of 30 September–1 October, with Grayson in particular in conciliatory mood. A union of Socialists outside the Labour Party seemed a realisable goal and a genuine atmosphere of unity and comradeship pervaded the proceedings.

Certainly attendance at the Conference was impressive. Delegates claimed to represent 41 ILP branches, 32 Clarion organisations, 85 SDF/SDP branches, 50 local Socialist Societies, and 12 branches of the new BSP, totalling some 35,000 members in all. A further 46 organisations, including 18 ILP branches, had sent messages of support. How successful then had been the appeal to the rank and file of the ILP? How accurate were the membership figures so proudly announced? To what extent were the various groupings united on policy?

On the surface the BSP progressed rapidly and smoothly after the Conference. ILP branches moving over to the new party included Failsworth, Maidstone, Romford, Wakefield, St. Helens, Crewe, Stretford, Balham, and Stoke Newington. The Colne Valley Socialist League seceded from the ILP and Conrad Noel, the 'red' vicar of Thaxted, resigned his membership and joined the BSP. Leonard Hall and Victor Grayson argued that one-third of the ILP had come over to the BSP.[41] There is little evidence however to support such a claim and indeed such evidence as there is suggests that initial estimates of membership were exaggerated. As Morris has pointed out there were no reliable membership figures for bodies represented at the Unity Conference other than the SDF and ILP branches. There was also 'a fair degree of over affiliation ... numerous cases of overlap.'[42] Delegates attended from SRCs and their affiliated bodies, from Clarion groups and SDF/ILP/BSP branches in the same town. As far as ILP recruitment is concerned precise figures are difficult to estimate. Grayson and Hall's analysis of 30 per cent was flatly denied by the *Labour Leader*, which put the figure as low as five per cent, presumably for propaganda purposes. Quite clearly temporary incursions into ILP support were made. Membership in the Lancashire division fell by 900 in

1911–12, and the 22 Lancashire branches represented at the Conference were a quarter of the divisional total. By 1913 Altrincham was the only branch left in its federation, many Cheshire branches having followed their NAC member into the BSP. Other groupings, the Colne Valley Socialist League and Openshaw Socialist Society for example, were ex-ILP branches which had already seceded.

Yet there were limits to these losses. They were concentrated in South Lancashire, the BSP failing to extend much beyond the SDF branches in the north-east of the county. 'It was also evident that few branches came over in total and that some which attended the Socialist Unity Conference remained in the ILP. The branches shed were generally smaller ones with traditions of disaffection and semi-autonomy.'[43] Keith Laybourn's research into the West Riding of Yorkshire suggests that at the height of its support, in March 1912, the BSP there could claim 2,000 members. Of these 'perhaps between 1,000 and 1,300 ILP members went … nearer 20 per cent than the 30 per cent Grayson claimed.'[44] Many of these were from the Colne Valley Socialist League, Grayson's heartland. It is obvious therefore that the BSP did appeal to dissident ILPers, but certainly not on the hoped-for scale. Many of the opponents of ILP policy, J. M. McLachlan for example – co-author of the 'Green Manifesto' with Hall and a director of the Manchester Clarion Cafe – did not cross over because they were not convinced that the BSP offered a realistic alternative to the Labour Alliance. The British Socialist Party had first to prove itself.

It had been decided at Conference that the SDF should retain its organisation intact until a new constitution had been ratified by the branches. A provisional committee drafted the constitution, to which the SDF agreed, and the first annual conference of the BSP was arranged for March 1912 in Manchester. Until this date the organisation had been run from two centres. David Reid had dealt with the *Clarion* operation, H. W. Lee had looked after affairs for the SDF. With the new party established, activities were now centralised at Chandos Hall, the SDF headquarters, but as Walter Kendall has observed

> Grayson quickly realised that he had been outwitted. The SDP had no intention of dissolving into the British Socialist Party before the next year's conference. In the meantime its organisation remained in being. By relinquishing the Workship Street office, and consenting to centralisation under Lee, Grayson had handed over organisational control of the new party to the SDP.[45]

Grayson aired his dissatisfaction publicly early in the New Year. He accused the SDF of duplicity and of taking steps for which it had 'not a scrap of delegated authority.' Thereafter he gradually reduced his activity and failed to attend the 1912 Conference. In fact Grayson had always been very much an individualist. In this he reflected the *Clarion* philosophy; neither he nor Blatchford was capable of sustained work within an organisation; like the

Clarion they worked best as free-lance operators for the movement at large. The SDF had no preconceived plan to 'capture' the BSP but the somewhat amorphous nature of the non-SDF elements, allied to the organisational incapacity of the Grayson group, made it easy for the Federation to assume control. Tom Groom of the Clarion Cycling Club also withdrew from active work for the party shortly after Grayson's departure. The Clarion element was thus severely weakened within the first six months.

Apart from the SDF and the Clarion groups the other major faction at the Unity Conference had been the Syndicalists. They had been encouraged by the new constitution which declared that political and industrial action were complementary to each other. A party 'Manifesto to Railway Workers' in December 1911, calling on them to unite with the miners, transport workers, and seamen, 'to act all together and simultaneously', seemed to suggest an awareness of the industrial situation and a move towards the syndicalist idea of a general strike. The illusion was soon shattered. In the New Year's edition of *Justice* Quelch and Thomas Kennedy, the London organiser of the BSP, reiterated the traditional SDF line that the Socialist party must be the political expression of the working class and, ominously, emphasised the need for party discipline. As the new year progressed supporters of Hyndman began to attack the syndicalists in *Justice* and the *British Socialist*. They insidiously suggested that syndicalist ideas were a 'foreign' irrelevance, that the industrial battlefield was a diversion from the question of political power. Fred Knee argued that mere industrial action was useless 'So long as the capitalist state remains with its army, navy and police, and its hand on the machine of administration'.[46] The failure of the BSP leadership lay in their inability to establish the relationship between industrial and political action, the significance of industrial struggle as a challenge to the state. In response Leonard Hall and his supporters combined their demand for priority to be given to industrial organisation with a plea for party democracy. E. C. Fairchild pleaded in vain for a synthesis of the political and the industrial: 'Let the strike and the vote, the industrial combination and the political party, be as the right arm and the left arm of the human body.'[47] A major battle would be fought at the 1912 Conference, and meanwhile the thorny questions of the suffrage and armaments had flared up again, with Zelda Kahan and Quelch engaging in a long-running dispute over the latter in the pages of the *British Socialist*.

What progress had the British Socialist Party made by the time of its First Annual Conference at the end of May 1912? Reports from around the country indicated increased membership. In London 59 branches were represented at a District Conference;[48] the Manchester District Council reported 37 branches, South Salford claiming 230 members and Stockport 300;[49] the West Yorkshire District Council announced 1,000 members;[50] with Hull claiming 110 members,[51] Sheffield 200,[52] Wakefield 70,[53] and Bradford 400.[54] Perhaps the only sour note had been struck by the movement abroad, which failed to grant its approbation. *Vorwarts*, the German Socialist journal, remarked that 'By Socialist Unity in England one has always understood the union of the

S.D.P. and I.L.P. That is the problem; there is no other.'[55] However that could not be achieved unless the BSP affiliated to the Labour Party and in 1912 that was not on the agenda. What the 1912 Conference would demonstrate was whether or not the BSP could maintain its own unity.

The national press made great play of disorderly scenes at the conference, but in one sense the outcome was satisfactory in that an open breach between conflicting wings of the party was avoided. The constitution offered hope to the syndicalists because it embraced both the 'industrial unity of all workers' and 'the establishment of a militant Socialist Party in Parliament.' The elections to the Executive reflected a balance between the old SDF and the newer intake of members. Hall and Russell Smart were both elected, along with Zelda Kahan and E. C. Fairchild representing the left wing of the SDF. Ben Tillett and Conrad Noel were closer to these than to the Hyndmanites, who were represented by Quelch, Dan Irving and F. Victor Fisher. What the Conference had revealed was the emergence of an increasingly sizeable opposition to the leadership which was prepared to stay within the party and fight its corner. Yet all the in-fighting and manoeuvring obscured the fact that organisationally the picture was far from encouraging.

The BSP claimed 370 branches and 40,000 members, but these figures disguised the true situation. Total dues reported were only £650 which, at one shilling per head, gave a total of only 13,000 paying members. This was scarcely an advance on the SDF's membership, and the BSP's total of 150 seats on local government bodies was similarly unimpressive. Compared with the ILP's paying membership of 30,000 and its 1,070 local government representatives then it is obvious that the British Socialist Party had not made the hoped-for breakthrough. A 'Great Propaganda Campaign' launched immediately after the Conference barely got off the ground. Even in its Lancashire stronghold there were complaints of branches defaulting on their dues. The Wigan branch had collapsed by June and others suffered from 'the slump which has been in evidence all over Manchester.'[56] The party was perpetually short of money and the problem was compounded by the failure of the Twentieth Century Press after a libel action. Meanwhile the 'Socialism versus Syndicalism' controversy continued to divide the BSP and eventually precipitated a damaging split.

In October 1912 the Executive issued a Manifesto on 'Political Action and Direct Action', emphasising the primacy of the former and denouncing supporters of the latter as anarchists, levellers and luddites. Hall, Smart and Conrad Noel dissociated themselves from the Manifesto, charging that they had not signed it and that it had been altered without their knowledge. Hall and Smart resigned from the Executive shortly afterwards and Hall soon left the BSP altogether, joining the Socialist Labour Party. The disruption severely weakened the BSP. In Birmingham, a syndicalist stronghold, of nine branches represented at the 1912 Conference only two sent delegates to that of 1913. Many of the Clarion groups also became disenchanted and drifted away. In December John Scurr, a long-time SDFer and ex-Executive member, announced his resignation from the BSP. The only basis for Socialist unity, said Scurr, was the fusion of the SDF and the ILP, and this had not been achieved. As Stanley Pierson quite rightly remarks of the BSP, 'Not only did it fail to unify the various groups but the Social Democrats themselves were increasingly divided.'[57]

At an Executive meeting on 14 December 1912 Zelda Kahan finally succeeded in her long struggle against Hyndman's views on national defence. Her resolution dissociating the BSP from the propaganda for increased naval expenditure was carried by a majority of one. The internationalist wing of the BSP had won a signal victory, but it was not yet a decisive one, as the 'Old Guard' of the SDF once more proved themselves masters of political intrigue. They used the pages of *Justice*, which they controlled, to pour scorn on their opponents and to accuse them of being 'comrades alien in blood and race.' An Executive meeting with only five members present suspended the armaments resolution, causing Kahan to resign from the Executive. A further split in the party seemed inevitable but the Blackpool Conference of May 1913 was anti-climactic. Hyndman, realising the strength of the opposition, compromised and agreed to keep his views to himself. In one sense therefore the outcome was inconclusive but in the long term it was significant. An opposition group, by remaining in the party, had won the first victory against an ageing leadership. It marked the beginning of a radical shift in policy for the BSP and the eventual defeat of the Hyndmanite wing in 1916. But in many ways it came too late, for the 1913 Conference also marked a party in decline.

In his opening address Dan Irving commented that they had not been as successful as they had hoped. 'They certainly had not gone back, but at any rate they had not had the adhesion to their ranks they anticipated from the Independent Labour Party.'[58] Even this was a somewhat sanguine appraisal of the party's fortunes, for the membership was claimed to be only 15,313, as compared to 40,000 at the previous conference. This was little more than the membership of the SDF before the unity campaign, and it seemed indeed that the party was once more centred on the old SDF heartlands of London and Lancashire. Recruitment from the ILP had been a transitional phenomenon, a picture reflected by the history of the BSP in Yorkshire.

As has already been noted the idea of Socialist unity, based upon the ILP and the SDF, had never attracted significant support in West Yorkshire, where the ILP was overwhelmingly predominant. The Dewsbury by-election of 1902 and the subsequent Socialist revival did however suggest a body of opinion supportive of the idea, although significantly no Socialist Representation Committee was formed in the area. Grayson, with his roots in the Colne Valley Socialist League, made determined efforts to woo over ILPers to the new party and there were 27 organisations from the county represented at the Unity Conference in 1911. BSP branches mushroomed in the early period of enthusiasm and some 42 branches can be traced at the height of the party's fortunes. Two District Councils were established in Yorkshire to co-ordinate activities. ILP defections, as we have noted. numbered some 1,300 with the

Wakefield branch and the Colne Valley Socialist League coming over. Skipton reported 15 ex-ILPers in its ranks and others were recruited in Keighley. In March 1912, when both locally and nationally the BSP was at its zenith, the West Yorkshire District Council claimed to represent 1,000 members. Add to this branches not represented on the Council and the membership of the Colne Valley Socialist League and a figure of 2,000 members in West Yorkshire seems reasonable. Yet significantly no prominent ILPer other than Grayson joined the BSP and leading ILP figures such as Fred Jowett and Willie Leach in Bradford were severely critical of the new party.

After March 1912 support fell away rapidly. Twenty-two branches were represented at the 1912 Conference but only 10 at that of 1913. Essentially the Yorkshire BSP had slimmed down to its pre-1911 SDF core. Bradford was the most successful BSP centre but even there it faded badly after 1912. When the national body imposed John Stokes, secretary of the London Trades Council, upon East Bradford as its parliamentary candidate the local branch was unable to gain ILP acquiescence and its chances of contesting the constituency it regarded as its own appeared slim. The Leeds branches remained active under the tutelage of Bert Killip, who was elected to the Executive in 1913, and Sheffield could also boast a reasonably strong branch, which inclined towards syndicalism. But in general, 'Ranged against the membership and successes of the ILP, the BSP's impact was embarrassingly poor and failure generated failure.'[59] Developments in Leeds clearly demonstrated this, for in April 1913 the Leeds BSP decided, by a substantial majority, to affiliate to the local Labour Party. Its correspondent wrote to the *Leeds Citizen* explaining that 'we sincerely believe it will place us as a B.S.P. branch in a far better position for helping the workers of the district in their political aspirations and will make us more effective in fighting the class struggle.'[60] The idea of uniting the ILP and the SDF outside the Labour Party had been tried and found wanting, and the branch therefore substituted Labour unity for Socialist unity.

Events in Leeds foreshadowed events at a national level and demonstrated the failure of the Socialist alternative to the Labour alliance. The rationale for pursuing Socialist unity had been that the Labour Party, by compromising with capitalism, was ensuring its survival. 'Reformism' simply ensured the postponement of Socialism. Conference after conference of the SDF had rejected affiliation to the Labour Party and this attitude had been carried over into the BSP. Indeed the BSP went further than the SDF in seeking separate affiliation to the International Socialist Bureau on the Grounds that the Labour Party was not a Socialist party. The ISB, however, refused to accept the application and pressured the BSP to affiliate to the Labour Party. It convened a conference of the BSP, the ILP, and the Fabian Society in London in July 1913 and suggested that a United Socialist Council be formed with all sections affiliating to the Labour Party. As the matter was debated it became clear that the mood within the BSP had changed. As *Justice* remarked, 'The late S.D.P. did its best for Socialist Unity in the formation of the B.S.P.', but 'the combination has not been as large as we could have wished.'[61] The paper declared that: 'Socialist Unity is of such paramount importance that almost everything ... may be waived if only it can be accomplished.'[62] Declining membership and the demise of *The British Socialist* encouraged the realisation that 'The Labour Party, with all its weakness, is an effort, however faltering, of the working class to take its destiny in its own hands, and as such should be encouraged and helped by us.'[63]

A referendum of the BSP membership in May 1914 showed a marginal vote in favour of affiliation to the Labour Party. Large-scale abstention and the narrow majority demonstrated the still considerable hostility to the idea and a number of branches seceded, notably in areas where the ILP had come over to the BSP in 1911. Nevertheless on 23 June 1914 the British Socialist Party made a formal application for admission to the Labour Party. This process of events effectively demonstrated the demise of the long-held desire for Socialist unity, the dream of a mass Socialist party. The BSP was now committed to a Labour as opposed to a Socialist alliance and had accepted the continued separate identity of the BSP and the ILP.

The Socialist movement in the 1880s and 1890s was a growing movement, not in the restricted sense of party membership, but in the sense that its message reached out to ever wider sections of the population. The circle of involvement was much larger than the actual membership would suggest, and many Socialists were members of more than one organisation. A feeling of fellowship pervaded the movement, an air of optimism abounded, there was a belief in imminent change. In such an atmosphere 'Socialist unity' stood its greatest chance of success. As Stephen Yeo has recalled,

> Socialism in that period had not yet become the prisoner of a particular party machine – a machine which would come to associate its own well being with the prospects for Socialism.[64]

There was a much greater democracy in the movement in the early days and it was from the rank and file that early pressure for unity arose. The failure of the SDF and the ILP to make the hoped-for advances in the mid-1890s meant that the leaderships responded to such pressure, spurred on without by Blatchford and the *Clarion*. However the extraordinary resilience of British capitalism and the retrenchment of the Liberal Party meant that the Socialist parties found themselves without a mass movement to lead and they retreated into their own particular shells. A group interested in bureaucratic consolidation gained a commanding position within the ILP, a group whose conception of Socialism differed in many respects from that of the SDF, and it wanted no part of Socialist unity. The blame for the collapse of Socialist unity in the 1890s can be laid fairly and squarely at the door of the ILP cabal of Hardie, Snowden, Glasier and MacDonald.

The appeal of Socialist unity however lived on, particularly as the alternative strategy offered by the ILP leaders seemed to lead them into the arms of the Liberal Party. As the Labour Party failed to establish a distinctive identity so did the appeal of Socialist unity revive. It manifested itself in a host of local initiatives, was fostered by the *Clarion*, and was encouraged by election results in places as diverse as Rochdale, Dewsbury, and above all the Colne Valley. The ILP's refusal to countenance unity was matched only by the dedication with which the SDF pursued it, a dedication fuelled by the Federation's own stagnation. A Socialist revival after 1906, allied to increasing industrial unrest, made 1911 appear a propitious moment to appeal to the rank and file of the ILP over the heads of their leaders.

The formation of the BSP failed to effect a mass organisation. The various groups which coalesced were divided from the start over the policy to be adopted. The only coherent grouping was the old SDF, yet it too was divided internally. A large proportion of the party's new recruits were alienated by the refusal of the SDF's leaders to relinquish control and even more so by its failure to adopt to new ideas and to move with events. Thus the failure of the second attempt at Socialist unity can be blamed on the 'Old Guard' of the SDF.

At a local level Socialist unity proved a realisable concept. Indeed the co-operation of ILP and SDF branches was instrumental in the emergence of the Labour Party in many areas. Developments at a national level however militated against local initiatives, and the failure of Socialist unity stemmed from a lack of imagination and resolve on the part of the leaderships of the two main Socialist organisations. The concept did not die with the failure of the BSP, but the battleground became very different. The unity attempt of 1911 had one very important result. It strengthened the opposition within the SDF/BSP to the Hyndmanites, who were eventually defeated in 1916. They reformed the SDF but the BSP, now a more definitely Marxist party, formed a major component of the Communist Party of Great Britain at its inception in 1921. For the first time there was a clear division between the revolutionary and reformist wings of the Socialist movement in Britain.

NOTES

1. *Justice*, 9 July 1892.
2. *Ibid.*, 21 Jan 1893.
3. J. Hill, 'Social-Democracy and the Labour Movement: The Social Democratic Federation in Lancashire', *The Bulletin of the North-West Labour History Society*, 8, 1982.
4. S. Yeo, 'A New Life: The Religion of Socialism in Britain 1883–1896', *History Workshop Journal*, No. 4, Autumn 1977, p.7.
5. *Justice*, 25 Aug 1894.
6. *Ibid.*, 8 Sept 1894.
7. *Labour Leader*, 6 Oct 1894.
8. D. Howell, *British Workers and the Independent Labour Party 1888–1906*, p.118.
9. *Justice*, 17 Apr 1897.
10. *ILP News*, Aug 1892.
11. *Justice*, 6 June 1896.

12. *ILP Annual Conference Report*, 1898, p.8.
13. *Justice*, 7 May 1898.
14. *Ibid.*, 25 June 1898.
15. *Ibid.*, 18 Feb 1899.
16. H. Pelling, *The Origins of the Labour Party 1880–1900*, p.118.
17. *Labour Echo*, 11 Apr 1896.
18. *Ethical World*, 8 Oct 1896.
19. S. Yeo, *Religion and Voluntary Organisations in Crisis*, p.262.
20. H. W. Lee and E. Archbold, *Social-Democracy in Britain*, p.159.
21. D. Howell, 'Was the Labour Party Inevitable?', *The Bulletin of the North-West Labour History Society*, 1984, p.17.
22. *Social-Democrat*, Jan 1897.
23. D. Howell, *British Workers and the Independent Labour Party 1888–1906*, p.211.
24. *ILP Annual Conference Report*, 1899, p.9.
25. *Clarion*, 7 Dec 1901.
26. E. R. Hartley, unpublished Diary, 21 Nov 1901, West Yorkshire Archive Service, Bradford.
27. P. Snowden to Keir Hardie, 17 Jan 1902, ILP Archive, Francis Johnson Collection, 02/9.
28. *Clarion*, 7 Feb 1902.
29. *Dewsbury Reporter*, 18 Jan 1902.
30. *ILP News*, Feb 1902.
31. *Labour Leader*, 18 Apr 1903.
32. *Justice*, 29 July 1911.
33. *Labour Leader*, 15 July 1904.
34. *Huddersfield Worker*, 2 May 1908.
35. *Let Us Reform the Labour Party*, (1910), p.1.
36. C. Tsuzuki, *H. M. Hyndman and British Socialism*, p.162.
37. *Clarion*, 25 Feb 1910.
38. *Ibid.*, 18 Aug 1911.
39. *Ibid.*, 11 Aug 1911.
40. *Ibid.*
41. *Clarion*, 13 Oct 1911.
42. D. Morris, 'The Origins of the British Socialist Party', *The Bulletin of the North-West Labour History Society*, 8, p.35.
43. *Ibid.*, p.36.
44. K. Laybourn, 'A Story of Buried Talents and Wasted Opportunities: The Failure of the Socialist Unity Movement in Yorkshire 1911–14', *The Journal of Regional and Local Studies*, 7, Autumn 1987, pp.12–13.
45. W. Kendall, *The Revolutionary Movement in Britain 1900–21*, p.40.
46. *British Socialist*, June 1912.
47. *Clarion*, 26 Apr 1912.
48. *Justice*, 13 Jan 1912.
49. *Ibid.*, 20 Jan 1912.
50. *Ibid.*, 2 Mar 1912.
51. *Ibid.*, 23 Dec 1911.
52. *Clarion*, 22 Dec 1911.
53. *Justice*, 9 Dec 1911.
54. *Clarion*, 1 Dec 1911.

55.   *Justice*, 4 Nov 1911.
56.   *Ibid.*, 15 June 1912.
57.   S. Pierson, *British Socialists: The Journey from Fantasy to Politics*, p.253.
58.   *Second Annual Conference Report of the British Socialist Party*, 1913, p.5.
59.   K. Laybourn and J. Reynolds, *Liberalism and the Rise of Labour*, p.163.
60.   *Bradford Pioneer*, 11 Apr 1913.
61.   *Justice*, 11 Oct 1913.
62.   *Ibid.*, 20 Dec 1913.
63.   *Ibid.*, 4 Oct 1913.
64.   S. Yeo, 'A New Life', p.31.

2. *Women and the ILP, 1890–1914*

June Hannam

> Where women walk in public processions in the streets the same as the men; where they enter the public assembly and take places the same as the men ... there the great city stands.[1]

From the beginning the Independent Labour Party prided itself on being the most sympathetic of all political groups to the 'woman question'. Keir Hardie claimed that 'ours is the one political organisation wherein women stand on terms of perfect equality with men. Women are eligible for election to the National Council of the Party, and to the various offices on the same terms as men. From its earliest inception the ILP has taken a decided stand on the side of women's claim for political equality. In the sphere of industry also the same claim is put forth: equal pay for equal work'.[2] Hardie's assessment of the ILP's attitude towards women members and to sex equality, made in 1913, was shared by most of his contemporaries. Men and women active in socialist politics before 1914, regardless of their own stand on feminist issues, presented a remarkably consistent view of the ILP's attitude to the 'woman question'.[3]

Joseph Clayton, secretary of the Leeds ILP in the 1890s and a historian of the socialist movement, noted that 'in the early ILP women were a great deal more than mere helpers to men, they were quite literally the co-leaders' and 'gave it a tendency to look upon women's suffrage as a reform of vital need'.[4] Isabella Ford, a suffragist and member of the NAC between 1903 and 1907, claimed that she had joined the ILP because it was the only party that 'stood for equality and opportunity for the whole race ... women had never had such equality before'.[5]

Once women's suffrage had become an accepted part of mainstream labour politics even those who had not initially been sympathetic to the campaign for women's enfranchisement echoed these views. Looking back from the vantage point of 1919, for example, John Bruce Glasier argued that 'the women's political agitation, like the political labour movement, may be said to have been cradled in the ILP ... and while as yet the question of the women's suffrage was wholly ignored on Liberal and Tory platforms, Hardie, Isabella Ford, Enid Stacey [sic] and others were urging it to the front in ILP meetings ... I am right I think, in saying that the ILP was the first political party to promote the candidature of women for election on public bodies. It has the distinction also of being the first political body to elect women on its National Executive'.[6]

The image presented of the ILP's commitment to sex equality was a powerful one and has proved to be long lasting. Historians interested in feminist politics have generally concurred the assessment of contemporaries.

Olive Banks, for example, suggests that the ILP was 'feminist from its inception', while Jill Liddington and Jill Norris claim that 'the ILP, more than any other party, was sympathetic to the aspirations of feminism'.[7] Liddington and Norris also, however, recognise that in many respects the ILP was ambivalent, in particular in its attitude to women' suffrage, and while the Party was undoubtedly keen to recruit women members, 'those who joined had to assert themselves if they wanted to do more than make the tea and run fund-raising bazaars ...'[8]

The apparent discrepancy between the confident assertions by contemporaries that the ILP was committed to sex equality and the ambiguities noted by historians needs to be explained. This is not simply an academic exercise, to determine at what point along the scale of commitment to feminist politics the ILP actually stood. Its importance lies in its practical political significance for the recruitment of female members and their participation in socialist politics.

A necessary first step is to analyse what the ILP actually meant by 'sex equality' and to examine the way in which the Party, and individual members, constructed a theory about the relationship between feminism and socialism, for theory was inextricably linked with political practice. In her stimulating study of the Social Democratic Federation Karen Hunt argues that the way in which socialist organisations understood the 'woman question' affected their practice towards actual and potential women members since it influenced their 'assessment of women's potential for politicisation and their actual organisation within the party'.[9] The importance of taking account of such questions is also demonstrated by Eleonor Gordon's work on women and the labour movement in Scotland. She suggest that the ILP's definition of sex equality conditioned its response to a range of practical, political questions of concern for women, including attitudes to women workers and their struggles, the demand for women' suffrage and the Party's view of women as participants in socialist politics.[10]

There was no shortage of discussion on the 'woman question' within the ILP in the 1890s and early 1900s, both in local branch meetings and in the pages of the socialist press. The consideration of this issue did not take place in a vacuum. It was part of a much wider debate within socialist organisation throughout Europe which was stimulated by the growth of a women's rights movement. There were several points of contact between the two movements, in particular in terms of ideas and membership. Women's rights campaigners were increasingly concerned with the social and economic problems faced by working-class women and could be seen as competitors for their allegiance. At the same time a number of articulate middle-class feminists were attracted to socialist groups where they drew attention to the importance of sex oppression for women of all classes.[11]

After the rise of Marxism, socialists found considerable difficulty in reconciling socialist theory with a feminist analysis. The emphasis of Marxism on class conflict at the point of production and the importance of waged work in developing a working-class identity meant that women's specific experiences, including their oppression by men, were largely ignored and their potential contribution to socialist struggle was marginalised. An attempt was made by Engels and Bebel to examine women's subordinate position within the family from a materialist perspective. They both stressed that women's economic dependence was derived from men's control of private property which made women into a proletariat in the domestic sphere. Their solution, however, was for women to enter social production so that they could achieve emancipation as members of the working class. Bebel was particularly important in identifying sex oppression as a separate issue, but both writers subsumed questions related to sex under class exploitation and neither challenged the view that women were naturally the most suited to undertake the responsibilities of child care.[12]

Such arguments had a considerable impact on political practice. Socialists could claim that campaigns around issues relating to sex oppression merely deviated from the more important struggle between classes and that women's emancipation could not be achieved until after socialism had been won. Moreover, if too much emphasis were placed on women's grievances as a sex this could harm the development of socialism since it would point up divisions between working-class men and women and weaken a sense of class solidarity.

Despite these obstacles, many members of the ILP did try to highlight the importance of sex oppression and to link together feminism and socialism. Their task was made somewhat easier because of the diverse sources from which ILP socialism was derived, with Marx providing only one of many different perspectives. The notion of class conflict, for example, was less central for the ILP than for many other socialist organisations. The most influential national leaders of the ILP, such as Keir Hardie and James Ramsay MacDonald, denied the importance of class struggle in the achievement of socialism. Indeed, Hardie argued that advocates of the 'class war' were postponing the triumph of socialism since 'socialism declares war upon a system, not upon a class; to carry it forward successfully we want to enlist conscious socialists irrespective of class'.[13]

ILP members have most often been described as 'ethical socialists'. Inspired by the writings of Edward Carpenter and Walt Whitman they argued that socialism would bring a moral transformation of all areas of people's lives and would lead to a society based on the principles of justice, love and beauty. This Utopian vision of the future went hand in hand with the desire to live a different way of life in the 'shell of the old society'. There was an emphasis on comradeship, the development of an alternative socialist culture, on 'personal change and the creation of new forms for everyday life', including a change in the relationship between the sexes.[14]

This vision of socialism was particularly attractive to women. Most of the early female propagandists for the ILP, such as Isabella Ford, Katherine St John Conway, Caroline Martyn, Enid Stacy and Isabella Bream Pearce were influenced by Carpenter's ideas which helped to shape their views on both feminism and socialism. Not all of them, however, emphasised feminist issues in their propaganda. Katherine St John Conway, for example, expected her marriage to John Bruce Glasier to be based on a democratic relationship, but her political work was not directed explicitly to women's needs. Nonetheless, it was more usual for members of Carpenter's circle to take an interest in the "woman question".

While sharing many of the aspiration of the women's movement, they focused in particular on the needs of working-class women and argued that only socialism would ensure women's full emancipation. At the same time they were unwilling to put the demands of women in second place and in their theory and practice attempted not to put either socialism or feminism above the other.[15] Socialist feminists within the ILP sought to improve all aspects of women's lives. Their analysis was not confined to issues of equal rights or to the material basis of women's oppression in the workplace and in the home. They also explored sexuality and the relationship between the sexes within marriage, arguing that personal experience and political activity were inextricably linked.

In the 1890s feminists within the ILP tried to further the cause of women in a variety of ways. They were active as propagandists, disseminating their ideas widely through articles in socialist newspapers, in particular in the *Clarion* and the *Labour Leader*, and in numerous speeches to local branches. Some also took part in industrial struggles and helped women workers to organise into trade unions. Enid Stacy (1868–1903) was one of the best known ILP speakers. In the late 1880s she risked her livelihood as a high school teacher to help women workers on strike in Bristol. As a result of this experience she became a member first of the Bristol Socialist Society, a group with links to the SDF, and then the Fabian Society before joining the ILP in 1893. She served as a member of the National Administrative Council for two years and became a paid lecturer for the Party. In 1894 alone she addressed 122 meetings in 33 townships in Lancashire, Cheshire and Cumberland on subjects which ranged from 'Causes of Poverty' and 'What Socialism is' to 'Women's Franchise'.[16]

Enid Stacy also wrote extensively about the relationship between feminism and socialism. She suggested that although women had already achieved a great deal by opening up new work opportunities and gaining many legal rights, they needed further changes to achieve real emancipation. These included the right to choose whether or not to have children, full legal and political rights, freedom as workers, with protective legislation applying to both sexes, and easier divorce.[17]

At a more local level Isabella Ford (1855–1924) was carrying out very similar propaganda. The daughter of well-to-do Leeds Quakers, who were noted for their involvement in radical liberal reform movements and women's rights campaigns, Isabella Ford took part in strikes among women workers in Leeds in the late 1880s and joined the ILP as soon as it was formed in 1893. For the next decade she concentrated on trying to organise tailoresses and textile workers into trade unions and travelled widely in Yorkshire as an ILP speaker. She addressed meetings on a broad range of issues, including women's suffrage, protective legislation and women's trade union organisation.[18]

Isabella Ford also put forward her ideas in a regular column in the local ILP newspaper, the *Leeds Forward*, where she livened up serious subjects with witty, humorous sayings and examples. She discussed women's involvement in revolutionary movements abroad, the resourcefulness of American women, state regulation of prostitution in India, the diseases suffered by women workers, such as 'phossy jaw', and the need for women's suffrage to bring improvement. In discussing the controversial question of protective legislation she called for both men and women to be included: 'I never can understand why night work and overtime are considered so desirable for men and so undesirable for women. Over-work brutalises people – why, therefore, should men be brutalised more than women?'[19]

Attitudes to protective legislation differentiated many ILP feminists from those women who were concerned to put labour unity first. In the 1880s and 1890s the middle-class leaders of the Women's Trade Union League wholeheartedly supported protective legislation for women, whereas Enid Stacy and Isabella Ford were far more ambivalent. Concerned that women had no say in laws which affected their work, they argued that both sexes should be included in any protective measures. They were wary of proposals to exclude women from areas of employment, such as chain and nail making, which seemed no more detrimental to women's health than many other occupations.[20] Their caution was shared by many working-class women who feared that some legislation was designed to protect male interests rather than their won.[21]

A similar range of ideas were discussed in the *Labour Leader*. The paper was owned and edited by Keir Hardie until 1904 and he clearly exercised considerable influence on its content. As Party Chairman, however, Hardie did represent the views of many in the ILP and , although circulation was not large, the paper provided a forum for national debate.[22] During the 1890s the *Labour Leader* carried numerous pieces on women's work, women's suffrage and women's politics. There was also a regular column, 'Matrons and Maidens', written under the pen name of 'Lily Bell', which drew considerable correspondence from readers. The identity of 'Lily Bell' is a controversial question, with some authors claiming that it was none other than Hardie himself. However, in her thesis on 'Lily Bell' Helen Lintell argues convincingly that she was Isabella Bream Pearce, vice President of the Glasgow Labour Party and the wife of Charles Bream Pearce, the ILP candidate for Camlachie. Isabella was elected to the Cathcart School Board in 1894 and attended ILP Annual Conferences in the early 1890s where she was a frequent speaker.[23]

Alongside pieces on equal rights and the need to improve women's employment conditions 'Lily Bell' also explored personal sexual politics and the links between these and political change. She discussed prostitution, the double standard of morality, the detrimental effects on women of their ignorance about sex and women's need to control their own bodies. She believed that men and women should behave differently towards each other and that this was a necessary prerequisite for achieving social change. 'Lily Bell' argues that attitudes towards, and behaviour within, marriage were a crucial test of a man's commitment to a socialist future and that domestic relationships were the central factor determining women's capacity for public action. Rejecting the view that a change in productive relations alone would bring emancipation for women, she called for legal and political equality and a transformation from within of male and female behaviour and attitudes.[24]

Marriage, the family and sexuality were subjects which always provoked controversy in the period and led to differences between feminists themselves, Caroline Martyn, for example was sympathetic to the view that men and women should live together. She argued that this would lead to a higher, more equal form of union than a legal marriage in which a woman was considered to be the property of a man. 'Lily Bell' on the other hand was not prepared to go so far. She was critical of the legal and economic subordination of women within marriage but was unwilling to advocate 'free unions'.[25] Nonetheless, feminists within the ILP all agreed that women's emancipation meant more than the achievement of economic, legal and political equality. They asked for nothing less than a re-definition of appropriate male and female behaviour and a transformation of attitudes towards personal and sexual relationship.

It was argued that such changes would never be brought about unless women took part alongside men in the struggle for socialism. There was always some ambivalence within the ILP about women's propensity to take political action which was shared by many feminists. Women were thought to be submissive and conservative in their attitudes or too bound up in domestic duties to take an interest in political affairs. Nonetheless, feminists tried to understand the reasons for this and were generally positive about women's capacity to take action. It was noted that conventional religious and social thought had conditioned women to be submissive and that this could be challenged.

Apart form the issue of equal rights socialist feminists believed that it was vital for women to take part in ILP politics because their contribution would be based on different experiences. Isabella Ford, for example, argued that because women suffered from so much inequality within the workplace and the home 'everywhere women have greater cause to cry for vengeance than men have, and that is why even for a peaceful revolution such as trade unionism or socialism, the presence and influence of women is absolutely essential'.[26] It was also suggested that women derived special qualities from their role as mothers and homemakers and that these should influence public affairs, since the country was everyone's home.

In raising the importance of differences between the sexes, socialist feminists of the 1890s were not suggesting that women's involvement in politics should only be based on their domestic experiences. Rather, they set out to provide a critique of masculinity and to challenge the view that male and female characteristics were unchangeable. 'Lily Bell', for example, argued that feminine qualities should be valued in the public sphere as much as, or more than, masculine values and the men and women should each adopt the best attributes of both sexes.

> To me Socialism in its fullest sense means the liberation of the feminine element in humanity, which so far has been held in bondage, and thus prevented from entering into the external life of society. The position of women simply represents the actual state of matters which in mankind has brought about present conditions the feminine qualities in man have been suppressed, and never allowed free outlet. His affections, his sympathies, all the finer feelings within himself have been by himself forcibly separated from his outward life. Their place was at home (as women are told now). They had nothing to do with the State, or affairs of the nation, which were solely the province of his intellect alone. They were hardly allowed at all to enter into his relations with his fellow-men, but were limited and confined in every direction – the result being that he has made a hell upon earth, where was meant to be a kingdom of heaven![27]

This feminist vision of the new society was broadly compatible with the more general ethical socialism of the ILP. It also shared similar problems of agency, that is how the desired changes were to be achieve. In 1894 Enid Stacy suggested that there should be an ILP Women's Association, but no action was taken on this and the question of whether women should organise separately within the ILP was not debated very extensively.[28] Locally, however, many branches formed separate women's groups which discussed gender politics and women's participation in the labour movement.

The Matrons and Maidens column was dropped from the *Labour Leader* in 1898, possibly following a disagreement between Keir Hardie and 'Lily Bell', and there was no separate section for women in the paper until 1906 when the Women's Outlook, written by Iona, the pseudonym of Katharine Bruce Glasier, was introduced. This new column was very different in tone from that of 'Lily Bell'. It was often condescending and emphasised the importance of women's role as homemakers. Several feminists, including Isabella Ford, Maud Keary of the Leeds ILP and Ethel Snowden wrote to complain that a mixed sex organisation should not be separating the interests of men and women members. Ethel Snowden thought that 'in matters of citizenship and on questions of the sexes ... for whose benefit is the remainder of the *Labour Leader*? If for men only, why so much more space for men than for women? If for both men and women, why a special column for women? I should like to suggest a special column for men'.[29] This controversy reflected the more general view in the ILP that the Party was so sympathetic to women's issues that there was no need for a separate organisation and therefore there was never a strong momentum to have a women's association at a national level.

The other issue of political strategy which faced ILP feminists in the 1890s was whether they should seek a close association with the women's movement.

A variety of positions were taken on this question. As a member of the Leeds Women's Suffrage Society, Isabella Ford would have liked to see co-operation between the ILP and the women's movement. She linked economic and political questions arguing that, whatever its imperfections, the vote was at least a recognition of equality, and most industrial evils arose from the fact that women were treated as inferiors. the emphasis of her own activities in the 1890s, however, was on the organisation of women into trade unions, coupled with socialist propaganda for the ILP.[30]

Enid Stacy on the other hand described women's rights as a 'middle-class fad', while 'Lily Bell' thought a focus on political rights eclipsed socio-cultural elements in women's oppression.[31] Writing a report on the women's conference at the International Socialist Congress of 1896, May Foster, a member of the Leeds ILP, commented that:

> While the bourgeois women's movement in all lands where it exists has points of great interest and has tended to open the minds of women generally to an examination of the questions which especially affect their sex, it cannot be compared in importance and significance with the organisations for working women ... and with the efforts of individual women working with men in the ranks of Socialism to advance the cause of labour and political freedom.[32]

Feminist socialists were not critical of the 'women's rights' campaign simply because it was identified with middle-class women or because it did not appear to address the needs of working women. They were also critical of the individualist, liberal philosophy which underpinned the movement. This was anathema to socialists who looked for the establishment of a co-operative commonwealth which would be based on collective responsibility. Returning to the theme of difference Enid Stacy, for example, criticised the notion of individual rights which was embedded in the demands of the women's movement. Instead she emphasised women's duties, derived from their role as wives and mothers, which they should exercise in the public sphere for the good of all.

> The question has been placed upon a broader basis, not woman's rights as a middle-class spinster, with a livelihood to fight for, against hostile male forces, but women's duties, not simply as a spinster, but also as a wife and mother, and, in order that she amply fulfil these duties, her freedom as an individual and her equality as a citizen.[33]

Feminists within the ILP, therefore, agreed that sex oppression needed to be discussed separately and should be challenged immediately, but thought that this would best be done by men and women working together within the socialist movement. They saw the oppression of women as multi-faceted, having material, legal, political and sexual causes and located the site of women's oppression within the family and domestic labour as well as within the workplace. While recognising differences in the experiences of men and women they did not seek to confine women to the domestic sphere. Rather, they sought improvement at the workplace as well as in the home, to foster collective action among working women and to extend the range of choices available in women's lives. They also called for socialist men to change their attitudes and behaviour towards women rather than simply seeking the removal of formal obstacles to equality.

These ideas were not accepted wholeheartedly within the ILP; a much narrower view of sex equality was often put forward and there was no agreement that priority should be given to issues of special interest to women. There was also little consistency in the opinions expressed about women's potential for political activity. A wide variety of images of women were juxtaposed in the *Labour Leader*. In contrast to the view of 'Lily Bell' that 'womanliness stands for strength and courage and endurance', much of the fiction, cartoons and more serious political articles in the paper variously portrayed women as 'insubstantially youthful ... lethargic, inferior, apathetic, full of pretence and hopelessly dominated by men',[34] without any sympathetic understanding the social conditioning which might have produced such characteristics. This led Isabella Ford to complain that 'it is so easy to rail at the tiresomeness, the stupidity of women – we all do it – and so pleasant to have a good supply of domestic scapegoats, that we never stop to think is our railing really justified ...'[35] Whether consciously or unconsciously appeals for members were often couched in male language; John Lindsley, secretary of Sunderland ILP, wrote a pamphlet with the title *Young Manhood and Socialism*, while even Hardie addressed his propaganda to 'Young Men in a Hurry!'[36]

ILP pamphlets which described the benefits of a socialist future made few specific references to the position of women. Instead, they made a more indirect appeal to women in suggesting that socialism would benefit family life by improving child health, education and living standards.[37] The identification of women's interests with changes in the domestic sphere became increasingly common. In her pamphlet *Why Women Want Socialism*, Julia Dawson claimed that under socialism every woman and child would be looked after by the State. The removal of poverty would alter relationships within the family and transform the quality of domestic life. Socialism would free women from the drudgery of family life by the collective organisation of cooking, cleaning and mending. This would not undermine the sex division of labour but free women to give a full-time commitment to the more important and pleasurable work of caring for children.[38]

The importance of women's role in the domestic sphere and the need to end their double burden of paid and unpaid work lay at the heart of ILP appeals to women. A leaflet produced in 1894, addressed *To the Women of the ILP*, claimed than none were so brutally enslaved as women who were forced to work in the mills and factories because their husbands could not earn enough to keep them at home. 'For a wife and mother to work all day and then to be called upon to do her housework at night, is sufficient to drive one to revolting point'.[39] The leaflet urged women to study the Labour problem, with help from their local branches, so that they could encourage children to understand social problems and join with men to achieve change. 'Labour women join with the men in raising Labour's standard, that real life shall become possible. Do not wait till it shall become more fashionable to endorse Labour politics; but right away embrace the labour gospel and work for social redemption'.[40]

Thus women received contradictory messages in the propaganda put out by the ILP. On the one hand they were viewed as conservative or uninterested in politics, because they were bound up in the details of family life. On the other hand, they were urged to take part in the struggle for socialism in order to bring improvements in the domestic sphere and because their influence on other family members could be so great. The failure to challenge the sex division of labour at the workplace or in the home had several advantages for a socialist organisation concerned to emphasise class exploitation and to forge links with the trade union movement. H. Russell Smart may have argued that the tyranny women suffered in the workplace was 'supplemented by a worse tyranny in the home',[41] but the mainstream view of the ILP was to deny a conflict of interest between the sexes in the working class and to emphasise capitalist exploitation rather than male power over women.[42]

As Margaret McMillan so perceptively noted, 'the Independent Labour Party was not formed to champion women. It was born to make war on capitalism and competition'.[43] In practice, therefore, issues which highlighted women's disabilities as a sex were not given a high profile or translated into specific campaigns. A resolution was passed at the 1895 Annual Conference to the effect that the 'Independent Labour Party is in favour of every proposal for extending electoral rights to both men and women and democratising the system of government', but this did not result in any sustained campaign on franchise questions.[44] During the 1890s the ILP concentrated on economic issues such as unemployment and building up links with the trade unions in order to further the cause of independent labour politics.

The ILP did aim to welcome women as members and there were no formal barriers to women's participation at all levels of the organisation. Nonetheless, little was done in any positive sense to attract women into socialist politics. Only a small number of women held any official positions which may have made it difficult for them to influence policy. In most years there was one female member on the NAC, usually one of the educated middle-class propagandists such as Enid Stacy, while approximately ten per cent of Conference delegates were women.[45]

At branch level, however, women, in particular working-class women, took the opportunity to be far more extensively involved in ILP politics. The encouragement given to women and the extent and nature of their participation varied from region to region and was affected by local work opportunities, the political traditions of a branch, the nature of local leadership and the culture of socialist politics in an area. Few women took on official posts, such as secretary or treasurer,[46] but they did take part in a wide range of other activities, in particular in Lancashire, the West Riding of Yorkshire and Scotland where they joined campaigns over housing, unemployment, rents and education. Eleonor Gordon has suggested that the emphasis on social and political, as well as industrial, struggles at a local level encouraged women's participation and provided them with space to make a contribution to socialist politics.[47]

Some branches, for example Glasgow and Bradford, set up separate women's groups to provide a non-threatening context in which working-class women could begin to express their political views. Very often they concentrated on organising social events, but these had a real significance at a time when socialists felt beleaguered in a hostile environment. The creation of a social world for all members of the family helped to 'make socialists' and contributed to feelings of solidarity and comradeship.[48]

On the other hand, many women gained a very varied political experience at a local level and were not confined to a 'tea-making' role. In Manchester Emmeline Pankhurst made her name at free speech demonstrations at Boggart Hole Clough in 1896 while in Leeds, the young schoolteacher Mary Gawthorpe, vice-president of the local ILP branch, was particularly active in unemployment campaigns. When property qualifications were removed in 1894 many ILP women stood for election to Boards of Guardians, including Selina Cooper and Harriet Beanland in Burnley, Hannah Mitchell in Ashton and Mary Taylor in Halifax. By 1908 their numbers had grown to 33.[49]

Local branches also became involved in he industrial struggles of women workers. In Crewe, for example, Ada Neild Chew received help from the ILP branch in her efforts to improve the work conditions of tailoresses and she became a member of the branch as a result. During the 1890s she travelled with the *Clarion* van as an ILP speaker and addressed numerous meetings on the need to improve the work conditions of both men and women. She was also elected to the Nantwich Board of Guardians. In 1900 Ada Neild Chew was appointed as a full-time organiser for the Women's Trade Union League but continued to be active in the ILP, speaking on numerous topics related to women such as 'Should Women Have the Vote?', 'Should Women Support Trade Unionism?' and 'My Work among Women'.[50]

Women involved in local socialist politics had many difficulties to overcome. They had to assert themselves if they were not just to be confined to a supportive social role and to challenge prejudices about their political capabilities. They rarely received much help within the home, even from socialist husbands, as Hannah Mitchell's frequently quoted autobiography shows.[51] When dealing with issues related to women they often had to walk a tightrope between loyalty to their class and to their sex. The industrial struggles of women workers, for example, frequently highlighted tensions between the sexes over protective legislation, the introduction of women into 'male' work and married women's employment.[52] Compromises were usually reached in order to preserve labour unity and emphasis was placed on improving women's work conditions while leaving men's position at the workplace unchallenged.

After the turn of the century, however, as women in ILP branches took a greater interest in the vote, it became more difficult to ignore the potential for conflict between the interests of men and women in the Party. The struggle for women's suffrage raised the profile of sex equality in the branches and also attracted more female members for the ILP. For a brief few years this one aspect of the 'woman question' became a topic of national importance, dividing ILP members over priorities and tactics and revealing in an acute form the tension between class and gender politics. The suffrage campaign focused on an inequality that was clearly based on sex and which affected all women. Moreover, it gave women a practical goal, the achievement of political equality, which, it was argued, could then provide the means to gain further changes.

Working-class women in Lancashire provided the main impetus for a revival of interest in the suffrage. Jill Liddington and Jill Norris' pioneering study of radical suffragists in Lancashire reveals how textile workers and trade unionists, members of the Women's Co-operative Guild, the ILP and the North of England Women's Suffrage Society all came together after 1900 to demand the enfranchisement of women.[53] They had already gained political experience in a variety of campaigns in the 1890s and were used to working with each other. The petition that they distributed to mill workers explicitly raised the needs of women as waged workers as well as homemakers. The text claimed that the denial of the franchise lowered women's position in the home, while in the factory 'their unrepresented condition places the regulation of their work in the hands of men who are often their rivals as well as their fellow workers'.[54] This brief reference to the conflict of interest between male and female workers provides an indication of why the suffrage was to become such a controversial issue for socialists Nonetheless, in the heady days of the petition the potential for disagreement was put to one side.

The enthusiasm shown by Lancashire working women for the vote encouraged Emmeline and Christabel Pankhurst, along with other members of the Manchester ILP, to set up the Women's Social and Political Union (WSPU) in 1903. They aimed to use direct action to publicise their claim for votes for women on the same terms as men and received financial help and moral support from the local ILP. For the next four years speakers from the WSPU carried out propaganda for both social and women's rights throughout the North of England. The sense of excitement generated by the campaign inspired many women to become members of the ILP. Eleonor Gordon suggests, for example, that the sympathetic coverage given to the women' suffrage campaign in the *Glasgow Forward* may have been one reason for the local ILP's success in attracting women members.[55]

Nationally too the campaign had an impact. The main debate now was not over whether socialists should work alongside a women's rights campaign, but whether they should support the demand for votes for women on the same terms as men. Only a small percentage of women would have received the vote under existing qualifications and therefore it was termed a limited franchise. In 1904 the ILP Annual Conference supported a resolution in favour of a limited franchise and reaffirmed this stand in subsequent years. Nonetheless there were many members of the ILP, including some of the leadership, who argued that a socialist party should be demanding nothing less than full adult suffrage for all.

On the surface, debate over the franchise question appeared to revolve around the details of who would gain the vote. Opponents of a limited franchise, for example, argued that only propertied women would receive the vote. This would be of no help to working-class women and could be detrimental to the electoral chances of the Labour Party. Ada Neild Chew thought that socialists should work for a Bill 'which would enable a man or a woman to vote simply because they are man and woman, not because they are more fortunate financially than their fellow men and women'.[56]

This was a logical position for a socialist to take, but it sidestepped the thorny issue of political priorities. Supporters of a limited franchise were no longer willing to wait for a distant future, when every adult might have the vote, and to ignore the fact that women, simply on account of their sex, were disenfranchised in the present. Thus support for the demand for votes for women on the same terms as men came to be seen as a test of socialist commitment to sex equality.

For Keir Hardie, a consistent supporter of a limited franchise, it was a point of principle that 'sex disability' should be eliminated before there could be any movement for adult suffrage. It was necessary to remove women 'from the sphere of "idiots, lunatics and paupers", and to recognise that, woman though she be, she is a human being who may become a citizen'.[57] Other supporters claimed that 'until the sex disability was removed the organisation of workers on class-conscious lines would be hindered by the cross current of women's interests' and that economic equality could never be achieved without political equality.[58]

Adult suffragists took almost the opposite point of view. One delegate to the Annual Conference of 1905 claimed that 'he looked upon this matter from a class point of view and refused to look at it from the point of view of sex'.[59] William Anderson, who later became a Labour MP and married the trade-union leader Mary Macarthur, feared that any attempt to focus on women's common oppression would undermine labour unity and divert attention from class exploitation:

> It is inconsistent for a Socialist Party to lend its support to a movement which is deliberately attempting to distract the attention of women workers from the wrongs of their class to the wrongs of their sex ... Lancashire working women were being taught that all their woes may be traced to their voteless condition, and they are kept blind to the fact that there is no sex in industry, and that lack of organisation is the primary cause of bad conditions.[60]

The high profile of the suffrage campaign affected the tone in which the ILP appealed to women and addressed their needs. As a member of the NAC between 1903 and 1907 Isabella Ford was able to exert more influence over official policy because she had a growing women's suffrage movement behind her. It is likely, for example, that she wrote the new leaflet *What Socialism Means for Women*, published as part of the Platform series in 1904. It contrasts in both content and style with an earlier one, *Women and Socialism*, which appeared as part of the same series in 1900.

In the earlier version concern was expressed that women were bounded in their outlook by the immediate concerns of their families and were disinterested in political life. The leaflet aimed to show women that public policies on education and social reform affected the family and therefore were of vital concern to women. 'By all means let the home and children to be the house-mother's first care, but let her recognise that she has not fulfilled here whole duty when the kitchen range is nicely swept, and the stockings neatly darned'. In a rather patronising statement the leaflet concluded by recognising that women were very busy, but 'it does not take long to give a little sympathetic attention to what is going on, to talk with the husband about the local or national politics he is interested in...'[61]

The later pamphlet takes a much more positive view of women's potential as political activists and is never condescending in tone. Its aim is to show what socialism would mean for women in all aspects of their lives and not just in their role as mothers and homemakers. The leaflet starts with the message that socialism means freedom for women just as much as for men. To obtain that freedom women must have the vote for 'nothing awakens peoples minds, nothing educates them so much as responsibility'. It goes on to make a series of demands which are in no way confined to women's domestic responsibilities: 'Women want better wages, better factory legislation, better conditions in the workshops. They want better houses ... they want good food ... they want an equal share with men in the custody of their children ... Socialism, when it demands freedom, demands it for all, and not as the other parties in the political world have hitherto done, for men first, for women second'.[62]

As the leaflet suggests feminists within the ILP did not narrow their focus to a demand for political equality alone and they continued to develop a theoretical perspective to link feminism and socialism. Nonetheless, the importance of the suffrage as a pre-requisite for change in women's social position now loomed larger in their analysis that it had done in the 1890s. Teresa Billington, a colleague of the Pankhursts in the Manchester ILP, a founder member of WSPU, and a paid organiser for the ILP from 1904–5, argued against the view so prevalent in socialist circles that women's emancipation could wait until after the revolution for 'sex equality is an absolutely indispensable preliminary to the reorganisation of society ...' She denied the right of male socialists to determine the basis on which women should vote, arguing that it was only just for women to have the vote on the same terms as men, even if those terms were less than ideal: 'Women are entitled to equal recognition now, not only when the millennium is reached. They are not entitled to the greater or less measure of freedom which men may be willing to give, they are entitled to equal freedom with men'.[63]

218

Political inequality was not the only cause of women's oppression, but the vote would provide the means to deal with other problems, Isabella Ford thought that women needed to have a say in legislation which affected their lives since 'to work for female factory legislation before demanding full political power for the women workers, so that they themselves may work out their industrial salvation as men have done, is hindering the emancipation of women's labour ...'[64] Similarly, she argued that trade unions were only likely to flourish among women when 'on election days the female union voice can make itself heard alongside of the male trade union voice'.[65]

By raising women's status and feelings of self worth political equality would also help to bring the inner change which was so necessary for women to be free. Teresa Billington sought women's emancipation from 'all shackles of law and custom, from all chains of sentiment and superstition, from all outer imposed disabilities and cherished inner bondages which unite to shut off liberty from the human soul borne in her body'.[66] In a passage reminiscent of Enid Stacy in the 1890s Billington demanded that women's dependent role should be changed by a recognition of women's rights at the workplace, motherhood by choice, the elimination of repressive marriage customs, changes in attitudes towards prostitution and 'unrecognized' sex relations, and a rejection of the family as the recognised unit of society.

It was from a similarly broad perspective that Isabella Ford wrote her pamphlet *Women and Socialism*, which was the most sustained attempt to date by an ILP member to theorise the relationship between class and sex oppression. Isabella was by then a member of the NAC, a close friend of the leaders of the Party and a frequent contributor to the *Labour Leader*. Her pamphlet was given official approval by the NAC and published under ILP auspices in 1904. A revised version was produced in 1906.[67]

Written in the midst of the revival of the suffrage movement the pamphlet aimed to persuade the ILP, and the labour movement, to make common cause with the women's movement. To that end Isabella Ford argued that both movements were inextricably linked. Male workers and all women were economically dependent on the owners of private property and their status had grown steadily worse since the fifteenth century. Women, however, were not only economically subordinate to the workplace but were also oppressed within the home.

She argued that the home life of the family was of key importance for social change, since it was there that men and women developed a sense of citizenship. And yet poor social conditions meant that homes were hardly fit places in which to rear children and to develop values of truth and justice. For these reasons she refused to sentimentalise motherhood and argued that social reforms were necessary before there could be any 'recognition or understanding of the real value of motherhood'.[68] In a revised edition of the pamphlet, published in 1906, Isabella suggested that men were the oppressors in the family since the two sexes stood in a false position of inequality towards each other and that 'falseness spreads, as a fungus spreads its evil growth, into their relationship with others'.[69] Personal life and politics, therefore, were closely intertwined. 'To destroy the injustice of sex disability will, many of us hold, so immensely help to clear the world's vision ... that we shall be able to see how to establish a true enfranchisement for all, and bring an ever widening justice, in which we shall then include love of the human race, into all the relationships of life'.[70]

Isabella Ford did not dwell on the oppression of women by men. She argued that although all women suffered from economic and social dependence on men, working-class men and women suffered from the injustices of capitalism and therefore needed to work together to achieve economic and political freedom. Moreover, men suffered economically from women's political slavery. Her task of integrating the needs of women of all classes with those of working-class men was made easier by her view of what socialism meant and how it could be achieved. Along with other ILP leaders she thought that the labour movement had gone beyond class war and she believed that all men and women could be persuaded by the justice of socialist claims to work together to achieve a 'cooperative commonwealth', once they realised that it implied a higher form of civilisation.[71]

It was at this point that she raised questions of difference. The Labour movement and the women's movement could benefit each other enormously since they brought different qualities; 'The Labour movement will keep the economic side in view, a side women are apt to overlook, and of which they frequently fail to understand the vast moral significance. Women will help to keep more clearly before our eyes, than is always possible now, those great ideals for which, after all, labour representation is but a means of accomplishment'.[72]

ILP suffragists also used the notion of women's different qualities in their attempts to persuade sceptical colleagues that women voters would bring positive benefits to society. Elizabeth Wolstenholme Elmy, who had been involved in women's rights campaigns since the 1860s, suggested that domestic life, far from making women conservative, could make them into a force for social change. The values derived from the home were ones of cooperation, love and caring which would be needed in the new collectivist state. She quoted approvingly from Darwin that 'woman seems to differ from man in mental disposition, chiefly in greater tenderness and less selfishness ...'[73] If women worked for socialism on a basis of equality with men they would 'insist that the ethics of the home shall be the ethics of public life, and the morality of man not lower than the morality of woman ... the society o the future ... must include the love and intuition of the woman, and the genius and strength of the man'.[74]

 Thus feminists sought equality, but did not deny difference, and part of their demand for sex equality was that motherhood and childcare should be valued equally with waged work. This did not mean, however, that they saw women as confined by their domestic role and they challenged any sentimentalising of family life. Isabella Ford, for example, wanted to wipe out the view that 'women are naturally more angelic than men, and somehow possess more first-hand knowledge about heaven'.[75] As in the 1890s they wanted to assert the positive values of feminine characteristics, to challenge aspects of masculinity and to use women's experience as workers and in the domestic sphere to change political life. In the hands of those in the ILP who had less of a feminist perspective, however, concepts of difference could be used to form the basis for drawing women into public support for the Party, while confining interest in their needs to domestic questions. At the same time men's privileged position at home and in the workplace was left unchallenged. This in turn affected the extent to which women made a contribution to the ILP, the development of its policies and the building of a popular politics before 1914.

The tendency to concentrate on difference was reinforced when many active suffragists began to give a full-time commitment to the suffrage campaign and withdrew for a time from socialist politics. Members of the WSPU in particular were growing increasingly impatient with the labour movement. At successive annual conferences the Labour Party refused to support a 'limited' suffrage position and even the ILP did not appear to be giving the campaign top priority. On the other hand ILP members were highly critical of the actions of the WSPU at the Cockermouth bye-election of 1906 when the women carried out propaganda against the Labour as well as the Liberal candidate.

This led to a fierce debate at the ILP Annual Conference of 1907 about the loyalty of WSPU activists. Feelings ran high, but Conference delegates were unwilling to censure WSPU members or to call for their resignation and proceeded to elect Mrs Pankhurst as a delegate to the Labour Party Annual Conference. Despite protests from John Bruce Glasier and others the Conference agreed, by a large majority, to send a telegram of support to imprisoned suffragettes 'for their fidelity to the cause of sex equality' and congratulating them on their 'courage in suffering the rigours of our inhuman prison system'.[76]

These sympathetic resolutions did not, however, prevent many of the leaders of the WSPU from resigning their membership of the ILP. They began to run their campaign from London and severed any formal links between the WSPU and the labour movement. Other ILP suffragists had taken a more conciliatory stand at the Conference; Isabella Ford, Ethel Snowden, Charlotte Despard and Annie Cobden Sanderson had pledged not to go into any constituency at an election unless it was to help the Labour candidate. Nonetheless, even they were now so committed to winning the suffrage before any other cause that they put all their energies into the suffrage movement rather than playing a large part in ILP politics.[77] This must have contributed to the fact that the ILP appeared to give only lukewarm support to women's suffrage after 1907; individual MPs such as Keir Hardie and Philip Snowden continued to champion the women's cause in Parliament, but the adult suffragists Mary Macarthur and Fred Jowett, chairman of the Party, were in positions of influence on the NAC. It was also suggested that the *Labour Leader* gave too little coverage to the suffrage campaign now that the adult suffragist John Bruce Glasier was editor. The growing influence of adult suffragists led Ethel Snowden to resign from the ILP, while Isabella Ford warned that if a limited suffrage were no longer ILP policy 'many of us will be compelled to leave that party for which we care so much'.[78]

At a local level the boundaries between groups were more fluid and women still combined socialist and suffragist politics. They frequently managed to remain as members of the WSPU and of the ILP even though this could cause tensions. Local branches invited a variety of speakers from all the different suffrage groups; in 1908, for example, the Gloucester ILP attracted a large audience for Christabel Pankhurst who was speaking on Votes for Women, while Selina Cooper, an ILP member and paid organiser for the National Union of Women's Suffrage Societies, Mrs Despard and Teresa Billington-Greig frequently spoke at ILP meetings throughout the North of England.[79]

After 1906, however, ILP women became increasingly involved in campaigns which emphasised their role within the domestic sphere. This was reinforced by their participation in a new organisation, the Women's Labour League (WLL), which was established in 1906 to encourage women to take a more active part in politics on behalf of the Labour Party. The early leaders, Margaret MacDonald and Mary Middleton, sought to educate women in political and social questions through meetings and discussions and to build up the confidence of working women as propagandists. Branches had considerable autonomy and emphasis was placed on women working from their own experience, in particular from within the home. On this basis many women were put forward for election to public bodies such as Boards of Guardians, and the League became associated with campaigns on baby clinics, school meals and health.[80]

The League did succeed in involving more women in labour politics, but adopted the view that in this way they could best serve their homes and families. At the founding conference it was claimed that 'they wanted to show the wives of trade unionists and cooperators particularly ... that the best way to look after their homes was by taking an interest in the life of the community'.[81] Caroline Rowan suggests that while this approach 'put the working conditions of housewives on the political agenda for the first time, it did so in a way that reinforced the existing sex division of labour'.[82]

Issues which caused most controversy for the League, therefore, were those which challenged the sex division of labour or which appeared to give priority to the oppression of women as a sex. There were lively debates, for example, on the question of women's suffrage. A compromise was reached whereby local branches were left free to decide whether to support a limited or an adult suffrage position, while at a national level the League did not take a particular stand. The economic independence of married women was another controversial issue. Some members advocated that mothers should receive a state endowment which would give them economic security and also make motherhood attractive. Opponents of the scheme feared that it would reduce male wages and remove men's responsibility for their families. Many labour men also feared that male privileges and authority within the home would be undermined. Given that the primary purpose of the League was to ensure support for the Labour Party it once again failed to take a stand on the issue in the interests of labour unity.[83]

Increasingly, in both the WLL and the ILP, women were welcomed as workers for socialism and labour politics and were able to carve a role for themselves, but it was one which was bound up with, rather than challenging, their domesticity and the differentiation of roles between the sexes. Thus women were actively encouraged to stand for election to Boards of Guardians, but very few were put forward as candidates for the more prestigious Borough Councils.[84] The NAC of the ILP claimed that it hoped to see ILP women becoming candidates in large numbers, but nothing concrete was done to ensure that this would happen.[85]

When the Labour Party finally agreed to support the cause of women's suffrage in 1912 suffragists were brought back into the fold of labour and socialist politics. It could be suggested, however, that this ensured that feminist aims would be subsumed in class politics, a trend that was reinforced by the war and the achievement of the vote itself. Women's active participation in labour and socialist politics was now assured, but their interests were seen to lie in social reforms affecting children and the home, rather than in challenging their unequal position at the workplace.[86] In some respects this had been encouraged by ILP suffragists who had emphasised women's special qualities derived from the domestic sphere, but it was a far cry from the vision of the socialist feminist pioneers that women's emancipation would mean a transformation in all areas of life – the political, the economic and the personal, and that all these aspects were inextricably linked.

Socialist feminists throughout Europe were sensitive to issues of male dominance and economic oppression, but constantly had to perform a balancing act between loyalty to party and furthering feminist demands.[87] They found a warmer welcome for their ideas within the ILP than in many other socialist groups and this may explain the very widespread belief among contemporaries, both male and female, that the ILP was committed to sex equality. The importance of women's suffrage for feminists in the pre-war years helped to reinforce this view. The ILP was the only political group in Britain to officially endorse the demand for votes for women on the same terms as men at its Annual Conferences and, apart from the Fabian Society, was alone in supporting a limited franchise at the 1907 International Socialist Congress at Stuttgart.[88] Even former opponents of a limited franchise, such as William Anderson and John Bruce Glasier, came to emphasise the role of the ILP in supporting suffragist demands.[89]

The broad, non-doctrinaire approach to socialism of the ILP meant that it was not a foregone conclusion that class issues would have priority over all other interests and there was room, as in the suffrage debate, to put an alternative point of view. Nonetheless, the influence of contemporary ideas on womanhood, sexuality and the family, coupled with involvement in a Labour

Party which had roots in the trade union as well as in the socialist movement, leant a certain ambivalence to the ILP's theory and practice concerning the oppression of women. Sex equality, therefore, came to have a multi-layered meaning.

On one level it clearly meant formal equality between the sexes, in the legal, political and economic sphere, although in practice the attitude of the ILP towards economic equality was ambiguous. The Party called for equal pay for equal work and supported efforts to improve women' conditions of employment, but only if this did to threaten the position of the male breadwinner at the workplace. The assumption that the aim of socialists should be to relieve women of their double burden of paid work and domestic labour, freeing them to concentrate on the family, meant that women's needs as wage earners were not given priority. Indeed, for the ILP sex equality also meant giving equal value to motherhood and domestic labour alongside waged work and women were encouraged to become involved in socialist politics on that basis.

Despite an increasing number of studies of women's involvement in labour politics, in particular at a local level, we still know far too little about the theory of the ILP in relation to the 'woman question' and the extent to which this affected its recruitment of female members and the nature of their participation in socialist politics. General histories of the ILP continue to either minimise the importance of the 'woman question' or are critical of claims made that the Party was sympathetic to feminist aims. Thus issues relating to gender politics are left, with notable exceptions, to specific studies of women and are not integrated into mainstream accounts of socialist organisations.[90]

Rather than seeking to test ILP statements about sex equality against an ideal that the Party clearly did not, and perhaps could not, live up to, historians need to explore the complexities of gender and class relations, in particular at a local level. There can be little doubt that issues around sex oppression, and the nature of women's involvement in socialist politics, were of vital interest to the ILP in this period. We need to know more, therefore, about what this meant on the ground, to what extent attitudes towards sex equality affected women's participation in ILP politics, what kind of campaigns involved women and in what ways and whether class and gender politics were linked in particular local areas. This would enhance our understanding of women's role, not only within the early ILP but also within the post-war Labour Party and contribute to the debate about the uneasy relationship between feminism and socialism which has continued to the present day.

NOTES

1. Walt Whitman, quoted in S. Bryher, *The Labour and Socialist Movement in Bristol* (Bristol, 1929), p.5.
2. K. Hardie, *After Twenty Years: All About the ILP* (ILP, 1913), p.13.

3. The term feminist is used throughout the chapter, although it was not used by contemporaries, to describe campaigns (and those who took part) in which women identified with each other in political struggles which challenged, and sought to improve, women's social position. See P. Levine, *Victorian Feminism, 1850–1900* (Hutchinson, 1987), Introduction.

4. J. Clayton, *The Rise and Decline of Socialism in Great Britain, 1884–1924* (Faber & Gwyer, 1926), pp.84–5.

5. I. O. Ford, 'Why Women Should Be Socialists', *Labour Leader*, 1 May 1913.

6. J. Bruce Glasier, *Keir Hardie: The Man and His Message* (ILP, 1913), p.9.

7. O. Banks, *Faces of Feminism* (Oxford, Martin Robertson, 1980), p.123.

8. Ibid., p.128.

9. K. Hunt, 'Equivocal Feminists: The Social Democratic Federation and the Woman Question, 1884–1911', unpublished PhD thesis, University of Manchester, 1988, p.2.

10. E. Gordon, *Women and the Labour Movement in Scotland, 1850–1914* (Oxford, Clarendon Press, 1991), pp.271–3.

11. See B. S. Anderson and J. P. Zinsser, *A History of Their Own: Women in Europe* (Harmondsworth, Penguin, 1988); R. J. Evans, *The Feminists* (Croom Helm, 1977); M. J. Boxer and J. H. Quataert, *Socialist Women: European Socialist Feminism in the Nineteenth and Early Twentieth Centuries* (New York, Elsevier, 1978).

12. For a discussion of the work of Engels and Bebel, see Hunt, 'Equivocal Feminists', chapter 2; L. C. Johnson, 'Socialist Feminisms', in S. Gunew, (ed.) *Feminist Knowledge: Critique and Construct* (Routledge, 1990).

13. J. K. Hardie, 'An Indictment of the Class War', *Labour Leader*, 2 Sept 1904. J. R. MacDonald also thought that socialism marked the growth of a society 'not the uprising of a class'. See A. Wright, *British Socialism* (Longman, 1983), p.12.

14. S. Rowbotham and J. Weeks, *Socialism and the New Life: The Personal and Sexual Politics of Edward Carpenter and Havelock Ellis* (Pluto, 1977), p.66. See also S. Yeo, 'A New Life: The Religion of Socialism in Britain, 1883–1896', *History Workshop Journal*, 4, Autumn 1977.

15. This contrasts with the attitudes of socialist feminists in other European countries who, it is suggested , put socialism first in any conflict between socialism and feminism. See Anderson and Zinsser, *op. cit.*, p.372 and Boxer and Quataert, *op. cit.*

16. A. Tuckett, 'Enid Stacy', *North West Labour History Society*, Bulletin 7, 1980–1. See also Bryher, *op. cit.*, and K. Bruce Glasier, *Enid Stacy* (ILP, 1924). Enid Stacy was a member of the NAC in 1895 and 1896.

17. E. Stacy, 'A Century of Women's Rights', in E. Carpenter (ed.) *Forecasts of the Coming Century* (Manchester, Labour Press, 1899).

18. J. Hannam, *Isabella Ford, 1855–1924* (Oxford, Blackwell, 1989).

19. *Leeds Forward*, Oct 1898.

20. Hannam, *op. cit.*, pp.64–6, 72–8 and A. Phillips, *Divided Loyalties: Dilemmas of Sex and Class* (Virago, 1987), chapter 4.

21. Liddington and Norris, *op. cit.*, pp.239–40.

22. K. O. Morgan, *Keir Hardie: Radical and Socialist* (Weidenfeld, 1975).

23. H. Lintell, 'Lily Bell: Socialist and Feminist, 1894–1898', unpublished MA thesis, Bristol Polytechnic, 1990. Authors who claim that Hardie was Lily Bell include Morgan, *op. cit.*, p.66; C. Collette, *For Labour and For Women: the Women's Labour League, 1906–18* (Manchester, Manchester University Press, 1987), p.19;

C. Stevens, 'The Objections of "Queer Hardie", "Lily Bell" and the Suffragette's Friend to Queen Victoria's Jubilee, 1897', *Victorian Periodical Review*, 21, 3, 1988.

24. Lintell, *op. cit.*
25. Both women expressed their views in reaction to the Elsa Lanchester case which is fully discussed in Hunt, *op. cit.*, chapter 5.
26. *Leeds Forward*, Dec 1898.
27. *Labour Leader*, 8 Feb 1896.
28. Collette, *op. cit.*, p.19.
29. *Labour Leader*, 23 Mar 1906.
30. I. O. Ford, 'The Woman's Movement', *Humanity*, iii, 50, Jan 1899.
31. *Justice*, 13 Oct 1894.
32. *Illustrated Report of the Proceedings of the Workers' Congress Held in London, July 1896* (Labour Leader, 1896), p.84.
33. Stacy, 'A Century of Women's Rights', quoted in Liddington and Norris, *op. cit.*, p.130.
34. Lintell, *op. cit.*, p.67.
35. I. O. Ford, 'Woman As She Was and Is', *Labour Leader*, 13 May 1904.
36. J. Lindsley, *Young Manhood and Socialism* (ILP, 1903); K. Hardie, *Young Men in A Hurry* (Labour Leader, 1898).
37. For example, see K. Bruce Glasier, *The Road to Socialism* (Manchester, Labour Press, 1895).
38. J. Dawson, *Why Women Want Socialism* (ILP, 1904).
39. 'To Women of the ILP', 1894, Francis Johnson Collection.
40. *Ibid.*
41. H. Russell Smart, *The Right to Work* (ILP, 1896).
42. For example, see Dawson, *op. cit.*
43. M. McMillan, *The Life of Rachel McMillan*, quoted in Liddington and Norris, *op. cit.*, p.131.
44. *ILP Annual Conference Report, 1895*, p.10.
45. Calculated from *ILP Annual Conference Reports*, 1893–1914.
46. *ILP Annual Conference Reports* list branch secretaries. In 1908, for example, there were only eight female secretaries in nearly 200 branches.
47. E. Gordon, *op. cit.*, pp.264–5.
48. See Yeo, *op. cit.*, for the importance of 'making socialists'.
49. *ILP Annual Conference Report, 1908*. For the local activities of ILP women, Gordon, *op. cit.*, Liddington and Norris, *op. cit.*; J. Hannam, '"In the Comradeship of the Sexes Lies the Hope of Progress and Social Regeneration": Women in the West Riding ILP, c.1890–1914', in J. Rendall (ed.), *Equal or Different: Women's Politics, 1800–1914* (Oxford: Blackwell, 1987)
50. D. N. Chew, *Ada Neild Chew: The Life and Writings of a Working Woman* (Virago, 1982).
51. H. Mitchell, *The Hard Way Up: The Autobiography of Hannah Mitchell, Suffragette and Rebel* (Virago, 1977).
52. For example, see Hannam, *Isabella Ford*, chapter 4.
53. Liddington and Norris, *op. cit.*, chapter 12.
54. *Ibid.*, p.145.
55. Gordon, *op. cit.*, p. 264.
56. Chew, *op. cit*, p.38. For a discussion of the arguments between limited and adult suffragists, see S. Holton, *Feminism and Democracy: Women's Suffrage and Reform*

Politics in Britain, 1900–1918 (Cambridge, Cambridge University Press, 1986).

57. K. Hardie, *The Citizenship of Women: A Plea for Women's Suffrage* (1906), p.11.

58. Mr. H. S. Wishart delegate from Woolwich, *ILP Annual Conference Report, 1905*, p.35. See also speech of Teresa Billington, Manchester.

59. Mr. Campbell, delegate from Walthamstow, *ibid.*, p.36.

60. *Labour Leader*, 18 Nov 1904.

61. *Women and Socialism* (ILP, Platform Series no. 104, 1900).

62. *What Socialism Means for Women* (ILP, Platform Series no. 131, 1904).

63. T. Billington-Greig, 'Socialism and Sex Equality', in *New Age*, 20 June 1907, in C. McPhee and A. Fitzgerald (eds.), *The Non-Violent Militant: Selected Writings of Teresa Billington-Greig* (Routledge & Kegan Paul, 1987), p.131.

64. *Labour Leader*, 16 Jan 1904.

65. I. O. Ford, *Industrial Women and How to Help Them* (Humanitarian League, 1901), p.10.

66. T. Billington-Greig, 'The Militant Suffrage Movement (1911)', p.137 in McPhee and Fitzgerald, *op. cit.*, p.9.

67. For the approval of the ILP, see *Labour Leader*, 16 Sept 1904.

68. I. O. Ford, *Women and Socialism* (ILP, 1904), p.10.

69. I. O. Ford, *Women and Socialism* (ILP, 1906), p.3.

70. *Ibid.*, p.13.

71. *Ibid.*, p.12.

72. *Ibid.*, p.13.

73. E. Wolstenholme Elmy, *Woman the Communist* (ILP, 1904), p.14. Isabella Ford made a similar point when she quoted approvingly from the Social Darwinist, Karl Pearson, that a woman was so used to thinking of others rather than herself that she 'may be able to submit her liberty to the restraints demanded by social welfare, and to the conditions needed for race permanence'. Ford, *Women and Socialism* (1904), pp.13–14.

74. Elmy, *op. cit.*, p.15.

75. I. O. Ford, 'Why Women Should Be Socialists'.

76. *ILP Annual Conference Report*, 1907.

77. For example, Mrs Despard, Teresa Billington-Greig and Annie Cobden Sanderson were active in the Women's Freedom League. Ethel Snowden, Isabella Ford and Selina Cooper worked for the National Union of Women's Suffrage Societies. Selina Cooper and Ada Nield Chew were paid organisers of the NUWSS.

78. *Labour Leader*, 5 Nov 1909.

79. Advertisements for meetings in the *Labour Leader*; leaflet of the Gloucester ILP, 1908, Francis Johnson Collection.

80. Collette, *op. cit.* See also P. Hollis, *Ladies Elect: Women in English Local Government, 1865–1914* (Oxford, Oxford University Press, 1987).

81. Report of the First Conference of the Women's Labour League, 1906, p.2.

82. C. Rowan, '"Mothers Vote Labour!" The State, the Labour Movement and Working-Class Mothers, 1900–1918', in R. Bunt and C. Rowan (eds.) *Feminism, Culture and Politics* (Lawrence and Wishart, 1982), p.74

83. For a discussion of these issues see C. Rowan, 'Women in the Labour Party, 1906–1920', *Feminist Review*, 12, 1982. Collette, *For Women and For Labour*, however, suggests that the WLL took a more independent stand in its relationship with the Labour Party.

84. Gordon, *Women and the Labour Movement in Scotland*, p.274; Hollis, *Ladies Elect*, pp.411–15.

85. NAC Report to *ILP Annual Conference*, 1907 and 1908.

86. Rowan, '"Mothers Vote Labour!"'

87. Anderson and Zinsser, *op. cit.*, p.372.

88. Letter from John Sosmer in *Freewoman*, 1 Aug 1912.

89. See W. Anderson, 'The Attitude of the Independent Labour Party towards the Woman's Movement', *Labour Leader*, 11 July 1912.

90. D. Howell, *British Workers and the Independent Labour Party, 1885–1906* (Manchester, Manchester University Press, 1983) gives little attention to women's role in the ILP or to gender politics. A recent study which analyses the interaction of class and gender at a local level is A. Mckinlay and R. J. Morris (eds.) *The ILP on Clydeside, 1893–1932: From Foundation to Integration* (Manchester, Manchester University Press, 1991).

3. 'Trailed on the tail of a comet': the Yorkshire Miners and the ILP, 1885–1908

Andrew Taylor

Studies of political change in the Yorkshire coalfield have focused on the conflict with the Liberal Party over parliamentary nominations. This is because, first, the conflict was visible and is documented in union records and the press. Second, the conflict was clearly 'political' in that it was concerned with the viability of competing political strategies of working-class politics. Third, the political shift in the Yorkshire coalfield can be seen as part of a wider transition in the labour movement and can be rationalised by reference to that wider experience. Finally, the decline of Lib-Labism and the rise of Labour fits neatly with the 'whig' interpretation of working-class history and politics. This chapter explores two propositions: first, parliamentary politics provide an incomplete and inadequate explanation of political change in the Yorkshire coalfield, and second, that the affiliation of the miners to the Labour Party does not represent a 'victory' for the ILP.

The politics of the YMA can only be understood by distinguishing between two facets of politics.[1] The first is *union politics*. This is a centripetal force and represents the mineworkers' collective goals expressed by the national organisation (the Mineworkers' Federation of Great Britain, MFGB) and more importantly the Yorkshire Miners' Association (YMA). Union politics tend towards cooperation, collaboration and compromise with employers in the interests of the membership whose material interests were enshrined within and expressed by the union as an organisation. This required the creation of a powerful ethos by union leaders supported by a patronage system, bolstered by a success on wages and condition to keep centrifugal forces within the union in check.

These centrifugal tendencies stemmed from *pit politics* which were, and remain, a volatile mixture of accommodation and conflict. Branch officials provided the organisational and political link between pit and union politics and were therefore in a complicated position. Local officials were the sanctioned local representatives of a wider organisation and were required to follow its policies. They, however, owed their position to election and much of their authority depended on their standing in the community and ability to manage, successfully, pit industrial relations.

Parliamentary politics are essentially the preserve of the leadership and activist stratum. The bulk of the union membership might, for example, regard a Liberal refusal to concede a parliamentary nomination as a slight and resent it but this is unlikely to be a major and direct influence on their attitudes and behaviour.[2] Attitudes and behaviour are largely determined by industrial experiences. It was conflict at pit level aggregated in the coalfield via the YMA Council (and official and unofficial panel meetings) and localised, bitter disputes (at, for example, South Kirkby (1897), Ravensthorpe (1900), Hemsworth (1906) and Glasshoughton (1907)) which were of great symbolic importance addressing wider issues and fuelling political change in the YMA.[3] Liberal reluctance to concede nominations was only one factor in this change.

This leads to the second proposition. Affiliation of the YMA (and MFGB) to the Labour Party does not represent the 'victory' of the ILP/socialist traditions over the Lib-Lab tradition as the former was simply too weak. Furthermore, many leading ILPers, locally and nationally, were seen in the YMA as 'anti-union'. YMA politics was driven by the tensions generated by the interplay of centripetal (union) and centrifugal (pit) politics. From the founding of the YMA in 1881 until the early-1900s union politics retained its dominance in the form of Lib-Labism. By the early-1900s the centripetal forces were weakening as the political, economic and social factors which had underpinned Lib-Labism weakened. This produced a relative increase in influence of centrifugal politics at pit level challenging union orthodoxy. This ushered in a period of conflict between these facets of YMA politics which ultimately resulted in the YMA's decision to affiliate to the Labour Party. Within the tension between union and pit politics the ILP served as a focal point for a small group of activists expressing wider discontents associated with the YMA's inability to respond effectively. The product of the conflict between union/pit politics and the Lib-Lab/socialist political traditions was the political compromise which formed the basis of labour movement politics for the next 80 years and received concrete expression in the figure of Herbert Smith (YMA President, 1906–1938).

Labourism: Pragmatism as Ideology

Labour history has often been concerned to explain why the mid-nineteenth century working class failed to develop an independent working-class party. After the collapse of Chartism, it has been argued, the working class were speedily subordinated to bourgeois ideas, notably the power of the vote and parliamentary sovereignty and the bifurcation of class conflict into industrial and political conflict. Working-class consciousness was therefore partial: economist at work and integrative in politics. This is usually defined as 'Labourism' which,

> recognized the working of political democracy of the parliamentary variety as the practicable means for achieving its own aims and objectives. Labourism was the theory and practice of class collaboration; it was a tradition which in theory (always) and in practice (mostly) emphasized the unity of Capital and Labour, and the importance of conciliation and arbitration in industrial disputes.[4]

The analysis of Labourism often implies it was a deformed reflection of 'true' class and political consciousness foisted on the working class by bourgeois ideologists and their working class dupes. This is inaccurate.

At Labourism's core was the demand for labour's acceptance as a legitimate participant in political and industrial life,

> Is a miner a Man? ... Is he part of the United Kingdom? ... Does he pay rates to support the Government of his country? ... Has he to obey the laws of the Country in which he resides? ... Why should it be a thing incredible that the miner should have a vote and a representative at the end of that vote? Why should he be debarred from assisting locally and imperially in swaying the destinies of this great nation? He helps to build it up.[5]

Labourism was not, of course, a challenge to existing society; 'The chasm, which divides the rich from the poor, wants bridging over, and working men must do it, [but] not by trenching on the interests of other classes'.[6] Lib-Labism involved using the ideology of liberal democratic capitalism by working people and their organisations to secure participation within liberal democracy. In securing participation workers accepted a subordinate role but what other realistic option was open to them?

Labour historians have tended to ignore non-socialist political traditions in the working-class, possibly a reflection of their own political preferences.[7] The obsession with the early socialist pioneers has mean that Lib-Labism and the solid, bearded, dark-suited men who were its chief exponents have been poorly served by labour historians. The political tradition they represented drew on roots deep in the working-class political experience which were laid down long before the revival of socialist ideas in the 1880s. Lib-Labism's strength ensured that socialism could never hope to supplant it, only reach an accommodation. Trade unionism is, by definition, sectional and economist and Lib-Labism was a distillation of union experience. Lib-Lab MPs, for example, were 'elected to advance the specific requirements of a single industry in a particular locality' at a time when a labour *movement* barely existed.[8]

Labourism spawned two major political strategies: Lib-Labism and Parliamentary Socialism. There is an understandable tendency to see the latter triumphing over the former but this chapter argues that Parliamentary Socialism – certainly in the case of the Yorkshire miners – was a synthesis of Lib-Labism and challengers. Many early socialist pioneers began as Liberals and remained staunch supporters of Liberal policies. These personnel linkages were supplemented by the continuity provided by organisations, notably the unions, the main forum for working-class politics. Within the synthesis of Parliamentary Socialism, Lib-Labism remained the dominant strain with socialist rhetoric (notably relating to nationalization) grafted on.

Men like Ben Pickard and Ned Cowey were pioneer trade union organisers, hardened negotiators and deeply committed to political reform. It is profoundly a-historical to accuse the Lib-Labs of sectionalism. Their political and industrial strategies were rationalizations of their trade union, not class, experiences (though the two were interconnected) in relation to the environment in which they grew to adulthood and activism. Lib-Labism in the Yorkshire coalfield was a rational response to the situation in which the mineworkers and their leaders found themselves and, moreover, in the 1880s and 1890s it delivered tangible benefits.[9] Of course, circumstances change and by the early twentieth century the environment which had underpinned Lib-Labism had altered so the YMA's strategy had to adapt. It is important to remember that we are concerned with the changing political loyalties of a trade union in which the perceived needs of the organisation and its members were the dominant consideration. The key word is adapt: Lib-Lab politics and personnel were not thrust into the dustbin of history by insurgent socialism. Both political traditions were reconciled to each other. Lib-Labism and socialism were competing but in the end complementary political strategies which were synthesised by and received expression in the Labour Party after 1906. Lib-Labism was, therefore, a very robust political tradition. 'There was', Saville writes, 'nothing soft or sentimental about the labourist tradition in the mining areas; and only when its strength is appreciated shall we be able to properly assess the tradition in its historical perspective'.[10]

The Yorkshire Miners and Lib-Lab Politics

The Yorkshire miners' political strategy and consciousness pre-dated the ILP. At the time of the Third Reform Act observers of coalfield politics noted the 'extreme importance' of reform to the mining communities, that their politics were moderate, they were unattracted by socialism, and they had absolute faith in Gladstone.[11] The Political Association established by the YMA (itself formed in 1881) was dominated by Liberals and saw its role as organising the miners in the Liberal interest.[12] The most tangible result was the selection and election of Ben Pickard as the Lib-Lab MP for Normanton in 1885. Pickard declared, 'In the name of gratitude for favours and rights secured, we appeal confidently to our fellow workmen to vote for the Grand Old Man and the Grand Old Cause of Progress ...'[13] and, although brought into the field as a Labour Candidate, I may safely say that I am as much a Liberal as any other candidate before our Yorkshire constituencies. I am a strong believer in Peace, Retrenchment, and Reform, and a firm supporter of the Right Honourable William Ewart Gladstone, MP![14] Lib-Labism in the Yorkshire coalfield grew from trade-union roots and the industrial experience of the miners, generating significant modifications in traditional Gladstonian political economy.

Pickard's Liberalism was a political tool designed to enhance the YMA's trade union activities. Thus Pickard, because of difficulties in securing an Eight Hours Act, adopted a pragmatic stance: 'I am not bound up altogether with the views of the Liberals as a party and I have my own opinions [on the party's stand] on many questions of great interest to the workers'.[15] The YMA were determined to 'set aside all rules of political economy ... they would not depend on the old systems which brought all the wealth to one section and all the hard work to another'. They rejected the notion that wages should follow the price of coal and challenge aggressively the coal owners' market economics, arguing 'these should not be ingredients in regulating and controlling the life and living wage of the miner'. This required firmness from the union in its dealings with the owners but did not mean conflict was either necessary or permanent. Lib-Labs believed conflict stemmed from a wilful refusal to recognise the benefits of cooperation. The 1893 lockout had 'fought the owners into a frame of mind which had induced them to meet them nearly half-way'. Owners were warned the YMA wanted collective bargaining to embrace all owners and none would enjoy the 'blessings' of non-unionism. The achievement of these industrial objectives depended on the maximisation of workforce solidarity.[16] At the 1897 MFGB Conference Pickard declared '(a) the principle of the Federation is that Political Economy as taught by the schools is not adopted or acted upon; (b) the principle of the living wage predominates and its members believe that the workers should have the first claim to live as a resultant of their labours; (c) that no condition of competition shall intervene between the worker and wages ... ; (d) they do not propose a sliding scale or wages board'.[17]

Lib-Labs like Pickard recognised industrial concessions could not be secured by industrial action and miners had to pursue their just claims by 'constitutional means'. He warned that strikes caused more hardship to the worker than the employer and 'They had seen that in a battle between the weak and the strong the empty stomachs had to succumb'.[18] Lib-Labism in the Yorkshire coalfield, therefore, had two distinct but connected elements: parliamentary and industrial,

> First, it believes in active legislation for securing an Eight Hours Day from Bank to Bank by law. Secondly, rightly or wrongly, it does not believe this can be obtained permanently for the country by Trade Union effort. Third, like all the older trade unions, this Federation believes in Parliamentary effort to ameliorate the workers' conditions. Fourth, as a matter of fact, everything on the Statute Book has been sought for and obtained by parliamentary action.[19]

A strong, united union was necessary to secure the membership's wages and conditions at the point of production but some interests (e.g. safety and hours) had to be decided nationally and enforced by legislation. This required the election of miners to Parliament to press for reform and the party most likely to grant reform were the Liberals. Lib-Labism in the political conditions of the late-nineteenth Yorkshire coalfield was a rational strategy but it had one major flaw; there was no guarantee a Liberal government would respond to the miners' wishes as was revealed in the struggle to secure an Eight Hours Act in the 1890s.[20]

In the early-1890s the YMA threatened to use their electoral influence to persuade Liberal MPs to support an Eight Hours Bill.[21] One local MP, H. J. Wilson, agreed with the YMA on the need for the limitation of hours but favoured allowing each coalfield to decide for itself and rejected the YMA's appeal for support.[22] Wilson was well aware of the YMA's opposition, warning this might split the Liberal vote and lose the seat. Furthermore, Wilson suggested, the local miners (orchestrated by Ned Cowey) were behaving unconstitutionally and threatening an MP's independence while others implied Cowey and the YMA were after the seat. It became clear that whatever the YMA's position neither it, nor the local YMA branches, would risk a split and Wilson was confident he could count on the miners' votes 'even against Mr Cowey'.[23] However, in 1897 Wilson's attitude changed as a result of the Engineers' Lockout, arguing that workers, when confronted by the combined power of the employers, might expect Parliament to redress the balance.[24] In February 1899 Wilson announced his conversion to the legislated eight-hour day without the local option. This provided support to both the supporters and critics of Lib-Labism. For supporters it showed that steady pressure combined with loyalty could produce political gains, for critics it showed that there were clear limits on the influence the miners (and by extension the working class) had over the Liberal Party and that independence offered greater opportunities.

The rise of independent labour and the founding of the ILP in 1893 represented a fundamental challenge to the Lib-Labism of the YMA and the miners' post-1885 strategy. Men like Pickard and Cowey resented the ILP's criticism of trade unionism as inherently sectional and of limited use in bettering working-class conditions. Anti-unionism was an important element in ILP thinking.[25] Lib-Lab animosity was personal as well as political and dated from before the ILP's formation. At the 1889 TUC Ned Cowey rejected calls for independent labour representation, claiming 'his constituents would not be willing to accept the gospel according to Keir Hardie'. He accused Socialists of wanting political power without having to work for it by capturing the unions, 'The simple fact was, they wanted a house that had been built by somebody else'.[26] Pickard saw the Bradford Conference as a conference of newcomers posing as the saviour of the working man. Lib-Labs like Pickard had spent 'their lives in the thick of the fight and many a sad and dreary day in the initial work of organisation', creating the conditions in which the ILP could develop. Pickard believed that the MFGB should have nothing to do with the ILP which had little support in the mining communities and that Keir Hardie would have served the Scottish miners better by working for a stronger union. The Liberals still offered the miners' best political hope.[27]

Personal resentment was a powerful motivation. 'I have been', Pickard declared, 'practically told that I am one of the effete, one of the worn out, that I don't understand what I am saying, don't know the meaning of words, and can't qualify as a Trades Unionist'.[28] From the Lib-Lab perspective the ILP posed a threat to the political and industrial settlement forged in the Yorkshire coalfield and based on the 1885 electoral pact with the Liberals and the Conciliation Board created as a result of the 1898 dispute. It also posed a personal challenge to the authority and dominance of the Lib-Lab leadership. In the 1894 Attercliffe by-election Pickard and the YMA made it clear that they stood behind the Liberal candidate and opposed the ILP candidature.[29] Studies of the politics of the Yorkshire coalfield and the YMA in the 1890s place great stress on the 1897 by-election as symbolic of the clash between Lib-Labism and the ILP and in a sense the by-election marks the high-point of Lib-Labism.[30]

As a result of the rescinding at the 1896 TUC of socialist resolutions passed in 1894, Page Arnot argues 'Pickard and the other Yorkshire leaders, at the end of 1896, decided that the time had come to "stop the rot"'.[31] Pickard's animus towards the ILP had been boosted by a speech Keir Hardie made at Rothwell on the 4th of July 1896 in which he was reported as declaring trade unionism was 'played out' and the future lay with the ILP (Hardie and his supporters denied he had made this statement). In his Presidential Address Pickard told the delegates they were to decide 'as to whether or not we are to work under a new law of Socialism instead of the old principles of Trade Unionism'. Pickard and the Yorkshire Lib-Labs dismissed the Scottish Federation resolution as impractical and its advocates as 'word painters', expressing 'no desire to be trailed on the tail of a comet until I don't know where I am'. At the end of the vitriolic two day debate Pickard hinted he would regard approval of the Scottish resolution as a vote of no confidence in himself.[32]

Cowey, moving a counter resolution, argued 'I am a Socialist to a certain extent, but I am a possibilist'. Committing the MFGB to socialism would be an unrealisable burden and he expressed resentment at the view that trade unionism was played out. Socialism would, he argued, fragment the union to no-one's advantage and he implied that the socialists in the MFGB would do better to direct their energies into securing 100% union membership before abandoning 'the good old beaten path we have been travelling for some time'.[33] The debate became increasingly ill-tempered with Pickard accusing socialists of impugning his integrity and socialists accusing him of misrepresentation. The debate clarified little. One delegate, for example, who asked Cowey how he proposed to separate trade unionism and socialism, received the enigmatic response, 'Trades Unionism is Trade Unionism, and Socialism is Socialism'.[34] Pragmatists on both sides sought a compromise by arguing the the dichotomy between trade unionism and socialism was false as they overlapped (particularly over nationalisation) and could be reconciled, but such delegates received short shrift. Pickard declared,

> this resolution is the core of the Independent Labour Party ... the doctrine laid down at East Bradford is the policy and tactics to be followed ... if Trade Unionists assembled here don't know where Trade Unionism begins and where it ends, it is about time they studied Adam Smith (A Delegate: Oh!) ... and John Stuart Mill.[35]

The Scottish resolution was crushed by 137,000 to 18,000 and Cowey's resolution reaffirming trade union action was approved by 134,000 to 21,000. Pickard was, however, wrong when he declared with satisfaction, 'That disposes of that'.

In the 1897 Barnsley by-election Pickard made support for Walton, the Liberal candidate, a vote of confidence in his own leadership and the YMA branch officials worked for Walton. The miners were urged to vote for Walton not as a coal owner but as a Liberal whilst the ILP and Keir Hardie were roundly condemned; '[the miners] were being told to bite the hand that fed them they could mould the Liberal Party to their liking'. The YMA's support for Walton was justified by the practicalities of working-class political representation and the Liberals' general support for the the eight-hour day so 'Every miner who does not vote for Mr Walton votes against the Eight-Hour Bill'.[36] Furthermore, Pickard claimed, Curran's candidature was in the interests of the Conservative Party, 'It was the Liberal Party that gave them the power they possessed and the ILP wanted to defeat that Party'. Conservatives hoped that if large numbers of miners supported ILP candidates middle-class Liberals would defect to them, splitting the progressive vote and undermining the YMA and MFGB's industrial strategy.[37]

The basis of the ILP's political challenge to the Lib-Labs came from a small number of geographically proximate YMA branches – Rothwell, Middleton, Glasshoughton and Hemsworth – which were dominated by a group of young ILP activists (notably, Willie Lunn, Isaac Burns, and John Walsh). In 1895 an ILP branch was formed at Rothwell where, a year later, Hardie delivered the speech which so incensed Pickard. In the by-election the Rothwell YMA branch unanimously urged the miners to vote for Curran. Walsh spoke frequently for Curran, and the South Kirkby branch's deprecation of Pickard's vitriolic attacks on Curran and the ILP were published in local newspapers.[38] The small number of ILP branches posed no serious threat to the Lib-Labs' political hegemony but it is clear from Pickard's reaction that they were regarded as a potentially very serious threat to the political solidarity of the YMA and the authority of the union leadership.[39] Whilst the Lib-Labs had no real difficulty in beating off the ILP's feeble electoral challenge its industrial challenge proved a different matter.

Union Politics, Industrial Militancy and Solidarity

The main forum for ILP politics and the basis for its challenge to the Lib-Labs came at branch level where activists in local disputes found themselves confronting the Lib-Lab machine. In union politics questions of political and electoral strategy could affect industrial policy (for example, over the eight-hour day) but the conduct of industrial politics was complicated by the importance attached to union solidarity and loyalty.

The YMA's leadership stressed the importance of solidarity as the mineworkers' basic defence and fount of their strength. Any threat to that solidarity from whatever source posed a challenge to the union as a whole and its members' interests. The problem, as Michels demonstrated, was that the membership's natural sentiments of solidarity and loyalty were a crucial support for union leaders in the face of dissent and could be manipulated in the leaderships' interest.[40] Critics of the YMA union bureaucracy would find that Pickard and the other leaders could and did deploy solidarity in defence of their own bureaucratic and political interests (which they identified as synonymous with those of both the union and its members) and as a means of controlling and suppressing dissent over the YMA's industrial and political policies. Dissent, political or industrial, could be marginalised by the leadership portraying dissenters as schismatics and wreckers, concerned to use the miners and the YMA for their own personal and political objectives.

The whole life experience of the Lib-Lab leadership pointed them towards a strategy designed to maintain and strengthen the YMA's effectiveness as an organisation expressing the political and industrial interests of the mineworkers. They were motivated by the need to institutionalise the union's influence and this required organisational stability and predictability. The ethos of solidarity and loyalty, when coupled with the delivery or denial of patronage by the leadership, ensured that most branch leaderships for most of the time consented to and collaborated in the leadership's strategy. There remained the possibility of a challenge welling up from within the more combative world of pit politics. Here solidarity was spontaneous not bureaucratised and flowed from shared work experiences within a closed occupational community. This, in turn, generated a high-level of inter-consciousness and involvement extending far beyond the formal branch meeting. Leaders emerging from this milieu were able to draw on common instincts of solidarity and loyalty as a basis for a challenge based on 'a blend of industrial experience, local patriotism and political conviction … Young ILPers could come to dominate the decisions of a local lodge as the result of a specific industrial question and could then attract support based on respect and patriotism'.[41] In the Yorkshire coalfield the political challenge to the Lib-Labs came from local leaders in a small number of geographically proximate branches, and these also provided the industrial challenge.

A dispute at South Kirkby colliery in the summer of 1897 gives an insight into the YMA's politics and ethos. This dispute seemed to confirm the worst fears of both the Lib-Labs and the ILPers about each other. The situation deteriorated and the South Kirkby men staged an unofficial strike contrary to union rules. The YMA Executive recommended they return to work and the officials were condemned for breaching union rules, threatening union solidarity, and acting on the advice of local leaders.[42] Attempts by the YMA leadership to secure a return to work were rejected by the branch which implied the district had no rights in the case, a stance which infuriated the Executive.[43]

Opinion in the YMA was, however, pulled in two directions: sympathy for a group of fellow mineworkers engaged in what was clearly, to them, a matter of principle, coupled with a recognition that individual branches could not be allowed to pursue their own interests and flout the union's rules. There was pressure for financial aid for the South Kirkby men and the Rothwell branch protested at the Executive's attitude, believing the conflict stemmed from 'the bitter personal prejudices that exist between the permanent officials of the association and the local officials of the association and the local officials of the South Kirkby branch'.[44] In September the South Kirkby request for strike pay was put to the district for a decision and the branch voted 573 to 375 in favour of the Executive's decision not to support the strike. The Area Council then voted by 90 to 38 to endorse the Executive's condemnation of the branch's refusal to accept the help and advice of the deputation sent by the Executive to help find a solution.[45] A second branch vote found 641 to 316 in favour of upholding the Executive's original position.

These votes convey an impression of the power of the Lib-Lab machine at work when combined with instincts of loyalty and solidarity. Branch officials would be well aware of which way Barnsley expected their members to vote and the minority attending branch meetings were likely to be the most solid, loyal, and conservative of the YMA's membership. Nonetheless there remained a considerable reservoir of support for South Kirkby and no less than 38 of the YMA's branches voted against upholding the Executive's censure of South Kirkby. The South Kirkby strikers returned to work two days before Barnsley by-election. The Barnsley by-election provided a political fillip for the ILPers and for those in the YMA unhappy with the direction of union industrial relations policy and, although these group overlapped, hostility to the union leadership should not be interpreted as support for socialism.[46] This raises the question of the nature and extent of Pickard's and Lib-Labism's grip on the Yorkshire miners.

The accepted historical picture of Ben Pickard is of an autocrat of Tsarist proportion. Contemporaries stressed his hold on the Yorkshire miners, implying an ability 'to whip the miners into the desired fold as if they were so many flocks of sheep'.[47] According to *The Barnsley Chronicle* 'Mr Pickard is a monarch among the miners of South Yorkshire, and very jealous is he of his Crown ... he pervades the whole vicinity, and allows no pretenders within a mile of it!'[48] Conversely, miners' loyalties (political and industrial) were deeply ingrained. It was 'the innate conservatism of the people which causes them to vote Radical now because they voted Radical before and because their fathers were Chartists and Radicals'.[49] There was, of course, no guarantee that trade unionists would follow their unions' political lead,

> They had some constituencies in Yorkshire where the Liberal Two Hundred was composed of three-parts working men who would not meet them, neither the Yorkshire Miners' Association nor any other association ... He had not forgotten the late War in South Africa, and had not forgotten how some of the miners' leaders said that war was not justified. The miners would not listen to them, but set them at defiance, and now they would not be able to convince the Yorkshire Miners' Association that the Liberals were no good.[50]

It was obviously the case that the miners and their leaders had powerful opinions but 'the miners have far more effect on Mr Pickard than Mr Pickard has on them'. Pickard's Lib-Labism reflected the preferences of the bulk of his members, even if Pickard had been converted to socialism it was unlikely his members would follow, Cowey's bluff had been called by Wilson in Holmfirth in 1892. Similarly, 'when the miners are converted it will not matter much whether Mr Pickard is converted or not'.[51] In the final analysis a union leadership and the policies it advocates depend on the endorsement (or at least the acquiescence) of the membership. The bureaucratic resources of leadership coupled with sentiments of loyalty and solidarity gives leaders a strategic advantage in the management of dissent and opposition but this is a wasting asset. By the end of the 1890s discontent was welling up within the YMA over pay, there were complaints from officials about unofficial meetings designed to subvert official policy and the presumption was that ILPers were behind these agitations and the leaking of confidential documents.[52] Studies of the Yorkshire miners (and the wider labour movement) in this period stress that the economic and political environment which had given Lib-Labism its validity was changing in ways hostile to Lib-Labism. For much of the 1890s Lib-Labism was a credible and rational strategy, and furthermore the bulk of the membership felt a deep sense of gratitude to the union's founders. This legacy protected the Lib-Labs from being challenged but it could not disguise the fact that events were moving on.

Policy, Performance and Political Change 1900–1908

To explain political change Gregory cites the growing antagonism between capital and labour, the death (between December 1903 and February 1904) of Pickard, Cowey and Frith, and adverse judicial decisions but concentrates on the vicissitudes of parliamentary politics.[53] Howell contrasts the relative stability of coalfield industrial relations after 1893 with the post-1900 deterioration in the industrial, legal and parliamentary position of the YMA.[54]

The physical replacement of the YMA's Lib-Lab leadership is the most visible reflection of change. The death of Pickard, Cowey and Frith undoubtedly eased the psychological inhibitions on the expression of dissent in the YMA. Critics were hitherto inhibited by the feeling that criticism of the YMA's policies was an attack on the union itself and the integrity of the founding fathers. Those Lib-Labs who replaced them, notably Wadsworth and Hall, were union bureaucrats and lacked the pioneers' authority when controlling dissent. In 1908 *The Yorkshire Post* commented 'The days of Pickard and Cowey had gone. However rebellious some of the men were in their day they could quieten them'.[55] The demise of the Lib-Lab leadership led to change (notably the rise of Herbert Smith, an ILP member, to the YMA Vice-Presidency and then to the Presidency in 1906) but their replacements came from the Lib-Lab tradition and remained loyal to that legacy. The elements of continuity were as important as the elements of change. The death of these three men was symbolic of the YMA's travails and the increasing complexity of coalfield politics as the social, industrial and legal environment deteriorated.

Table 1   Population Growth in the Yorkshire Coalfield 1871–1911

	1871	*1881*	*1891*	*1901*	*1911*	*Change*
Hemsworth						
Urban district	993	1665	2887	6383	10173	9180
Parish Council	7121	9441	11744	17096	29930	22809
Poor Law Union	8114	11106	14631	23379	40103	37989
Doncaster Area						
Adwick UDC	565	543	536	561	6973	6408
Bolton UDC	479	1002	1205	3828	8670	8191
Thurnscoe UDC	196	246	217	2360	4074	3878

Source: Derived from data in RD17/1/12–1/51.

In 1881 70,328 males were employed in mining in the Yorkshire coalfield (10.4% of total employment), in 1891 the figures were 89,995 (11.4%), rising to 113,628 (12.7%) in 1901 and 151,137 (14.8%) in 1911 .[56] The result was explosive population growth not only in the new mining villages to the east but also in the established communities (Table 1) with obvious consequences for social conditions. In 1901 the WRCC's Chief Medical Officer reported that smallpox, scarlet fever, diphtheria, typhus, measles and whooping cough were rife throughout the mining communities, producing very high death rates. In Wombwell, for example, the death rate for zymotic diseases was 5.6 per 1,000 persons, in Barnsley 5.4, Bolton-upon-Dearne 4.8, Monk Bretton 4.8, Hoyland Nether 4.4, Darfield 4.3, and Wath-upon-Dearne 4.1. Mining communities had always experienced high death rates but these were now exacerbated by the expansion of mining. This attracted a high number of internal and external migrants and the age structure of the workforce produced high birth rates.[57]

In the mining communities, where life had always been hard and was expected to be hard, there was a significant worsening of conditions.[58] The inability, reluctance and sometimes refusal of local authorities and coal companies to provide anything more than the minimum in terms of housing, sanitation and educational facilities underscored the miners' established conviction that neither the free market nor private capitalism could remedy the situation. The mineworker's experience in his community inevitably drew him to collectivist and statist (but not inevitably socialist) responses. A proposal by the Middleton branch to add to the YMA's objectives, 'To secure the return of the Members of the Association to Parliament, Municipal Bodies, and Board of Guardians who are pledged to run as direct Labour Candidates' was rejected by Council by 97 to 25.

Nonetheless, 25 branches represented a substantial minority in favour of independent parliamentary representation.[59] In 1904 three branches (Wath Main, Wheldale, and Allerton Silkstone) influenced by the ILP tried to open the question of union officials also being MPs, a common criticism of the ILP, but all three resolutions were rejected by 784 to 338.[60]

Although it is not possible to talk of an employers' offensive as a coherent strategy in the Yorkshire coalfield, the end of the South African War boom and the expansion of the coalfield eastwards made employers more cost conscious. From the coal-owners perspective (Table 2), the economic facts of life – rising output, falling productivity, declining receipts and increased competition – were unanswerable and pointed unequivocally to the need for wage cuts. A letter from the Ackton Hall branch secretary in 1903 described an instance of the new management style,

> Our Grievances are as follows: Alteration in mode of work, Silkstone Seam, thereby reducing men's wages by one-half; removal of [union] Collecting Box from Pit Yard, and not allowing any organising to be done; men having their places stopped on complaining of not being able to earn a day's wage; reducing Bye-workmen's wages, and several others. We have had nothing but trouble since Ellis Barraclough came, and the men are very uneasy … We have had Mr Wadsworth down on a Deputation, besides several locals, but have not been able to come to an understanding with them.[61]

This pressure of wages, furthermore, occurred at a time of rising prices.

In 1893 the YMA and MFGB successfully resisted a demand for a 25% pay cut, accepting a 10% reduction in 1894 (Table 3). The line on pay was held until 1898 and between 1898 and 1901 the YMA secured increases which added 60% to the 1888 standard. After the end of the boom there were cuts of 20% (1902–04) but increases of 15% (1906–08) then took the YMA back to the level of 1901. This was followed by a 10% cut in 1909 which meant miners' wages were back to the level of the 1890s.[62]

The legal battle between the YMA and the Denaby and Cadeby Collieries – the famous Bag Muck Strike – was a local manifestation of the turn of the century legal assault on the unions. The strike 'was a clear victory for the employers, a defeat for the MFGB and YMA, and a disaster for the workmen … Lost homes, lost jobs, and no wages for forty weeks or more.[63] In response to the House of Lords confirmation of Taff Vale the YMA advised members, 'however humiliating it may be, the only course is to resume work, and by that means put ourselves right and within the Rules and under the Law as now understood'.[64] These legal uncertainties forced the YMA to act cautiously in its dealings with employers for fear of further legal assaults.

These factors made it more difficult for the YMA to defend its members and contributed to growing conflict between pit and union politics. An impression of the state of coalfield and union politics can be gleaned from two sources. From the YMA's Annual Accounts can be calculated the percentage of total spending on strike, lockout and victim pay ('Conflict Expenditure') to provide an overall picture of the structure of pit politics. Strike, lockout, and victim pay can be expressed as a percentage of Conflict Expenditure to provide a measure of the balance of power between management and workforce. An

Table 2
The Economics of Coal Production in the Yorkshire Coalfield 1899–1909

| Year | Output | Output per: | | Value of Coal: | | Collieries |
		Hewer	Man	Total	Ton	
1899	26904	359	283	10322	0.35	391
1900	28243	357	280	14344	0.50	382
1901	26969	324	256	11575	0.40	391
1902	27960	327	265	11302	0.40	402
1903	28527	328	259	10697	0.35	418
1904	28832	325	257	10237	0.35	365
1905	29920	335	265	9993	0.30	375
1906	35247	386	304	10959	0.30	384
1907	35171	359	283	14221	0.40	385
1908	34927	327	258	14711	0.40	396
1909	35894	322	354	13437	0.35	399

Output = 000 tons; Output per Hewer/Man = tons p. a.; Value = £000/pence
Source: derived from data in *H.M. Inspector of Mines Annual Reports (Yorkshire Region)*.

Table 3
Changes in YMA Wages Rates (% Change +/- on Wage Standard of 1888)

Year	Change	Year	Change
1888	+10	1899	+7.5
1889	+10	1900	+10
1890	+20[1]	1901	+10[3]
1891	No change	1902	-10
1892	No change	1903	-5
1893	Major Dispute[2]	1904	-5
1894	-10	1905	No change
1895	No change	1906	+5
1896	No change	1907	+5
1897	No change	1908	+5[4]
1898	+2.5	1909	-10

Notes
1. 40% increase on Standard of 1888
2. The 1893 dispute concerned blocking the owners call for a 25% wage cut
3. 60% increase on Standard of 1888
4. 60% increase on Standard of 1888
Source: YMS Annual Report for 1909, pp.5–6

increase in the percentage spent on strike pay indicates the balance favoured the union, an increase in the percentage spent on lockout and victim pay indicates a shift in the balance in the employers' favour. The second source is the fortnightly data published in the YMA minute after 1904 of the number of individuals receiving strike, lockout, and victim pay. This provides an indication of the scale and direction of pit politics.

In Table 4 the early years are excluded because of missing data and the impact of the 1893 lockout. Between 1894 and 1909, in seven out of the 16 years, conflict expenditure was over half of total YMA spending and 6 of these years were after 1900. The worst year (apart from 1893) was 1902 due to the Lads Strike. The evidence of Table 4 is that conflict is a post-1900 phenomenon. Spending on strike pay increases (Table 5) more or less continuously through the 1890s, peaking in 1901. It declines thereafter (albeit with two revivals) as unions are less likely to strike in recession as power shifts to employers. Conversely, lockout pay peaked in 1893 and declined fairly consistently until 1901, being almost eliminated after 1899 and then increasing

Table 4   Total YMA Spending and Conflict Expenditure 1890–1910

Year	Conflict Expenditure (£000s)	Total Spending (£000s)	% of Total Spending
1890	—	—	—
1891	3018	117822	2.3
1892	—	—	—
1893	218418	268757	81.3
1894	11427	66605	17.1
1895	25245	51056	49.4
1896	18437	38504	48.0
1897	18017	40300	45.0
1898	35366	58745	60.2
1899	11768	32075	37.0
1900	7342	32236	23.0
1901	45326	74908	60.4
1902	77205	111614	69.2
1903	43669	73559	59.4
1904	41468	79916	52.0
1905	62231	97626	64.0
1906	50559	89135	57.0
1907	28408	63521	45.0
1908	17653	58208	30.3
1909	32179	78345	41.0

Conflict Expenditure = combined total of Strike, Lockout and Victim Pay.
Derived from data in YMA Annual Accounts.

Table 5   Strike, Lockout and Victim Pay
as Percentage of Conflict Expenditure 1893–1909

Year	Strike Pay	Lockout Pay	Victim Pay	Lockout/Victim Combined
1893	0.4	98.7	0.6	99.3
1894	23.7	59.8	16.3	76.1
1895	31.5	57.2	11.2	68.4
1896	22.1	66.8	11.0	77.8
1897	68.0	17.1	13.1	30.2
1898	67.1	27.5	5.5	33.0
1899	85.5	6.4	7.9	14.3
1900	81.2	9.7	9.0	18.7
1901	92.6	2.4	4.8	7.2
1902	27.3	72.6	4.1	76.7
1903	70.8	20.2	8.8	29.0
1904	38.4	53.0	8.4	61.4
1905	18.8	68.8	12.6	81.4
1906	27.0	63.1	9.7	72.8
1907	24.4	63.8	11.7	75.5
1908	26.8	50.1	22.9	73.0
1909	15.6	70.2	14.0	84.2

Derived from data in YMA General Accounts

sharply. Victim pay follows the same general pattern, a downwards drift to 1902 followed by a (gently) rising trajectory. This data indicates a shift in market conditions in favour of employers.

The deterioration in industrial relations had implications for the union's effectiveness. Council warned 'we still have a considerable number of men on the Funds, and Branches should be very cautious with regard to bringing any more men out under present circumstances'. The membership was warned that the union was now paying more out in strike pay than it was receiving in contributions; 'it is therefore necessary for the District to be very careful about bringing more men out on strike'.[65] In 1906 the Trustees warned about the huge sums being spent on strike, lockout and victim pay and argued that the membership 'ought to do all they possibly can to reduce the extraordinary expenditure that is taking place'.[66] Confronted by managerial pressure and a growing financial burden Council instructed Parrott to write to the Secretaries of the West and South Yorkshire Coal Owners' Associations to ask for their help in reducing the number of members on the funds.[67] Table 6 is based on a limited number of years but suggests the numbers on strike peaked in 1905, the low point being 1908; in the case of those locked out the equivalent years were 1905 and 1909 and for victimisation, 1905 and 1908.

The decline in the incidence of industrial action indicates neither improving

Table 6   YMA's Membership Receiving Strike, Lockout
and Victim Pay 1904–1909 (Fortnightly Average)

| Year | *Average Receiving:* | | | |
	Strike Pay	Lockout Pay	Victim Pay	Total
1904	290	1431	131	1825
1905	446	1448	229	2115
1906	326	1122	132	1750
1907	244	619	76	939
1908	137	292	91	706
1909	170	173	108	435

Calculated from fortnightly data in the YMA Minutes & Reports

industrial relations nor increased union effectiveness but the effect of a new rule (Rule 69) which made it possible for officials to bring disputes to an end and remove members from union funds. Frustration was expressed at some branches drawing on union funds for long periods. One branch secretary complained about the Ravensthorpe, Wheldale, Frystone No 1, Frystone No 2, and Wyke as 'it seems too much like a "Pension fund" the ways that monies are being paid out at these places'.[68] In November 1906 these branches were denied any further access to union funds under Rule 69. In April 1907 Glasshoughton, Halifax, and Soothill Wood were removed by an average of 665 to 427 votes so a considerable minority remained opposed to Rule 69. This rule change suppressed but did not resolve discontent.

A further indicator of the YMA's difficulties is union density (the % of the workforce in the union). Union density rose up to 1895 and held steady until 1900, thereafter declining for the next five years (Table 7). To some extent this was the result of employment growth in the coalfield but membership peaked in 1902 before the dramatic expansion in the east and the YMA lost members until 1906. Average union density in the coalfield was, it should be noted, an impressive 60.8% which again shows the employers did not mount a general anti-union offensive. Both the east and South Yorkshire coalowners 'recognised the right of workmen to belong to a Union or not as they deem fit, and raise no objection to their belonging but they do not consider themselves justified in interfering with the freedom of the Miners on such a question'.[69]

In this harsher industrial climate and faced by growing internal discontent the YMA's officials sought tighter control over the branches. During the Lads Strike (1902) large numbers of members applied for lockout pay which revealed the parlous state of many branches,

> Scores of men were found to be Unfinancial in the Books who were financial on their Cards ... a considerable number of Local officials are seriously neglecting their duty, and causing many men to be Unfinancial by their neglect or incompetency.

Table 7   A Stagnating Union?

Year	Employed	Members	Density
1890	76776	—	—
1891	82037	—	—
1892	86563	55000	63.5
1893	88590	55000	62.0
1894	90996	—	—
1895	88680	50000	56.3
1896	72104	50000	69.3
1897	71660	50000	69.7
1898	72556	50000	68.9
1899	74855	51000	68.1
1900	79053	54475	68.9
1900	105258	60000	57.0
1902	107730	60684	56.3
1903	109969	60504	55.0
1904	112105	56960	50.5
1905	112619	55211	49.0
1906	115508	62182	53.8
1907	123938	79052	63.7

Derived from H.M. Inspector of Mines Reports, and YMA
Minutes and Reports

The result of this incompetence (and in some cases embezzlement) was that
the officials in Barnsley were subject to 'much cursing and filthy abuse'. They,
in turn, sought to impose standardised procedures on the branches. A major
problem was the quality of branch officials,

> What is needed at present in many of our Branches is three capable and
> unprejudiced men as President, Secretary and Treasurer, who will carry on
> the work of this Association according to rule and common sense, *and not be
> biassed by a clique or party feeling, too much of which exists at the present time*.[70]

Barnsley was deeply worried by factionalism and the quality of local
officials but several branches embroiled in major local disputes (for example,
at Glasshoughton and most importantly at Hemsworth) claimed officials were
more concerned with protecting union funds than the members.

The Hemsworth Dispute (1904–1907) dated back to at least 1897. There
was a history of tension between Hemsworth and Barnsley. Hemsworth was,
as Wadsworth told the Joint Board in July 1905, a problem pit absorbing
union funds and officials' time.[71] Local leaders (notably Potts) accused YMA
officials of deserting the Hemsworth miners and of not visiting the camp of
evicted miners and their families at Kinsley. The local branch organised a

nationwide relief effort and the dispute was used by the ILP to mobilise support in an area with a history of pro-ILP sentiment. On 7 October 1905 Hardie, Ben Turner (ILP candidate for Dewsbury) and John Potts attended a meeting which did not overtly attack the YMA but was implicitly critical of its stance. In January 1906 John Potts wrote to the *Sheffield Daily Telegraph* attacking the YMA leadership.

This letter is usually cited as a critique of the YMA's parliamentary politics but it queried all aspects of the YMA's policies using Hemsworth as an example. Its basic point was that the main objective of YMA officials was to protect union funds and perpetuate existing union policies. The officials' reply in *The Sheffield Independent* charged Potts with damaging union solidarity and giving comfort to the YMA's enemies. In a sense the response was a sledgehammer to crack a very small nut but the vitriol directed at the ILP is significant. The response was particularly hostile to Hardie and expressed sentiments Pickard would have endorsed enthusiastically (Bob Smillie is referred to throughout as Smellie). It went back to 1893, resurrected the 'trade unionism was played out' charge, and claimed that the ILP was only after the YMA's money. Finally, the officials presented a spirited defence of the YMA, contrasting its strength with the numerical and financial weakness of the ILP. In February 1906 a second circular intended for internal union consumption was produced. Whilst repeating the same set of charges against the ILP it placed greater stress on the difficult legal and industrial environment facing the YMA. It appealed for maximum solidarity and unity in the face of external threats, warning that Potts' conduct jeopardised the union and that YMA policy could not be determined by the renegade Hemsworth branch. This produced a call from the Cortonwood branch that Potts be 'dismembered', a punishment not endorsed by the Executive who felt their point had been made.[72] Hemsworth assumed wider significance because of its political overtones and the manifest inability of the established machinery to solve the local price list problem. The dispute encapsulated the tension between union and pit politics and conforms to a persistent pattern in coalfield politics: dissent can be held in check by a strong leadership enjoying authority, legitimacy, and a modicum of success. By the early-1900s these factors had disappeared.

An outlet for suppressed discontent was the growth of unofficial meetings. In December 1898 Council has passed a resolution condemning illegal Panel meetings called to discuss union policy and secure joint votes in Council. This resolution was reaffirmed by Council in 1902.[73] By 1906 this had broadened to include elections of delegates to union and other conferences. Council condemned

> all Joint Panel Meetings to discuss the election of men to Conferences and congresses, or any other official position, and resolves that the men elected are illegally elected, and cannot be paid from the funds of this Association for attending any Conference or Congresses if they or their Branch have taken part in such illegal meeting.[74]

YMA officials identified 23 branches (with 313 votes) involved in such activities. Many of these branches crop up frequently as either 'problem' branches or branches opposed to YMA policy and it is reasonable to regard these branches (some with long-established ILP connections) as the 'opposition' in the YMA. At times restiveness took on a more public face. At the 1908 Annual Demonstration there was considerable unrest. As the speeches concluded,

> suddenly there was a great deal of hooting from the audience, and hats were knocked off when one miner shouted 'And what about Hemsworth?' Another spectator rose and cried 'And what about the trouble at Glasshoughton?' It was obvious that these people had a good deal of support among the crowd judging by the continued booing.

Introducing Will Crooks to a rowdy crowd Herbert Smith blamed the disturbances on men who would 'pay a bob on Saturday night and want a quid in strike pay on the Monday morning'. When heckled Crooks replied 'I am 56, you don't look 30, but if you do not keep order I will come and punch your head'.[75]

As the new century progressed many mineworkers could be forgiven for concluding their union's current policies were failing. At snap time, when waiting for the pit cage to ascend and descend, in the pubs and clubs, and on the streets of the pit villages, it is not hard to imagine mineworkers discussing stagnating wages, the harsher managerial climate, and the union's legal difficulties and so contributing to a climate conducive to change. It was in this context and in response to decisions of the MFGB Conference the YMA voted 1906 and 1908 to affiliate to the Labour Party (Table 8). This decision was

Table 8   YMA Votes on Labour Party Affiliation, 1906 and 1908

	For (% votes)	*Against (% votes)*	*Total Vote*	*% Turnout*	*Majority*
1906	17389 (57.7)	12730 (42.2)	30119	49.7	4659
1908	32991 (61.3)	20793 (38.6)	53738	76.8	12103

taken in the belief that affiliation would provide the MFGB with increased influence in the House of Commons and help secure the passage of an Eight Hours Act.

What were the political consequences of affiliation? At one level the consequences were minimal as the YMA's two MPs (Hall and Wadsworth) refused to sever their links with the Liberals. Significantly the Labour Party Executive made no attempt to compel conformity other than at a formal level.[76] The YMA and MFGB's decision to affiliate to Labour was part of a wider synthesis between Lib-Labism and socialism then taking place. The synthesis provided the core of the labour movement's doctrine and ethos for the next seventy years, receiving visible expression in the substantial shape of Herbert Smith. Smith's political evolution provides a valuable insight into the developing labourist tradition. In what ways did Smith differ from the Lib-Labs? Were there any similarities?

The obvious difference was Smith's ILP membership. In supporting Curran in 1897 Smith 'burnt his boats and took his place with those who stood for a separate political party which was pledged to pursue working-class interests irrespective of both great parties'. In so doing Smith 'took the opposite side to his leaders. That was not an easy thing to do when such leaders were so popular'.[77] Smith's incendiary decision however did not hinder his rise up the union hierarchy and this raises the question of the motivation behind his decision. Throughout his biography *The Man In The Cap*, Lawson reiterates Smith's 'practical', non-ideological approach to union affairs and suggests he 'did not see the logic of the whole line he took'.[78] According to Lawson, ILP membership was a reflection of a younger man's impatience with established leaders (although Smith was 35 when he joined the ILP), an impatience which faded once high office was achieved. Smith's attitudes to Communists in the 1920s and 1930s, for example, bears more than a passing similarity to Pickard's views on the ILP. Smith was an ILP member but he was a miner before he was a socialist and his socialism was an expression of his experiences as a miners' union official. Though he recognised the importance of parliamentary politics his political militancy never matched his industrial militancy and despite running against Hall for the YMA's nomination for the Normanton seat after Parrott's death his heart was not in electoral politics.[79] We may infer he stood not out of deep conviction but out of a sense of duty and because he was the obvious choice.

Press comment at the time noted there was little doctrinally to distinguish Hall and Smith apart from the question of cooperation with the Liberals.[80] What then did Smith stand for?

> Herbert Smith, of the younger generation, was definitely against the doctrine of the market determining the standard of a man's life. He was uncompromising on that. And in both the industrial and political field he stood with the forces that insisted on the Minimum Wage, Eight Hours Day, Nationalization of the Mines, Abolition of Royalties. All designed to regulate the industry and make life decent for the miner.[81]

There is nothing here that Lib-Labs like Pickard or Hall would oppose either on principle or pragmatically. There is an understandable tendency to see nationalisation as the touchstone of socialist politics but in fact Liberals could and did support nationalisation. A brief examination of the MFGB's approach to nationalisation shows the importance of personality in influencing union politics and policy towards the ILP. The 1892 TUC unanimously approved a resolution on the nationalisation of minerals and the coal industry and in 1894 the MFGB approved a similar resolution by 1558 to 50. This was not followed up and Pickard declared 'I am not a miners' [sic] nationalizer. I don't think that if the mines were nationalized the miners would be a penny better off then they are today'.[82] At the 1897 MFGB Conference a nationalisation resolution from Scotland was defeated. The disinterestedness of the MFGB executive over nationalisation – which was not regarded as practical politics nor as important as the eight-hour day – can be seen from the relegation of nationalisation either to the TUC or the International Miners' Federation. After Pickard's death mines nationalisation resolutions appeared on the MFGB Conference agenda in 1904 and 1905 and in 1906 the YMA was won over.[83] Several Lib-Labs and socialists at the 1897 Conference were bewildered by Pickard's obduracy over nationalisation, arguing that here was an issue over which all could cooperate. MFGB thinking on nationalisation remained underdeveloped but once the Eight-hour day had been achieved in 1908 and with the emergence Labour Party then nationalisation entered the political agenda as practical politics.

Despite Smith's ILP membership there is no evidence of personal animosity between Pickard and Smith, or between Smith and the other Lib-Labs. Lawson suggests Smith modelled himself on Pickard,

> That Herbert had for him [Pickard] a great admiration we know, and that the early miners' leaders deeply impressed those who followed is unquestioned. In this case both men used the bludgeon. That it was natural to Herbert Smith there is no doubt. But the close company of Pickard and the universal admiration for him among Yorkshire miners may have tended to develop the style of the younger man.[84]

Both Smith and Pickard were inspired by a passionate commitment to improve the miners' lot to be achieved by maximising the collective strength of the union which required unity and solidarity. This inclined both men towards an aggressive, often authoritarian, leadership style in which they identified their preferences with the interests of the union and its members. Thus,

> He didn't ask opinions – he gave them. He did not weakly wait to hear what others had to say before policy was decided. He made up his mind and told them. That was the old way. But there was one difficulty, there had been thirty years' education, and he had young men who did not like the old way.[85]

In the final analysis, there was little difference between the views of Pickard and Smith on the question of working-class consciousness and class politics,

> Though he had throughout life a contempt for theorising, the fact remains he was emphatically class conscious. To have said he was 'Miner conscious' would have pleased him most. He would have understood that better. Miners are real: classes are abstract – and Herbert Smith had no room for abstractions.[86]

It is therefore very easy to overestimate the political consequences of the death of the Lib-Lab generation.

One further reason for the blending of the Lib-Lab and socialist traditions derives from the paradoxical political behaviour of the Yorkshire miners. A major myth of political history is that Britain was a mature liberal democracy before 1914 whereas 47%–49% of the adult male population was excluded from the franchise.[87] Amongst these were millions of potential Labour supporters whose absence from the electoral lists gives a false impression of Liberal strength. If we divide the miners into those with the vote and those without and then compare parliamentary elections with the YMA's two votes on affiliation to the Labour Party a very interesting situation develops.

Electoral results show that when miners had the opportunity to vote for ILP and Labour Party candidates they voted Liberal (Table 9). The logical conclusion must be that the vast majority of miners with the voted continued to support the Liberal Party and exhibited little interest in Labour politics. In 1906 and 1908, however, the YMA voted to affiliate to the Labour Party. How can this paradox be resolved? The answer lies in the exclusivity of the franchise and the demographic change in the structure of the mining population. As we have seen, the coalfield was in a state of flux and it is a plausible hypothesis that in such a situation large numbers of miners would not meet the residence and/or property qualification and would therefore be disqualified from voting. As communities settled and population movements declined patterns of political behaviour would establish and be reflected in the electorate.[88] If many miners were excluded from the franchise none (assuming they were members and were financial) were excluded from voting in YMA ballots. The paradox of the Yorkshire miners' political behaviour can be resolved therefore if we assume that the union ballots on affiliation revealed a large pool of pro-Labour support which could not find expression in parliamentary elections.

The strength of the Yorkshire miners' commitment to the Liberal Party has been exaggerated by the emphasis given to parliamentary politics and those miners who had the vote. It was the large numbers of electorally disqualified miners who determined the political development of the YMA (and MFGB) in 1906 and 1908 and the decision to vote for affiliation can be plausibly portrayed as a reflection of, and response to, the difficulties faced by the YMA. Affiliation to the Labour Party did lead to an increase in the Labour vote but it was the impact of the First World and the extension of the franchise in 1918 which enabled the miners' support for Labour to become one of the key elements in the political development of the Labour Movement.

Conclusions

It is clear that the ILP had a limited impact on the YMA. This was because there were few major policy differences between the two (except on the question of cooperation with the Liberal Party) but more importantly because the ILP and its supporters were from its earliest days associated with 'anti-

Table 9   ILP/Labour Party Parliamentary Contests in the Yorkshire Coalfield

Constituency	% Turnout	ILP/Labour % Vote	Liberal % Vote	Miners in Electorate*
Attercliffe		°		
1894 (b)	79.0	13.5	48.6	10–20
1909 (b)	77.3	27.5	24.6	10–20
1910 (J)	83.9	56.1	43.9	10–20
1910 (D)	72.1	55.0	45.0	10–20
Barnsley				
1897 (b)	76.3	9.1	59.7	40–50
Hallamshire				
1910 (J)	82.2	62.2	—	30–40[1]
1910 (D)	73.0	59.9	—	30–40
Holmfirth				
1910 (J)	86.2	14.9	57.5	20–30
1912 (b)	86.9	28.2	42.0	20–30[2]
Morley				
1910 (J)	86.0	16.1	59.0	30–40[3]
Normanton				
1910 (J)	77.2	72.2	—	40–50[4]
Wakefield				
1902 (b)	79.0	13.5	48.6	10–20
1906 (b)	88.5	36.9	40.8	10–20
1910 (J)	90.5	45.5	54.5	10–20

b = By-election. * = Gregory's estimate for 1910.

Of the constituencies identified by Gregory as mining constituencies no ILP or Labour Party candidate stood in Osgoldcross, Doncaster, Rotherham, Pontefract, or Barkston Ash in the period up to 1914.

[1] YMA Candidate. John Wadsworth (Labour Party). First elected as a Lib-Lab in 1906 with 55.2% of the poll.
[2] YMA Candidate. William Lunn (Labour Party).
[3] YMA Candidate. Herbert Smith (Labour Party).
[4] YMA Candidate. Fred Hall (Labour Party). Elected unopposed as a Lib-Lab in the 1905 by-election, 1906 and December 1910. Parrott polled 70.2% as a Lib-Lab in the 1904 by-election and Pickard's average vote was 58.9%

Source: F.W.S. Craig, *British Parliamentary Election Results 1885–1918* (London: Macmillan 1974).

union' and disruptive elements in the YMA. ILPers challenged the authority of the YMA's founding fathers in ways that seemed to belittle their achievements, denigrate their supporters, and threaten union solidarity. Their advocacy and pursuit of political independence was seen to jeopardise the YMA's principle objective – the legislative eight-hour day – by threatening the longstanding relationship with the Liberal Party which was the only party likely to pass such an Act. Finally, the prominence of ILPers and occasionally the ILP itself in major local industrial disputes was seen as disrupting relations with the employers at a time when cooperation was required. One of the main gains of the 1893 struggle for the YMA had been to secure recognition from the employers that the union had a legitimate role in ordering coalfield industrial relations, one the main tenets of Lib-Labism. Thus, the ILP challenged every major aspect of union politics and policies, and its behaviour offended against the powerful political culture of the Yorkshire coalfield which stressed the supreme importance of solidarity and loyalty.

The conflict between the ILP and the Lib-Labs was fought out in the harsh arena of pit – union politics where union leaders are under challenge from those at the grassroots who see their policies, legitimised by the union's rules, as detrimental to their local interests and the wider interests of the mineworkers. In return, those challenging the leadership can expect to feel the weight of the union bureaucracy. The ever-present tension between pit and union politics provided the motor for union politics. Seen from this perspective politics in the Yorkshire coalfield becomes less concerned with the merits of independent parliamentary politics than with the conflict between the union bureaucracy and its supporters in the branches anxious to defend the policies with which they are associated and which they believe are in the membership's real interests, and their opponents who believed with equal passion they were too concerned with protecting union funds and their positions. The conflict over parliamentary representation is only part of a wider debate over the future of the YMA.

The critical events promoting change were the end of the South African War boom and the death of the Lib-Lab generation. The latter greatly eased the psychological and organisational restraints on the articulation of dissent and the former ushered in a period of recession which brought into question virtually all aspects of union policy. The YMA's protective capabilities were reduced by recession which as always shifted power to the employers. Declining effectiveness was reflected in stagnating wages and union density, whilst continued expansion in output in a harsher economic climate led to greater management assertiveness in controlling cost. This did not produce a general offensive against the YMA although there were a number of spectacular conflicts (notably at Denaby and Cadeby Collieries, and Hemsworth), and whilst union density remained quite high there was constant management pressure for changes in working practices which when coupled with the paralysis induced by the post-1900 legal uncertainties inhibited the YMA's ability to defend its members.

It is not surprising that this syndrome of failure led to a questioning of union policy and culminated in the decision to affiliate to the Labour Party. What was the ILP's role in this? By 1906 the ILP had branches in several part of the coalfield and the Labour vote in parliamentary elections was beginning to increase although the Liberal Party easily retained its dominance. There is evidence that support and sympathy for the ILP and its allies has been underestimated due to the exclusivity of the franchise and the pressure exerted by the YMA bureaucracy in favour of loyalty to the union and its leadership. Nonetheless, it is the case that the ILP as an organisation remained unimportant in union and coalfield politics except as an irritant. This is less true of individual ILPers. The influence of the ILP lies not in its organisational effectiveness but in the role that ILP members played at branch level as union officials elected by their members and reflecting their members' wishes. All union officials, at whatever level, must ultimately reflect the wishes of their members and what we see in the Yorkshire coalfield is a shift in the perceptions of the membership as to how their interests could best be advanced. By 1906 this meant the Labour Party.

The affiliation votes reflect a widespread sentiment amongst the membership that the YMA's current political orientation was an inadequate response to a harsher industrial climate. This sentiment sprang from the miners' industrial and community experience and it is not easy to draw a direct causal link between the miners' industrial experience and their political attitudes. There is little evidence of a dramatic shift in union policy, even less of an explosion of class consciousness amongst the miners as a result of affiliation to the Labour Party. What we see in the Yorkshire coalfield in the years up to 1908 is a local manifestation of a general phenomenon – the making of the working class between 1870 and 1914. In the coalfield this complex change received a dramatic visibility in the shape of Herbert Smith whom Hobsbawm, in an elegiac passage sees as representative not only of the miners but of the working class as a whole.[88] Labour Party affiliation, when seen in the context of the Yorkshire miners' political tradition, was not the result of ILP agitation but a response to a changed political and industrial environment and the result was a Labourist synthesis, not the transcendence of Lib-Labism by socialism.

Notes

1. P. Gibbon, 'Analysing the British miners' strike of 1984–5', *Economy and Society*, 17 (1988), part II, pp.152–154, for a similar distinction.
2. The refusal by the Labour Party NEC to accept the NUM candidate for the Hemsworth constituency in 1991 caused resentment but did not lead to mass defections from Labour. Similarly, massive pit closures, incomes policy and the loss of parliamentary nominations did not dent significantly the Yorkshire miners' electoral loyalty to Labour. Nonetheless, the period 1968–1973 sees a dramatic leftwards shift amongst the Yorkshire miners. See A. J. Taylor, *The Politics of the Yorkshire Miners* (Beckenham, Croom Helm, 1984), pp.191–211.

3. These disputes are examined in detail in C. Baylies, T*he History of the Yorkshire Miners, Volume II, 1881–1918* (London, Longmans, forthcoming).

4. J. Saville, 'The Ideology of Labourism', in R. Benewick *et al* (eds.), *Knowledge and Belief in Politics* (London, G. Allen & Unwin, 1973), pp.215–16.

5. *YMA Yearly Report for 1883*, p.9.

6. *Miners' National Union*, Working Men's Representatives in the House of Commons (Durham, 1884), p.3. This manifesto was signed by both Pickard and Cowey.

7. M. Pugh, *Tories and the People 1880–1935* (Oxford, Blackwell, 1985) notes (on p.2) that in 1900 the ILP had a total membership of 6,000, equivalent to the paid up membership of the Primrose League in Bolton.

8. M. Barker, *Gladstone and Radicalism, The Reconstruction of Liberal Policy in Britain 1885–1894* (Hassocks, Harvester Press 1975), pp.137–8. The YMA's political programme was described as 'broad enough for all working men to take part in, and it will require that the iron-workers, mill-hands and miners especially, co-operate together, in order that the objects aimed at may be successfully attained', *YMA Branch Circular*, 14 Jan 1885. The non-involvement of other groups of workers confirmed the Lib-Lab belief in the inevitability of political self-help by occupational groups.

9. D. Howell, *British Workers and the Independent Labour Party, 1888–1906* (Manchester, Manchester University Press, 1983), pp.17–18.

10. J. Saville, 'Notes on the Ideology of the Miners before World War I', *Bulletin of the Society for the Study of Labour History*, 23 (Autumn) 1971, p.26. See also Saville's *The Labour Movement in Britain* (London, Faber & Faber, 1988), chapter 2.

11. Bagshawe to Fitzwilliam, 4 June 1885, in *Bagshawe Papers*, Sheffield City Libraries.

12. *Yorkshire Miners' Political Association*, 14 Aug and 1 Oct 1884.

13. Ben Pickard's Election Address 1885, in *H. J. Wilson Papers* MD5942, Sheffield City Libraries.

14. YMA General Election Circular 1885, in *Miscellaneous Cuttings Book 1881–1886*.

15. *Wakefield Free Press*, 21 Jan 1893.

16. E. Cowey Speech in *Testimonial to Mr Benj. Pickard MP*, 24 July 1894, p.4.

17. *MFGB Conference*, Jan 1897, p.23.

18. *Sheffield Independent*, 11 May and 23 Apr 1891.

19. B. Pickard, *MFGB Conference*, Jan 1897, p.24. See also his speeches reported in *Sheffield & Rotherham Independent*, 2 Oct, and *Barnsley Chronicle*, 9 Oct 1897.

20. B. J. McKormick and J. E. Williams, 'The Miners and the Eight-Hour Day', *Economic History Review*, (2nd series) 12 (1959–60) gives a good account of the MFGB's politics.

21. See, for example, *Sheffield Independent*, 15 Apr and 11 May 1891 for speeches by Pickard, Frith and Murray.

22. *H. J. Wilson Papers*, MD2499–8, and *Sheffield Independent*, 15 Aug 1892.

23. *H. J. Wilson Papers*, MD2501–3.

24. *Holmfirth Express*, 22 Jan 1897 and 28 Apr 1898.

25. Howell, *op. cit.*, pp.356–7.

26. *Trades Union Congress*, Report of Annual Proceedings 1889, p.37. It should be noted that Hardie reciprocated Lib-Lab hostility. See D. Lowe, *From Pit to Parliament. The Story of the Early Life of James Keir Hardie* (London, Labour Publishing Co, 1926), p.56.

27. *Wakefield Free Press*, 21 Jan 1893.
28. *MFGB Annual Conference*, Jan 1897, pp.65–66.
29. J. Brown, 'Attercliffe 1894 – How One Local Liberal Party Failed To Meet The Challenge of Labour', *Journal of British Studies*, 1975, pp.44–77.
30. R. G. Neville, 'The Yorkshire Miners and the 1893 Lockout – the Featherstone Massacre', *International Review of Social History*, 1976, pp.313–36, and D. Rubinstein, 'The Independent Labour Party and the Yorkshire miners – the Barnsley By-Election of 1897', *International Review of Social History*, 1978, pp.102–134.
31. R. Page Arnot, *The Miners, A History of the MFGB 1889–1901* (London, G. Allen & Unwin, 1949), p.301.
32. *MFGB Annual Conference*, Jan 1897, p.24, p.42 and p.51.
33. *Ibid.*, pp.43–44
34. *Ibid.*, p.48.
35. *Ibid.*, p.65.
36. *Barnsley Chronicle*, 2 Oct 1897.
36. *Sheffield & Rotherham Independent*, 25 Sept 1897.
37. *Sheffield Daily Telegraph*, 25 Oct and 21 Oct 1897.
38. *Yorkshire Post*, 27 Sept 1897, and *Barnsley Chronicle*, 2 Oct and 9 Oct 1897.
39. *Yorkshire Post*, 27 Sept 1897.
40. R. Michels, *Political Parties. A Sociological Study of the Oligarchical Tendencies of Modern Democracy* (First published 1915; new edn. New York, Crowell-Collier, 1962).
41. Howell, *op. cit.*, p.21.
42. *YMA* Ordinary Executive Committee, 9 Aug 1897.
43. *Ibid.*, 13 Sept 1897.
44. *Ibid.*, 13 Sept 1897.
45. *YMA* Ordinary Council Meeting, 4 Oct 1897.
46. Howell, *op. cit.*, p.20.
47. *Sheffield Daily Telegraph*, 24 Sept 1897.
48. *Barnsley Chronicle* 2 Oct 1897. For a graphic portrayal of Pickard in his hey-day see R. Smillie, *My Life for Labour* (London, Mill & Boon, 1924), pp.68–69.
49. *Barnsley Chronicle*, 4 Oct 1897.
50. *MFGB Annual Conference*, Oct 1904, p.50.
51. *Barnsley Chronicle*, 6 Nov 1897.
52. *YMA* Ordinary Executive Committee, 28 Nov 1898, and Howell, *op. cit.*, p.21.
53. Gregory, *The Miners and British Politics*, p.10.
54. Howell, *op. cit.*, p.23.
55. *Yorkshire Post*, 7 July 1908.
56. C. H. Lee, *British Regional Employment Statistics 1841–1971* (Cambridge, Cambridge University Press, 1979) for data.
57. WRCC Clerk's Department RD17 1/1/12–1/1/51, *13th Annual Report of the Chief Medical Officer of Health* (15 Sept 1902), p.21.
58. RD17, *17th Report of the CMO* (10 Sept 1906), p.14.
59. *YMA* Special Council Meeting, 2 Feb 1903.
60. *YMA* Yearly Council Meeting, 28 Dec 1904.
61. Sam Earnshaw to Ben Pickard, 1 May 1903, in *YMA* Executive Committee Minutes, 4 May 1903.
62. *YMA* Annual Report 1901–2 (Oct 1902) for Pickard's analysis of the

consequences of trade depression for the YMA.

63. J. Macfarlane, *British Miners and the Taff Vale Judgement: the Bag-Muck Strike at Denaby and Cadeby Collieries 1902–3* (unpublished MS, nd), p.63.

64. *YMA* Special Council Meeting, 2 Feb 1903.

65. *YMA* Ordinary Council Meeting, 9 Sept, and Executive Committee Minutes, 17 Nov 1902.

66. *YMA* Annual Trustees Meeting, 24 Mar 1906.

67. *YMA* Ordinary Council Meeting, 31 Oct 1904

68. John Frith (Branch Secretary, Stanhope Silkstone) to J. Wadsworth, 13 July 1906 in *YMA* Executive Committee Minutes, 13 July 1906.

69. B. Day (Joint Secretary South and West Yorkshire Coal Owners' Associations) to J. Wadsworth, 2 July 1907.

70. *YMA* Executive Committee Minutes, 22 Sept 1902. Notes by the Financial Secretary (my emphasis).

71. *Joint Committee Meeting of WYCOA and the YMA*, 25 July 1905.

72. The documents relating to this controversy are too long for detailed consideration here. They can be found in *YMA* Executive Committee Meeting Minutes, 12 Feb 1906. Potts' habit of taking notes in Council for, it was widely presumed, transmission to Hardie and other ILPers led delegates to vote by 118 to 22 for his dismemberment unless he desisted (*YMA* Ordinary Council Meeting, 19 June 1906).

73. *YMA* Ordinary Council Meeting, 27 Jan 1902, and Sam Jones (Branch Secretary, Wharncliffe Woodmoor) to Ben Pickard, in *YMA* Ordinary Council Meeting, 30 Dec 1902.

74. *YMA* Special Council Meeting, 15 Oct 1906.

75. Quoted in S. Thompson, *Demonstration. The Pride of the Yorkshire Miners* (Barnsley, Yorkshire Area (NUM), 1987), p.29

76. Gregory, *op. cit.*, pp.111–19 for Labour Party-YMA relations after affiliation and R. McKibbin, *The Evolution of the Labour Party 1910–1924* (Oxford, Oxford University Press, 1974), pp.24–28 for an overview.

77. J. Lawson, *The Man In The Cap. The Life of Herbert Smith* (London, Methuen, 1941), pp.75–76.

78. *Ibid.*, p.76.

79. Smith stood for Labour in Morley in January 1910. He came third with 2,191 votes (16.1% of the vote) and as a result appears to have vowed never to stand for parliament again.

80. *Sheffield Independent*, 24 Nov 1905.

81. Lawson, *op. cit.*, p.90.

82. *MFGB Annual Conference*, January 1894, p.15

83. R. Page-Arnot, *The Miners. Years of Struggle* (London, G. Allen & Unwin, 1953), p.128. See E. Eldon-Barry, *Nationalisation in British Politics. The Historical Background* (London, Jonathan Cape, 1965), chapter 4 for an overview of mines nationalisation.

84. Lawson, *op. cit.*, p.85.

85. *Ibid.*, p.93.

86. *Ibid.*, p.33.

87. H. C. G. Mathew, R. I. McKibbin and J. A. Kay, 'The Franchise Factor in the Rise of the Labour Party', *English Historical Review*, 61, 1976, pp.723–52.

88. This hypothesis is derived from D. Friedlander and R. J. Roshier, 'A Study of

Internal Migration in England and Wales', *Population Studies*, 19/3, 1966, and D. Friedlander, 'Demographic Patterns and Socioeconomic Characteristics of the Coalmining Population in England and Wales in the Nineteenth Century', *Economic Development and Cultural Change*, 22, 1973.

89.   E. J. Hobsbawm, *Worlds of Labour. Further Studies in the History of Labour* (London, Weidenfeld & Nicholson, 1984), pp.211–13.

4. Religion and the ILP

Leonard Smith

Now look here Fred. Tha' knows they're an ignorant lot at Wibsey, so don't be trying any of that scientific socialism. We want no Karl Marx and surplus values and that sort of stuff. Make it plain and simple. Tha' can put in a long word now and then so as to make them think tha' knows a lot, but keep it simple, and then when tha'rt coming to t'finishing up, tha' mun put a bit of "Come to Jesus" in, like Philip does.

> Advice to Fred Bramley, later secretary of the TUC,
> by a chairman at Wibsey.[1]

The formation of the National ILP at Bradford in 1893 was preceded by three significant landmarks in the thrust for independent Labour representation. Of these, the foundation of the Scottish Labour Party, 1888, and the Manchester and Salford ILP, 1891, with its celebrated Fourth Clause, have accepted places in the annals of Labour history, but the third, the Labour Church movement, founded at Manchester in 1891, tends to be treated as if it were an aberration. The reasons for this may partly be explained by the mistake of trying to relate British labour history without reference to the strongly religious and ethical impulses motivating the movement's pioneers, and the fact that ILP leaders apparently preferred not to mention their earlier connections with religious denominations when writing their autobiographies. However, the evidence which this chapter seeks to explore suggests closer links between religion and the ILP, both through the Labour Church movement and the conventional churches, than the received view generally admits. This is not to argue that relationships were ever more than flimsy and fluctuating, but that there was a desire on the part of both the ILP leadership and influential religious leaders, particularly in the Free Churches, to forge an unofficial alliance, which ultimately seems to have foundered on attitudes towards the Boer War.

To begin, the Labour Church movement provides the main focus for an examination of religion and the ILP, especially in the period between the party's foundation in 1893 and the time when the Labour Church became moribund in 1902, after the earlier concern of socialist societies with brotherhood and fellowship, and the making of socialists, gave way to the creation of Labour's electoral machine.

Labour churches were mainly a response to the largely hostile position which the Liberal dominated Nonconformist chapels took towards working-class aspirations for Labour representation. John Trevor, the Unitarian minister at Upper Brook Street Chapel, Manchester, founded the Manchester and Salford Labour Church in 1891 as a solution to the problem which working men faced in their relations with Nonconformist chapels. How could they continue to feel at home in chapels which, whilst happily welcoming them for the fulfilment of their spiritual needs, were quite unsympathetic and often hostile to their economic and political emancipation? The difficulty was overcome by the formation of Labour Churches. The movement, which had its own journal, *The Labour Prophet*, spread rapidly nationwide, but mainly in the textile regions of Lancashire and Yorkshire, where the ILP was making most headway. Labour churches often existed side by side with ILP branches, with overlapping memberships. They attracted members from all denominations. The leaders included disaffected Conregationalists, Quakers, Unitarians and Wesleyan Methodists, but also several whose backgrounds were Anglican. Dissatisfaction seems to have been with the churches generally, rather than Nonconformity in particular, but it was more likely to be directed against the chapels because they had traditionally been thought of as being sympathetic to the improvement of the economic and political status of working people, whereas the Established church had an accepted record of opposition. In Manchester, Labour Church members played a leading role in the formation of the Manchester and Salford Independent Labour Party, in May 1892. Trevor also co-operated with Robert Blatchford in the commencement of Sunday Schools in connection with the Clarion movement's Cinderella Clubs. These were separate from the Socialist Sunday Schools that had their origin in the Crusader clubs recruited from Keir Hardie's column for young people in the *Labour Leader*, but both sprang from the same conditions and shared ethical outlook. And when the unsuccessful strike at Manningham Mills, Bradford, led to the inaugural conference of the National ILP at Bradford in 1893, Trevor was responsible for a Labour Church service at St George's Hall, attended by 5,000 people and addressed by Keir Hardie and George Bernard Shaw. The complementary nature of the Labour Church and ILP is emphasized by a resolution of the ILP's National Administrative Council in May 1894 advising 'that branches of the ILP wherever possible should run a Sunday meeting on Labour Church lines'.[2] The Sunday meetings provided a platform and a meeting point for Labour pioneers and ministers of religion who were supportive of independent Labour's advance, most of them either Congregationalists or Unitarians, but also a few High Anglican members of the Guild of Saint Matthew. Moreover, the Labour Church existed not only independently of the conventional Nonconformist churches, but there is some evidence, particularly amongst Swedenborgians, that 'Labour Church meetings' were held as part of a range of activities within an ordinary church.[3] After reaching a peak in 1895, when there were 54 congregations, the Labour Church movement suffered serious decline and by 1902 there were only 22 churches, most of these doing little more than provide a meeting ground for the different socialist groups – ILP, SDF and Fabian Society. The reason for the decline of the movement is not altogether clear, but suggestions have included the internal struggles between those, like Trevor, who regarded it as essentially concerned with the personal regeneration of Labour supporters, and those, like Fred Brocklehurst, its second General Secretary, a Cambridge graduate and former Anglican ordinand, who saw it as little more than an extension of the ILP's electoral machine. It has been argued that the disappointment of the 1895 General Election result – was a contributory factor. None of the ILP's 28 candidates was returned, and even Keir Hardie, who had previously been Labour's lone voice in the Commons, as the member for West Ham, lost his seat. It may also have been Trevor's own weak and ineffectual character which led to ossification. A year after his personal spiritual insight, that 'God was in the Labour Movement – working through it, as he had once worked through Christianity, for the further salvation of the world'[4] had led to the formation of the Labour Church, Trevor suffered a nervous breakdown. Refusing or unable to give his movement proper leadership it fell into the hands of those who had little concern about the personal regeneration which he believed must go hand-in-hand with social reconstruction. And, just as the movement was suffering under the disappointment of the poor election results, he appears to have offended the moral sensibilities of those who shared his own view of the Labour Church by re-marrying within three months of the death of his first wife, Eliza, without a respectful period of mourning. When Trevor wrote to tell of 'the strange circumstance' that led to the marriage, but left further explanation until there should be an opportunity to meet,[5] Keir Hardie replied: 'You have given the movement such a blow as it will not recover from in a hurry, and if you really desire to serve it you will now best do so by resigning all connection with the Labour Church – otherwise the organisation will go to pieces'.[6] Hardie's prophecy came uncannily true. The Labour Church movement was moribund by 1902. During the 1890s it had provided a meeting point for those with a wide variety of theological viewpoints who saw their religion and politics as part of a common hope, expressed on the one hand in terms of 'The Fatherhood of God and the Brotherhood of Man', and on the other in terms of the practical programme of the ILP, with its Eight-Hour Day. It had united those of many denominations who felt that there was no possible hope of persuading the conventional churches to support the Labour move-ment. For about a decade after 1891, the mutual responses of the Labour movement and Nonconformity found greatest expression in the Labour Church Movement, whose heartland was virtually co-terminus with that of the ILP. After that, any responses which the Labour movement made to religious interest was made more directly with the conventional churches, because the Labour Church was no longer an effective organization.[7]

Before proceeding to evaluate the relations between Labour and the conventional churches, it is appropriate to consider, briefly, the 'religion of socialism' which produced mutual sympathies between Labour pioneers and their supporters within the churches. The phrase had been used as early as 1885 in the peroration to the manifesto of the Socialist League, written by William Morris, and was used by many of the pioneers during the 1880s and 1890s. It described the processes of conversion which many early socialists felt they had undergone in their call to a radically different way of life; it included the sense of social ostracism – the breaking with family and friends – which becoming a socialist frequently involved; and, above all, the sense of brotherhood in the Fellowship of the New Life. The phenomenon was much broader than its institutional manifestations in bodies such as the Labour Church, the Brotherhood Church and the Socialist Sunday School Movement. It was by no means confined to the ILP ethical socialists, or to the areas where Labour advanced amidst strong traditions of religious Nonconformity. Even the meeting of the quasi-Marxist SDF often assumed a religious character. George Lansbury recalled his membership of the Bow and Bromley SDF branch where 'meetings were like revivalist gatherings. We opened with a song and closed with one, and often read together some extracts from economic and historical writings.'[9] Early socialists also recognized the need for ritual. A few Labour Churches adopted ceremonies for the reception of infants, marriage and the burial of the dead, although only Leeds Labour Church was registered for marriages. But the tendency to ritual was present in less obviously religious sectors of the Labour movement. In 1885, Eleanor Aveling Marx urged the council of the Socialist League to have a Christmas Tree, asking 'Is not socialism the real "new birth", and with its light will not the old darkness of the world disappear?'[10] The adoption of a cultic style of expression was a significant characteristic of the 'religion of socialism'. Religious and anti-religious socialists alike gave form and colour to their speeches with the words 'evangelists', 'apostles', 'disciples', 'new birth', and suggested that socialism would create the 'New Jerusalem'. It was also common to publish collected essays under the umbrella-title *The Religion of Socialism*: Katherine St. John Conway (Mrs Glasier) and Bruce Glasier did it for the Fabian Society in 1893, the Socialist League and the ILP did it in 1894, and Ernest Belfort Bax, the most anti-religious of Socialist League and SDF members, in 1885. Yeo has suggested that the period in which the Labour movement had the characteristics of a religious faith came to an end in 1896, after the total failure to win seats at the 1895 General Election, when it became necessary to develop the party machinery to secure Parliamentary representation.[11] Nonetheless, it continued in attenuated form until the advent of World War I, and in the case of a Labour Church and Socialist Sunday School at Hyde as late as the 1950s. Although very different from conventional Christianity, there were enough similarities to stimulate mutual fascination between non-dogmatic Socialists and Free Churchmen, and conflict between the more doctrinaire sections of Nonconformity and the Labour movement.

Another important factor which determined the nature of relations between the emergent Labour movement and the chapels was the fact that a large number of the Labour candidates elected at the 1906 General Election claimed to be Free Churchmen, although it is not established that more than a few of them had retained active church membership. It is quite possible that a claim meant no more than some family association with a chapel, a baptism, or attendance at a Sunday School, possibly extending to the Adult class. The survey conducted by W. T. Stead for his article 'The Labour Party and the

Books that have helped to make it' itself illustrates the problem.[12] Thomas Burt declined to allow any reference to religious affiliation to be included, adding 'I have struck out your entry under 'Religion,' as it might mislead. I am not a member – nor have I ever been – of the Primitive Methodist body. My father and mother were Primitives. I went to the P.M. Sunday school and chapel as a boy and youth. From the travelling preacher – who often came to our house – I derived intellectual stimulus, and benefit in other ways; but as I have said I never was a member of the denomination'.[13] Yet Burt has been claimed by both Methodists and Unitarians. Clearly, on his own testimony, there was no actual affiliation but the acknowledgement of considerable Nonconformist influence. This may have applied to others who claimed more definite religious affiliations, but who could not afford to be so open about the truth of their purely nominal churchmanship because they had been returned as Lib-Lab members, as a result of the unofficial agreement between Ramsay MacDonald and Herbert Gladstone, the Liberal Chief Whip, whereby Liberals did not oppose seats contested by the LRC. These members owed their return to the co-operation of the Liberal/Nonconformist alliance, and their acknowledgement of Free Church roots may have been little more than a mark of respect. Burt, although a Lib-Lab candidate, was a miner's MP and less dependent upon the Nonconformist Liberals than many others. K. D. Brown has pointed to a discrepancy between the 18 MPs who claimed membership of Nonconformist churches and the eight listed in the religious press.[14] The press mentioned Crooks, Gill, Hardie, Henderson, Hodge, Hudson, Jenkins and Taylor, but not Barnes, Clynes, Glover, Parker, MacDonald, Macpherson, Richards, Seddon, Shackleton or Wardle, yet some of those not mentioned are known to have had connections with Nonconformity. The discrepancy may, perhaps, be explained by the fact that the relations of Labour candidates were more likely to be with the Brotherhood Movement, an auxiliary of Nonconformity, rather than with its mainstream, and therefore less likely to be reported in the principal denominational organs. Brown states that of the nine LRC men who preached, only three did so within a traditional Free Church setting; the rest in the Brotherhood movement.[15] Another fact revealed by Stead's survey and Brown's analysis is that eight of the 18 claimed to be Methodists – five Wesleyans, two Primitives and one Free. This may seem surprising in view of the relatively minor role played by Methodism in the early years of the Labour movement. The fact is that by 1906 the Labour movement was developing at the confluence of two streams, the socialist movement and the trades union movement, in which Methodism found it possible to play a greater role because it was more concerned with class conciliation than with class conflict. Significantly, many of the Labour candidates had served as trade-union officials. Whether their claimed associations with Nonconformity were active or tenuous, the fact that almost two thirds of the Parliamentary Labour Party regarded themselves as Nonconformists created channels for at least limited co-operation with the Free Churches, as and when it seemed expedient.

The temperance movement provided another meeting point between Nonconformity and the ILP. From the mid-nineteenth century onwards the chapels had developed a culture to oppose that of the public house. Band of Hope meetings grew in number in the 1890s as the production of beer increased, taking a larger proportion of working-class income, until it began to decline after 1900.[16] The Labour movement was divided over the question of whether drink was a cause of working-class poverty, or merely a symptom. Sometimes the process of becoming a socialist involved the realization that the roots of destitution lay deeper than the drink problem. As a member of the Evangelical Union in the mid-Lanarkshire coalfield, Keir Hardie, a strong supporter of the temperance movement, had believed that intemperance was the cause of much working-class distress. But by 1887 he had changed his view and believed that poverty could not be completely eradicated until the means of production was out of private hands. Nonetheless he remained a strong advocate of teetotalism, a commitment he shared with other leaders of the ILP. All four of the Labour MPs who sat in the Commons before 1906 – Hardie, Shackleton, Crooks and Henderson – had associations with temperance, as well as being Nonconformists. Of these, Crooks, a Congregationalist, Shackleton, a Wesleyan, and Henderson, a Congregationalist until sixteen then a Wesleyan, were actively involved in trying to persuade labour that drink was an enemy. They took a leading part in the Trades Union and Labour Officials' Temperance Fellowship, as did many other of the Labour members of parliament elected in 1906.[17] Henderson was its President and Shackleton the treasurer; MacDonald and T. F. Richards belonged to its executive committee; and among its vice-presidents were Barnes, Crooks, Duncan, Gill, Hodge, Snowden, J. W. Taylor and Walsh. For the first three years of its existence signing 'the pledge' was a condition of membership of the ILP. It reflected a continuing belief that drink was still a factor standing in the path of working-class emancipation, if not the fundamental cause of their bondage. And, in part, it was an attempt to give the emergent Labour party credibility and respectability, to show that working men could behave responsibly and were worthy of election to positions of influence and power. Significantly, when members of the party held divergent views, they were more often criticised for being intoxicated than for their opinions, as in the case of Hardie and Snowden's criticism Victor Grayson for the speech that led to his suspension from the Commons.[18] But there were critics of the ILP's temperance tradition and 'the pledge' was abandoned for new members in 1896.[19] This was, no doubt, partly a response to the depressing 1895 General Election results, and the realization that if the ILP was to make headway in securing Labour representation it would have to broaden its base by more readily accepting the public-house culture of working-class life; and partly because of the necessity to raise funds by engaging in the sale of drink and tobacco at ILP clubs. Some, like Ben Tillett, were also critical of Labour MPs appearing on temperance platforms in the company of Liberals, thus blurring in the public's eye the image of the Labour movement as an independent party.

Nonetheless, the party leadership remained committed to temperance and frequently joined with Nonconformists in the promotion of the temperance cause. On the other side, for Nonconformists, particularly in north-east Lancashire, attitudes to drink seem to have been crucial in determining the kind of Socialist advance they were prepared to support. Around Burnley, a stronghold of the SDF, Labour did not secure much, if any, Nonconformist support until the ILP emerged, with unequivocal teetotallers amongst its front rank leadership.

The Brotherhood movement on the fringe of Nonconformity, with its Pleasant Sunday Afternoon meetings, provided yet another interface with the Labour movement. The Movement helped to spread formative influences in favour of socialism through its book prize scheme, and shared common objectives with the Labour movement in supporting measures for social reform, particularly the provision of Old-Age Pensions. The PSAs also had links with the trade unions, who frequently made use of Brotherhood halls for their meetings and the payment of welfare benefits. Labour leaders accepted invitations to address Pleasant Sunday Afternoon meetings with the same readiness with which they had once responded to the opportunities provided by the Labour Churches, but with the benefits of a much larger and more enduring organization of working men. One important reason why the Labour leaders may have taken so great an interest in the Brotherhood Movement is that it was a large and efficiently organized association of working men. At Hyde, in the 1890s, the whole area served by the thriving PSA was divided into wards, with a committee to oversee visiting.[20] It could have been seen as providing an unofficial electoral registration society, as the chapels had once performed a similar function for the Liberal Party.

In areas where chapel were not so hospitable to Labour pioneers, it was necessary to seek secular venues, but often the meetings nonetheless had a religious flavour. In South Wales, where the coalowners were strongly represented in the chapels, Keir Hardie was refused permission to speak in the vestry of Sharon Welsh Congregational Chapel in Aberaman, Aberdare.[21] In 1898, Willie Wright reported to the ILP's National Administrative Council that on Sunday afternoon, 7 August, 'we had a good meeting on Penydarren 'Tips' between Merthyr and Dowlais. The meeting was of a religious character, opened by Hymn, Lesson and Prayer, and Keir preached the sermon to a large and attentive audience.'[22] Wright went on to say how on the following Sunday he 'continued the work commenced on the Tips. A smaller but better audience; they wanted me to take up the work as a regular thing, weekly.' Of course, giving a religious character to political meetings on a Sunday may have been no more than a way of circumventing laws which would have prevented them, but it seems there was more to it than this. Many in the Labour movement believed that its roots ran deep, as deep as the Sermon on the Mount, and had enough respect for religious traditions not to disregard them in places where they were strong, and where sections of the working class still took inspiration from them.

In general, the leadership of the ILP responded positively to the development of socialist support within the churches, and in the late 1890s was encouraged by the formation of a number of Free Church socialist societies. In 1894, under the leadership of John Clifford, a distinguished Baptist minister and active member of the Fabian Society, the Christian Socialist League was formed out of The Ministers' Union, which declared that 'this country cannot accurately be called Christian so long as people in their collective capacity, by their social, industrial and commercial arrangements, practically deny the Fatherhood of God and the brotherhood of man'. Christ's teaching is 'directly applicable to all questions of sociology and economics', said the union. The union's president was Clifford; its vice president, J. Bruce Wallace, a Congregationalist; and its secretary J. H. Belcher, a former Congregationalist who had become Unitarian. The Union under its openly socialist title of Christian Socialist League, which was adopted by an almost unanimous vote, cut across denominational boundaries and co-ordinated Nonconformist support for the Labour movement between 1894 and 1898, during which time a number of important Free Church ministers left the Liberal Party and joined the ILP, including Dr Charles Leach.[23] More sectarian were the Quaker Socialist Society (1898), which included Arthur Tuke Priestman, the prominent Bradford Quaker and socialist, and the New Church Socialist Society (1895),[24] whose journal, *Uses*, was edited by T. D. Benson. In November 1898 Priestman and Benson accepted the National Administrative Council's invitations to serve as trustees of the ILP Election Fund, and Benson eventually became treasurer of the ILP.[25] The denominational societies had limited influence on the Labour movement and were mainly concerned with trying to convert the members of their churches to socialism. The title of an article, 'The Building of the Bridge', which appeared in the organ of the New Church Socialist Society in 1898[26] epitomizes the efforts being made by sympathizers within the churches at this time, to which many ILP leaders were pleased to respond encouragingly.

Relations between the Labour movement and sections of the Nonconformist churches, which seemed to be developing harmoniously as the nineteenth century drew to a close, suffered serious disruption in January 1903, when, in the *Clarion*, Robert Blatchford delivered a devastating onslaught on religion as part of a review of a new edition of Haeckel's *Riddle of the Universe*, declaring that 'the book demolishes the entire structure upon which the religions of the world are built. There is no escape from that conclusion. The case for science is complete.'[27] The verdict incensed the largely northern readership of the paper, many of whom had strong associations with the Nonconformist churches. For a whole year the columns of the paper were filled with responses, including those of prominent socialist Nonconformist ministers, T. Rhondda Williams, R. H. Horton, S. E. Keeble and R. J. Campbell.[28] A *Clarion* contributor, the Rev. Cartmel Robinson, wrote to Alex. Thompson (Dangle), 'Can you not prevail on Blatchford to cut this controversial wreckage loose and let it go? I am for Unity, but if it is on condition that I apostasize, then — !'[29] And Thompson could see why hundreds of the paper's readers shared Robinson's distress: 'Many leaders of Labour, especially amongst the Trade Union officials, had been local preachers; most of them were more deeply rooted in Christianity than in Socialism.'[30] But Blatchford was unrepentant and reiterated his argument in a book, *God and my Neighbour*, which was followed by a series of articles entitled *Not Guilty or the Defence of Bottom Dog*, in which the theory of Determinism was pressed further. The *Clarion* staff was not altogether out of sympathy with religion, if it had a rational flavour. Blatchford had co-operated with John Trevor when he founded the Labour Church, by speaking at Labour Church Services and advertising services free of charge in his paper. He had joined with Labour Church members to form a Sunday school in connection with one of his Cinderella Clubs, the aim being that 'it should be a place where children can be trained to think and not merely become Socialist or Labour Church members.'[31] For conventional Christianity the *Clarion* staff 'proposed to substitute a theology of Socialism, based on the expansive humanity of the Carpenter of Nazareth.'[32] In the light of the subsequent theological developments when R. J. Campbell, minister of The City Temple, and T. Rhondda Williams, minister of Greenfield Church, Bradford, were saying similar things under the banner of the New Theology movement, it is surprising that Blatchford caused such a furore, but even the more progressive elements in the churches were not ready for it and took more exception to it coming from someone outside organized religion than they might have done had it come from within. However, although in the short term relations between Labour and Nonconformity were seriously disturbed by Blatchford's outspoken rejection of religion, the conflict was widely reported and discussed, and questions of the affinities between the two movements were constantly brought to the attention of the Labour movement and the churches over a period of two or more years. In the long term the '*God and my Neighbour* affair' probably did more to bring Labour and Nonconformity together than to separate them. Blatchford, at this time, was not only out of favour with those in the churches, but his attitude to the Boer War had not helped him in the ILP. Because he was not particularly interested in party organization, he was losing touch with the LRC leadership, amongst whom were some who saw that no advantage could be gained from being at odds with potential Labour voters who, whilst they might not be active in chapel life or agree with Nonconformist opposition to Labour representation, were sufficiently fair to admit that they owed much to chapel culture. This was particularly true of the strongly Nonconformist industrial districts, like Lancashire, the West Riding and South Wales, where Labour had most chance of an electoral breakthrough.

While Blatchford was alienating potential Nonconformist voters, other ILP leaders were courting them, and none more skillfully than one of the party's most outstanding propagandists, Philip Snowden. Born in 1864 at Cowling, a West Riding weaving village situated only four miles from the Lancashire districts of Nelson and Colne, as a child Snowden 'witnessed the vigour of non-conformity, its Radical politics, its temperance zeal, its emphasis on self-improvement' which left a profound mark upon him as 'a life-long temperance enthusiast, attached to Radical icons, most notably Free Trade'.[33] In the debates which surrounded the formation of the ILP in Bradford, Snowden had been recruited by local Liberals to argue their case, but if he had 'come to scoff he stayed to pray' and became a leading ILP propagandist, who, more than any other, adopted the style of an evangelical preacher. Asked by W. T. Stead, in 1906, for his article, 'Books that have made the Labour Party', Ethel, his wife, gave his religion as Wesleyan.[34] But there seems little doubt that he abandoned his parents' formal attachment to Methodism at an early age, possibly soon after reaching the age of eight, when be failed to have a conversion experience at an evangelical meeting.[35] Writing for the *Labour Prophet*, the journal of the Labour Church movement, in 1898, Snowden described how this had led him to see the necessity for two salvations. He believed 'salvation from hell for original sin is getting out of date. With another generation of School Board education it will disappear altogether.' There needed to be personal salvation and social salvation, and they 'are like two palm trees which bear no fruit unless they grow side by side'. The individualistic faith of the churches had confined itself to the preaching of personal salvation as the cure for worldly ills, and 'it has done nothing, unless by accident, for the social amelioration of the people'. Yet he had 'seen everywhere men upon whom the principles of Socialism have had a remarkable effect in raising their personal character. Socialism has regenerated them in the truest sense'.[36] This type of commitment had given birth to the Labour Church movement, as a reaction to the individualism of the chapels and their preoccupation with personal salvation for a future life. But, although he appears to have abandoned the narrow theology of his childhood at an early date, Snowden retained strong local ties and living for some years in Nelson courted and married Ethel Annakin, a Wesleyan Methodist Sunday School teacher.[37] Here, where religion and temperance underlay all social and cultural life, Socialists were compelled to adopt a positive attitude towards both. In doing so, in 1903, the same year as the *Clarion* was disrupting relationships between the Labour movement and Nonconformity, the ILP published a lecture by Snowden entitled *The Christ that is to be* under a text from Tennyson's *In Memoriam*: 'Ring in the valiant man and free,/ The larger heart, the kindlier hand;/ Ring out the darkness of the land,/ Ring in the Christ that is to be.'[38]

The lecture was the most positive expression of the emergent Labour movement's attempts to win the support of Nonconformists, and in the range of its appeal is a remarkable example of Snowden's skill as a propagandist. It includes theological ideas and religious terminology that would have appealed on the one hand to the liberal, near agnostic, and to the narrowly Evangelical nonconformist on the other hand. 'The life of Christ is the great example of human perfection'.[39] Despite all the inadequacies of the Christian Church and its role as 'the slave of rich men', and admitting every count in the indictment which the anti-Christian can bring against the Church', there still remains 'the great and potent fact that Christ has been the greatest influence in the world's history'.[40] This particular point would have had special appeal for those Lancashire and West Riding workers, who, whilst they did not recognize much true Christianity within the churches, and had ceased to attend, except for rites of passage – baptisms, weddings and funerals – nonetheless continued to understand ethical behaviour in terms of Christ's teaching. Snowden, from his own knowledge of the strongly Nonconformist textile districts, clearly recognized that working-class rejection of the churches did not mean that they had rejected religion. His estimate of Christ as differing 'in degree but not in kind from all great teachers' may not have satisfied some, but it was tempered by the qualification that 'in the life of Christ we find ... principles and truths more fully stated than in the life and teachings of any other master.'[41] Christ's law of sacrifice, love and cooperation is the foundation of all the great ethical religions of the world and of all schools of morality, and there is 'a sense in which all – Christian, agnostic and atheist – can accept him as a teacher able to make us wise unto salvation.'[42] United by this fact, he argued, 'the religion of the future will recognise ... the complete organic unity of the whole human race. And this religion will be a political religion ... which will seek to realise its ideal in our industrial and social affairs by the application and use of political methods.'[43] All this would certainly have appealed to theologically-progressive Nonconformists, whose commitment to socialism was gradually developing. It could not have had much appeal for the Evangelicals, whose all-sufficient scheme of redemption was based on the uniqueness of Christ, and who rejected politics. Yet, for all its progressive theological outlook, *The Christ that is to be* ends with Snowden expressing the socialist vision with a religiosity that would have appealed to Nonconformists at home with the terminology of an Evangelical revivalist meeting: 'the only way to regain the earthly paradise is by the old, hard road to Calvary – through persecution, through poverty, through temptation, by the agony and bloody sweat, by the crown of thorns, by the agonising death. And then the resurrection to the New Humanity – purified by suffering, triumphant through Sacrifice.'[44] In the scope of one lecture, Snowden, with his outstanding propagandist skills, had achieved the almost impossible task of appealing to the broad spectrum of Nonconformity. And nowhere was this kind of material more useful than in pressing the ILP cause in the industrial districts where Nonconformity was intricately intertwined with all aspect of the local culture. The pamphlet's importance for the relations between Nonconformity and the early Labour movement has been widely recognized, although its significance is partly missed by Jones who incorrectly attributes it to 1905, when in fact it was printed at Keighley in 1903. The earlier date not only suggests that Blatchford's onslaught on religion was not shared by important Labour propagandists, but also that the theological basis of R. J. Campbell's 'New Theology' movement, which emerged after 1904, was as early as 1903 the view of religion held by some Labour leaders, who believed electoral advantage could be gained by cultivating the common ground. Labour pioneers may have used religious terminology naturally, given that they often had backgrounds in Nonconformity, but it seems more likely that in most cases they deliberately adopted it as a vehicle to carry the socialist message to the strongly Nonconformist areas.

The effectiveness of Snowden's 'Come to Jesus' technique was understood, particularly by the Wibsey chairman. Victor Grayson, a former student for the Unitarian ministry, also made use of biblical imagery in his political speeches, when he successfully contested the Colne Valley seat in 1907, without official ILP support; and when he was defeated in 1910 it was by another Nonconformist preacher, Dr Charles Leach, who had returned to the Liberal Party from the ILP. Grayson received support from a number of clergymen and Nonconformist ministers, including the giant Rev. W. B. Graham, curate of Thongsbridge, described by Blatchford as 'six foot a socialist and five inches a parson'. The editor of the local paper complained that 'The presence in the valley of men wearing the habiliments of the cleric may have had some effect on the election, but it will have more on the church. There is surely something lax in an institution when men ostensibly devoted to spiritual matters can so forget themselves as to promenade a town with a big red banner on which is 'Socialism is God's Gospel for today'. We know of no other place where the presence of these men would be tolerated – a prostitution of their high calling to associate God's gospel with modern Socialism.'[46] It would appear that candidates with backgrounds in Nonconformist preaching had a particular appeal in those constituencies where chapels and their ministers played an important part in the local culture, particularly amongst the somewhat isolated townships of the West Riding ILP heartland.

That sympathetic approaches by the Labour movement did lead to an influx of Nonconformists into the Labour movement is suggested by a resolution of the National Administrative Council, in October 1904, under the heading 'Hymn Book', 'that J. Bruce Glasier compile a Songbook for the use of the Party and that T. D. Benson, I. O. Ford and Philip Snowden compile a song sheet.'[47] The idea was not new. The first edition of the *Labour Church Hymnbook*, published by John Trevor in September 1892, had a run of 10,000 copies, and more were needed before the end of the year. A second edition was published in 1898. As the Labour Church had only 54 congregations at the peak of its expansion in 1895, and because, with the exception of Manchester and Bradford, each with about 300 members, the membership of Labour Church congregations was small, it is clear that the hymnbook was used more widely than for Labour Church services, by ILP branches and for other Labour movement gatherings. The Rev. Aubrey Martin, whose father was secretary of the Gorsemoin ILP branch, South Wales, just before the 1914 war, recounts that the first English hymnbook he ever saw was the Labour Church hymnbook.[48] One explanation of the need of a hymn book may be the choice which had to be made between attendance at church and participation in Labour movement meetings, most of which were held on Sundays. If it had been possible, some Nonconformists who were attracted into the work of the Labour movement might have preferred to continue to worship in their chapels, but sooner or later a choice had to be made, and the hymn, reading and prayer before the ILP branch meeting provided a truncated form of Sunday observance. K. D. Brown has drawn attention to Pierson's conclusion that Labour leaders in the West Riding of Yorkshire tended to abandon their church activity once they became involved in the Labour movement, though they were inclined to regard both in the same light – as a sort of moral crusade.[49]

However, because of their livelihoods, ministers could not so easily make a choice between church and party, although a few did. For example, the Rev. R. Swan, the Congregational minister at Marsden in the West Riding of Yorkshire, resigned his charge in 1907 to become a full-time speaker for the Colne Valley Labour League, which was followed by a further three months as full-time registration agent in Colne Valley. Eventually, for many years until his death in 1938, Swan was treasurer of the *Daily Herald*.[50] But generally, Nonconformist ministers tended to play a supportive, rather than an active, role in Labour movement activities because they were severely limited by their Sunday duties. When J. H. Belcher, the former secretary of the Minister's Union, wrote from the Unitarian Church, Treville Street, Plymouth, to J. Ramsay MacDonald offering his services as an LRC candidate, he received the reply 'you are, of course, heavily handicapped because you cannot give us Sundays'.[51] The difficulties of transferring loyalties from chapels to the Labour movement did not go unnoticed, and by the publication of song sheets and the provision of a substitute for religious worship at the opening of meetings the transference was made a little easier.

Influences also developed which attempted to reconcile the old doctrines with the new social thought and suggested that Socialism was not as incompatible with chapel membership as Liberals liked to argue. For example, R. J. Campbell's 'New Theology', 'the religious articulation of the Labour movement', sought to widen the social content of religion. As well as in Bradford, where there was a small coterie of New Theology men, led by T. Rhondda Williams, the minister of Greenfield Congregational Church, the movement had a strong influence in Wales, where, coupled with the Religious Revival of 1904–5, it led not only to the invigoration of the devotional life of the chapels, but to concern for social questions broader than the traditional ones of education and Disestablishment. Whilst, with the exception of John Clifford, English Baptist ministers showed less interest in the Labour movement than the other denominations, some of their Welsh colleagues were prominent among the pioneers of the Labour Party. 'The Rev. Daniel Hughes, minister at Calfaria Welsh Baptist chapel, Llanelli, was a well-known member of the ILP, whose Socialism produced a reaction when he moved to the English Baptist Church, Crane Street, Pontypool, which was 'full of solicitors, etc.' Hughes was allowed plenty of time to campaign on behalf of Welsh Disestablishment, but when he began to do propaganda work for the

ILP, the congregation secured an injunction and locked the chapel door against him. His breaking of the lock with a sledge hammer did not improve relationships with the staunchly Liberal and respectable membership and he moved to the more tolerant Baptist Church at Machen, Monmouthshire, but apparently without the approval of the denomination, since his name ceased to appear in the Baptist diary. He served for many years as a Labour member on Monmouthshire County Council.

Labour leaders must also have been encouraged because of the influence which Socialism appeared to be having upon those who were to be the next generation of Nonconformist ministers. In the year of the ILP's inaugural conference, Yorkshire United Independent College, Bradford, which trained Congregational ministers, introduced lectures on Political Economy and Social Reconstruction. And, under the influence of the currently fashionable liberal theology, which emphasized the centrality of the Kingdom of God, to be realized on earth, theological students were apt to see no demarcation between religion and politics, and to anticipate the fulfilment of religious aspirations in political processes. This was particularly true in the denominations which most readily accepted modernist theological ideas. Theological students were inclined to adopt either political or ministerial careers as opportunities proved favourable and advantageous. It was not a question of choosing between religion or politics, for they regarded the two spheres as all-of-a-piece. Victor Grayson was a student at the Unitarian Home Missionary College, Manchester, from 1903 to 1907, and resigned from his course only shortly before winning the Colne Valley seat as Labour candidate, without the support of the LRC, in the by-election of 1907.[52] A fellow student, S. E. Bowen described how they used to unlock the door of the college after it had been shut for the night, to admit Grayson when he returned from speaking at ILP meetings. Students at Manchester College, Oxford, were also politically active in support of Labour, and R. V. Holt, later to become Principal of The Unitarian College, Manchester, was responsible for making arrangements for Keir Hardie's visit to the University of Oxford in March 1909.[53]

The Labour movement must also have noticed that the Free Church Council, which had been formed in 1892 to represent the interests of Evangelical Nonconformity, was becoming more concerned with social reform, and this led, in 1906, to the the Council's Social Questions Committee putting forward a Scheme of Social Reconstruction pleading for a number of necessary and urgent reforms. The rapprochement between sections of the Labour movement and the Free Churches was, therefore, sufficiently close in 1905 for the ILP's National Administrative Council to expect that it might secure the co-operation of local Free Church Councils for a demonstration on behalf of the unemployed, which was to take place simultaneously in London and the provinces on 24th June. In July 1905, the National Council of the Evangelical Free Churches made a further response by arranging a special conference to meet representatives of working men's organizations. In his invitation to Ramsay MacDonald, the secretary of the LRC, the Rev. Thomas

Law said that 'some members of Parliament who are working men leaders have already consented to be present and take part', and that 'the conference will be perfectly private so that there can be free and frank expression of opinion on all matters'.[54] MacDonald's replies, however, illustrate the ambivalence with which even the section of the Labour movement most sympathetic to co-operating with the Free Churches, the ILP, viewed relations between Labour and the Churches at this time. He was of the opinion that conferences were 'not particularly profitable because what we want to do is not meet and take part in something that is half conversation and half a speech, but rather, in much smaller gatherings, we should discuss certain underlying principles ... Given a common outlook and understanding and all the rest will follow, but unless we have that common outlook sympathy may be professed and fine things said and done, but there will still be a want of organic relationship between us.'[55] MacDonald's request for a list of those who would be attending the conference suggests that he had reservations about appearing in public with any labour and trade union leaders who, because of their association with the Liberal Party, blurred the image of the Labour movement as an independent political force.[56] But the main uncertainty about the usefulness of co-operating with the Free Churches rested upon the imperialist stance taken by prominent Free Churchmen during the South African War. 'I might say', wrote MacDonald, 'that one of the reasons why I have almost given up hope that the Free Churches will help us very much is the attitude which your leading men, with one or two exceptions, took upon the war.' He referred to names on the letterhead of the National Council of the Evangelical Free Churches, Rev. J. G. Greenhough, R. Perks and Compton Rickett MP, and told Law 'If you seriously consider that a Christian organisation associated with these men can do anything for righteousness' sake, to say nothing of mercy's sake, I think you are very much deluded.' MacDonald doubted whether he would be able to attend the meeting because of another engagement, but if it were possible he would feel bound to say something on these lines, 'so that Free Churchman as I am by all my prejudices and inclinations, I should probably not be able to contribute anything very helpful to the discussion.'[57]

Both the churches and the Labour movement were divided over the war; Pelling's comment that it caused 'a remarkable re-alignment of friendships and hostilities among the British Socialists' can be applied almost equally to the situation in the churches.[58] The Fabian Society by a small minority decided to make no official pronouncement on issues raised by the war, anxious on the one hand to avoid, as G. B. Shaw said, any commitment to 'a non-Socialist point of policy', and on the other crippling the Society by going against the tide of popular Imperialism. Blatchford, an ex-sergeant in the 103rd Fusiliers, was strongly patriotic, although his view was not shared by other members of the *Clarion* staff. MacDonald resigned from the Fabian Society for its refusal to denounce the war, and Keir Hardie was thoroughly pro-Boer, believing that 'their Republican form of government bespeaks freedom.'[59] Although Hardie's support for the Boers was extreme, the ILP was opposed to the war and after it was over remained strongly suspicious of the Imperialist tendencies which it had highlighted. In the churches, the anti-war faction, although not always small, had difficulty in keeping the issue before meetings because of the fear that it would be a cause of acrimonious division. In the Manchester District Association of Unitarian and Free Christian Churches, an anti-war motion was discussed after an unsuccessful attempt to prevent it by the moving of 'The Previous Question', but after a brief debate the meeting became so small that the proposer asked leave to withdraw it, and the matter was not again raised during 1900.[60] The London Baptist Association avoided discussing the war in the autumn of 1901, for fear of revealing its divided counsels; but a leading Baptist minister, J. G. Greenhough, president of the National Council of the Evangelical Free Churches in 1901, one of the men mentioned by MacDonald in his letter to Law, was a firm imperialist.[61] So also was the leading Methodist MP, Robert Perks, another subject of MacDonald's criticism, who for his lead in organising the Liberal imperialists was referred to as 'Imperial Perks'.[62] The prevailing Nonconformist response to the war is explained by a general growth of nationalism and racialism, which was intensified by British support for the Americans in the Spanish-American War of 1898, and a belief that the extension of British rule would benefit the human race. Three quarters of the Wesleyans are estimated to have supported the war and, in July 1901, only four of the 94 ministers serving Liverpool circuits opposed it.[63] In spite of some strong opposition, such as that of the Rev. S. E. Keeble, who in 1909 founded the Sigma Society, an association of socialist Methodist ministers, Nonconformity as a whole was seen to endorse the imperialism that fuelled the war. As a result, the ILP, which had so strongly opposed it, was unlikely to be very ready to take up suggestions from the churches for closer co-operation, at least at official level, and this was perhaps the most important fact determining the nature of the rather cool relationship of the ILP to the churches in the early years of the twentieth century.

NOTES

1. Cited by P. d'A. Jones, *The Christian Socialist Revival 1877–1914* (Princeton University Press, Princeton, New Jersey, 1968), p.353.
2. Independent Labour Party, National Administrative Council Minutes, 28 May 1894.
3. Jones, *op. cit.*, p.361.
4. J. Trevor, *My Quest for God* (Labour Prophet Office, London, 1897) p.241.
5. J. Trevor to J. K. Hardie, 20 Apr 1895, Archives of the ILP, Series III, *The Francis Johnson Correspondence*, 1888–1950, 1895/75 (Harvester Press Microfilm).
6. J. K. Hardie to J. Trevor, 23 Apr 1895, Archives of the ILP, Series III, *The Francis Johnson Correspondence*, 1888–1950, 1895/78 (Harvester Press Microfilm).
7. See L. Smith, 'John Trevor and the Labour Church Movement', Huddersfield Polytechnic MA dissertation, 1986.

8. Printed as Appendix I in E. P. Thompson, *William Morris, Romantic to Revolutionary* (Revised Edition, Merlin, London, 1977).

9. G. Lansbury, *My Life* (Constable, London, 1928), p.78.

10. Eleanor Marx Aveling to Council, Socialist League, 5 Oct 1885, in Socialist League Papers, Amsterdam, cited by S. Yeo in 'A New Life: The Religion of Socialism in Britain, 1883–1896', *History Workshop Journal*, 4-6, 1978–9, p.6.

11. Yeo, *op. cit.*, pp.5–56.

12. W. T. Stead, 'The Labour Party and the books that helped to make it', *The Review of Reviews*, 1906, pp.568–582.

13. *Ibid.*, p.570.

14. K. D. Brown, 'Nonconformity and the British Labour Movement: A Case Study', *Journal of Social History*, VIII, 1975, p.116.

15. *Ibid.*, pp.116–117.

16. D. E. Martin, '"The Instruments of the People"?: The Labour Parliamentary Party in 1906' in D. E. Martin and D. Rubinstein (eds.), *Ideology and the Labour Movement* (Croom Helm, London, 1979) p.133.

17. *Ibid.*, p.132.

18. *Ibid.*, p.133.

19. Independent Labour Party, National Administrative Council Minute, 2 Jan 1896.

20. Hyde, Pleasant Sunday Afternoon, Minutes, 1894–1900. (Tameside Public Library).

21. Miss D. Price, Flat 15, Llys Pedr, Lampeter, Dyfed, to L. Smith.

22. Independent Labour Party, National Administrative Council Minutes, Aug 1898.

23. Charles Leach to Keir Hardie, 20 Aug 1894, Archives of the ILP, Series III, *The Francis Johnson Correspondence*, 1888–1950, 1894/184 (Harvester Press Microfilm).

24. Jones, *op. cit.*, pp.353–367.

25. Independent Labour Party, National Administrative Council Minutes, Nov 1898.

26. *Uses*, A Monthly New-Church Journal of Evolutionary Reform, Vol.III, No 31, Oct 1898.

27. *Clarion*, 23 Jan 1903.

28. *Ibid.*, 1 May 1903, 17 July 1903, 23 Oct 1903 and 11 Dec 1903.

29. A. Thompson, *Here I Lie* (George Routledge and Sons, London, 1937), p.109.

30. *Ibid.*

31. Quoted by F. Reid, 'Socialist Sunday Schools in Britain, 1892–1939', *International Review of Social History*, 1966.

32. Thompson, *op. cit.*, p.107.

33. D. Howell, *British Workers and the Independent Labour Party, 1888–1906* (Manchester University Press, Manchester, 1983), p.4.; See also P. Viscount Snowden, *An Autobiography* (Ivor Nicholson and Watson, London, 1934), vol. 1, pp.20, 25–29; Keith Laybourn, *Philip Snowden: A Biography* (Gower, Aldershot, 1988).

34. Stead, *op. cit.*, p.580.

35. *The Labour Prophet*, Apr 1898, pp.169–170.

36. *Ibid.*

37. P. Firth, 'Socialism and the Origins of the Labour Party in Nelson and Colne', unpublished MA thesis, University of Manchester, 1975, p.33n.

38. P. Snowden, *The Christ that is to be* (Independent Labour Party, London, 1903).
39. *Ibid.*, p.3.
40. *Ibid.*, p.5.
41. *Ibid.*, p.5.
42. *Ibid.*, p.5.
43. *Ibid.*, p.7.
44. *Ibid.*, p.13.
45. D. Clark, *Victor Grayson, Labour's Lost Leader* (Quartet Books, London, 1985).
46. *Colne Valley Guardian*, 26 July 1907.
47. Independent Labour Party, National Administrative Council Minutes, 31 Oct and 1 Nov 1904.
48. Rev. Aubrey Martin, Garwen, Rhydowen, Llandysul, Dyfed, to L. Smith, 30th June 1986.
49. Brown, *op. cit.*, p.118.
50. D. Clark, *Colne Valley: Radicalism to Socialism* (Longman, London, 1981), p.148.
51. R. MacDonald to J. H. Belcher, 29 Dec 1905, Archive of the LP, Series III, *General Correspondence and Political Records*, LRC28/13 (Harvester Press Microfilm).
52. For Grayson, see David Clark, *Victor Grayson, Labour's Lost Leader* (Quartet Books, London, 1985).
53. R. Holt to J. K. Hardie, 9 and 14 Mar 1905, Archives of the ILP, Series III, *The Francis Johnson Correspondence*, 1888–1950, 1909/100 and 106.
54. T. Law to J. R. MacDonald, 16 June 1905, Archives of the LP, Series III, *General Correspondence and Political Records*, LRC24/119 (Harvester Press Microfilm).
55. J. R. MacDonald to T. Law, 20 June 1905, Archives of the LP, Series III, *General Correspondence and Political Records*, LRC24/120 (Harvester Press Microfilm).
56. J. R. MacDonald to T. Law, 6 July 1905, Archives of the LP, Series III, *General Correspondence and Political Records*, LRC24/123 (Harvester Press Microfilm).
57. J. R. MacDonald to T. Law, 20 June 1905, Archives of the LP, Series III, Series III, *General Correspondence and Political Records*, LRC24/120 (Harvester Press Microfilm).
58. H. Pelling, *Origins of the Labour Party* (Oxford University Press, Oxford, 1965), p.187.
59. *Ibid.*, pp.188–189.
60. G. Head, 'Unitarians and the Peace Movement, 1899', *The Inquirer*, 7 Jan 1984.
61. D. W. Bebbington, *The Nonconformist Conscience* (George Allen and Unwin, London, 1982), p.122; J. R. MacDonald to T. Law, 20 June 1905, Archives of the LP, Series III, Series III, *General Correspondence and Political Records*, LRC24/120 (Harvester Press Microfilm).
62. Bebbington, *op. cit.*, p.122.
63   *Ibid.*, pp.122–123.

5. The ILP and Education: the Bradford Charter

Carolyn Steedman

There is no existing body of work on the Independent Labour Party and education, and so discussion has to begin with arguments about education and the Labour movement in general, arguments that are both constraining and illuminating of any new set of questions about the ILP. In the historiography of the Labour Party and education, an implicit model has been constructed, of a 'background' to Labour thinking, in which the ILP and other socialist groups provide educational policy for the Trades Union Congress, and trade Unionists in their turn, inform and influence the Labour Party. When the relationship between the ILP and the TUC over educational questions in the period before 1906 has been discussed at all, it has been considered in terms of individuals, and their dual membership of the two bodies. It is that kind of individual and autobiographical link that has provided Clive Griggs's map of the connection between the education policy of the TUC and the Labour Party, and his suggestion that the Labour Party 'directly imported' Congress's policy.[1] As he points out, Labour MPs and prominent trades unionists were likely to attend the annual meetings of the Party and the Congress. At Congress, resolutions on education were usually brought forward by delegates who also belonged to the SDF or the ILP. 'This source of ideas,' says Griggs, 'partly explains why TUC views on education were radical in an organisation heavily influenced by liberalism'.[2]

We know then, a good deal about the TUC source of Labour Party thinking on education, particularly over the questions of secular education and social welfare provisions for school children. The campaigns for school meals and for medical inspection after 1905 have been used to illustrate the trajectory of ideas from the SDF, through the TUC to the Labour Party.[3] However, Margaret McMillan's experience with the Parliamentary members of her own party, who she found particularly obtuse and ungiving over the question of medical inspection, suggests that this member of the ILP found an important source of support and perhaps of her thinking in the TUC. There are grounds here for speculating about a reversal of the model of influence, from 'the smaller socialist parties', through the TUC, to the Labour Party. That model however is still – implicitly again – in use, when the First World War is under discussion, and analysis turns to the relationship of 'the smaller socialist groups' with the Labour Party, the brief flowering of ILP expertise and influence on the Labour Party Advisory Committees set up in the autumn of 1918, and its fate as a party under the structural reorganisation of Labour that these years saw.[4]

By telling the story in this way, the historian is dealing with two unspoken problems. The first is to do with what several ILP-ers of the early 20th century were quite open about, and that is that education 'is supposed to very dull and not very important.'[5] The second is to do with the way in which ILP policy on education did not seem to have very much to do with *education*; that the ILP published little pamphlet material on educational questions at the national level; and every year at Conference between 1894 and 1914 carefully walked the boundary between the idea of the full life for all and the compulsions of child-labour.[6] In some accounts of child labour and the half-time system (the half-time exemption of children from schooling between the ages of 12 and 14, particularly for work in the textile trades) the ILP has had a good press and been described as a major mover for its abolition.[7] But seeing the ILP's careful consideration of its trade union members and its cautious manoeuvres on this question as a crusade can only arise from confusing McMillan's mission with that of her party.

In its first year of existence, the ILP in Conference called for the abolition of 'overtime, piece-work and child labour'[8] and a year later fixed an age limit of 14 years to the last.[9] In 1895, whilst the resolution carried on this point asserted that 'no intelligent and humane community will permit its children to be exploited for wages under at least 13 years of age', and the NAC recommended 15 years as Party policy, Conference actually voted to recommend the minimum age of half-time labour for children to be raised from 11 to 12, in the Factories and Workshops Bill then before Parliament.[10] This same Conference (1895) settled the categories of its national programme, and 'Education' was one of them (the others were Agriculture, Industry, Social and Fiscal). Conference was to call for 'free primary, secondary and university education' as it now did for the next twenty years;[11] but 'free' was not at all the same thing as 'compulsory', which is a point to bear in mind when the Bradford Charter is discussed.

In 1897, proposals for the state maintenance of children 'while under teaching' were brought up against two ILP anxieties, the first embodied in Enid Stacy on this occasion, who thought they 'appeared to affirm that it was no longer the duty of any parent to bring up his children'; and the second that of those representatives who were quite clear that what was really at issue was *not* extended elementary or secondary education, but rather half-time labour and the role of children in the family economy of the textile districts. The formula agreed on in 1897, about the desirability of the 'ultimate abolition' of child labour (ultimately, but not now), was to serve Conference well for many years to come.[12] Conference could vote resolutely on the child-labour involved in street trading,[13] but the regulated employment of children in the cotton and woollen trades was a different matter. Resolutions to raise the age for half-time exemption from schooling were defeated in 1903,[14] and in 1909 Margaret McMillan regretted the weakness of the proposal on half-time at the annual Conference, wishing that the Party would select educational reforms in sequence and put some work into them instead of reiterating long lists of pious hopes.[5]

Trawling ILP Conference reports in this way, for discussion of child labour and education, does of course ignore the Party's other intense preoccupations, with secular education (in training colleges no less than elementary schools), with the analysis that developed in common with the TUC and later the Labour Party in the aftermath of the 1902 Education Act, of secondary education as 'the monopoly of the middle class'[16] and of course, after 1906, with the medical inspection and treatment of school children.[17] The question of medical attention to children and their physical education (which in contemporary terms involved feeding them) that was forced on the ILP agenda by McMillan, was not dealt with by Conference as a question of child-welfare or child rescue, nor as an aspect of an emerging 'welfare state', but as part and parcel of an analysis of education in a divided society, that the TUC had developed and that the 1902 Act had sharpened.[18] Medical inspection, the treatment of children, the vision that saw schools providing children with beds and baths were understood to be about equality of access to a cultural good.[19]

It is with this observation that the historian may begin to find the historiography of the Labour movement and education in Britain in the period 1890–1920 illuminating rather than constraining. In historical discussion of the Labour Party, there has developed a powerful commonplace, of 'education' seen as the cultural commodity of which large numbers of men in the Labour movement (this is a configuration ascribed to men, not to women: a history of the relationship of working-class women to these ideas remains to be written) had been deprived and thus as the cultural commodity – the good – that they sought to have bestowed upon new generations, that were representative of the children they themselves had once been.[20]

Clive Griggs develops this argument in his *Trades Union Congress and the Struggle for Education*, showing how a sense of educational deprivation operated in the autobiographies of trade union members of the Labour Party, providing them with a means of analysing and interpreting working-class childhoods of the late 19th century. These were childhoods remembered in early 20th century autobiographical writing, and often given meaning by depicting a particular type of schooling or lack of schooling.[21] Rodney Barker used similar evidence to support his claim that 'it was not commonly believed within the Labour Party that the actual material of the curriculum was the main cause of whatever social and political effects education might have.'[22]

In making a sketch map for a history of 'the ILP and education', we might well anticipate that same sense – of being cut off from the educational goods of the earth – to operate in the political life-stories of trade union members of the ILP; but we would then speculate about the shaping force of other factors. First, we would recognise that from 1893 (rather than from 1900, or 1906) the local and national ILP provided a focus for the political interpretation of individual life-stories. Certainly, the TUC had provided such a focus for even longer, but we should note as particular to the ILP the fact that up to 1902 the Party had its most consistent electoral successes and was most politically effective under the local School Board system. The ILP had its attention consistently drawn to local political management as a context for educational questions, educational policies and, indeed, for shaping memories of educational deprivation.[23] Then, we might wonder about the shaping imaginative

279

and practical force of a party that defined 'education' in the broad sense as 'the making of socialists', in William Morris's project of moulding thought and feeling in 'the education of desire.'[24]

We might then remind ourselves, over the question of redistributing the 'goods' of education (for there is a strong sense of disapproval in the accounts that have highlighted it) that we were warned a long time ago by Brian Simon against interpreting these attitudes of the labour movement as a purblind and unthinking effort to redistribute cultural capital (rather than subjecting it to rigorous scrutiny in the construction of new policies and new curricula). The Labour movement quite clearly understood the education system of Victorian and Edwardian England and Wales mirrored the class system. The way in which 'a cordon of gold' had been drawn around the secondary schools by the Education Act of 1902,[25] the Act's effective blocking of the developing system of secondary education for working-class children in the Higher Grade Schools, and the end of the School Board system, all offered a very recent example of the class drama that the question of secondary education in particular embodied for the Labour movement.[26]

Secondary schooling had developed as middle-class education, as a separate system from that of the elementary school, with a separate curriculum and a different set of age-boundaries. Infant and elementary schools catered for working-class children from 4 or 5 to 12 years (effectively from 1902) or to 14 (after 1918). The course of elementary education lasted until 14 years, and local education authorities (School Boards until 1902, Education Committees of Councils after that date) had the power to compel attendance until that age was reached. They equally had powers to grant certificates of partial exemption from schooling, when a child reached the age of 12 and a certain educational standard. The extraordinarily complex relationship of the Factory Acts and post-1870 educational legislation, and the way in which they together determined the shape of half-time child labour, presents us with three important factors for understanding Labour movement attitudes to it, and the development of programmes and policies concerning it.[27] First, to the contemporary ear, 'elementary' education meant (not as it now does to the historian of education, 'a system of education experienced by children under 14') but basic, simple, restricted and rudimentary education. It was understood as a cheap education for cheap children, developed for them, and more and more vigorously separated from 'secondary' education. Second, the system of half-time labour had been the first compulsory education in Britain, developed under the Factory Acts from 1833 onwards.[28] Some of its adherents were moved to defend it not only as fundamental to profit in the textile trades, but as a proper education (Karl Marx praised it as polytechnic education) for working-class children.[29] Third, its existence in two bodies of legislation, had led to forty years of arguments and litigation over the question of the power of bye-laws under the Education Acts to override the Factory Acts.[30] Since the 1870s, the question had been one of noisy publicity in the localities.

In this divided system, the Liberal administration did help provide a narrow ladder for a small minority of working-class children to the secondary schools at the age of 11 under the Free Places regulations of 1907.[31] But it is clear that in the pre-First World War period, the curricula of the elementary and secondary schools were more consciously divided from each other than they had been before. One case-study of reading material provided for elementary school children by the London County Council shows the practical force of new ideas, about a plain, elementary and 'natural' language, that was deemed appropriate for the elementary school children of the Metropolis: *Peter Pan*, as rewritten by the L.C.C. School Books Sub-Committee in 1915, was purged of the cultural referents and allusions that marked the language and the literature prescribed for secondary school children.[32]

In *Keywords*, Raymond Williams alerted us to a wider context – a history of culture in society – to these understandings and definitions of education. 'It remains remarkable' he comments, 'that after nearly a century of universal education in Britain the majority of the population should be seen as *uneducated* or *half-educated*.' Indeed, he locates the development of the word *educated* to mean those who had received a particular kind of education in literary and linguistic culture in precisely the period of organised and universal education in Britain (from about 1880 to 1920) and remarks that there was 'a strong class sense in this use, and the level indicated by *educated* has been continually adjusted to leave the majority of people who have received an education below it.'[33]

When R. H. Farrah, delegate of the National General Workers to the TUC in 1916, observed that 'the whole system is rotten, and since University men have been established at Whitehall, the line of partition between the middle and working-classes is greater than ever', it seems likely that he too was working with that same history of keywords in English culture and society, and with a history of legislative provision for increased class division in the form and content of education – a history that he had actually lived through.[34]

William Leach of Bradford (of whom, much more: in the end, this will be a local story) made those same points to the local Trades Council (and to the Liberals who made up the Education Committee on which he sat), those men (all men now, after the 1902 Act, for women could not be elected to urban and district councils, as they were to the School Boards) who 'smiled tolerantly in a superior fashion' at the thought of their own progressiveness in educational matters. He described a society divided into 'the governed and the governors', divided by the Act of 1902 and a ratio of one to fifteen, the one getting beyond 'the elementary process' and going to secondary school, the fifteen left behind as adolescent workers, to get 'a spasmodic and makeshift smattering of languages, handicrafts, book-keeping … in the evening schools.' He observed that

> no well-to-do parent would regard this demi-semi-training as in any sense satisfactory. Secondary education … as its title indicates, is the real process of training which follows preparation for training. Literature, languages,

the arts, the sciences, the technological studies, the physical development on the playing fields are reserved for one in fifteen of the nation's children.[35]

A recent account of 'Labour and Education' in the period 1906–1914, places the most successful aspect of the Parliamentary Labour Party's educational programme, that of child welfare, under this heading. Clive Griggs shows how enthusiasm – where it existed – for the feeding of school children and their medical inspection (later, their treatment) arose from a perception of 'the social conditions which prevented children from gaining the most that the educational system had to offer.'[36]

Arguments like these were not so much moved by belief that 'education was valuable for its own sake'.[37] Rather, these men understood quite clearly what was the cultural and monetary value of the commodity they sought, for as Clive Griggs points out, 'technical education might raise a worker to the rank of foreman, but it was secondary education ... which was more likely to provide the social mobility to join the ranks of the white collar workers.'[38] The Shipwrights' representative at the 1917 TUC thought that there was 'a real danger of this country losing its own soul in order to gain the whole world. I appeal to the Parliamentary Committee to see that classical and higher education shall not be neglected at the expense of mere science.'[39] This rhetoric was part of a political perception, available to anyone who knew the post-1902 history of education in a class society.

From 1893 onwards, these were the understandings and perceptions of childhood, culture and class that had framed ILP policy on education. The questions of child-labour and the half-time system were no mere adjunct to an educational policy, rather, child-labour *was* the educational issue of the years 1893–1918. We could remember at this point as well how symbolically important the half-time system was to ILP members in imagining social injustice. When Katharine Bruce Glasier was asked to join the Nursery School Association's campaign in 1927, what immediately sprang to mind was a system of child-labour that had been outlawed ten years before under the Fisher Act: 'the obsession returns upon me,' she wrote, ' – just as I felt the horror of half-time in Bristol in 1891 ...'[40] It is not possible then, to disentangle these questions, of education and child labour, from each other, and indeed, it would be historically misleading to make the attempt, for all questions of elementary education were also and at the same time questions about what a society *did* with its working-class children. We see here one example among many available from Western societies in this period, of large-scale cultural adjustments to the transformation of the majority of a society's children from workers into scholars. It was understanding this point that allowed Brian Simon to argue that the Fisher Education Act of 1918 was not a stage in educational advance at all, but rather a measure that finally abolished the half-time system.[41]

This chapter is concerned with these questions of class, culture and education – secondary education in particular – that were forced by the development of universal education after 1880. It will focus on a particular educational programme developed by the local Trades Council and the ILP in Bradford in the autumn of 1916 – 'the Bradford Charter' – and its rapid adoption as Labour Party (never Independent Labour Party) policy. It will be argued that a way in which the Bradford Charter might finally be understood is as an attempt to imagine (at a local level, but within a long national trajectory) what a working-class child who was not a worker, might look like. This act of imagination was forced by Liberal legislation on secondary education from 1902 onwards to be sure, and trade union analysis at Congress, from the late 1880s onwards, of schooling in a class society, was an important source for the Charter. But in an important way, this new kind of child could not have been imagined anywhere but Bradford or a place like Bradford where the conflict between the schooled child and the working child remained a question of local politics for so long, where the local ILP worked so closely with the local Trades Council and trade unionists in the city,[42] and where war conditions sharpened that conflict of definitions between scholars and workers in a way quite particular to Bradford.

In October 1916 the Bradford Trades Council organised a conference to discuss 'Education After the War', which had as a major agenda item a policy 'formulated by local trade unionists.'[43] Existing accounts of the Charter point out how much resemblance it bore to the TUC programme for educational reform, which had been developed over the previous twenty years. It has also been pointed out that the Charter moved beyond all existing Labour movement programmes, in calling for *compulsory* secondary schooling for all children until the age of 16. Under the terms of the Charter, this extended education was to take place in 'a common secondary school', to which all forms of competitive entry had been abolished, and within the framework of 'a unified national system of education', which stretched from the nursery school to the university. The Charter also embodied provisions that Brian Simon, in his early account of it, saw as 'proper coming from Bradford,' that is 'a great extension of medical services to children and expectant mothers, for gymnasia, swimming bath, playing fields ... school meals ...'[44]

A more recent account of the Charter has paid it attention as a response to a WEA initiative of 1916, which, along with other programmes for reform devised in this year, mark stages in the 'evolution' of a Labour Party policy for educational reconstruction.[45] J. R. Brooks suggests that none of these schemes was put forward as 'a final definitive statement; all were intended by their authors as a continuing debate on postwar reconstruction ...'[46] Of course, we are not to know what was in William Leach's mind when, as main author and promoter of the Charter, he told Bradford trade unionists that 'we can make this Charter law in the early future';[47] but that is what he *wrote*, and he does not seem to have been aware of contributing to a consensus over the reform of secondary education. Certainly the Charter had deeper and more complex origins than the circulation of the WEA pamphlet *What Labour Wants from Education* in August 1916.[48]

Brian Simon's account of 1965 is the one that is usually used to describe the swift passage of the Bradford Charter through the Labour Party and Independent Labour Party Conferences of 1917, and its enshrinement as Labour Party policy on education: William Leach (prominent member of the Bradford ILP, local manufacturer and editor of the *Pioneer*) proposed the adoption of the Charter to the delegates gathered in Bradford in October; the conference resolved to forward the plan to the Board of Education, to all Trades Council across the country and to local MPs.[49] Three months later Meredith Frank Titterington, member of the Bradford Trades Council, Stuff and Woollen Warehousemen delegate to the TUC and delegate to the Labour Party Conference, proposed the Charter to the Conference, whereupon it is unanimously accepted.[50] It is interesting (though perhaps not particularly important) to note what these accounts do not point out, which is that the Bradford Charter never became Independent Labour Party policy on education. The Charter was proposed to the ILP in Leeds in April. It was not voted upon, but forwarded to the National Administrative Council for consideration.[51] It was thought that it might form the focus of discussion at the ILP Summer School that year. A year later the NAC reported that it had done nothing to or with the Charter, given 'the unsettled state of industry and of finance and economics'.[52] The delegates to the 1918 ILP Conference did not discuss the Charter at all (it was anyway by now Labour Party policy). When they dealt with questions of education and schooling, they did so by giving a cautious welcome to the Fisher Bill, noting the hardship that parents would experience in feeding and clothing their children under its provisions for raising the school leaving age. Conference urged ILP Members of Parliament to press for an amendment providing a family allowance (called 'a mainte-nance grant') of 7s. (35p) a week for all children under 14 years. But they did not mention Clause 3 of the Bradford Charter, which had called for a graded system of allowances for all children under 16.[53] The eventual fate of the Charter is implied in several ways. J. R. Brooks suggests that Leach's proposal was a basic model for the first generation of comprehensive schools half a century later.[54] Meredith Titterington (who had proposed the Bradford Charter to the Labour Party Conference in 1917), continued to promote his – very Bradfordian – interest in the physical conditions of elementary schooling to the TUC,[55] (against the grain, as Griggs's work suggests[56]) though he had by now long ceased to be an executive member of the Bradford Trades and Labour Council, the body which, working closely with the local ILP, had developed the Charter in the first place.

It is in fact to the Bradford Trades and Labour Council that we must now turn our attention. On the eve of the First World War, it was one of the observers of the educational scene that told Bradford it was living on the fat of its reputation for progressivism, and that its predominantly Liberal Education Committee was practising retrenchment whilst pretending otherwise.[57] Nevertheless, cooperation between the Labour group on the Education Committee with key progressive Liberals had allowed the formulation of plans for the wholesale reorganisation of child welfare in the city, through the co-ordination of the Health and Education Committees. William Leach (formerly on both committees as ILP representative for Great Horton Ward, and writing in the newspaper he edited[58]) called these schemes 'cherished pieces of work', a practical possibility to be distinguished from 'more remote' aspects of ILP policy, such as 'the advance of public ownership, the destruction of exploitation of labour, the abolition of idleness … and the speed of communal goodwill.'[59] Certain cherished hopes, he argued, lay within administrative grasp: every baby born in Bradford might become a municipal responsibility, the whole educational system could be remodelled to secure maximum health for all children; secondary education could be made free; and the homes which scarred children's bodies with ill-health could be torn down by the assumption of 'municipal responsibility for the provision of good houses and the destruction of bad.'[60] Not only did all this lie within the realm of practical politics (much of it made possible by 'two of the most wonderful acts in matters educational that had ever been passed … the 1906 Schools Meals Act and the 1907 Administrative Provisions Act'[61]), but it was already happening in Bradford, measurable improvement shown by 'a notable reduction in the demand for babies' coffins'.[62] Official Liberalism however was preventing the development of the system by blocking the initiative of their own Chair and deputy Chair of the Health Committee.

The enemy of working-class children's education was not only to be seen at work in the city. The *Pioneer* scrutinised the proposal for 'vocational training' embodied in the Education Bill of 1913, and said 'why not discard fancy names and call it "Trade School Training?" … Who demands it? The commercial interests, goaded by the fear of better continental systems. A plentiful supply of efficient workers – not educated workers – is what they seek …'[63] In these months as well, educational experts seemed to be supporting reactionary political arguments. William Leach was twice outraged in his report of the North of England Education Conference held in Bradford in January 1914, first because Margaret McMillan's name was not once mentioned, and second at Alfred Mumford's paper of which one of the headings was "Some Gathering Doubts as to the Benefits of School Education for all Children of the Working Class".[64]

Two years later Bradford manufacturers could pursue more openly what Leach saw as their true ends and interests. Under war conditions, and with the country-wide demand for child labour, the Board of Education and the Home Office showed a willingness to countenance the employment of school-age children.[65] In December 1915, Bradford Chamber of Commerce sent a deputation to the Elementary School Sub-Committee of the Education Committee, asking for a lowering of the school-leaving age, and an extension of the system of half-time exemption. Leach's *Pioneer* thought theirs the most cynical use of the language of national interest, and praised the Committee's refusal to take part in the 'moral torpor induced by war conditions.'[66] These men were an old history, wearing new clothes, the same manufacturers you could have found twenty years before, who did 'not believe in child labour for their own children, but who ardently [believed] in it for the children of others.' Were they to have their way, 'we should expect to see Oastler's monument crash to the earth of its own accord in Forster Square through the vast increase of clattering little clogs on the hard pavements of the city.[67]

By May, the children had been 'thrown to the wolves,' and exemption for full-time labour at the age of 13 granted.[68] The Education Authority's decision had a symbolic importance at a national level, the *Highway* noting that

> Bradford Local Education Authority, the Mecca of English Educationalists, has 'fallen from grace.' The factory system has claimed a few more young souls, and out of the broken lives of Bradford's children it will coin a little more gold for the spinning masters.[69]

The Spinners' Association was particularly implicated.[70] Old arguments had resurfaced, about the need to train little fingers early. According to William Leach, 'child labour ... [had] received an enormous stimulus, and our education ... set back a generation.[71] What is more, a conjunction of the particular system of half-time labour in Bradford, and the impact of the Education Committee's decision on that system, would result in 'the double curse', of half-time labour from the age of 12, and full-time employment from the age of 13. By the beginning of 1917, it was clear that the new ruling had precisely this effect, that halftimers were leaving school for good at thirteen, accompanied by 'a heavy proportion of 13 year-olds who never would have gone half time at all.'[72]

In February 1916, three months before the Education Committee's decision had toppled Oastler's statue, the Bradford No.1 branch of the NUR had ordered a hundred copies of the WEA pamphlet *Fair Play to the Children* to support the campaign that its members saw they would have to mount against the national increase in children's employment.[73] A month later, in March, members of the local WEA visited the Trades Council to suggest the formation of study circles and a joint conference on 'Trade Union Problems After the War'.[74] A Bradford branch of the WEA had been formed in 1909, and its most popular classes in the six years of its existence had been in social and economic history, particularly when they focused on the locality and its industrial past.[75] Indeed, the Association's Secretary had recently published a pamphlet on the history of a topic that was just about to engage the attention of the Trades Council and the WEA,[76] for by May, the immediate focus of attention switched from post-War reconstruction to the lowering of the school leaving age and the rapid growth of child-labour in the city. Three days before the Conference on 'Trade Union Problems After the War' was due to take place, the Trades Council Executive met to form a committee of local teachers and the local WEA to promote condemnation of a move bound to lead to 'physical deterioration and unfitness for the children'.[77] A public meeting on the question was arranged for June,[78] and William Leach was fixed on as one of the two speakers who might represent the Trades Council position.[79] By the end of the summer he had assumed the shaping responsibility for the Trades Council's educational programme, the 'Bradford Charter'.[80]

It is frequently described how William Leach (1871–1949), the Bradford textile manufacturer of Valley Mill who had once employed Fred Jowett as an overlooker, was drawn into ILP politics by his former employee.[81] His name, as an editor of the Bradford ILP newspapers *Forward* (between 1904 and 1909) and the *Pioneer* (from October 1915 until Frank Betts took over), flickers through the pages of Bradford ILP history and existing accounts of the Bradford Charter. He presented himself to his various publics as an educational thinker pressed in the mould of Margaret McMillan, and his editorials and articles he commissioned for the *Forward* in particular strove to keep her memory alive for readers of the new century.[82] He thought that McMillan was 'the greatest living educationalist,' and that by 1914 'every single advance made in the last fifteen or twenty years is directly traceable to her genius. This wonderful seer and prophetess has disturbed and harassed and trained the public conscience ... one woman has set going an entire revolution'.[83] McMillan kept up with his work in the city long after she had left it, telling readers of the *Labour Leader* in 1908, for instance, about his proposal to the Bradford Education Committee that they properly ascertain the state of health of the children asking for half-time exemption who came before them.[84] He had been involved in the Bradford Cinderella Club since 1892,[85] voluntary work over which he and McMillan cannot always have seen eye to eye, given her disapproval of Cinderella's views on supplying children with 'jolly good blow-outs' instead of imparting physiological education through good food eaten in tasteful surroundings.[86] He stood successfully as municipal candidate for Great Horton Ward in 1907 and sat on the Education Committee until 1913 when he lost his seat, not regaining it until the election of 1920 when he stood for Bradford Moor. He was elected as MP for Bradford Central three times during the inter-war years.[87]

As early as 1905 *Forward* was promoting the same kind of 'complete scheme of national education for the use of all classes of the community' that the Charter was later to embody, though the focus was on infant and elementary education rather than secondary.[88] The regular column of 'Bradford Trades Council' news was started in 1907, and switched the paper's attention to the secondary stages of education in the conviction that 'there was a manifest attempt to turn the secondary education system of this city into a middle class channel ...'[89] By now, the kind of educational perception in which McMillan had tried to school Bradford was in decline. She had worked for twenty-five years for the physical and educational welfare (what she called the 'physiological education') of not only 'the very poorest' children of the unskilled labouring poor but also of the very youngest.[90] In 1907 the Liberal administration at the Board of Education had introduced the Free Places Regulations ('Regulations for Secondary Schools'), increasing capitation for those schools offering a quarter of their places free to elementary school graduates.[91] From now on, according to Rodney Barker, 'the interest of the

Labour Party switched to the secondary schools'[92] McMillan's political and educational concern with nursery, infant and elementary school children was out of political fashion, in the Labour movement as a whole, in her own party and among trades unionists in Bradford. When, in the years after *Forward* folded in 1909, William Leach contributed to the Trades Council *Year Book* and wrote on educational topics, it was secondary schooling on which he concentrated .

When the *Pioneer* noted in July 1916 that the WEA had sent a memorandum on educational reconstruction to the Board of Education, Leach observed with pleasure that it showed the organisation becoming 'bolder and more courageous since the war.' He summarised its contents for his readers, highlighting a proposed school leaving age of 15 (this left provisions for claiming exemption from full-time education altered but intact, he noted) and concluded that it was 'good as far as it goes, [but] makes no reference to the powers of the local Education Authority to assist by grant the parents of such children as are hampered by poverty conditions'.[93] (He had written before, of course, of the 'most wonderful' act which granted such powers, the Education (Administrative Provisions) Act of 1907.[94]) By October, Leach was able to report on 'A Larger Programme' than that of the WEA for the Bradford Trades Council had appointed a committee to draw up a programme of 'educational reform' in 'the name of Bradford Labour'.[95]

The Trades Council had met on September 15 and considered the matter of 'Educational Questions After the War', setting a provisional date of October 21st for a Conference on this topic. There were plans to invite the local WEA to participate, and invitations were extended to the Vice-Chancellors of Leeds and Sheffield Universities. They also made the decision to open their planning meetings to local members of the ILP with educational interests, asking William Leach among others to 'draft an Educational programme'.[96] A week later, the task of making a final draft of the programme was given to Leach, Richard Lishman and Alderman Michael Conway.[97] The Conference booking form also devised at this meeting flagged the key question of education in a class society. It was a question prompted by the lessons of 1902, given recent sharpness by the lowering of the school-leaving age in the city: 'if the workers' children are to be provided with the necessary armament of Education to provide them for the coming battle, we must see to it that our children have equal opportunities with the rich man's child ...'[98] Sometime in the following week the sub-committee met again and gave the final job of tidying up and proof-reading the Charter to Lishman and Conway, strongly suggesting what Leach himself never claimed, that the Charter was very largely his own work.[99]

In the Trades Council *Year Book* for 1917, Leach took his readers through the Charter, paragraph by paragraph, explaining why it mattered. The 1902 Act had to be amended so that all schools were owned and managed 'by the community,' not, as in the case of the non-provided schools, by charity, which sought to give 'a church atmosphere ... to the teaching of arithmetic and geography'. The abolition of all school fees would indeed save the wealthy money, but they would pay increased education rates. The scholarship system, which was 'merely a plan to subsidise the precocious at the expense of the normal,' would then disappear. The school-leaving age had to be raised to 16, and means-tested maintenance grants simultaneously introduced, for this 'in a single clause, [was] Labour's great educational stumbling block. Raising the school leaving age [meant] postponing wages to ill-to-do families'.

Secondary education had to be compulsory:

To make the country a happier and more pleasant place in which to live every grownup citizen ought to be able to discuss music, science, literature, the arts, politics and history, and to be able to make his or her wants known in two foreign languages. The night-woolcomber should have this common equipment in the interests of wool well-combed. This ... then is one of the necessary preliminaries to a nicer Britain.

There was to be no specialisation under the age of 15. All higher education was to be completely free and co-ordinated under public control. This would happily 'make short work of the exclusiveness now enjoyed by Oxford and Cambridge. It would also solve the problem of misused endowments. It would further be useful for the democratisation of the children of dukes and peers of the realm who would be deprived of a place in which to idle their time away.' There was to be no half-time exemption before the age of 16, and even after this every child should be seen by the school doctor before taking employment. Education authorities, then, had to be given the same power over the exemption system for half time employment in the textile trades as they had over other forms of juvenile labour,[100] and the children had to be seen by their doctor rather than the employer's doctor: 'Any one who has seen [the employer's] doctor at a Bradford spinning mill, passing children, will know why this department should be ... undertaken by the children's doctor.' A much larger proportion of educational expenses had to be borne by central government, as all education authorities knew that ratepayers were mean in a way that taxpayers were not. Pension rights had to be extended to secondary school teachers, and the 'intellectual and financial status of teachers' had to be raised, for 'in no professions are brains so little regarded or purchased so cheaply as in that of teaching the child of the workman. In no market are the results of cheap labour so disastrous ...' Class sizes in elementary schools had to be reduced from 60 to 30, the ratio for secondary schools: 'this huge discrepancy springs ... from the fact that anything, or almost anything will be docilely accepted by the workman for his child.' The amount of air and space made available to children in elementary schools needed to brought up to the minimum standard of existing secondary schools. A scheme of free medical care for pre-school children had to be properly co-ordinated with the school medical service: 'the war has made this proposal even more important than it was before. A school medical service is badly hampered by having to deal with ailing children who could have been quite healthy ...' There had to be swimming baths, gymnasia and proper physical education for all school children, including playing fields for elementary school children (this demand was made in the light of 'the silly statement about the Battle of Waterloo,' and to emphasise 'the need for less of the shocking submissiveness to conditions of insulting inferiority so long displayed by Labour.') After compulsory schooling ended, a scheme for 16 to 20-year-olds had to be devised. They themselves would demand it, and it was particularly recommended to 'all those good people who are concerned with the nightly promenading of the young and who never know what to do about it.' Open-air schools were to flourish, and a system of camp-schools, vacation centres and 'travel studies' set in motion ('after the war it may be possible to make use of the battleships of the world as travelling schools to teach geography ... to the world's children ...'). Parents able to pay for but who refused to let their children have school meals at public expense were to be 'legislatively overruled.'[101]

It seems then, that this was not an attempt to redistribute the goods of education, for there was nothing in existence like it to disperse; and it certainly was a proposal for much more than 'the broad liberal curriculum that [Leach] had experienced at Bradford Grammar School'.[102] The timing of the Charter was influenced by a WEA initiative, but its shape and contents had to do with an educational programme prefigured in the columns of the *Forward* and the *Pioneer*, and by Bradford's particular position at the interface of education and child labour in the crucial months after the school leaving age was lowered in the city.

William Leach himself believed that Bradford had brought forth the Charter because 'the Bradford Labour Movement [was] more alive to the real meaning of the war of the classes as expressed in terms of education than any other part of the country.[103] Margaret McMillan, in praising Leach's educational politics to the *Labour Leader* in 1908, had written of 'the dream of Socialists of an indefinitely enlarged life and culture for all',[104] and the Charter had a good deal to do with that dream too. It was also directly to do with what Leach had learned from McMillan's work and writing, that homes alone could not make any kind of new child, that 'new forms of association than those that prevail ... must be created in our social and civic life ...'[105]

Councillor Palin was disappointed in the Conference held on October 21st to launch the Charter. The vice-chancellor of Leeds University failed to turn up, and 'the so-called educationalists of the district were absent,' including members of the WEA, 'who failed to send any delegates, [though] how this came about requires some explanation as it was understood delegates had been appointed ...' Palin suggested ignoring this lukewarm response, and going forward, particularly to the TUC, which 'had passed many resolutions upon education, but ... never formulated a complete programme ... why should they not adopt it and try to get an enlightened public opinion as will secure its adoption by the nation?'[106] The *Yorkshire Observer* reporter had found the Conference members 'more concerned with Socialist propaganda than with a real desire to promote the interests of education. There was much talk of the children of the working class being exploited in the interests of capitalism ...'[107] The Yorkshire Divisional Conference of the ILP endorsed the Charter for submission to the national Conference at Easter,[108] but – as we have already noted – it was never formally adopted as ILP policy.

As J. R. Brooks observes, the trickle of programmes for educational reconstruction now became a flood.[109] From his editor's desk at the *Pioneer*, William Leach noted that of the British Socialist Party, which he pointedly refrained from criticising, though his readership must by now have been well-trained enough to note the 'cordon of gold' still encircling secondary education in its recommendation of 'free secondary training for the arts, crafts or professions *according to capacity*.' [my italics][110] The Bradford Charter emphasised that there should be no specialisation until the last year of secondary school for, as Leach explained, 'if Labour does not put its foot down, educational development will proceed on the lines of training boys and girls of perhaps ten or eleven how to become good mill-hands, under the high-sounding term "specialisation". Before becoming a workman or work-woman the child must receive its full heritage as a scholar. In just so far as it does not is your education plan a fraud ...'[111] In these terms, the WEA programme was a fraud too, because it retained elementary education as the education fitting for working-class children.

Despite the major differences between them, 1917 saw co-operation between the Trades Council and the local WEA,[112] though by the end of the year co-operation had turned into WEA efforts to secure Trade Union support for the Fisher Education Bill.[113] Relations between the two bodies were evidently tense and difficult by now, and Trades Council members were in no doubt that their plans and proposals were in conflict. At a meeting in November 'a long discussion took place regarding the attitude of the [WEA] speakers when addressing Trades Unionists. It was resolved that speakers be at liberty to deal with either or both Education Programmes, the Worker's Educational Association Programme or the Trades Council Programme and that they be allowed full liberty in answering questions.'[114]

Is the Bradford Charter story one of this kind of inconsequence, an educational programme that gets lost in the Labour Party's acceptance of the educational experts' view of children and learning, and the type of school most suitable for working-class children in the years after the War? To be sure, J. R. Brooks gives the Charter a revival of interest, a kind if rising from the dead in the 1960s and in planning for comprehensive education.[115] But these terms, of 'evolution', of whole schemes of education made tributary to the mighty flow of 'consensus', seem to me to deflect from the historical task of understanding what trade unionists and members of the ILP understood, in one place and at one time, of what was – in its turn – another history, a recent history of childhood, child labour and education, in one city. And it does seem odd to call Willie Leach an educational 'expert' whose membership of the Labour Party Advisory Committee on Education – according to which account is perused – represented a rise in the 'political fortunes of the party's intellectuals' in the two years after the War,[116] but who is soon also to offer an example of the way in which 'the unions were giving form and character to the Labour Party and also ... the simultaneous decline in influence of the socialist societies, whose members for the main part staffed the Committees;[117] or who, on the Sub-Committee on Continuing Education, can be seen converting Professor Percy Nunn from 'a class-based vocational education for working-class children', an education for 'the residue', to the idea of 'a liberal education' for all'.[118]

William Leach was not the only ILP-er with a writer's reputation on educational questions to be appointed to the Advisory Committee on Education. As members of it, both he and Margaret McMillan produced long memoranda on nursery education, but neither of them attended any meetings after June (the Committee was set up in April), and their work (particularly that of McMillan) was subject to quite severe revision.[119] Leach and McMillan themselves clashed over the question of parental contribution (Leach objected to parents paying anything; McMillan thought that even the poor had 'a right to choose ... to make new sacrifices for their children'); but they clashed only on paper, as by the time Professor Nunn got hold of the drafts, reduced the training period for nursery school teachers and the entrance requirement to such training courses,[120] both of them had stopped going to meetings anyway. Both Leach and McMillan were the victims of the new regime of the educational 'expert'.

NOTES

1. Clive Griggs, *The Trades Union Congress and the Struggle for Education, 1868–1925* (Falmer, Lewes, 1983), pp.159–160.
2. *Ibid.*, p.161.
3. *Ibid.*, pp.141–58. Rodney Barker, *Education and Politics, 1900–1951. A Study of the Labour Party* (Clarendon Press, Oxford, 1972), pp.17–18.
4. *Ibid.*, pp.34-5. Ross McKibbin, *The Evolution of the Labour Party, 1910–1924* (Clarendon Press, Oxford, 1974), pp.94–5, 98, 218–221. J. M. Winter, *Socialism and the Challenge of War. Ideas and Politics in Britain, 1912–1918* (Routledge and Kegan Paul, 1974), pp.272–3.
5. William Leach, 'Labour's Education Charter. Why It Matters', Bradford and District Trades and Labour Council, *Year Book*, No.18, 1917, p.49. See Ramsay MacDonald on this point, ILP, *Report of the Ninth Annual Conference of the Independent Labour Party, held in the Cook Memorial Hall, Leicester, on April 8th and 9th, 1901*, (ILP Office, 1901), p.42.
6. David Howell, *British Workers and the Independent Labour Party, 1888–1906* (Manchester University Press, Manchester, 1983), pp.344–8. For most extensive and illuminating discussion of children categorised as scholars and/or workers (and as the children of working-class parents) see ILP, *Report of the Fifth Annual Conference of the Independent Labour Party. Held in the Essex Hall, London, on April 19th and 20th, 1897, with Revised Constitution and Rules*, (1897), pp.21–2.

7. Edmund and Ruth Frow, *A Survey of the Half-time System in Education* (E. J. Morten, Manchester, 1970), pp.42–55.

8. ILP, *Report of the First General Conference* (Labour Literature Society, Glasgow, 1893), p.10.

9. ILP, *Minutes of the Second Annual Conference of the Independent Labour Party, held in the Lesser Free Trade Hall, Manchester, February 2nd and 3rd, 1894* (Labour Literature Society, Glasgow, 1894), p.13.

10. ILP, *Minutes of the Third Annual Conference of the Independent Labour Party, held in the Geographical Institute, St Mary's Place, Newcastle-on-Tyne, April 15th, 16th and 17th, 1895* (1895), pp.9, 27.

11. *Ibid.*, p.21.

12. ILP, *Report ...,1897*, pp.7–8, pp.21–22.

13. ILP, *Report of the Eighth Annual Conference of the Independent Labour Party, held in the Waterloo Rooms, Glasgow, April 16th and 17th, 1900* (ILP Office, 1900), pp.30, 32. ILP, *Report of the Ninth Annual Conference of the Independent Labour Party, held in the Cook Memorial Hall, Leicester, April 8th and 9th, 1901* (ILP Office, 1901), p.38.

14. ILP, *Report of the Eleventh Annual Conference of the Independent Labour Party, held in the Co-operative Hall, April 13th and 14th, 1903, Railway Street, York* (ILP Office, 1903), p.32.

15. Margaret McMillan, letter to the *Labour Leader*, 5 Feb 1909.

16. ILP, *Report of the Fifteenth Annual Conference, Temperance Hall, Derby, April 1st and 2nd, 1907* (ILP, 1907), p.45.

17. Debates about secular or 'moral' education represent direct intervention in questions of what children actually experienced in school – particularly between 9.00 and 9.30 in the morning at assembly time – and could allow the argument that the ILP was directly concerned with 'the actual material of the curriculum'. See below, note 20. Arthur Fallows, *Moral Teaching in the Board Schools* (Midland Socialist Pamphlets Number Two, (Birmingham Socialist Centre, 1900). ILP, *Report of the Twelfth Annual Conference of the Independent Labour Party, held in the City Hall, Cardiff on April 4th and 5th, 1904* (ILP, 1904), where the Keighley delegate proposed that branch members simply keep their children out of school during morning assembly and religious studies lessons.

18. ILP, *Report of the Sixteenth Annual Conference, Town Hall, Huddersfield, April 19th, 20th and 21st, 1908* (ILP, 1908), pp.61–4; *Report of the 20th Annual Conference, held at Merthyr, 27th, 28th May, 1912* (ILP, 1912), p.98.

19. The term 'equality of opportunity' is not anachronistic here, and was frequently used in programmes of education reform of the First World War period. See for instance the WEA pamphlet *Fair Play to the Children* (WEA 1916), p.6, p.10.

20. Rodney Barker, 'The Labour Party and Education for Socialism', *International Review of Social History*, 15, 1969, pp.22–53.

21. Griggs, *op. cit.*, pp.214–33.

22. Barker, 1969, *op. cit.*, p.23. See also Barker, 1972, *op. cit.*, pp.17–21, p.121.

23. Carolyn Steedman, *Childhood, Culture and Class in Britain. Margaret McMillan, 1860–1931* (Virago, 1990), pp.33–61. Keith Laybourn, '"The Defence of the Bottom Dog"; The Independent Labour Party in Local Politics,' in D. G. Wright and J. A. Jowitt, *Victorian Bradford. Essays in Honour of Jack Reynolds* (City of Bradford Metropolitan Council, Bradford, 1981), p.224. 1902 is the date of the Education Act that abolished the School Boards. See Brian Simon,

Education and the Labour Movement, 1870–1920 (Lawrence and Wishart, 1965), pp.208–46.

24. Steedman, *op. cit.*, pp.173–4.

25. Margaret McMillan, 'The Government and the People's Schools,' *Ethical World*, September 29, 1900 for 'the cordon of gold'. Robert Roberts, 'The People's Schools,', Labour Leader, January 5, 1901. Simon, *op. cit.*, pp.208–46.

26. Simon, *op. cit.*, p.344. Steedman, *op. cit.*, pp.49–50.

27. For the actual relationship of the Factory Acts to the Education Acts, the best account is still to be found in Frederic Keeling, *Child Labour in the United Kingdom* (P. S. King, 1914), pp.viii–xxxii.

28. Keeling, *op. cit.*, p.ix.

29. Frow, *op. cit.*, p.21. Karl Marx, *Capital*, Volume 1, (Penguin, Harmondsworth, 1976), pp.610–35.

30. Keeling, *op. cit.*, p.xxi.

31. Geoffrey Sherington, *English Education, Social Change and War. 1911–20* (Manchester University Press, Manchester, 1981), p.7.

32. Jacqueline Rose, 'State and Language: *Peter Pan* as written for the child', in Carolyn Steedman, Valerie Walkerdine and Cathy Urwin, *Language, Gender and Childhood* (Routledge and Kegan Paul, 1985), pp.88–112. William Leach still believed as late as 1918 that one of his functions on the Labour Party Advisory Committee on Education was to tell it that 'the attempt to separate the earlier forms of education into two kinds calling one Elementary and the other secondary is an error. Grammar schools, intended for the offspring of the well-to-do's make no such distinction.' National Museum of Labour History, Labour Party Advisory Committee on Education, memos 1–20. William Leach, 'Elementary and Secondary Education ...', memo, 9 Oct 1918.

33. Raymond Williams, *Keywords. A Vocabulary of Culture and Society*, (1988), pp.111–12.

34. C. W. Bowerman (ed.), *Report of the Proceedings of the Forty-eighth Annual Trades Union Congress, held in the Town Hall, Birmingham on September 4th to 9th, 1916* (Co-operative Printing Society, 1916), p.370, quoted by Simon, *op. cit.*, p.344.

35. William Leach, 'What Is Secondary Education?', Bradford and District Trades and Labour Council, *Year Book*, No.12, 1911, pp.49–51.

36. Griggs, *op. cit.*, p.171.

37. Simon, *op. cit.*, p.360.

38. Griggs, *op. cit.*, pp.116–17.

39. C. W. Bowerman (ed.), *Report of the Proceedings of the Forty-ninth Annual Trades Union Congress, held in Palace Hall, Blackpool, September 3rd to 8th, 1917* (Co-operative Printing Society, 1917), p.354.

40. London School of Economics, Archives of the British Association for Early Childhood Education, Nursery School Association Records, Box 18, Katharine Bruce Glasier to Grace Owen, 7 Jun 1927.

41. Simon, *op. cit.*, p.357.

42. For the relationship between the ILP and local trade unionists, see Keith Laybourn and Jack Reynolds, *Liberalism and the Rise of Labour, 1890–1918* (Croom Helm, 1984), pp.178–202; and Keith Laybourn, '"One of the Little Breezes Blowing Across Bradford": The Bradford Independent Labour Party and Trade Unionism c.1890–1914,' in Keith Laybourn and David James (eds.), *The Rising Sun of Socialism: The Independent Labour Party in the Textile District of*

the *West Riding of Yorkshire between 1890 and 1914* (West Yorkshire Archive Service, Bradford, 1991).

43. *Times Educational Supplement*, 19, 26 Oct 1916.

44. Simon, *op. cit.*, p.348–50. Sherington, *op. cit.*, pp.64–5. These accounts have their source in 'A Bradford Scheme', *The Times Educational Supplement*, 19 Oct 1916, and the *Bradford Daily Telegraph and Argus*, 21 Oct 1916, p.5.

45. J. R. Brooks, 'Labour and Educational Reconstruction, 1916–1926: a case study in the evolution of policy,' *History of Education*, 20:3, 1991, pp.245–59.

46. *Ibid.*, p.245.

47. William Leach, 'Labour's Education Charter. Why It Matters,' Bradford and District Trades and Labour Council, *Year Book*, No. 18, 1917, pp.49–58.

48. Brooks, *op. cit.*, p.247. WEA, *What Labour Wants from Education* (WEA, 1916) was a penny pamphlet, containing a series of questions and proposals about educational reform, 'distributed to all trades councils, trade union branches, co-operative societies, adult schools, etc., in England and Wales.' Responses to the questionnaire were used in the formulation of the WEA's programme for educational reconstruction, published in November, 1916. WEA, *Educational Reconstruction: Being the Recommendations of the Workers' Educational Association to the Reconstruction Committee* (WEA, 1916) gives an account of the distribution and use of *What Labour Wants*. See also *Highway*, Vol. IX, No.99 (Dec 1916), pp.51–6.

49. Simon, *op. cit.*, pp.346–50; Griggs, *op. cit.*, p.139; Sherington, *op. cit.*, pp.64–5; Brooks, *op. cit.*, p.245, pp.247–8.

50. Labour Party, *Report of the Annual Conference of the Labour Party held in the Albert Hall, Peter Street, Manchester, on Tuesday January 23rd, 1917, and three following days*, 1917, pp.135–6. Meredith F. Titterington, 'The Labour Party. Sixteenth Annual Conference ... Impressions', *Bradford Pioneer*, February 2, 1917, p.7.

51. It was one of last rushed resolutions, a victim of timetabling. 'The ILP Conference at Leeds', *Bradford Pioneer*, 13 Apr 1917, p.5.

52. ILP, *Report of the Annual Conference held at Leeds, April, 1917*, p.76. *Report of the National Administrative Council: To be presented to the Conference of the Independent Labour Party, on April 1st and 2nd, 1918* (ILP, 1918), pp.27–28. *Report of the Twenty-Sixth Annual Conference, Leicester. April, 1918* (ILP, 1918), p.82. *ILP Summer School, Bryn Corach, Conway, N. Wales, June 30th to July 13th, l1917*7. *Programme.*

53. ILP, *Report*, 1918, *op. cit.*, p.82.

54. Brooks, *op. cit.*, p.48,

55. TUC, *Report of the Fifty-Sixth Annual Trades Union Congress, Hull* (Co-operative Publishing Society, 1924), pp.418–9.

56. Griggs, *op. cit.*, p.54: 'Whilst the Labour Party was calling for secondary education for all, from 1922 onwards the TUC's demands for secondary education were still linked to a view that only the most intelligent of the working class children [sic] could go to secondary school'.

57. M. Conway, 'Municipal Enterprise 11. What the Education Committee Are Doing', *Bradford Pioneer*, 28 Feb 1913, p.8. 'What the Education Committee Could Do', *Bradford Pioneer*, 7 Mar 1913, p.3.

58. 'Fighters for Freedom', *Bradford Pioneer*, 17 Oct 1913, p.6. City of Bradford, Education Committee Minutes. 1907–1913

59. William Leach, 'A Liberal Conspiracy Afoot. Labour Must Thwart It', *Bradford Pioneer*, 31 July 1914, p.3.

60. For debate within the ILP on these proposals, see R. Roberts, 'Health and Education', *Bradford Pioneer*, 25 Apr 1913, p.7.

61. Leach, 'Educational Possibilities', *op. cit.* See J. H. Palin telling the ILP in Conference about the usefulness of this legislation. ILP, *Report of the Annual Conference held at Newcastle-upon-Tyne, April 1916* (Independent Labour Party, 1916), p.91.

62. Leach, 'A Liberal Conspiracy', *op. cit.*, 31 July, 1914, p.2.

63. 'The Forthcoming Education Bill. The New "Red Herring"', *Bradford Pioneer*, 6 June 1913, p.5.

64. Alfred A. Mumford, medical officer to and historian of Manchester Grammar School. His extensive research on growth in children and adolescents was presented in *Healthy Growth* (Oxford University Press, 1927). See J. M. Tanner, *A History of the Study of Human Growth* (Cambridge University Press, Cambridge, 1981), pp.228–9. For Leach's response to his 1914 paper, William Leach, 'The North of England Education Conference. A Frankly Biased View of It,' *Bradford Pioneer*, 9 Jan 1914, p.4. Margaret McMillan was none too pleased with what Alfred Mumford had to say either: 'she had listened with pleasure to [his] able paper … with much of which she was not in agreement. What she particularly regretted was that the general mass of children were not considered … as worthy of any higher education at all. She did not think that could be the final decision of the nation, for if these millions of people did not constitute the nation, what was the nation? We were told that most of the children were unfit for the strain of higher education, but surely this was rather ironical when we did not consider them unfit for the strain of the industrial system …' *Yorkshire Observer*, 5 Jan 1914, p.x.

65. Sherington, *op. cit.*, pp.49–51. Simon, *op. cit.*, pp.351–5.

66. *Bradford Pioneer*, 14 Jan 1916, p.6; 4 Feb 1916, p. 1.

67. *Bradford Pioneer*, 4 Feb 1916, p.3. On the symbolic use of this statue in ILP thought and propaganda, see Steedman, *op. cit.*, pp.102–3, and Plate.

68. 'School Children Thrown to the Wolves: The Extreme of Reaction,' *Bradford Pioneer*, 26 May 1916, p.4.

69. 'The Need for Educational Reform,' *Highway*, Vol. VIII, No.95 (August 1916), pp.188–9.

70. For the Spinners' pressure group, see *Bradford Pioneer*, 12 May 1916, p.8; 23 June 1916, p.6; 21 July 1916, p.6. See also 'The Woollen Industry's Future. Addressed to the Bradford Textile Society. Spinning and Education,' *Yorkshire Observer*, 21 Oct 1916, p.7.

71. William Leach, 'The War After the War', Bradford Trades and Labour Council, *Year Book*, No.17 1916, pp.50–60.

72. 'More Child Wage Slaves,' *Bradford Pioneer*, 16 Feb 1917, p.1. See also 'Bradford's Child Workers,' *Bradford Pioneer*, 9 Feb 1917, p.l.

73. *Bradford Pioneer*, 11 Feb 1916, p.7. WEA, *Fair Play to the Children* (WEA, 1916). 'Our largest sales [of *Fair Play*] have been to the National Union of Railwaymen and to the Workers' Union …' *Highway*, Vol. VIII, No.91 (April 1916), pp.111–12. *Fair Play*, p.7, noted that across the country 'by April 30th, 1915, 6,170 boys and girls had been exempted from school and set to work, who would in normal times have remained at school.'

74. The conference was arranged for May 8th, and was addressed by Arthur Greenwood. Bradford Trades Council Minutes. 56D80/1/9. Bradford and

District Trades and Labour Council (BDTLC) Minutes from 18 Nov 1915 to 31 Dec 1919. BDTLC, Minutes, p.48: Special Executive Committee Meeting, 26 May 1916. West Yorkshire Archive Service, Bradford.

75. Hilda M. Snowden, 'Founders of the Workers' Educational Association in Bradford,' *Journal of the Bradford Historical and Antiquarian Society*, 3:3, 1987, pp.21–6; 'The Story of the Workers' Educational Association in Bradford,' *History of Education in Bradford*, Bulletin 2 (Apr 1968), pp.28–31.

76. Isaac Holmes, *From Hand Industry to Factory System: the effects of the transition upon the Working Classes of Bradford* (WEA, Bradford n.d. [1913]). See Snowden (1968), *op. cit.*, p.30.

77. BDTLC Minutes, p.54: Special Executive Committee Meeting, 22 May 1916.

78. *Ibid.*, p.52.

79. BDTLC Minutes, p.54: Special Executive Meeting, 26 May 1916.

80. The Trades Council's programme was first given the title of 'Bradford Education Charter' in an article by J. H. Palin, in the *Bradford Pioneer*, 27 Oct 1916, p.5.

81. Keith Laybourn and Jack Reynolds, *Liberalism and the Rise of Labour, 1890–1918* (Croom Helm, 1984), pp.181–2; Laybourn (1981), *op. cit.*, p.234.

82. See Verax, 'School Children Under Five Years of Age', *Forward*, 3 June 1905, p.4; 'An Educational Utopia', *Forward*, 10 June 1905, p.5; 17 June 1905, p.6; 24 June 1905, p.5; 1 July 1905, p.3; 'The School Curriculum,' 21 July 1906, p.4. Margaret McMillan, 'Baths for Children,' *Forward*, 10 June, 1905, p.7.

83. Leach, 'North of England Education Conference,' *op. cit.*

84. Margaret McMillan, 'Mr Leech's [sic] Reform', *Labour Leader*, 10 July 1908.

85. He was a Vice-President by 1907. Bradford Central Library Local History Collection, *Bradford Cinderella Clubs Annual Reports*, 19th Annual Report, 1907–8; 25th Annual Report, 1913–14. *Bradford Forward*, 8 Oct 1907, p.5. J. H. Palin, *Bradford's Children and How They Are Fed* (ILP, n.d.), p.4.

86. Steedman, *op. cit.*, p.111. But for Bradford Labour Church's professionalisation of Robert Blatchford's original Rabelesian conception, see Palin, *op. cit.*, pp.3–4; and Keith Laybourn, 'The Issue of School Feeding in Bradford, 1904–1907, *Journal of Educational Administration and History*, 14:2 (July, 1982), pp.30–8.

87. *Bradford Telegraph and Argus*, 22 Nov 1949; Yorkshire Post, 22 Nov 1949.

88. 'Education and Democracy', *Forward*, 22 Apr 1905, p.5; Verax, 'The Infant School Question', 20 May 1905, p.5; 'School Children Under Five Years of Age', 3 June 1905, p.4.

89. *Forward*, 3 Mar 1907, p.3.

90. Steedman, *op. cit.*, p.58.

91. Griggs, *op. cit.*, p.164.

92. Barker (1972), *op. cit.*, p.22.

93. 'The WEA Programme', *Bradford Pioneer*, 14 July 1916, p.1.

94. See above, p. 24.

95. 'A Larger Education Programme', *Bradford Pioneer*, 20 Oct 1916, p.1.

96. BDTLC Minutes, p.76, p.78: Sub-committee Meeting, 15 Sept 1916. Miss Beszant, one time head of the Belle Vue Higher Grade School, and (along with Margaret McMillan) a director of the Labour Institute in the 1890s, also joined the committee.

97. *Ibid.*, p.80: Special Sub-committee Meeting, 22 Sept 1916.

98. *Ibid.*, p.81.

99. *Ibid.*, p.82.

100. See Keeling, *op. cit.*, pp.xx–xxi.
101. Leach, 'Bradford's Education Charter,' *op. cit.*, pp.49–58.
102. Brooks, *op. cit.*, p.248.
103. Leech, 'Bradford's Education Charter,' *op. cit.*, p.49.
104. McMillan, 'Mr Leech's Reform,' *op. cit.*
105. McMillan, 'Letter,' *op. cit.*
106. *Bradford Pioneer*, 27 Oct 1916, p.5.
107. *Yorkshire Observer*, 23 Oct 1916, p.6.
108. *Bradford Pioneer*, 26 Jan 1917, p.3.
109. Brooks, *op. cit.*, p.245.
110. 'Another Education Programme', *Bradford Pioneer*, 16 Feb 1917, p.2.
111. Leach, 'Labour's Education Charter', *op. cit.*, p.58.
112. BDTLC, Minutes, p.152: Council Meeting, 15 Feb 1917.
113. *Ibid.*, p.169: Council Meeting, 18 Oct 1917.
114. *Ibid.*, p.163: Education Sub-Committee, 13 Nov 1917.
116. Winter, *op cit*, pp.272–3. See also Barker (1972), *op. cit.*, pp.36–42.
117. McKibbin, *op. cit.*, pp.218–21.
118. Brooks, *op. cit.*, pp.256–9.
119. National Museum of Labour History, Labour Party Advisory Committee on Education, Minutes 1919–1932. Correspondence 1920–21 (this actually includes material from 1918). Minutes of Meetings held on 8 Apr, 15 May, 1 June, 12 Sept 1918. Memos 1–20, Memo. 3, Oct 1918, R.H Tawney and William Leach, '"Brief" on Nursery Schools.' Memo 4, Oct 1918, (Margaret McMillan), 'Nursery Schools'. 'Advisory Committee on Education. Amended Memorandum on Nursery Schools.' 'Advisory Committee on Education. Draft Suggestions for Deputation from Labour Party Executive to Board of Education.' This last Memo. recommended either a two-year course of nursery training, or a Montessori, Froebelian or kindergarten course, supplemented by a 'short course in infant welfare work'.
120. Memo dated 25 Oct 1918. T. P. Nunn, 'The Training of Teachers for Nursery Schools.'

6. The ILP and the Second International: the Early Years, 1893–1905

Chris Wrigley

> Debout! les damnés de la terre!
> Debout! les forçats de la faim!
> La raison tonne en son cratère,
> C'est l'eruption de la fin.
> Du passé faisons table rase,
> Foule esclave, debout, debout,
> Le monde va changer de base,
> Nous ne sommes rien, soyons tout!
> C'est la lutte finale
> Groupons-nous, et, demain
> L'Internationale
> Sera le genre humain.
>
> (*L'Internationale*, Eugene Pottier)

In spite of all that had been said about the socialists he thought English trades unionism was the best sort of socialism and labourism. He wished to capture the trade unionists of this country, a body of men well organized, who paid their money, and were socialists at their work every day and not merely on the platform, who did not shout for blood-red revolution, and when it came to revolution, sneaked under the nearest bed. Let them remember that there was a vast organisation of men in this country who were treading in the direction of their economic salvation and who, for hard work, would compare most favourably with any of the socialist teachers of men. With his experience of unions he was glad to say that if there were fifty such red revolutionary parties as there was in Germany, he would sooner have the solid, progressive, matter-of-fact fighting trade unionism of England than all the harebrained chatterers and magpies of continental revolutionaries.[1]

(Ben Tillett at ILP inaugural conference, 13 January 1893)[1]

Attitudes within the early Independent Labour Party to the Second International were often ambivalent. The Second International offered a broad socialist vision and also a connection with continental parties whose electoral successes were tangible. Yet for many in the ILP the continental comrade's Utopia was the wrong one. It was Marxist. The way to it was proclaimed in the rhetoric of class war, not in the language of either a puritanical, ethical socialism or an economistic labourism.

Most members of the ILP saw the need to win the support of organised labour. In the 1890s internationalism aroused little enthusiasm, indeed often hostility, among many trade unionists. From the outset of the Second International it was apparent that in such circles the pull of nationalism was much more powerful than ideals of workers having no country. The Boer and First World Wars were to make that quite clear. In making chauvinist comments at the ILP foundation conference Ben Tillett was not only blatantly courting such trade unionist support but was also distancing himself from the various fragmented Marxist groupings in London who looked to German Social Democracy as a model.

Indeed until the mid-1890s some of the leading ILP figures retained residual sympathies for less extreme anarchism. This was exhibited at the Second International's 1896 Congress in London. There, Keir Hardie and Tom Mann breached their mandate as delegates of the ILP's National Advisory Council (NAC) by urging the Congress that anarchist delegates should be permitted to participate in its proceedings.[2] Earlier the NAC, responding to a request from Mann, had resolved that 'the instruction was to support the decision arrived at by the Zurich Congress which excludes anarchists'. Later, after this had been dropped on the pretext of the long time that had elapsed since Zurich, the NAC had adopted a resolution that those to be admitted should 'believe in industrial or political organisation for the realisation of common ownership and control of all means of production'. The case that Hardie made to his fellow ILP delegates before speaking up for the anarchists at the Congress was:

> It might be alleged that if they supported these people's claims they were sympathising with Anarchists. For his part, he was more afraid of doing an unfair thing towards a body of Socialists with whom he did not see eye to eye, than he was of being called an Anarchist.

Hardie and Mann went on to compound their offence in the eyes of such ILP stalwarts as Fred Brocklehurst by speaking at a major 'Anarchist-Communist' meeting at Holborn Town Hall. When Hardie and Mann's conduct was challenged afterwards, Hardie rather disingenuously argued that at the Congress they had not actually voted contrary to their instructions and that 'credential forms had been refused to certain *bona fide* socialist organisations'. (This latter point was in itself true and had been remedied quickly; but he and Mann had not confined their comments to these anyway.) As for the Holborn Town Hall meeting they wrote in their report on the Congress: 'Both explained that they were not there in their official capacity, but felt that they were interpreting the spirit of the ILP in welcoming such distinguished workers for the cause as Prince Peter Kropotkin, Domela Nieuwenhuis, Louise Michel, [Errico] Malatesta, [Christiaan] Cornelissen, [Elisée] Reclus and others'.[3] This, of course, evaded the point as to what cause, these 'distinguished workers' being the leaders of international anarchism.

Bruce Glasier was even more sympathetic to the anarchists. He was a great admirer of William Morris and had been secretary of the Glasgow branch of the Socialist League. He had continued to contribute to the League's newspaper even after Morris had broken with the League due to the violent proposals expressed by some anarchists.[4] Thereafter Glasier's sympathies continued to lie more with Morris' outlook rather than with the Marxist approaches of H. M. Hyndman or Friedrich Engels. At the time of the 1896 International Congress he took the chair at a Trafalgar Square demonstration which called for the early release from prison of the Walsall anarchists, a rally at which the main speakers were the internationally famous anarchists Domela Nieuwenhuis and Louise Michel.[5] While Hardie and several prominent trade unionists also supported the campaign for an amnesty, Glasier was notable for the degree of interest he took in their cause, seeing two of the Walsall anarchists (in 1897 and 1910) after their release. A few days after the Trafalgar Square rally Glasier stayed with A. M. Thompson (the *Clarion* writer 'Dangle') and two of the French delegates to the International Congress. He noted with apparent approval in his diary:

> Dangle during the evening spoke strongly against German Social Democratic Party. Accuses them of struggling for power, which they would use as relentlessly as the bourgeois. They would show no tolerance to any socialism but their own. He evidently dreads parliamentarianism, not however from an anarchist, but [from a] broad democratic standpoint.[6]

The 1896 London Congress effectively set the international movement firmly along a Marxist road, or at least on a route marked by Marxist rhetoric but which permitted the travellers to arrive at a democratic electoral destination. Glasier continued to battle with this Marxist line both at the international and national level. He remained hostile to Hyndman and the SDF. From the 1904 International Congress at Amsterdam he wrote home to his wife that at an outside demonstration:

> All the speakers with the exception of Bebel seemed to rant away at the phantom enemy 'Capitalisme' and I less than ever felt drawn to the typical 'continental socialist'.
>
> Hardie was not asked to take part. Hyndman and Quelch as usual did the British serio-comic turn – nay I am wroth when I think of the ineptitude of it all.[7]

There is an ironic element in him selecting August Bebel for such praise, as Bebel had been the hammer of revisionism within the German Social Democrats (though he was not of that party's left wing) and wished to commit the International to following the German road to socialism (as confirmed at its 1903 Congress at Dresden).

Glasier set off a row with the SDF and also began again a debate among British socialists thereafter by condemning the Dresden resolution when it was under consideration at the Amsterdam International Congress. After his speech to a meeting of the British Delegates, he wrote to his sister Lizzie: 'I have boldly tackled the SDF on the "class war" and much upset them too'. In his letters from the Congress to his wife, Glasier made it very clear that he hoped to isolate the SDF. For example on the 17 August he wrote:

This morning at the British Section [David] Shackleton and I put in an enquiry asking specifically whether the resolution adopted last Sunday morning (when I made my anti-class war speech) implied either directly or indirectly censure or disapproval of our ILP or LRC policy. It was a highly strategic move. If the SDF carried the day we and the trade unionists would have retired from the SDF [perhaps he meant British Section?] – and if the SDF declared no, it virtually meant an admission that their own attitude to us and the International movement has not been candid. To our and most of his own side's surprise [Harry] Quelch rose and declared that he and the SDF had not a word of quarrel with the ILP and LRC policy except that the SDF claimed the right to use the word 'socialist'. We don't know how to account for this declaration except that he and his friends are in a state of funk between us and the irreconcilables.[8]

The International Congress passed the Dresden resolution in a slightly altered form, with the SDF voting for it and the ILP voting within the small minority which opposed it. While the ILP was overshadowed on this matter, the 1904 Congress did mark a growing awareness among the continental socialists of the importance of the ILP and the Labour Representation Committee. As Glasier put it in his letter to his sister:

The SDF has been much subdued by our joint ILP and trade union influence, and for the first time the continental movement begins to realise the real position of the Labour Socialist movement in this country.

When he returned to Britain Glasier kept the issue of 'class war' at the forefront for some months, a matter which he could more readily do as Hardie's successor in 1904 as editor of the *Labour Leader*. That September Glasier noted in his diary with considerable satisfaction:

Hardie comes out with a strong pronouncement against the 'class war' dogma. My anti-class war protest at Amsterdam has then proved a real gain. It is a great thing that our British movement should take the lead in emancipating the socialist world from this error.

Glasier clearly relished taking the SDF on in this matter and, from his own austere and puritanical position, did not hesitate to denigrate Hyndman personally. He noted of a public meeting at Burnley in late September:

Two SDF men rudely questioned me on the 'class war'. I replied effectively instancing the case of Hyndman and Maddison, the one the socialist and the other the Liberal candidate for the town. 'But the socialist is a capitalist and the Liberal a workingman – yet you will vote for the capitalist', I exclaimed. After the meeting one of them insisted that Hyndman had renounced his class. 'Nothing of the kind – he sticks to every advantage of it including exploiting poor African negroes', I said.[9]

Glasier's ethical socialism was shared by many of the ILP leaders. The Amsterdam Congress and then his editorship of the *Labour Leader* enabled

Glasier to bring to the fore in 1904 the issue of the nature of ILP, as opposed to 'continental', socialism. After further SDF or much continental writing on the subject in the *Labour Leader* in mid-November 1904, he commented:

I have now said all I want to say on the subject, unless fresh controversy compels me to enter the lists again. I am glad to have had an opportunity of putting the anti-class war position from my own standpoint before the movement, as I feel that it has enabled me to reveal more clearly than ever I have yet seen done, the true and vital meaning of modern socialism.[10]

Yet while ILP socialism was of a very different kind to the predominant socialism of most continental European countries, the early ILP was undoubtedly attracted to the international socialist movement. One reason for this was that electoral encouragement could be drawn from the successes of the German and some other continental European parties. In the golden age of European socialism – the era of the Second International, before the First World War – the German Social Democrat Party was a model not to ignore. Its representation in the Reichstag rose from 35 to 81 between 1890 and 1903, with its share of the vote rising from 20 to 32 per cent. In the latter year it was polling over 60 per cent of the vote in the industrialised provinces of Berlin and Hamburg and just under in Saxony.[11] Thus the NAC really meant what it said when it resolved that it:

... sends fraternal greetings to [its] comrades in Germany, France and Belgium and congratulates them most heartily on the magnificent results of recent elections. The Council is glad to assure its comrades abroad that their success has materially aided the cause of socialism in this country.[12]

Moreover the continental socialists were also seen as heroes and martyrs to the socialist cause. Eduard Bernstein received cheers at the ILP inaugural conference when he denounced Tillett:

The workers on the continent were not all very wise. They made mistakes, and they even claimed the right of making mistakes, as they conceded it to others. They had done what they could in the circumstances in which they were situated ...

... men in Germany had been condemned to a total of eighty years, two months and twenty six days' hard labour, and thirty six years and ten months' penal servitude for their actions on behalf of the emancipation of the workers .... They had not sneaked and run away.

In 1896 the ILP leadership readily condemned the German government for sentencing Liebknecht to imprisonment for a sixteenth time, after he had allegedly insulted the Emperor.[13] While in the mid 1890s the ILP struggled for free speech in Walthamstow and Boggart Hole Clough, Manchester, with members such as Fred Brocklehurst suffering in prison, they were well aware of the greater struggles in Germany and elsewhere.

Another reason for the attraction was that the International Socialist

303

movement's rhetoric reinforced the millenarian vein of the ILP. It was not a great leap to the Second International rhetoric of the brotherhood of man from such attitudes as that expressed in *The Labour Annual 1895*: 'Hence, to develop the Religion of the Labour movement, to destroy all forms of slavery, to work for true Comradeship, and to fill the hearts of the people with new confidence in themselves, in each other, and in God, the Labour Church has come'.[14] As David Howell has remarked, the ILP leaders were 'typical Victorian Radicals' in their optimism:

> In the end, the forces of progress were irresistible. It was "The Springtime of Nations ... a Springtime of Society". The weight of history was on the side of the ILP.[15]

Both the ILP and the Second International benefited from the social upsurge which occurred across Europe in the late 1880s. In Britain working-class socialists fostered the New Unionism, and the New Unionism played an important part in bringing out the huge crowds which attended the early British May Days. Indeed the European successes of the early May Days ensured that the Second International's socialist celebrities appeared more than just the leaders of their national movements. Herein lay an early strength of the Second International; but one which in 1914 was to be shown to amount to little when nationalist pressures swept aside most remnants of supra-national authority.

However in the 1890s the link with International Socialism associated the early ILP with a larger body which also seemed to be marching inevitably forward. By this it also acquired part of a wider socialist tradition. One part of this was the memory of the Paris Commune, 1871, a powerful symbol. As Lenin recognised in the period 1901–5, the Commune could be made relevant to all socialist viewpoints, and its legend became as important as the event.[16] It was taken up particularly by the London branches. Thus, for example, in 1895, the General Council of the London Federation agreed that for the next year an approach should be made to 'all the socialist bodies of London with a view to a united meeting and demonstration on the anniversary of the Commune, March 18th'.[17]

May Day was an especially potent international socialist occasion in the early days of the ILP. It was redolent with images of renewal and hope. May Day iconography often chose such images as the rising sun behind the emergent and soon to be triumphant working class or spring flowers representing the start of a new season. May Day as the workers' holiday fitted in very well with the British socialists' need for a unifying tradition. James Leatham, an Aberdeen admirer of William Morris, wrote in 1895:

> As the churches celebrate Christmas and Easter so should the workers celebrate May Day ... with enthusiastic demonstration and exhortation ... No party can afford to neglect its festivals. Festivals furnish a ceremonial and mechanical aid in retrospection ... They give outward and visible sign

to the inward and spiritual significance of the great principles which at ordinary times are mere words.[18]

The success of the first May Day demonstrations put labour issues and socialism at the front of public affairs. Even before 300,000 people crowded into Hyde Park for the first Sunday May Day demonstration in London on 4 May 1890, the *Times* observed of those organising demonstrations across Europe:

> They have brought forcibly to the notice of the civilised world the existence of working class grievances or demands, and have concurrently given proof of a novel and unexpected capacity for concerted action on the most extended scale. Throughout the Christian world the universal topic this morning is the demonstration of labour.[19]

Though there was a falling off in numbers in London and elsewhere after 1892, the Sunday May Day demonstrations of the mid 1890s provided large audiences for ILP orators. Bruce Glasier moved the socialist resolution on Glasgow Green in 1893, 1894, 1895 and 1896, with crowds of 12–16,000 present on the latter two occasions. Hardie was a great draw at May Day rallies in those years; indeed he had been a speaker in East Meadows, Edinburgh for the first of the socialist May Days in 1890.[20] The London May Days in particular were cosmopolitan affairs, with distinguished emigres on the platforms. In March 1895 the London Federation sent as a resolution for the 1895 ILP Conference the resolution

> ... that this Council views with satisfaction the growth of the movement in favour of Labour Day in this country, and believes that the movement would be strengthened internationally by the Independent Labour Party Conference of 1895 sending Comrade J. Keir Hardie to Berlin on May 1st.[21]

It is not surprising that the NAC, when revising the ILP programme in January 1897 included: 'A maximum eight-hour day, with the retention of all existing holidays and Labour Day, May 1st, secured by law'.[22] By then, however, the early popular enthusiasm for May Days was abating, due partly to changed economic circumstances and partly to a lack of powerful and currently vital issues to mobilise support for them.[23]

Yet another vital element in the attraction of internationalism was the hope that it would be the surest way of ensuring decent working conditions. It might provide an international equivalent of the London County Council and other municipal authorities operating as model employers. The demand for a legally enforced eight-hour working day was the major unifying international cause of the late 1880s and early 1890s. It was a key issue for the Scottish Miners' National Federation and for Keir Hardie. Hardie spoke on the issue at the 1888 TUC held at Bradford. At a miners' international conference held in Belgium in May 1890 he called for all European miners to co-ordinate strike action to achieve the legal eight-hour day.

Hardie became a strong advocate of international trade union action. At the 1888 TUC he had chaired a fringe meeting for French and British delegates to exchange views. Soon after, at the International Trades Congress held in London in November 1888, he proposed:

First.   That all unions of one trade in one country combine in electing an Executive Central body for that trade in that country.

Second.   That the Central bodies of the various trades in the different countries elect a General Council for all trades.

Third.   That the central bodies of the various trades in the different countries shall meet in conference annually and an international conference shall be held at intervals of not less than three years.

Such moves brought Hardie into contact with London-based Marxists, notably in 1888 with Friedrich Engels and Eleanor Marx.[24] Hardie attended both the Marxist and the non-Marxist conferences held in Paris in 1889 to mark the centenary of the storming of the Bastille, the former gathering being deemed in retrospect the founding meeting of the Second International.

Hardie's internationalism sprang initially from his trade unionism. As Fred Reid has commented:

He was drawn towards international socialist politics by his experience a miner. It had made him aware of the international character of capitalist production.[25]

Earlier, in 1887, he himself had written when some Lithuanian miners had arrived in Ayrshire: 'decent men are not going to be turned adrift to make room for beastly, filthy foreigners without knowing the reason why'. Over several years Hardie rose above such attitudes.[26] Such use of foreign labour was a major worry to the international socialist movement at that time. In May 1892, at the request of Bebel and Paul Singer of the German Social Democrats, Eleanor Marx travelled to Ayrshire and spoke to German miners, urging them to become bilingual and not to damage the international miners' movement by being exploited as cheap labour.[27]

Thus Hardie emerged to be the international man of the ILP and its main international spokesperson. This was put on a formal footing in July 1900 at the time of a bitter dispute between the ILP and SDF over recognition by the International. The NAC minutes record:

Hardie urged on the Council the importance of cultivating closer relations with the continental socialists in order to counteract the damaging statements that were frequently made with regard to the position and standing of the ILP. With the approval of the Council he undertook to work up the international correspondence of the party.[28]

The ILP leaders were further attracted to internationalism by their sheer admiration for the big names of the continental European and American labour movements, whether they be emigrés in Britain or still active in their own countries. Men and women such as Prince Peter Kropotkin, Stepniak (Sergei Mikhailovich Kravchinsky), Friedrich Engels, Wilhelm Liebknecht, Louise Michel, Eugene Debs and Jean Jaurès were revered, often regardless of their ideological positions. Stepniak was a star speaker at a *Labour Leader* dinner in December 1895, just two days before he was killed while crossing a railway line.[29] Kropotkin was widely admired. Bruce Glasier, not surprisingly given his views and acquaintanceship with him, noted of a speech by Kropotkin in March 1897:

> I was glad to hear him say 'that socialism and anarchism are not enemies but complements of each other'. His whole speech was eminently tolerant.

But he was equally enthusiastic about other international 'big names'. Thus of Liebknecht speaking in Glasgow in 1896, he wrote:

> He speaks slowly and with a remarkable choice of phrase in English. Although 70 years he hardly looks much over 50. Impresses one as a man of great breadth of vision and largeness of wisdom. Very simple and unaffected.

After Liebknecht's death in 1900, he noted:

> The only socialist who was *personally* international. A great man. Fatherly, grave, good humoured, so like many an old Scotsman I have known. I was entirely charmed with him alike during his lecture tour four years ago, and at the International Congress, London though I differed from him on the treatment of the anarchists.
>
> His recent articles in the *Clarion* against imperialism and militarism were so gracious, so big hearted and friendly to us in Britain.[30]

While such enthusiasm was widespread among the leading ILP figures, in the early days its internationalism was often prompted by the activities of Edward Aveling, Eleanor Marx and other London-based associates of Friedrich Engels. Having broken both with Hyndman and the SDF and with Morris and his Socialist League, Edward Aveling and Eleanor Marx's activities centred on the Bloomsbury Socialist Society (a former branch of the League) and their socialist and radical Legal Eight Hours Committee. Aveling's political importance, such as it was, depended on his access to major continental Marxists through his Marx and Engels connections as well as on the key role that the Legal Eight Hours group played in organising the very successful early London May Day demonstrations.[31]

Aveling brought these international interests with him when he became involved with the ILP. He was a delegate to the ILP's inaugural conference in January 1893 and a member of its first National Administrative Council. Soon after the foundation conference, Aveling took steps to become involved in the London District of the ILP, which had been set up the previous June. London was one of the ILP's weakest areas.[32] Although the ILP constitution prevented the Bloomsbury Socialist Society from affiliating as a body, Aveling nevertheless became a major figure in the London ILP for much of 1893. In this period the London District ILP became very internationally minded. Great care was taken over the 1893 May Day preparations, considerable attention was given to the German and French socialists' electoral struggles and much interest shown in various aspects of the 1893 International Congress held at Zurich. At the executive committee meeting on 5 June 1893 Eleanor Marx urged that the ILP should make a donation to the German Social Democrats' election fund. This suggestion was taken up and resulted in the ILP nationally making a donation and an additional sum being raised by Fred Pickles in Bradford.[33] Aveling eventually over-reached himself with his May Day connections. Having been eased out of his ILP positions, in 1894 he acted in spite to exclude the London ILP from the May Day platforms. Because of this, his resort to lying and his failure to turn up to back up his spurious claims about his role in the incident, he was expelled from the London ILP. It is interesting to note that his associates thereafter tried to wield their international connections in a forlorn attempt to get him back into favour, suggesting that Liebknecht would be willing 'to speak for the ILP at the next May Day Demonstration, providing that he receives a proper invitation'.[34]

The cosmopolitan influence of London on the early ILP's internationalism did not only depend on the Engels circle or major figures such as Kropotkin and Stepniak. Successive waves of political refugees from continental Europe had settled in the capital and there played a major role in the radical and socialist clubs and in bodies such as the Manhood Suffrage League.[35] London was also the most likely base for visiting continental socialists, such as Eduard Bernstein. As the reputation of the ILP rose among continental socialists, they gravitated increasingly towards the London homes of Keir Hardie and James Ramsay MacDonald.

They in turn travelled abroad and renewed contacts with continental European and American socialists.[36] In the case of the United States, Hardie toured there for fifteen weeks in late 1895 and MacDonald for a similar period in the autumn of 1897. For both the trips were 'more like political progresses' than holidays.[37] Before MacDonald left, the ILP NAC provided him with credentials to the American Labour associations.[38] Hardie on his visit addressed the American Labor Congress at Chicago on Labor Day. Thereafter the ILP leadership was especially aware of American labour developments and in particular of the splits in the socialist movement. In the autumn of 1899, before the outbreak of the Boer War, MacDonald was quite advanced in making arrangements for Eugene Debs to undertake a six-week lecture tour of Britain. Hardie had got on well with Debs, when he had visited Debs in Woodstock gaol in 1895. In 1898, when Joseph Chamberlain tried to obtain an alliance with the US at a time of tension when Russia and Britain were forcing the Chinese into leasing territory, the NAC agreed to issue

... a manifesto ... to the workers of Britain and America protesting against the jingoistic spirit manifested in certain quarters with regard to the suggested Anglo-American Alliance, but expressing gratification that the prospects of good understanding between the democracies of the two countries are becoming brighter.[39]

Yet for all this, before 1905 the ILP brand of socialism remained something apart from much of the contemporary continental socialism. Sam Hobson, an early ILP pioneer, when later reflecting on the ILP activists of the 1890s, observed:

> They were desperately in earnest ... Unless we understand their [northern industrial centres] social, religious, and political atmosphere, we shall never understand British socialism. One has only to attend an international socialist conference to realise our intellectual and moral insularity. It will never bridge the English Channel.[40]

At the time of the 1904 Amsterdam Congress, Hardie commented that many of his ILP colleagues were 'out of touch with those currents and cross-currents which are always at work in the great ocean of Continental Socialism'.[41] The ILP's motions to the International Congresses rarely engaged in the current ideological debates; indeed they tended to be insular in outlook and sometimes even quirky. Before the London Congress of 1896 the NAC approved the resolution:

> Firstly to ascertain what is actually the most practical or convenient language to employ as the official language of international congresses; that is to say what languages would be best understood by the majority of delegates and nationalities likely to attend such Congresses for some years to come, each nationality be separately asked to state what language other than their own language it would prefer.
>
> Secondly: that with a view of uniting future generations by the knowledge of one fixed international language, which all children in primary schools should be compelled to learn, the Congress be invited to decide whether that future international language should be English, French, German, Holapuk [similar to Esperanto] or Latin.[42]

The intentions were splendid, but the prescriptions were politically unrealistic to say the least.

The Second International, with its ill-fated efforts to prepare to take action to ensure peace in the event of a European crisis, is easily debunked, both by the Left and by the Right.[43] Nevertheless it did provide a focus for efforts to prevent international war and the plundering by Europe and the US of poorer parts of the world.

For many in the ILP it widened horizons and discouraged chauvinism and racism. J. R. Clynes, who attended the Zurich International Congress of 1893, later recalled: 'For the first time I realised that, bad as labour conditions were in Britain, they were infinitely worse in certain other parts of the world'.[44] Something of the growing awareness of 'a wider world out there' also comes through in the leaflet that the ILP issued in English, French and German ahead of the 1896 London International Congress. The text, after surveying developments in Britain and, somewhat awkwardly, those in continental Europe, the United States and the British Empire, concluded:

> ... we express a hope that our greetings will be reciprocated by all the comrades to whom these messages may come. We are one with them in heart and mind. we feel with them in all their sufferings and have joy in all their triumphs. It would alike cheer us to know that the same sentiments inspire their breast. We invite responses to our fraternal greetings from all Socialist and Revolutionary movements throughout the world, and we trust that when the International Socialist Congress assembles in London next year, we may have an opportunity of meeting their delegates fact to face, and of hearing from their lips the growth and prosperity of our Common Cause.[45]

The contact with the continental socialists helped crystallise the ILP leaders' critical attitudes to British imperial actions in the Sudan, South Africa and elsewhere and also to the menacing Great Power rivalries.[46] Of course in this, they also had a rich British radical heritage on which to build. At the time of the 1898 Fashoda Incident, the ILP sent Lord Salisbury the message:

> That having regard to the best interests of the French and British peoples and the fearful horrors which war would entail, we hereby enter our own emphatic protest against the suggestion that war should be resorted to over the Fashoda difficulty and call upon Her Majesty's Ministers to offer to submit to the arbitration of some just and equitable tribunal all the points in dispute between Great Britain and France with a view to their equitable adjustment.[47]

This was very much in the Gladstonian tradition of arbitration. The links with the Second International only provided added strength to go in a direction that was to be their route anyway. The Labour Representation Committee (LRC) accepted the basic lines of ILP international policy. Its 1901 conference gave unanimous support to the ILP call to settle the Boer War by arbitration and also to its condemnation that 'modern imperialism with its attendant militarism is a reversion to one of the worst phases of barbarism'.[48] In 1905 the LRC joined the Second International.

By 1905 the ILP's outlook was much less insular than it had been in 1893. Now leaders such as Hardie and MacDonald were accepted as major figures of international socialism. No longer was there a role for intermediaries such as Edward Aveling in bringing the leading lights of continental European socialism into contact with the leaders of the British democratic labour and socialist movement.

NOTES

1. ILP, *Report of the First Annual Conference, 1893*, p.3.
2. Tuesday morning, 28 July 1896. *Report of the International Socialist Workers and Trade Union Congress, London 1896*, pp.9–11.
3. ILP, NAC minutes, 2 Jan, 22 Apr, 3 July and 1 Oct 1896 and 26 Feb 1897; Independent Labour Party Papers (hereafter ILP), 1/2; British Library of Political and Economic Science, LSE. W. Stewart, *J. Keir Hardie* (1921), p.129.
4. J. Bruce Glasier, *William Morris and the Early Days of the Socialist Movement* (1921). E. P. Thompson, *William Morris: Romantic to Revolutionary* (1955), pp.886–99. L. Thompson, *The Enthusiasts* (1971), pp.34–52. S. Pierson, *Marxism and the Origins of British Socialism* (1973), pp.141–6.
5. The other speakers were Dan Irving and C. A. Gibson of the SDF and Pete Curran of the ILP. Glasier went on to Kelmscott House (Morris himself was then away). Diary entry, 2 Aug 1896; J. Bruce Glasier Papers, 1/2, Sydney Jones Library, Liverpool University. For the Walsall anarchists, whose imprisonment owed much to the action of a police agent provocateur, see J. Quail, *The Slow Burning Fuse* (1978), pp.103–43 and 200–2.
6. Diary entry, 7 August 1896. When the Empress of Austria was assassinated, he wrote in his diary (12 Sept 1898): 'How hard it must be upon the few anarchists of the nobler sort'. Glasier Papers, 1/2.
7. J. Bruce Glasier to Katharine Glasier, 14 August 1904; Glasier Papers, 1/1. 04/22. D. J. Newton, *British Labour, European Socialism and the Struggle for Peace 1889–1914* (Oxford, 1985), pp.44–6.
8. J. Bruce Glasier to Elizabeth Bruce Glasier and to K. Bruce Glasier, 17 August 1904; Glasier Papers 1/1 04/15 and 25. For the background to the Amsterdam Congress see G. D. H. Cole, *A History of Socialist Thought, Vol. 3, Part 1, The Second International 1889–1914* (1956), pp.45–59, J. Joll, *The Second International 1889–1914* (second edition, 1974), pp.102–7, as well as Newton.
9. J. Bruce Glasier diary, 3 and 25 September 1904; Glasier Papers 1/2.
10. J. Bruce Glasier to Elizabeth Bruce Glasier, 18 November 1904; Glasier Papers 1.1. 04/17.
11. W. L. Guttsmann, *The German Social Democratic Party 1875–1933* (1981), pp.78–127.
12. ILP, NAC minutes, 1 July 1898; ILP Papers 1/3. Similarly, following the ILP's 1895 conference, Mann sent a telegram from it congratulating the 'comrades of Denmark' on their electoral success; Harvester Press microform of pamphlets and papers of the ILP (hereafter 'Harvester microform').
13. *Report of First Annual Conference*, p.5. R. H. Dominick, *Wilhelm Liebknecht* (Chapel Hill, North Carolina, 1982), pp.407–8. ILP, NAC minutes, 2 Jan 1896; ILP 1/2.
14. Quoted in S. Yeo, 'A New Life: The Religion of Socialism in Britain 1883–1896', *History Workshop*, 4 (1977), pp.5–56.
15. D. Howell, *British Workers and the Independent Labour Party 1888–1906* (Manchester, 1983), p.362.
16. On this see G. Haupt, 'The Commune as symbol and example' in his *Aspects of International Socialism 1871–1914* (Cambridge, 1986), pp.23–47.
17. London Federation of ILP branches, General Council minutes, 6 December 1895 and 6 March 1896; ILP London District minute books (hereafter ILP

311

London), available on Harvester microform.

18. Quoted in Pierson, *op. cit.*, p.227 On May Days see E. J. Hobsbawm, 'Mass Producing Traditions: Europe 1870–1914' in E. Hobsbawm and T. Ranger (eds), *The Invention of Tradition* (Cambridge, 1983), pp.283–6 and 'Birth of a Holiday: The First of May' in C. J. Wrigley and J. Shepherd (eds), *On The Move* (1991), pp.l04–22; A. Panaccione (ed.), *The Memory of May Day* (Venice, 1989) and C. J. Wrigley, 'May Day and After' in *History Today* (June 1990), pp.35–41.

19. *Times*, 1 May 1890.

20. J. Bruce Glasier diary, 5 May 1895, 3 May 1896 and 1 May 1897. *Edinburgh Evening News*, 5 May 1890.

21. London Federation of ILP branches, General Council minutes, 15 March 1895. Hardie did not go (and the London motion was sent in too late for the Conference).

22. ILP, NAC minutes, 5 Jan 1897; ILP 1/2.

23. Bruce Glasier was no doubt right to see the failure of the 1897 Glasgow demonstration having much to do with switching it to a Saturday ('Boys brigade and Volunteer Review and several great football matches are against us') but his 1904 general explanation for the 'slump in May Day sentiment' is unconvincing: 'Processions and village festivals are evidently archaic now: they are forms of celebrations which city life makes difficult and unreal'. J. Bruce Glasier diary, 1 May 1897 and 1 May 1904; Glasier Papers 1/2.

24 . Stewart, pp.48–52. F. Reid, *Keir Hardie: The Making of a Socialist* (1978), pp.123 and 96. K. O. Morgan, *Keir Hardie: Radical and Socialist* (1975), pp.39–41.

25. Reid, *op. cit.*, pp.121–2

26. Reid, *op. cit.*, p.122

27. C. Tsuzuki, *The Life of Eleanor Marx, 1855–1898* (1967), pp.219–21. Y. Kapp, *Eleanor Marx, Vol. 2* (1976), p.532.

28. ILP, NAC minutes, 28 July 1900; ILP 1/4.

29. Stewart, *op. cit.*, pp.l26–8. ILP, NAC minutes, 2 Jan 1896; ILP 1/2

30. J. Bruce Glasier diary, 4 Mar 1897, 26 May 1896 and 8 Aug 1900; Glasier Papers, 1/2.

31. Engels was naturally seen as an authority on German Social Democracy, and Joseph Burgess was eager to get him to write on the subject for his *Workman's Times*. ILP London minutes 28 Nov 1892; Harvester microform. More generally, for the background see H. Pelling, *The Origins of the Labour Party* (Oxford, 1954).

32. P. Thompson, *Socialists, Liberals and Labour: The Struggle for London 1885–1914* (1967), pp. 157–65 and Howell, pp.255–65.

33. ILP London minutes, 5,12 and 19 June 1893; Harvester microform.

34. ILP London minutes, 24 Aug 1894; Harvester microform. Aveling had earlier acted equally petulantly in excluding the SDF from the 1891 London May Day Demonstration. Tsuzuki, pp.211–12.

35. S. Shipley, *Club Life and Socialism in Mid Victorian London* (1983).

36. On Hardie's travels and contacts see especially Morgan, pp.85–7 and 181–200. For MacDonald, see D. Marquand, *Ramsay MacDonald* (1977), pp.57–9, 76–8.

37. As Jane Cox put it in her edition of Ramsay and Margaret MacDonald's letter, *A Singular Marriage* (1988), p.179.

38. ILP, NAC minutes, 21 Apr 1897; ILP 1/2/

39. ILP, NAC minutes, 14 Mar 1899 and 1 July 1898; ILP 1/3.

40. S. G. Hobson, *Pilgrim To The Left: Memoirs of a Modern Revolutionist* (1938), p.30.

41. Newton, *op. cit.*, p.45 (quoting *Labour Leader*, 26 Aug 1904).

42. The motion originated with Adolph Smith, who had acted as an interpreter at the 1888 International Trades Congress in London. ILP, NAC minutes, 22 April 1896; ILP 1/2.

43. For two often shrewd and lively assessments see A. J. P. Taylor, 'The Second International' (a review of Cole), reprinted in his *Europe: Grandeur and Decline* (Harmondsworth, 1967), pp.138–42, and G. Niemeyer, 'The Second International: 1889–1914' in M. M. Drachkovitch (ed.), *The Revolutionary Internationals 1864–1943* (Stanford, California, 1966), pp.95–127. The latter observes, 'Without the International, European labor might have become as integrated a part of the existing society as labor did in America in the twentieth century ...' (p.126).

44. Though it has to be said that otherwise his recollections of that Congress reinforce the worst 'wild foreigner' stereotypes. J. R. Clynes, *Memoirs 1869– 1924* (1937), pp.72–3.

45. *Socialists of all Countries Unite!* (actually published, May 1895). While this may be period-piece flowery rhetoric, the whole leaflet has an air of striving for international socialist recognition. Indeed a little earlier the NAC had been very surprised to learn that they were financially committed in regard to the arrangements for the 1896 International Congress. This only came to light after their February 1895 meeting (the commitment only being known to their former secretary, Shaw Maxwell). ILP, NAC minutes, 6 and 7 Feb 1895; ILP 1/1/

46. Newton provides an excellent account of British socialists' attitudes to war and imperialism in the 1890s and of their campaigns during the Boer War. See in particular Newton, pp.50–138.

47. ILP, NAC minutes, 26 Nov 1898; ILP 1/3.

48. 1 Feb 1901. *Report of the First Annual Conference of the Labour Representation Committee* (1901), p.20.

SECTION IV

REVIEW OF LITERATURE
AND RECORDS

1. Recent Writing on the History of the ILP, 1893–1932

Keith Laybourn

The Independent Labour Party was formed as a national body in Bradford on 13 and 14 January 1893. From its formation until its secession from the Labour Party, in 1932, it was and remained essentially an amalgam of provincial organisations. As E. P. Thompson has emphasised, 'the ILP grew from the bottom up; its birthplaces were in those shadowy parts known as the provinces'.[1] Indeed, the first meeting was effectively a gathering of provincial bodies – socialist clubs, Labour unions and the like – which had emerged in the North, Lancashire and Yorkshire, during the late 1880s and early 1890s. As a provincial organisation the new party mediated with a variety of regional and local working-class cultures and trade union organisations, working within an intricate pattern of relationships. Even though the ILP was not always able to make a significant impact upon local politics it could claim some major breakthroughs in towns such as Bradford, Leicester and Halifax, and rightly lays claim to being the first socialist party to gain widespread, if not mass, support in Britain. Yet, until twenty-five years ago it was one of the least studied of Britain's political parties. However, since then much research on the ILP has unearthed the wide range of its activities and revealed the vitally important role it played in the development of the Labour Party. It is now obvious that the ILP provided the platform from which the British Labour Party was launched, even if its child was eventually hijacked by the trade union movement.

The ILP was a formative influence in British Labour politics from 1893 until 1932. Its support had risen quickly up to 1895, when the defeat of all its candidates in the general election set back its political fortunes. In 1900 it helped form the Labour Representation Committee, which became the Labour Party. During the Edwardian age its support increased rapidly, as did that of the wider Labour movement, until it was checked by the First World War, when its official opposition to war lost it much trade-union support to the reorganised and more patriotic Labour Party. The ILP revived in the early 1920s, under the middle-class leadership of Clifford Allen, until it was divided in the late 1920s and early 1930s by rival Scottish and proletarian demands of Jimmy Maxton who, in August 1932, led the ILP out of the Labour Party and into the political wilderness. More than forty years later, in May 1975, the party changed its name to Independent Labour Publications, subsequently re-entering the Labour Party.

Inevitably, many of the ILP's achievements have been ignored, obscured by its departure from the Labour Party in 1932. Historians have normally focused upon the national developments in Labour history. Yet the last twenty years have seen a revival of interest in the ILP as historians have risen to the challenge of E. P. Thompson and Asa Briggs to become more involved in detailed local investigation. Also, the concern of Labour politicians about the future of the Labour Party in the 1980s has revived interest in the reasons for Labour's past successes and thus the vital contribution played by the ILP.

Until the 1970s the vast majority of publications on the history of the Independent Labour Party dealt with national themes. Henry Pelling's *Origins of the Labour Party*, written in the early 1950s, and R. E. Dowse's *Left in the Centre*, are of this type, even though they did draw upon illustrative local information.[2] Even the studies of nationally important ILP leaders focused upon the national rather than local events. This was particularly true of Fenner Brockway's *Socialism over Sixty Years*, which dealt with the life of Fred Jowett, and Colin Cross's *Philip Snowden*. Both studies forsook the local for the national after their preliminary chapters.[3] Since then there have been many books and articles on the local history of the ILP which have sought to set it into its local and regional context.[4] In particular, there have been two monumental attempts, by David Howell and Duncan Tanner, to combine the national and the local approaches, recognising that there is a two-way relationship in labour history and that local developments can influence national developments just as much as national developments can affect local political trends.[5] In general, what recent research has revealed is the vibrant and lively nature of early Labour politics and its immense variety of form. The move from national to local research has done much to undermine the notion of the declining salience of local politics in the twentieth century. As Bill Lancaster has stressed, in his study of working-class politics of Leicester, local traditions could shape Labour politics:

> The early Leicester Labour Party possessed a Janus face: on the one side the party with MacDonald at the helm appeared to prefigure the future process of bureaucratizing and centralizing Labour politics; on the other the Leicester movement manifests itself as a product of a specific local political tradition deeply entrenched in, and taking direction from, issues rooted in the local community.[6]

With the burgeoning of local and rank and file studies, historians are now looking again at the questions and issues which have so troubled them in explaining the early development of the ILP and the Labour Party.

Recent research has clearly influenced thinking on the history of the British Labour movement. On the origins of the ILP, it has provided evidence about the relative importance of the trade union movement, social activities and club life to its early development, and there is now a wider understanding of the distribution and nature of ILP support. Even more important, new research has offered insights into the relationship between the ILP and the Labour Party which qualify previous assumptions that the ILP was simply a tributary, albeit an important one, to the development of the Labour Party. In many respects the ILP helped to shape the socialism which the Labour Party eventually adopted, and also helped to formulate many of its attitudes towards dealing with the poor, the unemployed, the uneducated and ill-housed. Yet there has also been some modifying evidence to suggest that the ILP may not have been the only routeway to the formation of a mass socialist party; in some areas the Social Democratic Federation seems to have carried influence as part of a wider Labour protest. The ILP also appears to have drawn its support more widely than the working class and, according to Carl Levy, was strongly influenced by the significant presence of the lower-middle classes, the white-collar section of the community, within its ranks.[7] Although the First World War and the post-war years have attracted much less attention than the years before 1914 yet there has been some research on the First World War which has called into question the assumption that the ILP was simply the 'peace party', and research on the inter-war years has indicated the uneasy relationship which existed between the ILP and the Labour Party at the local level.[8] The whole body of this new evidence has inevitably adjusted assessments of when the Labour Party began to seriously challenge the political hegemony of the Liberal Party. In some areas, the ILP/Labour Party had clearly challenged and seriously undermined the position of the Liberal Party before 1914, whilst in others this was not the case.

Despite the conflicting nature of much recent research, several themes are beginning to emerge. First, it appears that the impact of the ILP varied from region to region and from town to town. Secondly, the ILP was clearly the largest and most successful socialist party in Britain until 1918, even though it was but one of several socialist organisations pushing forward the cause of the political Labour movement. Thirdly, the ILP's political future was damaged much more by the emergence of a Labour Party committed, albeit loosely, to socialism in 1918 than by its official opposition to the First World War. Fourthly, whilst it was a predominantly working-class party it drew significant support from the lower middle classes and even from some sections of the business community. Fifthly, the ILP's secession from Labour in 1932 was an inevitable consequence of an intensely regional and semi-autonomous type of ILP organisation which could not easily adjust to the national Labour movement whose focus was very much judged and defined by the burgeoning influence of the trade union movement.

Past and Present Research

Traditionally, the ILP has been presented as being a rather small political tributary in the development of the Labour Party and its history has often emerged through the biographies of Labour leaders, such as Keir Hardie, Fred Jowett and Philip Snowden, or more general histories of the political Labour movement. Quite naturally, the much larger Labour Representation Committee/Labour Party has occupied centre stage. At best the ILP appeared to play a fringe role in the development of the wider Labour movement and was considered to have failed to be the effective propagator of a mass socialist movement. At worst the ILP was considered to be a quaint and ineffective organisation after 1895. Indeed, its failure in the 1895 General Election, and its subsequent general decline in the late 1890s, is considered to have forced it to contemplate a wider, and initially non-Socialist, Labour alliance in the form of the Labour Representation Committee/Labour Party in 1900. The LRC superseded the ILP, almost immediately.

Such a Whiggish approach, which emphasised progress and the discarding of redundant influences along the route, obviously played down the importance of the ILP. This was all too evident in George Dangerfield's *Strange Death of Liberal England* and in the writings of G. D. H. Cole, and other Fabian writers, which emphasised the rival claims of the Labour Party and the Fabian society.[9] The problem with this national approach is that it rather assumed that twentieth century politics moved, almost inexorably, from domination by local politics to domination by national politics. Yet, Ian Donnachie, Christopher Harvie and Ian Wood in the case of Scotland have demonstrated that local politics can affect the attitudes of national parties and that to ignore the local perspective is to disregard a vital component in the make-up of national politics.[10]

A change in focus began to emerge in the 1950s, especially once Henry Pelling reminded his readers, in his book T*he Origins of the Labour Party*, that

> Whatever the future might hold, the very birth of the I.L.P., the creation of this institutional form, was an event of primary importance not only in labour history but also in the general political and constitutional evolution of the country.[11]

The importance of the ILP had been rediscovered and re-emphasised. Yet Pelling's contribution was to revive interest in the national rather than local importance of the ILP, although it led on to some distinguished efforts to reconstruct the ILP's national impact.[12] It was six years later, in 1960, that the renewed interest in the ILP was focused upon local developments by E. P. Thompson in his seminal article 'Homage to Tom Maguire'.[13] Thompson noted the provincial nature of much early socialist growth and focused upon the experience of industrial conflict, most notably the Manningham Mills strike which took place in Bradford in 1890 and 1891 and was responsible for the the first detachment of working-class support from the Liberal Party to the embryonic ILP. Thompson's dominating argument was that the industrial defeat of the Manningham operatives by Samuel Cunliffe Lister and his directors was of more than an ordinary importance. It attracted the support of trade unionists in Yorkshire and throughout Britain, divided the middle classes and the working classes in Bradford, raised questions of free speech and, in the wake of the defeat of the workers, led to the formation of the Bradford Labour Union in May 1891, the Colne Valley Labour Union in July 1891, and many others similar organisations over the next few years. Many new trades councils were formed in the textile district of Yorkshire, most of whom soon attached themselves to the new Labour unions and to the ILP once it was formed in January 1893. Thompson maintained that the defeat of the Manningham operatives speeded up the formation of the independent Labour movement.

Thompson's pioneering work on the textile district of Yorkshire soon stimulated others to examine the history of the ILP within its local and regional context, and to question the typicality of the experience. In the mid 1960s R. K. Middlemass produced his book *The Clydesiders: a left wing struggle for Parliamentary Power*, which examined the history of the ILP in Glasgow and the emergence of the Scottish ILP's working-class ideals into the national ILP, the Labour Party and Parliament in the 1920s.[14] Ten years later Jack Reynolds and Keith Laybourn examined the emergence of the ILP in Bradford.[15] Their main theme was that it was the capture of trade-union support which was largely responsible for the success of the Bradford ILP, whilst acknowledging that other factors, such as anti-Liberalism, club life and the Labour Church, contributed to the ILP's rapid and sustained growth in the community. Since then, and particularly throughout the 1980s, there have been numerous articles and books examining the local development, policy and membership, of the ILP.[16] These have changed the way in which the history of the ILP is now perceived.

Trade Unionism, Socialist Societies, Club Life and the Distribution of ILP support

There have been two pressing questions in recent research. First, why did the independent Labour movement emerge? Secondly, how widespread and influential was the ILP before 1914? On the first question, there have been divergent explanations offered, many of them relating to the importance, or otherwise, of trade unionism. On the second question, there has been a serious debate between those who maintain that that there was widespread support for the ILP/Labour Party and those who argue that its support was shallow and thinly spread throughout the country.

What emerges is that the working classes reacted in different ways in different communities and that a multitude of factors help to explain the growth of the ILP. In particular, trade-union support appears to have been important. Many studies have stressed that trade unionism underpinned much of the early growth of the ILP. Thompson, in 1960, and Reynolds and Laybourn, in 1975 and 1984, emphasised that trade union support was vital to the development of the ILP in the textile district of the West Riding.[17] Jeff Hill also accepted that trade unionism was one of the prime factors in the growth of the ILP in Manchester and south Lancashire, although the Social Democratic Federation and other bodies were important.[18] Patricia Dawson and Robert Perks, on Halifax and Huddersfield, respectively, have also tended to confirm the importance of the trade union movement in Labour's early growth.[19] Bill Lancaster's work on Leicester also strongly confirms that industrial struggles, such as the boot lock-out of 1895, paved the way for the emergence of the ILP and the Labour movement, as socialists amongst the National Union of Boot and Shoe Operatives and the Trades Council began to make inroads into a trade union movement which had once been largely attached to the Liberal Party.[20] Yet the impression one gains from this and other research is that structural conflict was by no means universal and that trade unions remained loyal to the Liberal Party in some areas or were too weak to make a significant contribution to the early successes of the ILP.

Chris Wrigley, in his study of 'Liberals and the Desire for Working-Class Representation in Battersea, 1886–1922'[21] notes that 'The local MP, John Burns, increasingly drifted towards the liberals in the 1890s, and the Battersea Trades and Labour Council worked with the Liberal and Radical Associations, taking on a marked lib-lab hue after 1897.'[22] Indeed, he adds that 'In the 1890s and up to 1906 Battersea liberalism and radicalism came to work closely with the Labour League and the local trade unions. This was particularly so at the local level, through the Battersea Trades and Labour Council.'[23] The progressive alliance operated effectively between the early 1890s and 1906, attracted widespread working-class support, but from 1906 onwards it came under pressure from the LRC/Labour Party, which began to capture widespread working-class support, got its supporters to leave the Trades Council, and pushed forward the issue of unemployment. The Progressive Alliance collapsed during the war and the Labour Party replaced it. As for the socialist activists, the Battersea branch of the Social Democratic Federation was active on the issue of unemployment and the ILP barely made a mark. In this particular case the relatively powerful trade union movement sided with the Progressive Alliance until 1906 and gradually drifted to the Labour Party thereafter.

A similar situation prevailed in Rochdale until 1906.[24] In Wales, it appears that the Liberals were overwhelmingly powerful in the north and south before 1914. According to Kenneth Morgan, this was due to the control which Liberalism held over Nonconformity, and the national and popular aspirations of Welsh society. But it was also partly due to the fact that many of the unions, such as the South Wales Miners' Federation, were dominated by Liberal leaders such as William Abraham, 'Mabon', and Liberal supporters, despite the fact that the Miners' Federation Great Britain voted for affiliation with the Labour Party in 1908.[25] In other areas, such as Leeds, the Trades Council retained a neutral stand until about 1895 and gradually drifted towards the ILP, although it was the Labour Party which exerted a more effective presence in the early twentieth century.[26] And in Barnsley, the ILP found it very difficult to make headway in the face of the staunch opposition of Ben Pickard and the Yorkshire Miners' Association. As David Rubinstein has noted, Peter Curran, the ILP candidate in the 1897 by-election, obtained only 1,091 votes against the Liberal candidate's 6,744 and the Conservative's 3,454:

322

The most important lesson which the ILP leaders drew from the campaign was that only by working with, rather than against trade unions, could real progress be made. Jim Connell wrote immediately after the election in the *Labour Leader*:

'Nearly all the organised workers in the division are miners, and the miners' organisation was opposed to us. Mistakenly, wrongly, wickedly, if you please; but still it was opposed to us. [...] If the Yorkshire Miners' Association were with us, the result would be just as startling the other way. If we are to succeed, the trade unions of this country must be officered with Socialists. In the present stage of development the average Britisher cannot rise above the trade-union level. Let our aim be to win the trade unions for Socialism.'[27]

Trade unionists could often be slow to move over to the ILP/Labour Party. And, as implied in some of the above-mentioned research, it was the Labour Party rather than the ILP as such which eventually, after 1906, became the great beneficiary. But what happened in areas where trade unionism was simply weak rather than vacillating?

David James has indicated that the Keighley ILP, which was one of the most active in Yorkshire and produced Philip Snowden, lacked a sound trade union base. The local Trades Council was small, barely mustering 1,000 members – although its numbers appear to have risen to 1,302 in 1902, at a time when it had far more branches than in the early 1890s.[28] There was an uneasy relationship between the ILP and the Trades Council from time to time, but the vast majority of ILP members appear to have been trade unionists and the ILP put forward trade-union policies in the municipal election, advocating fair wages and municipal workshops. Yet the ILP movement was not able to make a major impact upon Keighley until after the First World War, and was firmly opposed by an intransigent old Liberal leadership prior to 1914. What seems to have sustained the Keighley ILP was club life, clubs, the Labour Church and the Clarion movement. 'The realisation of the kingdom of heaven upon earth' became the main focus of ILP activity. The Labour Church, which could often attract as many as 400 or 500 people, was regaled by Philip Snowden's famous lecture 'The Christ that is to be', and with speeches by Margaret McMillan, Caroline Martyn and Fred Brocklehurst.[29]

Whilst James suggests that Keighley's weak trade unionism blended with other factors to create a viable ILP, albeit one which gained only modest success in the face of intransigent old Liberalism, there have been others who have argued that trade unionism played a much less important role than is often suggested. David Clark, for instance, argues that the the ethical and moral aspects of socialism were the driving force behind the ILP in Colne Valley.[30] With only about 1,500 trade unionists in Colne Valley, meaning that only about 2.6 per cent of the total population were trade unionists compared with more than twice that level for the West Riding of Yorkshire, it is obvious that trade unionism was weak in this constituency.[31] Whilst Clark

323

acknowledges the contribution of the trade unions he emphasises that 'The emergence of Socialism in Colne Valley came not as a rupture with the past but as a natural progression of radical thought which had been associated with advanced Liberalism.'[32] He particularly underlines the importance of the Colne Valley Labour League, groups and club life in sustaining and developing a movement which was able to return Victor Grayson in the parliamentary by-election of 1907:

> It was the Labour clubs which were to be crucial factors in the successful development of the new political party in the Colne Valley and elsewhere. Not only did they provide the permanency upon which the activities of the party could be based but they symbolised the emancipation of the members from the existing political parties. In turn they were instrumental in persuading the new movement to adopt a Socialist outlook.[33]

In other communities, such as Leicester, trade unionism and ethical factors combined with co-operation and other factors to develop the ILP. As Bill Lancaster writes:

> The concept of cooperative production touched a nerve that ran to the heart of young socialist trade unionists during the early 1890s. The main tenets of this idea hinged upon the fact that where socialism did exist in Britain during the 1890s it tended to be intensely local. Conflict and struggle occurred within specific communities and socialist solutions, if they were to have any popular currency, had to be dressed in local garbs. Thus while a cursory glance at NUBSO's conference and monthly reports for the period show that the Leicester socialists spent most of their energy pursuing cooperative aims, these aims were the core of the emerging local socialist programme.[34]

The role of religion in the growth of the ILP has also been subject to intense debate. At one extreme, Len Smith has suggested that the connections were incidental, dependent very much upon the quirks of individual ministers in the free churches, an argument which might also apply to the Anglican Church. At the other extreme, Tony Jowitt suggests that the connection was more potent than is often suggested because much of the link is to be found in attitudes, morals and forms not just in the incidental links between ministers, vicars, and the early ILP, a factor which Stephen Yeo was aware of in his seminal article on the 'Religion of Socialism'.[35] This is clearly an area for further research, most particularly upon the extent to which the political actions of ministers of religion reflected a more pervasive commitment by religion to the ILP. This could be important given the fact that in just about every community in the country the active members of churches and chapels vastly outnumbered the active members in the ILP, or even the Labour Party. What significance, then, might be drawn from the fact that Rev. Roberts, a Congregationalist, sat on the Bradford School Board beside Margaret McMillan, or that the Rev. W. B. Graham, an Anglican, campaigned for Victor Grayson in the Colne Valley parliamentary by-election in 1907.[36]

The balance of political and social forces which contributed to the growth of the ILP and the early political Labour movement is, of course, subject to immense variation. Certainly it is not to be expected that influences would be equally important in all constituencies. Nevertheless, it still remains the fact that trade unionism generally underpinned the support of those areas where the ILP registered a major presence, whilst the ILP barely grew in areas, such as Battersea and Rochdale, where the Liberal Party appears to have retained the support of most trade unionists until at least 1906. In areas such as Keighley and Colne Valley, where trade unionism was weak, the Labour cause seems to have been slow to develop or the trade union support appears to have been fitful. One might also reflect that there is no necessary antipathy between collective and ethical movements. The fact is that even in the Colne Valley those ILP/Colne Valley Labour Union activists who could be members of trade unions usually were, a situation witnessed in the fact that many of those who attended the inaugural meeting of the CVLU were union members. Trade unionism and ethical socialism could, and did, go hand in hand. As Reynolds and Laybourn indicated, ILPers saw membership of the ILP and the trade unions to be two sides of the same coin but also attended ILP clubs and Labour churches in abundance. In Bradford there were at least 28 ILP clubs and groups formed between 1891 and 1895, and 23 at the most at any one time. In 1893 they had about 2,000 members and, although the ILP's support dwindled and clubs disappeared in the mid and late 1890s, the Bradford ILP still had the distinction of having the largest membership by far, at around 1,000 by the end of the 1890s. Halifax, which also had a strong trade-union presence, particularly from the engineers after the 1897 engineering lockout, still had a club membership exceeding 500 in the late 1890s.[37] Trade unionism and ethical socialism were complementary to each other, although, with its greater membership, the trade union movement always provided the true base of support at municipal and parliamentary elections.

Yet the ILP was not the only socialist society active in many areas. And the question which has been asked most often is – was an alternative socialist strategy available? Clearly, the Battersea branch of the Social Democratic Federation, which had been formed in the mid 1880s, carried considerable local influence.[38] The SDF was also active in Burnley, Manchester and other areas of Lancashire politics.[39] It was also deeply involved in the Labour politics of Dewsbury, where Harry Quelch stood in a parliamentary by-election in 1902.[40] Yet there is evidence against the possibility of a quasi-Marxist group offering a realistic alternative to the gradualist, municipal and parliamentary ILP. P. Watmough has indicated that the majority of SDF branches and members were to be found in London and Lancashire – in other words its influence was not as widespread as that of the ILP.[41] And Jeff Hill has indicated that its influence in Lancashire stemmed from its willingness to identify with the wider Labour cause rather than to cut itself off from the ILP, the Fabians and other Labour groups after its withdrawal from the Labour Representation Committee in 1901.[42] Even in the case of Dewsbury the position has been hotly debated by Martin Crick, Keith Laybourn and Jack Reynolds. Crick argues that the SDF had wide support for its actions in putting forward Harry Quelch as his parliamentary candidate in 1902, whilst Laybourn and Reynolds, using the ILP archives, strongly suggest that there was much ILP disquiet and frustration within ILP ranks at the way in which the SDF insinuated itself into Dewsbury Labour politics.[43] And one might remember that the SDF carried little support throughout the West Riding of Yorkshire, unlike Lancashire, and that the Bradford SDF, and indeed other branches, were often a small 'collection of oddities'.[44]

The dominating feature of much of this local research has been the diverse nature of the ILP. In those areas where there was strong trade-union support its growth was often rapid and well founded. In those areas where trade unionism was weak or slow to emerge, the growth of the ILP was often fitful and became heavily dependent upon local ethical and cultural factors. But how widespread was its support in any case? This is far more difficult to assess since the studies produced deal with but a small fraction of those communities where the ILP was present. And it is clear that the ten thousand or so fee-paying members of the mid 1890s, (although Keir Hardie claimed 50,000), were but the tip of the iceberg of actual support. It may not be possible, given the overlapping of the ILP and the Labour Party in some areas, to fully and accurately assess the ILP's overall spread and influence. Nevertheless, this aim, in part, has been the objective of two recent books by David Howell and Duncan Tanner.

David Howell's book, *British Workers and the Independent Labour Party 1888–1906*, contains a section on 'political spaces', in which he examines the development of the ILP in Scotland, the Yorkshire woollen district, Lancashire, and in a variety of other ILP islands of support. Concluding his survey, he notes the many contradictions which emerge in ILP politics – most notably that the ILP grew in comparatively weak trade union areas such as the Yorkshire textile areas and yet failed to develop amongst the unorganised workers of large cities.[45] In part, that type of problem has been answered by Bill Lancaster who has argued that the culture and traditions of the locality are vital in explaining the development of local ILP/Labour organisations. In addition, Laybourn and Reynolds pointed out that the most difficult workers to organise were those who were unskilled and in poverty. The ILP depended upon semi-skilled and skilled workers, most of whom would have been in a trade union given the opportunity. In the case of the West Riding of Yorkshire textile belt some workers joined the textile unions in the wake of the Manningham Mills strike of 1890/1. Also, as Howell suggests, the attitude of the local Liberal organisations could be vital. Where such organisations were relatively weak, as they were in Lancashire, the Liberals were more inclined to keep trade union support because of their willingness to compromise. Yet in other areas, such as the Yorkshire textile belt, where Liberalism was well entrenched and remained relatively unthreatened in the early 1890s, a Liberal willingness to compromise with the trade unions and the emergent Labour and socialist groups was much less evident.

The abiding impression one gets from Howell's book is that ILP fortunes were immensely variable. And, in the debate about the rise of Labour and the decline of Liberalism, one has to admit that the ILP was but a small part of the overall Labour movement once the Labour Representation Committee/ Labour Party began to emerge with trade union support from 1900 onwards. Tanner's book, *Political change and the Labour Party*, examines the wider framework of the Liberal vs Labour Party debate, surveys the state of the Labour Party between 1900 and 1918, and concludes that by 1914:

> Labour had not developed the ideological/political strength to support the expansionist strategy. It had not created a solid 'class' vote, based upon cultural unities which were common to working-class voters in all areas. It had not even the uniform support of trade unionists. The assumption that it did is based upon inadequate theory and shaky and partial empirical analysis. In reality, electoral politics followed a pattern in which past political parties and current economic interests combined to create an extremely uneven electoral map. The distribution of support was such that it was comparatively strong where the Liberal party was weak, and unable to seriously rival it in most Liberal areas. Cooperation was therefore possible.[46]

Later in the conclusion, he forces home his point;by stating that

> The Labour Party was not on the verge of replacing the Liberals in 1914. [....] The Liberal party stood for prosperity, improvement and security. The Labour left had no *generally* successful region. It had not created a 'class-based' political allegiance which would undermine the Liberal party on a broad front.[47]

In reflecting upon Tanner's comments, it is first wise to recognise that he is dealing with the wider debate about the reasons for the Labour Party replacing the Liberal Party as the progressive party of British politics. He is dismissing the views of a large group of historians who, despite their varied explanations, maintain that the inexorable rise of Labour was occurring due to the emergence of class politics before the First World War.[48] He is supporting the alternative viewpoint, that the First World War, in destroying the principles, organisation and fundaments of Liberalism, permitted the Labour Party to fill the lacuna which occurred in British wartime politics.[49] To Tanner, there is much evidence that Nonconformity, 'New Liberalism' and a combination of the 'Old' and 'New' Liberalism were more than sufficient to keep the Labour Party at bay before 1914.

Now there is no doubting the impressive nature of what Tanner has written, but equally there is no doubting some of the failings of the work. Subsuming the contribution of the ILP within that of the wider Labour Party, the first point that must be made is that the regional studies which Tanner makes tend to be, perhaps inevitably, thin and undeveloped. Above all, as in the case of Yorkshire, they fail to demonstrate an intimate knowledge of what is going on at the local level. Despite Tanner's claims to the contrary, the fact is that the thrust of his work is parliamentary in nature. The successes of Labour at the most immediate local sources of power – in municipal, board of guardians, parish council, county council, urban district council and rural district council elections – are not examined. Between 1906 and 1914 the number of such representatives in West Yorkshire alone rose from at least 89 to at least 202, with a surge of success after 1909.[50] Such local success also appears to be borne out in the country as a whole by M. G. Sheppard and J. L. Halstead.[51]

Secondly, on particular points the study is simply wrong, as for instance in the suggestion that in Bradford and Leeds Labour made most progress before 1906, when the Liberals were extremely conservative. All one can presume is that Tanner is thinking of the events leading to the parliamentary successes of 1905/1906 because thereafter, in both towns, municipal representation increased dramatically and in Bradford the Labour Party held the balance of power on the city council from 1906 until the First World War, although this was partly negated by the fact that the Liberals and Tories operated a municipal pact in 16 of the 21 wards in Bradford. In addition, the number of Labour councillors in Bradford rose from 11 in 1906 to 20 in 1913, and in Leeds from 9 to 16.[52]

Thirdly, few of those historians who maintain that the Labour Party had broken the political mould before 1914 assume that there is an homogeneity about the response of the working class. Many accept Professor John Benson's point that there was no unified working class and accept that there were differences in employment situation, family arrangements, and the cultural traditions of the working class or classes of different areas. This is explicit in the work of Reynolds and Laybourn, David Clark, Bill Lancaster, and others.[53] The cultural diversity of the working classes has been recognised by a wide variety of Labour historians. As already noted, they have recognised that trade unionists have varied enormously in their commitment to the ILP/Labour Party and that in some areas it was ethical socialism which carried more weight and, taking Stephen Yeo's point, might have been stifled by the development of trade unionism.[54] The fact is that most historians who have argued that the working class were increasingly voting upon class lines before 1914 have recognised the major differences existing between the various sections of the working class. They are not at odds but suggest that just as the Liberal Party could be a party of alliances and cooperate with trade unionists, whose views they were out of sympathy with whether they were 'Old' or 'New' Liberals, so working-class groups coming from different directions and with different objectives could come to identify with the demand for independent political action for Labour. Before the First World War a substantial proportion of the trade union movement was associated with the Labour Party. Just over two-thirds of the four million plus trade unionists were members of the Trades Union Congress in 1914 and of these 1,572,931 were affiliated to the Labour Party, up from 904,496 in 1906, due largely to the miners voting in favour of affiliation in 1908. By the beginning of 1914 trade unions with a membership of 1,207,841 members had voted on the necessity of establishing political funds for the Labour Party. Of more than 420,000 members who voted, 298,702 voted in favour and 125,310 against.[55] As Chris Wrigley writes, 'In Britain in the fifteen years before the First World War the dominant Lib-Labism of the trade unions was replaced by a socialist-flavoured Labourism.'[56] He also adds that 'These votes [in favour of political funds] ensured Labour's post-First World War electoral finances, and, in themselves reflect an element of the explanation for the rise of the Labour party and the decline of the Liberal party in the early twentieth century.'[57] That such support was not turned into parliamentary success has more to do with the system of property franchise, which left fewer than two-thirds of working men with the vote, than Tanner would admit.[58]

Contrary to Tanner, there is sufficient evidence to suggest that the Labour Party was strengthening its position before 1914, and that working men, drawn from many different backgrounds and experiences, were beginning to see in a generalised way that it was the Labour Party which was going, in future, to be the vehicle for their political aspirations. The ILP, although only a small part of the Labour Party, made its contribution to this process of political change.

The Membership of the ILP

Although much emphasis has been placed upon the ILP and Labour Party, it is clear that the ILP, probably rather more than the Labour Party, drew a significant amount of its support from the middle classes, and particularly the white-collar sections of the lower-middle classes. This has been evident in much recent work, and the point has been emphasised in an excellent survey article on this theme by Carl Levy.[59]

Reynolds and Laybourn have stressed that the ILP in Bradford, Halifax, and several other areas of the West Riding of Yorkshire, drew its support mainly from the working class.[60] Nevertheless, they have also noted the presence of clerks and teachers within ILP ranks. In addition, there was some small, but significant, support from employers and landowners. Amongst the landowners, John Lister, who owned the Shibden Hall estates in Halifax, was the main benefactor of the Halifax ILP and acted as a guarantor for the national ILP in the 1895 general election. He was, in fact, the first Treasurer of the national ILP.[61] Arthur Priestman, a Bradford manufacturer, was prominent in the Bradford ILP and took over from Fred Jowett as its chairman when Jowett was returned to Parliament in 1906. At the same time his brother, H. B. Priestman, was the chairman of the Bradford Liberal Association.[62]

Similar evidence has emerged in the works of David Howell, Jeff Hill, Bill Lancaster and just about every survey of the local developments of the ILP.[63] It is difficult to quantify the evidence of middle-class support for the 1890s but Deian Hopkin has identified a group of 1,700 nationally-orientated activists and lower-middle-class ILP workers, about ten per cent of the formal membership, in the years 1904 to 1910.[64] It would be unwise to exaggerate their importance in terms of membership, or to suggest that they carried enormous weight within the wider Labour Party, but, as Carl Levy suggests, their influence was rather more pervasive than their numbers would suggest. The presence of the lower-middle-class men, the middle-class women and the aspiring trade unionists served to professionalise the politics of the age through the proliferation of Labour-inclined newspapers, such as the *Labour Leader* and the *Clarion*, and through the public speaking and lecturing activities which formed such an important part of ILP activities. These middle-class aspirants were intent upon making the working-class supporters of the ILP think about their socialism and to them the concept of the ILP being no more than a party of the trade unions and the working class was anathema.[65] Levy's points are well made for the ILP, and even the Labour Party, through its domination by the MacDonalds and Snowdens of the movement, may have reflected some of these concerns before the almost inexorable rise of trade unionism undermined their influence.

The body of evidence suggests that the ILP was a party of the semi-skilled and skilled working classes but that it also attracted significant middle-class support which felt that support for socialism as more than simply a working-class objective. Yet one must recognise that whilst it was the largest socialist party in Britain up to 1918, its numbers were small, normally in the 10,000 to 20,000 range, although it fancifully claimed up to 50,000 active supporters from time to time before declining rapidly in the 1930s.[66] Clearly its support was volatile. But why was this the case?

The Growth, Development and Social Policies of the ILP from the 1890s to 1932

The body of recent research tends to confirm the generally recognised pattern of ILP growth. It supports the view that the ILP expanded in the early 1890s, waned in the late nineteenth century, began to expand again between about 1900 and 1913, was set back by the First World War but expanded during the early 1920s before fading in importance and influence between 1926 to 1932. The differences occur in the explanations offered.

There has been comparatively little adjustment to received opinion on the history of the ILP throughout the 1890s. The ILP grew, for a variety of reasons, in the early 1890s but faded badly after the defeats in the 1895 general election. This change of fortunes is evident in most communities which have been studied. In Bradford the ILP declined from about 2,000 members in 1893 to around a thousand in 1898.[67] In Halifax, the loss was less dramatic, falling from about 700 to between 500 and 600 in the same period.[68] Also, a wide variety of evidence tends to suggest that the ILP, in common with the LRC, began to expand rapidly from 1903 onwards.[69]

330

According to Keith Laybourn the reason for some of this Edwardian growth in Bradford was the fact that the ILP offered social policies to deal with unemployment, school feeding, housing and the extension of municipal control which built up its support on the firm base which already existed. The fact that municipal socialism was insufficient to deal with the problems of poverty and unemployment which afflicted the nation was irrelevant to the immediate ambition of the ILP in Bradford. Michael Cahill has also endorsed this particular view, arguing that 'Keir Hardie's contention of 1906 that "it became increasingly evident that socialism in this country would come through the municipality" seemed to belong to another age.'[71] In the end, evidence suggests that local initiative was not enough to solve the social problems of Britain, although it clearly provided the platform for the ILP's campaigns and its brief Edwardian and pre-First World War successes.

It was the First World War which provided the ILP with its first main test in the twentieth century. The general opinion used to be that the ILP lost membership as a result of its official policy of opposing the war. That interpretation is now being challenged. A recent article by Jowitt and Laybourn suggests that, at least in Bradford, the ILP was divided on the war issue and that despite the national policy of opposition a very substantial proportion of the membership were prepared to and did fight in the First World War.[72] Bradford's Revis Barber may have been imprisoned as a conscientious objector, but a large number of ILPers were more equivocal. Fred Jowett, whose stance amounted to a belief in the need for National Defence and individual liberty of thought on the war, thought it should be pushed to a speedy conclusion. Indeed, when the *Bradford Daily Telegraph* attacked the ILP for its unwillingness to 'raise a single finger to help the country prosecute the war successfully', Jowett replied that 'In proportion to its membership the ILP has more adherents serving in the army and navy by far than either of the two other political parties.'[73] Censuses of the Bradford ILP membership confirm this impression. One census in February 1916 indicated that of 461 young men in the local party membership of 1473, 113 were in the trenches, four had been killed and one was missing, nine had been wounded, three were prisoners of war, 118 were in training in England, six were in the Navy and 207 were attested under the Derby scheme as necessary home workers.[74] A similar survey in 1918 found that of the 492 members liable for service, 351 were serving in the forces whilst 48 were conscientious objectors or on national work.[75]

Nevertheless, the ILP as a national movement did decline as a result of the First World War, although in some regions, such as Clydeside, its support was maintained or even increased.[76] Yet its real threat was not the war but the emergence of the Labour Party as a socialist party. With a more or less universal organisation throughout Britain, and burgeoning trade union support, the Labour Party effectively left the ILP wondering about its future and its continuation as a separate political party. Although it did continue, it was never again going to be more than a fringe socialist conscience to the

Labour Party. Its power and influence was to be relatively less in the inter-war years than it had been before the war.

Comparatively little has been written on the inter-war ILP since the works of Dowse, Middlemass, Brockway and Marwick, all works produced more than a quarter of a century ago.[77] They outlined the ILP's growth in the early 1920s and its decline, from the mid 1920s, as Clifford Allen was replaced by Jimmy Maxton as the leading force within the ILP. In *Labour Heartland*, Jack Reynolds and Keith Laybourn have endorsed this impression, noting that the ILP declined in the late 1920s once it began to come into conflict with the Labour Party over the issues of the 'Socialism in Our Time' campaign, and particularly *The Living Wage*, and over the question of accepting the Labour Whip.[78] In Bradford, particularly, there were tensions between the Labour Party and the ILP organisations.

Such tensions were finally resolved by the decision of the ILP to disaffiliate from the Labour Party at Jowett Hall, Bradford on 30 July 1932. Dowse referred to this decision as being due to a clash of personalities and policies whilst Middlemass referred to it as 'suicide during a fit of insanity'.[79] Keith Laybourn, in a recent article, has suggested that whilst disaffiliation was irrational it was highly predictable, given the history of the ILP in the 1930s and the events which followed Ramsay MacDonald's desertion of the second Labour government in 1931: 'The fact is that the commitment to the development of socialist principles and actions led the ILP to follow a course which could only lead to its political obscurity.'[80] He concludes by maintaining that

> A small group of ILP leaders seem to have convinced themselves, in a period of intense conflict with the Labour Party, that they could offer a viable and enduring Socialist alternative to the Labour Party, when it was obvious, to even the least politically astute of political observers, that the Labour Party's support had waned due to the unusual circumstances of the 1931 general election. In the end, Willie Leach was correct and the 'total sterility' of the ILP was assured.[....] The irony was that having been formed in Bradford in 1893 it effectively committed suicide there in 1932.[81]

Conclusion

The study of the ILP has changed dramatically over the last twenty-five years. In the first place, there has been a substantial amount of local research to complement the national histories of the movement. Secondly, it is obvious that the ILP played a vital role in the early development of the Labour Party, even though the importance of its role diminished rapidly after 1914. Thirdly, it is clear that the history of the movement varies considerably from area to area, according to local cultural, religious, industrial and political factors and it should not be expected that every area would sport a viable ILP. Fourthly, it appears that ILP attracted much middle-class support and that there was a general ILP objective that it should attract support form all social classes, not just the working class, even if the semi-skilled and skilled working class predominated. Obviously, our knowledge of the history of the ILP is now wider and more sophisticated than it once was, and many myths about its attitudes and development have been dispelled. Yet there is still a dearth of information on many aspects of its activities – most notably on education, on religion, on women, on socialist Sunday schools and their relation to the ILP, and the history of some regions and localities. The role of individuals, such as the commercial traveller who moves from region to region, might also be rather more important than is often suggested. This centenary volume is designed to widen the scope of our knowledge of the history of the ILP. Hopefully, it will also act to stimulate further research into the local development of the ILP and the themes, policies and issues which it pursued for it is clear that the ILP was an important, if not a vital, component in the process by which the Labour Party challenged, and undermined, Liberal political hegemony in the years before the First World War.

NOTES

1. E. P. Thompson, 'Homage to Tom Maguire', in A. Briggs and J. Saville (eds.), *Essays in Labour History* (London, Macmillan, 1960), p.277.
2. H. Pelling, *The Origins of the Labour Party* (London, Macmillan, 1954); R. E. Dowse, *Left in the Centre* (London, 1966).
3. F. Brockway, *Socialism over Sixty Years: The Life of Jowett of Bradford* (London, George Allen & Unwin, 1946); C. Cross, *Philip Snowden* (London, Barrie & Rockcliffe, 1966).
4. For instance, D. Clark, *Colne Valley: radicalism to Socialism: The portrait of a Northern constituency in the formative years of the Labour Party 1890-1910* (London, Longman, 1981); D. Cox, 'The Labour Party in Leicester: a study in branch development', *International Review of Social History*, VI, 1961; K. Laybourn and D. James, *The Rising Sun of Socialism: The Independent Labour Party in the Textile District of the West Riding of Yorkshire between 1890 and 1914* (Wakefield, West Yorkshire Archive Service, 1991); K. Laybourn and J. Reynolds (eds.), *Liberalism and the Rise of Labour 1890–1918* (London, Croom Helm, 1984); B. Lancaster, *Radicalism, Co-operation and Socialism: Leicester working-class politics 1860–1906* (Leicester, Leicester University Press, 1987); M. Savage, 'The Rise of the Labour Party in Local Perspective', *The Journal of Regional and Local Studies*, 10, summer 1990. K. Laybourn, *Philip Snowden* (Aldershot, Temple Smith/Gower, 1988) also contains detailed work on the ILP in Keighley and Blackburn.
5. D. Howell, *British Workers and the Independent Labour Party 1888–1906* (Manchester, Manchester University Press, 1983); D. Tanner, *Political change and the Labour Party* (Cambridge, Cambridge University Press, 1990).
6. Lancaster, *op. cit.*, p.xviii.
7. C. Levy, 'Education and self-education: staffing the early ILP', in C. Levy, *Socialism and the Intelligentsia 1880–1914* (London, History Workshop Series,

Routledge & Kegan Paul, 1987).

8. J. A. Jowitt and K. Laybourn, 'War and Socialism: The Experience of the Bradford Independent Labour Party 1914–1918', *The Journal of Regional and Local Studies*, 4, no. 2, autumn 1984.

9. G. Dangerfield, *The Strange Death of Liberal England* (1935, London; MacGibbon & Kee edition, 1966).

10. I. Donnachie, C. Harvie, and I. S. Wood, *Forward! Labour Politics in Scotland 1888–1988* (Edinburgh, Polygon, 1989).

11. Pelling, *op. cit.*, p.131.

12. Most particularly, Dowse, *op. cit.*

13. Thompson, *op. cit.*

14. R. K. Middlemass, *The Clydesiders: a left wing struggle for Parliamentary Power* (London, Hutchinson, 1965).

15. J. Reynolds and K. Laybourn, 'The Emergence of the Independent Labour Party in Bradford', *International Review of Social History*, XX (1975).

16. S. Carter, 'The Independent Labour Party in Ashton-under-Lyne 1893–1900', *North West Labour History Society*, no. 4, 1977–8; Clark, *op. cit.*; J. Hill, 'The early ILP in Manchester and Salford', *International Review of Social History*, XXVI, 1981; D. Hopkin, 'The Membership of the Independent Labour Party, 1904–1910: a spatial and occupational analysis', *International Review of Social History*, XX, (1975); Laybourn and James, *The Rising Sun of Socialism*; Laybourn and Reynolds, *op. cit.*; D. Rubinstein, 'The Independent Labour Party and the Yorkshire Miners: The Barnsley By-Election of 1897', *International Review of Social History*, XXIII, 1978.

17. Thompson, *op. cit.*; Reynolds and Laybourn, 'Emergence'; Laybourn and Reynolds, *op. cit.*

18. J. Hill, 'Social Democracy and the Labour Movement: the Social Democratic Federation in Lancashire', *North West Labour History Society*, Bulletin 8, 1982–83.

19. P. A. Dawson, 'The Halifax Independent Labour Movement: Labour and Liberalism 1890–1914' and R. B. Perks, '"The Rising Sun of Socialism": Trade Unionism and the Emergence of the Independent Labour Party in Huddersfield', in Laybourn and James, *The Rising Sun of Socialism*.

20. Lancaster, *op. cit.*

21. C. Wrigley, 'Liberals and the Desire for Working-Class Representation in Battersea, 1886–1922', in K. D. Brown, *Essays in Anti-Labour History* (London, Macmillan, 1974).

22. *Ibid.*, p.126.

23. *Ibid.*, p.135.

24. M. Coneys, 'The Labour Movement and the Liberal Party in Rochdale, 1890–1906', unpublished MA dissertation, The Polytechnic, Huddersfield, 1982.

25. K. O. Morgan, 'The New Liberalism and the Challenge of Labour: The Welsh Experience, 1885–1929', in Brown (ed.) *Essays in Anti-Labour History*, pp.159–182.

26. T. Woodhouse, 'Trade Unions and Independent Labour Politics in Leeds, 1885–1914' unpublished paper produced in the mid 1970s; T. Woodhouse, 'The working class', in D. Fraser (ed.), *A History of Modern Leeds* (Manchester, Manchester University Press, 1980).

27. Rubinstein, *op. cit.*, p.132, quoting *Labour Leader*, 6 Nov 1897.

28. D. James, 'Local Politics and the Independent Labour Party in Keighley', in Laybourn and James, *Rising Sun of Socialism*, pp.111–112; D. James, 'The Keighley Independent Labour Party 1892–1900', in J. A. Jowitt and R. K. S. Taylor, *Bradford 1890–1914: The Cradle of the ILP* (Bradford Centre Occasional Papers, 2, 1980).

29. D. James, 'Local Politics', p.118.

30. Clark, *op. cit.*

31. *Ibid.*, p.88–89.

32. *Ibid.*, p.181

33. *Ibid.*, p.182

34. Lancaster, *op. cit.*, p.148.

35. T. Jowitt, 'Religion and the Independent Labour Party', in Laybourn and James, *The Rising Sun of Socialism*; L. Smith, 'Nonconformity and the Emergence of the Independent Labour Movement, c. 1880–1914, with particular reference to Lancashire and the West Riding of Yorkshire', unpublished PhD, CNAA, Huddersfield, 1989; S. Yeo, 'A New Life: The Religion of Socialism in Britain 1883–1896', *History Workshop Journal*, 4, autumn, 1977.

36. Laybourn and Reynolds, *op. cit.*, p.34; Clark, *op. cit.*, pp.148–9.

37. Laybourn and Reynolds, *op. cit.*, p.60; Reynolds and Laybourn, 'The emergence'; Dawson, *op. cit.*, p.51.

38. Wrigley, *op. cit.*

39. Hill, 'Social Democracy'.

40. M. Crick, 'Labour Alliance or Socialist Unity? The Independent Labour Party in the Heavy Woollen Areas of West Yorkshire c 1893–1902', in Laybourn and James, *The Rising Sun of Socialism*, pp.38–41.

41. P. A. Watmough, 'The Membership of the Social Democratic Federation, 1885–1902', *Society for the Study of Labour History*, Bulletin 34, Spring 1977, pp.35–40.

42. Hill, 'Social Democracy'.

43. M. Crick, 'Labour Alliance or Socialist Unity'; Laybourn and Reynolds, *op. cit.*, pp.125–7.

44. M. Crick,' "A Collection of Oddities" : The Bradford branch of the Social-Democratic Federation', *The Bradford Antiquary*, Third series, no. 5, 1991, pp.24–40.

45. Howell, *op. cit.*, particularly pp.277–82.

46. Tanner, *Political Change*, p.317.

47. *Ibid.*, pp.441–2.

48. The views put forward by R. McKibbin, *The Evolution of the Labour Party 1910–1924* (London, Oxford University Press, 1974); Laybourn and Reynolds, *op. cit.*, and many others.

49. P. F. Clarke, *Lancashire and the New Liberalism* (Cambridge, Cambridge University Press, 1971); R. Douglas, 'Labour in Decline, 1910–1914', in K. D. Brown (ed,), *Essays in Anti-Labour History* (London, Macmillan, 1974); T. Wilson, *The Downfall of the Liberal Party 1914–1935* (London, Collins, 1966).

50. Laybourn and Reynolds, *op. cit.*, p.149.

51. M. G. Sheppard and J. L. Halstead, 'Labour's Municipal Election Performance in Provincial England and Wales 1901–1913', *Society for the Study of Labour History*, Bulletin 45, autumn 1982, pp.19–25. D. Tanner has suggested that municipal results need to be examined more closely in order to detect political

change in 'Elections, Statistics, and the Rise of the Labour Party, 1906–1931', *Historical Journal*, 34, 4 (1991), pp.893–908.

52. Laybourn and Reynolds, *op. cit.*, p.149.
53. J. Benson, *The Working Class in Britain 1850–1914* (London, Longman, 1989).
54. Yeo, *op. cit.*
55. C. Wrigley, 'Labour and the Trade Unions', in K. D. Brown, *The First Labour Party 1906–1914* (London, Croom Helm, 1985), p.152.
56. *Ibid.*, p.129.
57. *Ibid.*, p.151.
58. Tanner, *op. cit.*
59. Levy, *op. cit.*
60. Reynolds and Laybourn, 'The emergence'.
61. Laybourn and Reynolds, *op. cit.*, pp.34–6, 60–1, 69–70, 89–94.
62. *Ibid.*, pp.34, 60, 181.
63. Levy, *op. cit.*, for a survey of various evidence.
64. Hopkin, *op. cit.*
65. Levy, *op. cit.*
66. Pelling, *op. cit.*, p.243.
67. *Labour Union Journal*, for 1891 and 1892; *Bradford Labour Echo*, 17 Nov 1897; *I.L.P. News*, May and June 1898.
68. Dawson, *op. cit.*, p.51; *Clarion*, 2 Nov 1894; I.L.P. News, May and June 1898.
69. Clark, *op. cit.*, pp.114–26; Laybourn and Reynolds, *op. cit.*, p.109.
70. K. Laybourn, '"The Defence of Bottom Dog": the Independent Labour Party in Local Politics', in D. G. Wright and J. A. Jowitt, *Victorian Bradford* (Bradford, City of Bradford Libraries Division, 1981), pp.223–244.
71. M. Cahill, 'Socialism and the City', in *Bradford 1890–1914: The Cradle of the Independent Labour Party* (Bradford, Bradford Centre Occasional Papers, 2, 1980), pp.45–55; M. Cahill, 'Labour in the Municipalities', in K. D. Brown (ed.), *The First Labour Party 1906–1914* (London, Croom Helm, 1985), p.101.
72. Jowitt and Laybourn, 'War and Socialism'.
73. *Bradford Pioneer*, 21 May 1915.
74. *Ibid.*, 25 Feb 1916.
75. *Ibid.*, 1 Mar 1918.
76. Middlemass, *op. cit.*; J. Foster, 'Strike Action and Working-Class Politics on Clydeside 1914–1919', *International Review of Social History*, xxxv, 1990; J. Melling, 'Whatever happened to Red Clydeside? Industrial Conflict and the Politics of Skill in the First World War', *International Review of Social History*, xxxv, 1990; A. McKinley and R. J. Morris (eds.), *The ILP on Clydeside 1893–1932* (Manchester, Manchester University Press, 1991).
77. Brockway, *op. cit.*, Dowse, *op. cit.*; A. Marwick,, *Clifford Allen: The Open Conspirator* (London, Oliver & Boyd, 1964); Middlemass, *op. cit.*
78. J. Reynolds and K. Laybourn, *Labour Heartland* (Bradford, Bradford University Press, 1987), pp.71–4.
79. Middlemass, *op. cit.*, chapter 12.
80. K. Laybourn, '"Suicide during a Fit of Insanity" or the Defence of Socialism?: The secession of the Independent Labour Party from the Labour Party at the special conference at Bradford, July 1932', *The Bradford Antiquary*, Third series, no. 5, 1991, p.41.
81. *Ibid.*, p.52.

2. Researching the History of the ILP [1]

David James

Philip Snowden wrote in his *Autobiography*

> A National Conference of Labour and Socialist Organisations was held at Bradford in January of 1893, at which the Independent Labour Party was formed. This was the most important political event of the nineteenth century.[2]

Snowden was not an unprejudiced commentator, but the ILP is important in shaping the structure of labour politics in the years since 1893. ILP members were instrumental in founding the Labour Representation Committee in 1900 and the Labour Party in 1906. Many of the Labour Party's leaders, such as Keir Hardie, Philip Snowden and Ramsay MacDonald, were ILPers and numerous trade union officials served their political apprenticeship in the party. The ILP provided training for Labour backbench MPs, for local councillors, and for political activists at all levels. For the historian researching the political left the history of the ILP is important.

There are, by now, numerous studies, both national and local, of the ILP and many of them have bibliographies and notes on sources. Still valuable is Henry Pelling's *Origins of the Labour Party*,[3] while David Howell's more recent *British Workers and the Independent Labour Party 1888–1906*[4] contains a list of primary and secondary material which gives a good indication of what is useful to the student of the early years of the movement. R. E. Dowse's *Left in the Centre*,[5] although published in 1966 contains a bibliographical essay which outlines the material, both printed and archival, available to the researcher for the years after 1918. More recent works include Keith Laybourn's *The Rise of Labour: the British Labour Party 1890–1979* and *The Labour Party 1881–1951: a Reader in History*,[6] both of which in their footnotes and bibliographies mention relevant collections of documents as well as secondary sources. Works concentrating on localities include Keith Laybourn and Jack Reynolds *Liberalism and the Rise of Labour* and *Labour Heartland*[7] which trace the rise of Labour, including the ILP, in West Yorkshire. Each of these volumes has an extensive bibliography. The same region is the subject of the studies in '*The Rising Sun of Socialism':The Independent Labour Party in the Textile District of the West Riding of Yorkshire between 1890 and 1914*,[8] which contains abundant footnotes pointing out sources. Bill Lancaster has written about Leicester, one of the midland strongholds of the ILP.[9] Another recent work has researched the ILP on Clydeside, which after 1918 became the party's main centre of support.[10] Still other studies have examined the role of individuals who spent either part or all their careers within the ILP. Thus there are biographies of such leading ILPers as Bruce Glasier, Keir Hardie, Ramsay MacDonald and

Philip Snowden.[11] Later ILP leaders such as James Maxton have their own studies[12] and Keith Middlemas has examined the Scottish ILP group in *The Clydesiders*.[13] Lesser, but still important, ILPers, or activists connected with the ILP for some period of time have also had been the subject of books and articles. Victor Grayson, Fred Jowett, John Maclean, Margaret McMillan and Tom Mann are only a few examples of such people.[14] Others prominent in the labour movement such as Robert Blatchford, H. M. Hyndman, the Fabians, William Morris[15] and many trade unionists may have been involved with the ILP to a greater or lesser extent, and their biographies tell us of the importance or unimportance of the party in the wider political context. The *Dictionary of Labour Biography*[16] is an on-going publication which contains short biographies of those connected with the labour movement in its widest form, and as such includes numerous accounts of the lives of ILPers of all levels of distinction.

In addition to printed works many undergraduate and postgraduate studies exist, and these are often of value to the researcher. Frequently they have not been published, or only in part. For example, in West Yorkshire recent studies have examined the ILP, as part of a larger study or as a special topic, in Dewsbury, Halifax, Keighley, and Huddersfield.[17] Before embarking on any research, therefore, it is advisable to check what has already been produced. Many academic journals review the latest works of labour history and some, such as *History Workshop*, specialise in the history of the labour movement, printing reviews of recent publications and occasionally articles on archives and other sources. The *Bulletin of the Society for the Study of Labour History* produces an annual bibliography of labour publications and completed research projects and should be consulted to see what has been written on a particular area or on a particular person or aspect.

The *Bulletin of the Society of Labour History* also publishes an annual list of deposits of archives of interest to labour historians which have been made in record offices and libraries. Recent additions of ILP material can be readily identified by studying this list. In Scotland the student is fortunate indeed in having available *A Catalogue of some Labour Records in Scotland and some Scots Records outside Scotland*, compiled and edited by Ian MacDougal, and published by the Scottish Labour History Society, which in 598 closely printed pages lists many of the labour records kept in that country, including those for the ILP.[18] England and Wales have, as yet, nothing comparable with this but in addition to the lists in the *Bulletin of the Society for the Study of Labour History* and articles on sources in publications such as *History Workshop* the researcher should contact the National Register of Archives,[19] held by the Royal Commission on Historical Manuscripts, who will be able to give advice on where relevant material has been deposited in archive departments and record offices.

In studying the ILP it is necessary to understand the importance of the local branches in its history, for the ILP is different from the older parties in that decisions made at branch level could be as, or even more, important than what was done or said in the National Administrative Council. David Clark, in his case study of the Colne Valley Labour Union, which later became the Colne Valley ILP, emphasised this when he wrote that,

> In their efforts to understand the origins, emergence and development of Labour representation in Great Britain, historians have principally concentrated upon the trade union movement and national political activities. This is a valuable but rather limited perspective especially in relation to the Independent Labour Party (ILP) and to a lesser extent the Labour Representation Committee (LRC). The broad canvas is there but the details are lacking and without them full appreciation is impossible.[20]

'The strength of the ILP' he continues 'depended upon enthusiasm at branch level and the ability to adapt its agitation to the local situation'.[21] E. P. Thompson made the same point when he wrote that the 'ILP grew from the bottom up: its birthplaces were in those shadowy places known as "the provinces"'.[22]

Thus throughout its history the ILP remained a party whose branches and their activities were as important as its central administration. This remains true wherever its heartland lay, whether in the West Riding or urban Scotland. This essay, therefore, will concentrate on the sources likely to be of use to the researcher examining the impact of the party in a particular locality.

Nevertheless, the records of the central administrative body of the ILP – the National Administrative Council (NAC) – are of essential importance and have survived in considerable detail. The NAC was formed at the 1893 Bradford Conference – which was essentially the product of local initiatives – and local autonomy was seen by the new party as crucial. Any executive was to be given only limited powers, and it is significant that Conference gave its central body the title the National Administrative Council rather than the National Executive Council. The duties of the Council were strictly demarcated. They were: to carry out the resolutions of the annual conference; to raise money for propaganda work such as holding public meetings or distributing literature; to raise an election fund to aid districts which were running Parliamentary candidates; to take any necessary action in constituencies where there was no Independent Labour grouping when an election was pending. However, it was not to 'interfere with the rules, constitution, or internal affairs of any local organisation.' Nevertheless, the Council soon found it necessary to create an organisation if it was to function effectively. Soon, it was arranging the distribution of circulars to the branches informing them of the NAC's activities and decisions; forming various sub-committees, and establishing a central office. A publications department produced the monthly *ILP News*, and later the party acquired Keir Hardie's newspaper the *Labour Leader*. After the 1900 election, a Propaganda Fund was instituted, which funnelled finance into seats where there was a chance of winning, and paid for lecture tours and made grants to districts for the maintenance of organisers. These lecture tours and organisers promoted the NAC's views in any debates and disputes which took place, and slowly the

NAC became the governing body of the ILP, taking command of the annual conference and shaping policy.[23] Nevertheless, there was a constant tension between the NAC and the branches, which could show itself in resentment of the Council. Thus in 1905 the Keighley ILP wrote protesting against the NAC's nomination of delegates to go to the Labour Representation Committee Conference, being of the opinion that 'such delegates should be elected at the Annual Conference of the Party'.[24] The following year they objected to the continued dominance of the big four – Glasier, Hardie, Snowden and MacDonald – in the NAC, putting forward the motion for the annual conference 'that any member of the NAC after five (5) consecutive years service on such Council shall not be eligible for re-election until twelve (12) months have expired from the end of his five years' service'.[25] This conflict between the branches and the centre continued throughout the ILP's history. In the 1920s the internal reforms instituted by Clifford Allen to enable the NAC to guide and control the party after its post-war growth, met with considerable resistance. This can be explained in part by the antipathy of the older ILPers towards the new men who had joined the party during and after the war, and who were often middle-class, sometimes pacifists, sometimes intellectuals, and were often based in London. Yet, it was also a clash between the provincial centres of the party and its central administration. R. E. Dowse has shown how this struggle led to great divisions within the party and weakened its political strength.[26]

The records of the NAC are held in the Francis Johnson collection deposited in the British Library of Political and Economic Science.[27] The collection contains minutes of the NAC from 1893 until 1950, although they are not entirely complete. It also contains sets of minutes of other committees, financial records and circulars also for the period 1894–1950, although again some are missing. The correspondence of the General Secretary of the ILP, largely that of Francis Johnson, who became Secretary in 1903, has also survived and covers the same period. In addition there are reports, material from branches and ephemera, and a large number of pamphlets published by the ILP between 1893 and 1975. These collections have been microfilmed and were originally published by Harvester Press Ltd., now Research Publications Inc. They are available in a number of public and university libraries, or through the inter-Library loan system.[28] They give information not just on what was being discussed and decided by the NAC, but also on much of what was going on throughout the country, as the branches were continually corresponding with the NAC. Thus between 1904 and 1907 the Keighley ILP wrote twenty seven time to Francis Johnson, largely on routine matters, but occasionally on items of policy or protesting against the decisions of the NAC.[29]

The activities of ILP branches have to be researched in a number of sources. Relatively few branch records have survived and fewer still are anything like complete. A recent survey of over one hundred record offices and archive departments revealed that the minutes of slightly more than fifty branches had been deposited (see Appendix 1).[30] This is a disappointing number when it is remembered that at its peak in the years between 1922 and 1926 the ILP had over 1,000 branches. Many of the minutes, moreover, survive for comparatively short periods. Thus the Barrow in Furness branch minutes only cover two years, 1921–1922, those for Gloucester the period 1906–1908, for Macclesfield 1894–1897, for Nottingham 1927–1931, and Ystrad Mynach from 1925–1927. Of course, it is possible that some of these branches only existed for short periods, but in other cases the minutes have been lost or split up or not deposited. Even when minutes have survived for longer periods it is unusual for them to extend to twenty years. Thus, for example, the Birmingham branch minutes survive for 1904 to 1914; those for Colne Valley from 1892 to 1910; for East Ham from 1908 to 1921; for Gillingham from 1920 to 1931; for Meltham from 1893 to 1910; and for Wrexham from 1912 to 1921. Branches such as Keighley whose minutes continue for most of the ILP's existence as an important political movement are rare. Keighley has minute books, with gaps, for the period 1892 to 1951.[31]

Surviving minute books are, therefore, relatively rare, and minutes for periods longer than a few years scarcer still. In addition, the branches whose minutes have survived were not necessarily the most important centres of ILP activity. Thus, although Keighley was an active ILP area in the 1890s it was never as important as its near neighbour Bradford, yet only two minute books survive for all the branches in that city. Similarly one minute book remains for Halifax, the party's largest single branch during the 1890s; and many of the party's other strongholds have few extant records. Thus Leicester, where Ramsay MacDonald was MP, has no party records at all, and in Nottingham, active in the 1890s but languishing by the turn of the century, there are only minutes for 1927 to 1931.

The historical value of those minutes that have survived varies. Some are fairly full whilst others make merely the briefest mention of decisions arrived at. Their quality depends very much on the branch secretary and the care with which they are written up. Often their historical value differs with each change of secretary. In Keighley, for example, the early minutes are very informative, giving details of who were at the meetings, how often the officers attended and how the votes went, summarising the debates and discussions, and providing a useful picture of how a branch functioned. Thus a meeting of 1 June 1897 includes information on arrangements for distributing propaganda leaflets; the transfer of funds to the Club; the election of new members; the posting of bills; agreements with Bradford for a joint meeting of the Clarion Cycling Club; the advertising of visiting lecturers' talks; and the proposed reorganisation of branches throughout the district.[32] By contrast later minutes, after about 1905, are much less informative giving the barest details of decisions arrived at, and motions passed. Thus at the meeting on 6 May 1907 the resolutions read merely,

That correspondence be passed
That E.C. recommendation be passed

341

That LRC report as given by the Secretary be accepted

That the best thanks of the meeting be given to Mr W Pickles for his exhaustive report on the recent ILP Conference[33]

This does not mean that the later years in Keighley were less interesting than the 1890s. It was, in fact, a time of considerable interest both to contemporaries and historians, with the branch struggling to maintain its political credibility in the face of a series of local election defeats yet buoyed up by its creditable performance in the 1906 election, but with the branch also on the verge of a disintegration due to a divergence of views between the older largely ethical socialists and those more influenced by trade unionism. This tension may, of course, account for the pithiness of the minutes. However, their brevity makes the debate within the branch difficult to follow, or even to identify, which again may be deliberate. Overall, therefore, minutes are often of varying quality.

Surviving minutes do not always just refer to the main committees of the branch. Thus the Attercliffe ILP records include the minutes of the Building Committee; the Birmingham ILP's Finance Committee minutes survive for a short period; minutes of several of the Glasgow ILP Federation committees remain, although again for a relatively brief duration, and different branches have minutes for Lecture Committees, Clarion Clubs, Guilds of Youth and Women's Sections.[34] All these can be helpful in deducing how a branch functioned.

At least minutes exist for some branches. Other records, such as accounts, letters or membership lists are even more inadequate, and those that have survived are often only for short periods. This is unfortunate as material of this kind can be revealing for researchers. The nine hundred or so letters that have survived for the Keighley branch illuminate the many problems encountered by the ILPers. Some were self inflicted – the branch was well known for its internal bickering; some political – the difficulties of finding candidates to stand for office are exposed; some administrative – the problems of finding adequate speakers are clear; some financial – the branch never had enough money. Among the letters are, of course, many of a routine nature, but even these indicate how much work was entailed in managing a branch. Similarly account books reveal just how difficult finances were in most branches. Lastly membership rolls allow the historian to discover what kind of people joined the ILP. By comparing the names with other sources such as Directories, and particularly with the 1891 census returns it should be possible to locate members occupations, family sizes, and addresses and to identify their place within their communities. Once the name and occupation of members is known, newspaper reports, Year Books and similar sources make it possible, with patience, to build up a profile of a branch and its members.

Branch records, however, will never give a complete history. Additional primary sources will always need to be consulted. The most important of these are newspapers.

Researchers should initially check whether an ILP branch produced its own newspaper and whether it has survived either locally or at the British Museum Newspaper Library at Colindale.[35] The newspapers produced by the branches varied considerably in size, number of pages, frequency of publication and length of time they survived. Many had ephemeral lives for the cost of printing and publishing was substantial, and could impose a crippling burden on the finances of a branch. The Keighley ILP, with a well defined membership and significant popular support finally had to give up its struggle to keep publishing its newspaper. First printed in 1894 it was originally called the *ILP Journal*, then *'the Organ of the Keighley Labour Union'*, and finally the *Keighley Labour Journal*, and was for much of its life a weekly.[36] It eventually became a monthly and ceased printing in 1902. It was revived at election times and other occasions as an irregular publication. In 1905 it began regular publication again, but collapsed after six months. The branch was quite unable to find the small but necessary sum of 10s.6d (52.5p) a week required by the printers to produce the paper.[37]

Before it closed, however, the *Keighley Labour Journal* demonstrated how valuable such a paper was in spreading the message of socialism throughout its distribution area, and also how useful such a source is to the researcher. It was started as a free news sheet, only four pages in size, and eventually reached a claimed circulation of 5,000. Its first editor was G. J. Wardle, who later became an MP, and he was succeeded by Philip Snowden, who expanded the paper in both size, circulation and local importance. It provided comprehensive accounts of the ILP's activities in the town, and commented on local politics. It helped direct local political campaigns, telling sympathisers who the ILP candidates were, and when and how to vote for them. It advertised which speakers visited the area, outlined the main points in their speeches, and described how they were received by their audiences. It gave accounts of the various social and cultural activities of the branch, the Clarion Vocal Union meetings, the Clarion Cycling Club outings, the Free and Easy's, the Ham teas, the walks, the recruiting expeditions, the Socialist Sunday School and Labour Church meetings. After Snowden became editor he felt able to charge 0.5p a copy, and used the paper not just as a propaganda sheet for the ILP, but also as a muck raking journal exposing what he saw as the corruption of local public affairs. Thus 'one week he was attacking the decision to raise from £300 to £400 the salary of the Borough Surveyor while at the same time the wages of the night soil men were being reduced. Then he turned to the expenses charged by Council officials for trips outside Keighley.'[38] By exposing these and similar activities the *Keighley Labour Journal* became an important source of information not just for committed socialists, but for every politically aware person living in Keighley.

The Leicester *Pioneer* was another labour newspaper which gave its audience a lively read. It too had a claimed circulation of 5,000 and provided a sports page, reviews of performances at local music halls and theatres, book reviews and serialisations of novels. There was also a page devoted to national politics as well as extensive coverage of the local political scene, and it served as a notice board for all the organisations involved in the Labour movement. It helped to build up a sense of unity and community in the local labour movement. At the same time papers like the *Pioneer* aimed to provide a complete newspaper, not just a propaganda sheet, and were intended to attract all the people who were sympathetic to the socialist cause regardless of whether they were politically active, or indeed whether they were members of the ILP or some other group.[39]

A number of socialist newspapers were remarkably successful. In West Yorkshire, for example, by the end of the First World War there were three established labour newspapers which gave space to the ILP viewpoint. These were the *Bradford Pioneer*, the Leeds *Weekly Citizen*, and the Huddersfield *Worker*. The *Worker* expired in 1920 but the *Huddersfield Citizen* replaced it in 1926 and survived until the 1960s.[40]

In its day the most prestigious of these newspapers was the *Bradford Pioneer*. Amongst its editors was Joseph Burgess, the journalist whose call led to the formation of the national ILP at Bradford in 1893, and Willie Leach, Fred Jowett, the first Labour MP for Bradford, and Frank Betts, the father of Barbara Castle, were among its regular contributors. Victor Grayson Feather, later General Secretary of the TUC, was one of its correspondents and its cartoonist, until he left Bradford in 1926. Others who wrote for it included Margaret McMillan, Ramsay MacDonald and Philip Snowden.

Other local ILP papers were equally important, and just as valuable to the historian. Deian Hopkin has shown just how widespread the ILP newspapers were, and they seem to have survived rather better than branch records.[41] In Bradford, for example, in addition to the *Bradford Pioneer*, there was, at various times, the *Bradford Labour Echo*, the *Labour Union Journal*, *Bottom Dog*,[42] and other shorter lived productions. Ian MacDougall lists those Scottish papers which are available.[43] In many cases they are not complete runs, but it is remarkable what is available, albeit spread through different collections and deposits. Of course, not all labour newspapers were published by the ILP, but most of them have information on the activities of the party together with leaders and comments where appropriate.

In addition to local publications more general labour newspapers, either regional or national, often contain details of the activities of the ILP. In Yorkshire the most important paper for the early years of the party is the *Yorkshire Factory Times*, which was started in 1889, and which acted as the organ of the Yorkshire textile workers until it ceased publication in 1926. Although seen by its proprietor as a trade union paper, it included reports on the establishment and progress of local ILP branches throughout the region. Joseph Burgess who was its editor moved on to London to edit the *Workman's Times* and it was here that he printed an article about the need for an Independent Labour Party in April 1892. From then until January 1893 Burgess claimed to have written 5,000 words a week on the need for a national ILP. Throughout this period the *Workman's Times* carried details of the work of local groups, sometimes reproducing the programmes of these nascent ILP branches. Although some of these groups proved durable, others were to have only a brief existence, and a report in the *Workman's Times* may be the only evidence of their existence. The *Workman's Times* folded in 1894, its end hastened by the success of the *Clarion*.

The *Clarion* was the most successful of the Labour papers. It aimed to be a complete paper, advertising itself as 'an illustrated weekly journal of Literature, Politics, Fiction, Philosophy, Theatricals, pastimes, Criticism and everything else'. It combined entertainment with socialism, for the background of Robert Blatchford, the owner and editor, was as a journalist and he and his collaborators knew that he had to keep his readers interested, if the paper was to be successful.[44] Blatchford started the paper in December 1891 and printed it in Manchester until 1895, when it moved to London. Although it was often sympathetic to the ILP, Blatchford could be strongly critical of the party and frequently pursued his own line of argument. He divided many branches over the Manchester Fourth Clause, and his strong support of the British during the Boer War alienated him from many ILPers. All these debates are covered in detail in the paper which provides much material on the various policies available to socialists in the years of its greatest popularity. For example, Blatchford argued strongly for a united socialist party embracing the ILP, the Social Democratic Federation and other interested groups. This policy was disliked by the ILP leadership, though many branches found it attractive at different times. It is thus essential reading for students interested in the alternatives open to the labour movement in the years when there was potential for a number of different policy choices.

The paper also included a great deal of information about ILP branches and their relations with other socialists, both in its reports and its letter columns. It also has detailed accounts of the *Clarion* groups such as the Clarion Vocal Unions, Clarion Scouts, Clarion Fellowship and Clarion Cycling Clubs. As the name suggests these organizations originated with the *Clarion* and their activities were encouraged by the paper. They were frequently incorporated into the activities of ILP branches and would constitute much of its social life, as well as aiding in political propaganda. Thus the Keighley ILP had a well known Clarion Vocal Union which made political meetings more of an event and who often preceded or followed well known speakers. In 1897, for example, they toured the locality with Keir Hardie rendering 'valuable assistance at all meetings'.[45] Later Keighley formed a Clarion Scouts, a Clarion Fellowship and a Clarion Cycling Club. The justification for forming these organisations was the idea of brotherhood and living the life of a socialist. Socialism was a moral commitment as well as a political one, as the *Keighley Labour Journal* said about the Clarion cyclists:

> Apart, however, from the social advantages to be acquired by membership, there is work to be done which only cyclists can do, and the way to do it effectively is by some organised, systematic method, this method can most

easily be developed by a well disciplined Clarion Cycling Club, composed of men who are willing to do something, however humble, to spread the truths of socialism.[46]

The *Clarion* is thus a major source of information on the non-political side of ILP life.

In contrast to the cheerful, bohemian tone of the *Clarion*, the *Labour Leader* was more serious. The *Leader* was founded and edited by Keir Hardie. It had started life in 1887 as the *Miner*; in 1889 it had changed to the *Labour Leader*; in 1890 it was absorbed into the *Labour Elector*, which disappeared in the same year. In 1894 Hardie revived the *Leader*, and in 1904 it was acquired by the ILP as its official newspaper. Even before then it was regarded as the mouthpiece of the Party, and it competed directly with the *Clarion* for readers. There was a real antagonism between the two papers and between Blatchford and Hardie. Blatchford wanted to make socialists, Hardie to create a viable political party. For Blatchford the ILP was

the party of humanity. Our religion is the religion of humanity. 'The black with his woolly head, the felon, the deceased, the illiterate are not denied'. The thief on the Cross, the Magdalen at the well, are our brother and sister; bone of our bone, flesh of our flesh.[47]

Hardie thought Blatchford and the *Clarion* were destroying 'the fibre of the Socialist movement ... by a spirit of irresponsible levity',[48] and he regarded the whisky-drinking habits of the *Clarion* staff as downright sinful. Blatchford, for his part, declared of Hardie, 'I have tried hard to believe in that man but I cannot stand him'.[49] Like the *Clarion*, however, the *Leader* contains a great deal of information about the activities of the ILP. Its opinions are the official views of the ILP and, as such, it is a key source for the historian. It also contains extensive reports of branch activities. Herbert Horner, for example, regularly sent reports on the performance of the Keighley branch, and he was only one of many who did this.

The *Labour Leader* was replaced in 1923 by the *New Leader* which under its editor H. N. Brailsford became 'one of the most brilliant journalistic ventures in the history of British labour',[50] with circulation rising from 38,000 copies in November 1923 to 60,000 by April 1924. Brailsford resigned in 1926, and was succeeded by Frederick Pickles who had been Keir Hardie's secretary. His papers are in the National Museum of Labour History.[51] However, without Brailsford's inspired editorship the paper never recovered its intellectual supremacy. Nevertheless, it remains authoritative on the policy of the party and the debates which took place within it.

Other newspapers and journals contain information about ILP activities. The *ILP News*, the monthly publication started by the National Administrative Council in 1897 as a newsletter, aimed to keep the branches in touch with the leadership. It contains useful reports on what is happening to the party both at the centre and in the regions. For a short time it printed branch membership returns, so that some conclusions can be drawn on the size of ILP groups and the geographical spread of the party. *Justice*, the newspaper of the Social Democratic Federation, is valuable when examining the differences between the ILP and other parts of the socialist movement and their attempts to work together particularly at branch level; the *Labour Prophet* was the paper of the Labour Church whose history is inextricably entwined with that of the ILP. These productions can be supplemented by a whole flotilla of occasional broadsheets, trade-union quarterlies and Labour journals which illustrate the activities of the Labour movement generally, but also throw light on the ILP.

In addition to those works which had a national sale, researchers interested in particular branches need to examine the reports on ILP activity in local newspapers. These usually give extensive accounts of branch meetings, political programmes, election and other campaigns, visiting speakers, and recruitment drives. They often have obituaries of local labour leaders, and details of their careers when, for example, they leave the neighbourhood to pursue their activities elsewhere. Local papers reflect the different responses that were prevalent towards the ILP, but the bias of the paper is usually clear and can be taken into account when using their reports. In a few cases papers are sympathetic to the socialist cause, in others implacably opposed, and in others their views varied as their proprietors or editors felt appropriate; but whatever else they do they do not ignore the new movement. A Liberal paper will often give a cautious sympathy towards the socialists in the early 1890s, when the reluctance of local parties to give ordinary people the chance to stand in local elections was often thought short sighted. The *Keighley News*, for example, welcomed the election of ILP representatives on to the School Board in 1893 on the grounds that it would make them fit for office when they returned to the Liberals, as they surely must when the ILP inevitably collapsed,

> the responsibility of office is in itself a valuable training .. the heedless and illguarded utterances of the platform and the public hall find their best corrective in the toilsome and patient details of the Board and Committee Room, where the problems of actual administration have to be faced from week to week and month to month.[52]

As the ILP became an permanent part of the political scene, in parts of the country at least, the tone of local papers changed. In Liberal areas, such as West Yorkshire, the ILP came to be seen as weakening the Liberal vote and thus helping the Conservatives. By 1895 the *Keighley News* was writing bitterly about the municipal elections, 'in claiming the chief honour for the representatives of piety and the pothouse [the Conservatives] we are not unmindful of the debt of gratitude which they owe to their allies of the Labour party.' For 'nothing that Liberals do is or can be right with men who hate their old comrades with that malignant bitterness which men who change their colours always show.'[53]

Despite their bias, for most places local newspapers are the single most important source for the history of branches of the ILP. They report what they did and said, reveal the attitudes of the established political parties towards them, and show the development of the slow realisation that a Labour Party had become a permanent part of the political scene. Of course, newspapers also bring home the inescapable truth that the local Liberals and Conservatives were for many years far more important than the ILP; and that for most of the people politics were in any case only a part of their lives. In all newspapers sport gets far more coverage than the activities of the local political parties, and for the vast majority of readers this accurately reflected their priorities.

Other publications are also significant. The ILP, both from its headquarters and in its branches produced a continuous stream of leaflets, pamphlets and broadsheets, which in all are numbered in thousands. They range from Reports of the Annual Conference of the Party and major policy documents such as *The Living Wage*, to local election ephemera. There is no one place where all this material is gathered together, although the Harvester Press has produced microfilm copies of those kept in the ILP collection at the British Library of Political and Economic Science, and these are available in a number of local and academic libraries. The local history departments of the larger public Libraries and local Record Offices may also have selections of such pamphlets, usually those published locally. Others may appear in the papers or libraries of labour activists; for example, Keighley Reference Library houses the library of Philip Snowden, which contains several hundred socialist and ILP pamphlets. All these works, whether they are a tightly argued case for some point of ILP policy or a single election sheet are of value when examining the history of the party.

Further information on the work of the Party can be found in personal papers. Of the ILP big four Hardie and Snowden left few papers – indeed Snowden left instructions for his wife to destroy his papers. Bruce Glasier and Ramsay MacDonald, however, left large collections of personal papers[54] which have been extensively used by their biographers. Other major figures have also left archives; the Maxton family papers at Strathclyde Regional Archives, for example, include James Maxton's correspondence, speeches, diaries and other writings, as well as parliamentary and political papers and press cuttings.[55] The magisterial *Catalogue of Some Labour Records in Scotland* lists over four columns of Maxton entries and contains numerous other references to him among other collections.[56] However, the existence of such papers is very much a matter of chance. Fred Jowett of Bradford destroyed his papers after being advised by Snowden that he could not see the point in keeping them. Edward Hartley of the same town, an ILPer of local and some national importance, on the other hand, kept his diaries and various other records which have survived to be deposited in the local archives.[57] It is the same throughout the country, and although the chances of finding the records of a particular activist are not particularly good, it is always worth contacting the local library or record office to ascertain what is available. Papers of ILPers are still being deposited in archive departments and record offices; recently the National Museum of Labour History acquired the papers of Bob Edwards, who led the ILP contingent in the Spanish Civil War and later became President of the Party. Other such papers may still be in private hands, and in this case locating them may well be through word of mouth or other informal means.

The papers of individuals who were not party members, or were only members for a short time or only nominally members, can also be useful. The diaries of Beatrice Webb,[58] for example, contain some incisive comments on the ILP and ILPers. After the 1895 election, which was disappointing for the ILP, for example, she remarked, 'the ILP has completed its suicide. Its policy of abstention and deliberate wrecking has proved to be futile and absurd.'[59] The papers of figures as diverse as John Burns, Edward Carpenter, and Lloyd George[60] as well as many others can provide insights into how the ILP was regarded across the political spectrum.

Some ILPers wrote their biographies or reminiscences and these can be valuable, although they should be treated with care. Often one of the objects of writing the work is to justify the actions of the author. Philip Snowden's *Autobiography*,[61] for example is described as 'shallow on his personal life and pawky and partial on more political matters'.[62] J. H. Thomas's *My Story*[63] is described by one historian as being 'distinguished by some remarkable lapses of memory'.[64] Other works were written by less important figures who felt less need to vindicate their actions. For example, John Gilray produced a short typescript of 'Early Days of the Socialist Movement in Edinburgh', John Lister wrote the 'Early History of the ILP Movement in Halifax', and S. Bryher 'An Account of the Labour and Socialist Movement in Bristol'.[65] There are undoubtedly other works of this kind, sometimes buried in newspaper articles or reminiscences. Such books are an important source for researchers, as are biographies such as Fenner Brockway's study of Fred Jowett, *Sixty years of Socialism*, or his *Bermondsey Story, the Life of Alfred Salter* or G. McAllister's *James Maxton, Portrait of a Rebel*.[66] These and similar works may not be objective studies, but they do allow historians to understand why their subjects were so admired and in some cases loved.

One last category of records should be noted. These are the documents of other organisations who may have had relations with the ILP, whether friendly or antagonistic, or whose members may also have been ILPers. Many ILPers belonged to a whole series of different associations, whether within the labour movement or without. Thus an ILP activist might also be a trade unionist, a member of the Labour Church or Socialist Sunday School, active in his local Fabian Society or the various Clarion groups, sit on the local Council, School Board or Board of Guardians, be a church or chapel goer, or involved in charitable or other voluntary organisations. He would also probably have a job. A recent biography of Alfred Orage the Leeds socialist, teacher, and artist shows how many-sided the lives of some socialists could be, and Jill Liddington illustrates the same point in her life of the Lancashire radical Selina Cooper.[67] All these groups may have left records which may throw light on the local ILPer or his branch. In particular the archives of trade unions or Trade Councils should be consulted, for many early socialists were prominent in the movement to organise labour. At the same time records of other political parties may also repay examination.

There was, of course, always a close relationship between the ILP and the Labour Party. Often the records of the two parties have survived in the same place and in some cases they complement each other or are even intermingled. Thus as the minutes of the Colne Valley Socialist League (one of the several names that the ILP called itself in that locality) finish, those of the Colne Valley Divisional Labour Party begin.[68]

Before 1918 it was often the case that the ILP was the major constituency organisation of the local Labour Party and its main source of policy. Its heroes, MacDonald, Snowden, Glasier and many others, led the Labour Party in and out of Parliament, and their hegemony was virtually unchallenged. Far more than the Fabian Society the ILP was the 'brains' of the Labour party and as a constituency organisation it held pride of place. It was the biggest socialist body affiliated to the Labour Party, so that throughout the greatest part of the Midlands and North, membership of the ILP was synonymous with membership of the Labour Party, and it was the major propagandist wing of that Party.

After 1918 when the Labour Party acquired a socialist programme and an embryonic constituency organisation, serious questions were raised about the future role of the ILP. Nevertheless, many labour activists belonged to both parties, and *The Observer* noted that 'in every place where there is an ILP, its members dominate the local Labour Party. It is the ILP spirit, the ILP enthusiasm, and the ILP conception of social philosophy and economics which animate and dominate the bigger Labour Party.'[69]

Often the most active ILPers became absorbed by the constituency Labour parties and concentrated their work in them,'[70] and in many constituencies Labour Parties or Divisional Labour Parties connected different organisations including the ILP. For example, in 1918 Labour Constituency parties were formed for all four of the Bradford seats uniting the ILP, the Trades Council, and the Workers' Municipal Federation into one Labour organisation. The Huddersfield Labour movement was transformed into the Huddersfield Divisional Labour Party in the spring and summer of 1918, following meetings between the ILP, the Trades Council and other interested groups. Thus in places where the ILP was a political force, Labour Party records, which have generally survived better than those of ILP branches, will almost certainly have information about the ILP and their activities. It is likely that they will contain details of the struggles that ensued between the ILP and the Labour Party in the 1920s and 1930s when the ILP sought to define a role for itself. The national Labour Party, too, has considerable information on the ILP, including the activities of many of its branches. The papers of the Labour

Representation Committee and the Labour Party can be consulted in the National Museum of Labour History in Manchester.

The archives of other political parties can also be revealing. Many ILPers often received their apprenticeship in local Liberal branches and the records of these groups, particularly for the early 1890s, may reveal the political background of early ILPers. In a later period some ILPers were tempted to join the Social Democratic Party, the Communist Party, or even the fascists, and an examination of these sources, where they exist, can be valuable to the researcher.

It is not just documents which are of importance to the researcher. In recent years the discipline of oral history has become increasingly used by historians. The practice of interviewing people about their lives is now commonplace and there are already large collections of oral testimony available to students. Personal recollections, where they are available, can be valuable to the historian of the ILP, for a number of reasons. There is the paucity of branch records which oral testimony can sometimes fill. It can provide the personal view of important events which is often missing. It enables surviving documents to be looked at with fresh insight. It can provide information on the dynamics of meetings and branch life generally – the importance of the Socialist Sunday Schools, the Clarion activities, the walks, the lectures, and all the activities that went into living the life of a socialist. Lastly, it can illuminate the neglected aspects of the ILP, in particular the role of women.

The researcher will be unlikely to find many recordings of the first generation of ILP activists. The oldest surviving recording seems to be that of Ben Tillett in 1915, appealing for more munitions to fight Germany. Keir Hardie, Philip Snowden, and Bruce Glasier have left little or nothing and Ramsay MacDonald was rarely recorded before 1931. Nevertheless, it is worth enquiring about recorded material, even if most of it understandably relates to peoples activities in the 1930s rather than earlier. Sometimes these tapes are housed in libraries, museums or record offices, sometimes elsewhere.[71] On occasion the tapes have been indexed or transcribed, and in such cases their ease of use is much increased.

If the researcher is fortunate, he or she will find some or all of the sources mentioned above accessible, but it is more likely that evidence will be fragmented and difficult to come by and it will require considerable time and patience before the full story of the ILP in a town or area can be discovered. Nevertheless, this research is worth what can seem an endless effort, for it is only by a detailed examination of the activities of the Party both in its heartlands, and where it failed to make significant headway that its true importance in British political history can be appreciated.

Appendix 1

A list of those ILP branch records which have been deposited in Libraries or Record Offices. Some ephemeral records have not been included.

Aberdare Socialist Society, later ILP
Minutes	1901–1906

Cynon Valley, Borough Library.
List of officers, subscriptions and committees	1895–1908

Glamorgan Archive Service.

Attercliffe ILP
Building Committee Minutes	1903–1905
Executive Committee Minutes	1903–1923
Building Committee, secretary's cash book	1903–1904
Subscription books	1903–1906
	1916–1922

Sheffield Archives, Sheffield City Council, Libraries and Information Department.

Barnsley and District ILP Federation
Monthly returns from branches	1915–1921

Barnsley District Archives Department, Barnsley Libraries.

Barrow ILP
Minutes	1921–1922

Cumbria County Council Archive Service, Barrow in Furness.

Bermondsey ILP
Cash book	1925–1941
Membership cards, notices, rules and letters	1908–1914
Subscriptions book	1925–1941

Southwark Local Studies and Archives, Southwark Leisure and Recreation Department.

Birmingham City Branch of the ILP
Minutes	1915–1923

Birmingham Library Service, Social Sciences Department.

Birmingham ILP Federation
Federation Delegate Meetings, Minutes	1909–1914
Finance Committee Minutes	1912–1915

Birmingham Library Service, Social Sciences Department.
Year Book	1908–1909

Birmingham Library Service, Local Studies Department.

Birmingham Socialist Centre
Minutes   1902–1912
Birmingham Library Services, Archives Department.

Birmingham Labour Church
Minutes   1894–1910
Birmingham Library Services, Archives Department.

Birmingham, Hay Mills ILP
Minutes   1908–1911
Birmingham Library Services, Social Sciences Department.

Birmingham, King's Heath ILP
Minutes   1906–1919
Birmingham Library Services, Social Sciences Department.

Bradford ILP
Cash Book   1935–1958
Members Subscriptions, Operatic Section   1926–1927
Workers Municipal Federation, Minutes   1902–1919
West Yorkshire Archive Service, Bradford.

Bradford, Allerton ILP
Members Subscriptions   1924–1935
Membership List   1920–1940
Membership figures   1930–1931
West Yorkshire Archive Service, Bradford.

Bradford, Bolton ILP
Membership List   1920–1940
Membership figures   1930–1931
West Yorkshire Archive Service, Bradford.

Bradford, Central ILP
Membership List   1920–1940
Membership figures   1930–1931
West Yorkshire Archive Service, Bradford.

Bradford, East Bowling ILP
Membership List, Women's Section   1920–1940
Membership figures   1930–1931
West Yorkshire Archive Service, Bradford.

Bradford, Great Horton ILP
Membership List   1920–1940
West Yorkshire Archive Service, Bradford.

Bradford, Heaton ILP

Minutes	1928–1932
Members Subscription	1931
Membership List	1920–1940
Membership figures	1930–1931

West Yorkshire Archive Service, Bradford.

Bradford, Listerhills ILP

Membership List	1920–1940
Membership figures	1930–1931

West Yorkshire Archive Service, Bradford.

Bradford, Little Horton ILP

Members Subscription	1926–1931
Membership List	1920–1940
Membership figures	1930–1931

West Yorkshire Archive Service, Bradford.

Bradford, Manningham ILP

Minutes	1899
Membership List	1920–1940
Membership figures	1930–1931

West Yorkshire Archive Service, Bradford.

Bradford, Thornton ILP

Membership List	1920–1940
Membership figures	1930–1931

West Yorkshire Archive Service, Bradford.

Bradford, West Bowling ILP

Membership List	1920–1940
Membership figures	1930–1931

West Yorkshire Archive Service, Bradford.

Bristol ILP

Annual Report	1924
Correspondence etc. re donations for outings	
Correspondence re booking of speakers	1917–1933
Correspondence re Kingsley Hall (ILP Hall)	1919–1924
Letters and circulars re ILP-Labour Party split	1922–1923
Statement of accounts	1934

Bristol Record Office.

Cambridge ILP
Minutes   1906–1912
Quarterly Balance Sheet   Aug. 1911–Feb. 1912
Cambridgeshire County Record Office.

Colne Valley ILP, also known as Colne Valley Labour Union, the Colne Valley Labour League and the Colne Valley Socialist League
Minutes   1891–1918
Membership register   1901–1904
Annual report   1912–1917
University of Huddersfield Library

Colne Valley Independent Labour Party Federation
Minutes   1919–1928
University of Huddersfield Library

Darnall Ward ILP, see Sheffield

East Anglia Division of the ILP, Norwich, Ipswich, Great Yarmouth and March
Minutes   1931–1951
British Library of Political and Economic Science

East Ham ILP
Minutes   1908–1921
British Library of Political and Economic Science.

Edinburgh Central ILP
Minutes   1893–1897
Edinburgh Public Library
Minutes   1918–1919
Minutes of joint meetings with Edinburgh Labour Party   1917–1918
Correspondence   1917–1918
Notes for branch meetings   1917–1918
Papers and leaflets   1911–1934
Reports and balance sheets   1917–1918
National Library of Scotland

Finsbury, Central Finsbury ILP
Minutes   1898–1901
Membership list and rules   1898–1901
(Contained in Minute Book)
British Library of Political and Economic Science

Forfar ILP District Committee
Minutes   1908–1918
1920–1932
Arbroath Public Library.

Gillingham ILP
Minutes   1920–1931
British Library of Political and Economic Science.

Glasgow ILP Federation
Bi-Monthly and Special Aggregate Minutes 1917–1930
Draft Minutes   1920–1922
Executive Council Minutes   1917–1933
Elections Committee, Minutes   1918–1922
General Purposes Committee, Minutes   1922–1923
Lectures Committee, Minutes   1918–1923
Management Committee Minutes   1918–1933
Organising Committee Minutes   1918–1923
Released Conscientious Objectors
Assistance Fund Committee   1919
Socialist Star Board of Management
Minutes   1933
Annual Reports   1917/18–1927/28
Cash Books   1936–1953
Mitchell Library, Glasgow.

Glasgow ILP, Bridgeton Branch
Minutes   1951–1960
Financial statements   1943–1962
Social Committee cash book   1935–1953
Mitchell Library, Glasgow.

Gloucester ILP
Branch Meeting Minutes   1907–1909
Management Committee Minutes   1906–1908
Members subscription book, and list of speakers & subjects   1899
Gloucestershire County Record Office.

Gloucester Labour Club
Finance and Trading Committee Minutes   1915–1916
Gloucestershire County Record Office.

Great Yarmouth ILP, see East Anglia Division

Halifax ILP
Minutes   1936–1953
Socialist Hall and ILP Account Books   1895–1947
West Yorkshire Archive Service, Calderdale.

Hay Mills ILP, See Birmingham

Hoyland Common, Birdwell and District ILP
Minutes   1914–1929
Barnsley District Archive Department, Barnsley Libraries.

Ipswich ILP, see East Anglia Division

Keighley ILP
Minute Books   1893–1951
Woman's Labour League Minutes   1911–1925
Social Committee Minutes   1918–1924
Letter Books   1901–1911
Account Book   1897–1907
Accounts, Lectures and Socials   1904
Keighley Reference Library.

Kings Heath ILP, see Birmingham

Liverpool LRC
Minutes   1903–1920
Annual reports and accounts   1906–1917
                                                           1919–1920
Liverpool Record Office.

London and Southern Counties Division of the ILP
Minutes   1909–1921
Correspondence   1909–1921
British Library of Political and Economic Science

London, City of London ILP
Minutes   1908–1922
Correspondence   1908–1922
British Library of Political and Economic Science.

London, Bermondsey, see Bermondsey

London, East Ham, see East Ham

London, Finsbury, see Finsbury

London, Metropolitan ILP District Council
Minutes 1906–1919
British Library of Political and Economic Science.

London, North London Federation
Miscellaneous papers 1910–1912
British Library of Political and Economic Science.

London, Southwark, see Southwark

Macclesfield ILP
Minutes 1894–1897
Cheshire Record Office.

Manchester Central ILP
Minutes 1902–1919
Letters to Manchester, Salford Joint Disarmament Council 1932
Manchester Central Library, Local Studies Unit.

Manchester Clarion Club
Minutes 1913–1921
Newspaper cuttings 1903–1910
Manchester Central Library, Local Studies Unit.

March, see East Anglia Division

Meltham ILP
Minutes 1893–1908
  1914–1929
Accounts and membership roll 1893–1910
University of Huddersfield Library.

Middlesbrough ILP
Minutes 1898–1913
Cleveland County Council, Libraries and Leisure Department, Archives Section.

National Administrative Council
Minutes 1893–1918
Minutes 1894–1950
Minutes of committees, financial records, circulars etc.,
 (incomplete) 1894–1950
Correspondence of General Secretary of the ILP 1880–1950
Summaries of branches and branch membership 1918–1921
Head Office papers 1898–1899

Pamphlets and leaflets published by the ILP	1893–1975
Circulars, material from branches and ephemera	1904–1922
Papers relating to New Leader	1922–1931

British Library of Political and Economic Science.

Norwich, see East Anglia Division

Nottingham ILP
Executive Committee, Minutes	1927–1931

Nottingham University Library, Department of Manuscripts.

Pendlebury, Swinton and Clifton ILP
Minutes	1919–1921
Statements of income and expenditure	1919–1921

City of Salford, Archive Department.

Saltcoats ILP
Minutes	1917–29
	1935–36
	1939–49

North Ayrshire Museum, Saltcoats.

Scottish Socialist Party
Minutes	1920–1932

Arbroath Public Library

Sheffield ILP
Minutes	1910–1923

Sheffield Archives, Sheffield City Council, Libraries and Information Department.

Sheffield ILP
Darnall Ward Committee of the Sheffield LRC, Minutes	1906–1909

Sheffield Archives, Sheffield City Council, Libraries and Information Department.

Slaithwaite Labour Club
Minutes of the County Council Election Committee	1892–1901
Miscellaneous papers	1892–1906

University of Huddersfield Library.

Southwark ILP
Minutes	1906–1908

British Library of Political and Economic Science.

Stockport ILP
Minutes 1896–1898
1916–1922
Accounts 1896–1898
Stockport Central Library, Archives Section.

Vale of Leven ILP
Minutes 1904–1906
Baillie's Library, Glasgow.

Wallasey ILP
Minutes 1894–1901
Warwick University, Modern Records Centre.

Warrington ILP
Minutes 1920–1927
Guild of Youth Minute Book 1932
Accounts 1929–1933
Receipt book 1929–1933
Cheshire Libraries, Arts and Archives, Area Headquarters, Warrington.

Warrington Workers' Unity Council
Minutes 1933
Cheshire Libraries, Arts and Archives, Area Headquarters, Warrington.

Watford ILP
Minutes 1904–1910
Correspondence 1904–1910
British Library of Political and Economic Science.

Welsh Divisional Council
Circulars and Press Cuttings 1922–1828
British Library of Political and Economic Science.

Wrexham ILP
Minutes 1912–1921
Clwyd Record Office.

Ystrad Mynach ILP
Minutes 1925–1927
Glamorgan Record Office.

NOTES

1. I should like to thank Professor Laybourn of the Department of Humanities, Huddersfield University and Sylvia Thomas of the West Yorkshire Archive Service for reading and commenting on an earlier draft of this article. I must also thank those archivists and librarians who were kind enough to answer my enquiry about surviving ILP records. Mrs S. Hoyle of Bradford Libraries was kind enough to find me various items, both in Bradford Libraries and through the inter-library loan system.

2. P. Snowden, *An Autobiography* (London, Ivor Nicholson and Watson, 1934), p.53.

3. H. Pelling, *Origins of the Labour Party, 1880–1900* (Oxford, Oxford University Press, second edition, 1965).

4. D. Howell, *British Workers and the Independent Labour Party 1888–1906* (Manchester, Manchester University Press, 1983).

5. R. E. Dowse, *Left in the Centre: The Independent Labour Party 1893–1940* (London, Longmans, 1966).

6. K. Laybourn, *The Rise of Labour: the British Labour Party 1890–1979* (London, Edward Arnold, 1988); K. Laybourn, *The Labour Party 1881–1951* (Gloucester, Alan Sutton, 1988).

7. K. Laybourn and J. Reynolds, *Liberalism and the Rise of Labour 1890–1918* (London, Croom Helm, 1984); J. Reynolds and K. Laybourn, *Labour Heartland: The History of the Labour Party in West Yorkshire during the inter-war years, 1918–1939* (Bradford, University of Bradford, 1987).

8. K. Laybourn and D. James (eds), *'The Rising Sun of Socialism': The Independent Labour Party in the Textile District of the West Riding of Yorkshire between 1890 and 1914* (Wakefield, West Yorkshire Archive Service, West Yorkshire Archives and Archaeology Joint Committee and Bradford Library Service, 1991).

9. B. Lancaster, *Radicalism, Cooperation and Socialism: Leicester Working-Class Politics 1860–1906* (Leicester, Leicester University Press, 1987).

10. A. Mackinley and R. J. Morris (eds), *The ILP on Clydeside 1893–1932* (Manchester, Manchester University Press, 1991).

11. L. Thompson, *The Enthusiasts: A Biography of John and Katharine Bruce Glasier* (London, Victor Gollancz, 1971); F. Reid, *Keir Hardie: The Making of a Socialist* (London, Croom Helm, 1978).

12. K. O. Morgan, *Keir Hardie, Radical and Socialist* (London, Weidenfeld, 1975); I. Mclean, *Keir Hardie* (London, Allen Lane, 1975); D. Marquand, *Ramsay MacDonald* (London, Cape, 1977); K. Laybourn, *Philip Snowden: A Biography 1864–1937* (Aldershot, Wildwood House, 1988).

12. J. McNair, *James Maxton, the Beloved Rebel* (London, George Allen and Unwin 1935).

13. R. K. Middlemas, *The Clydesiders: A Left Wing Struggle for Parliamentary Power* (London, Hutchinson, 1965).

14. D. Clark, *Victor Grayson, Labour's Lost Leader* (London, Quartet Books, 1985); F. Brockway, *Socialism Over Sixty years: The Life of Jowett of Bradford* (London, Allen and Unwin, 1946); J. Broom, *John Maclean*, (Midlothian, MacDonald, 1973); C. Steadman, *Childhood, Culture and Class in Britain: Margaret McMillan 1860–1931* (London, Virago, 1990); D. Torr, *Tom Mann and His Times*, vol. 1 1856–1890 (London, Lawrence and Wishart, 1956).

15. L. Thompson, *Robert Blatchford: Portrait of an Englishman* (London, Victor Gollancz, 1951); G. Tsuziki, *H.M. Hyndman and British Socialism* (London, Heinemann and Oxford University Press, 1961); A. W. McBriar, *Fabian Socialism and English Politics 1884–1918* (Cambridge, Cambridge University Press, 1962); E. P. Thompson, *William Morris: From Romantic to Revolutionary* (London, Merlin Press, 1977).

16. *Dictionary of Labour Biography* (London, MacMillan, dates various).

17. For Dewsbury see M. Crick, 'The History of the Social Democratic Federation' (Halifax, Ryburn Publishing, in press); P. A. Dawson, 'Halifax Politics, 1890–1914', unpublished PhD thesis, Huddersfield Polytechnic, 1987; D. James, 'The Social and Political development of Keighley with special reference to the response of the Liberal Party to the rise of Labour 1885–1914', unpublished PhD. thesis, Huddersfield Polytechnic, 1991; For Huddersfield see, R. Perks, 'Liberalism and the Challenge of Labour, 1885–1914', unpublished PhD thesis, Huddersfield Polytechnic, 1989.

18. I. MacDougall (ed), *A Catalogue of some Labour Records in Scotland and some Scots records outside Scotland* (Edinburgh, Scottish Labour History Society, 1978).

19. The Royal Commission on Historical Manuscripts, Quality House, Quality Court, Chancery Lane, London, WC2A 1HP. The Royal Commission on Historical Monuments acts as a clearing house for information about the nature and location of manuscripts outside the public records.

20. D. Clark, *Colne Valley: Radicalism to Socialism. The Portrait of a Northern Constituency in the formative years of the Labour Party 1890–1910* (London, Longman, 1981), p.1.

21. *Ibid.*, p.1.

22. E. P. Thompson, 'Homage to Tom Maguire' in Briggs and Saville (eds), *Essays in Labour History* (London, MacMillan, 1960), p.277.

23. Howell, *op. cit.*, pp.314–315.

24. Keighley Independent Labour Party Letter Book, 7 Jan 1905. Housed in Keighley Reference Library, ref. no. BK 11.

25. *Ibid.*, February 1906 (no day given).

26. Dowse, *op. cit.*, pp.76–102.

27. British Library of Political and Economic Science, London School of Economics and Political Science, 10 Portugal Street, London, WC2A 2HD. The archives of the ILP are divided into two sections. The first contains the Archives of the ILP National Administrative Council and the General Secretary; the minutes of the NAC; Head Office Circulars, correspondence and pamphlets and leaflets. The second includes the records of branches and individual members.

28. These microfilm collections consist of:
Independent Labour Party, Part 1. Early Minute Books, not included in the Research Publications package;
Independent Labour Party, Part 2, Head Office Circulars, not included in the Research Publications package;
Independent Labour Party, Part 3, Later NAC Minutes, minutes and related records of the Independent Labour Party: Part 1, National Administrative Council minutes and related records, 1894–1950, Brighton, Harvester Press Microform Publications, 1979;
Independent Labour Party, Part 4, Correspondence of the Secretary, Francis Johnson.
The Archives of the Independent Labour Party, Series 3, The Francis Johnson

Correspondence, Brighton, Harvester Press, Microform Publications, 1979–1980;

Independent Labour Party, Part 5 Pamphlets and Leaflets, The Archives of the Independent Labour party, Series 1, Pamphlets and Leaflets, Brighton, Harvester Press, 1978.

29. Keighley ILP Letter Book, *op. cit.*

30. Letters asking for information on deposits of ILP material were circulated to local authority Record Offices in England, Wales and Scotland and selected University and other Archive Departments in October 1991. Among the replies were details of over fifty branches whose records had been deposited.

Many places of deposit had references to the activities of the ILP or ILPers among the records of other collections, and these are valuable sources of information.

Records of other ILP branches may be deposited in places which were not contacted by this survey, or may be in private hands. It would be strange if no more than this comparatively small number of records are all that remains of the many thousands of documents produced by the party's branches.

31. For details of the surviving records of the above branches, see Appendix 1.

32. Keighley ILP records, *op. cit.*, Minutes, 1 June 1897.

33. *Ibid.*, Minutes, 6 May 1907.

34. For details of these minutes, see Appendix 1.

35. Colindale Newspaper Library, Colindale Avenue, London, NW9, 5HE.

36. The most complete run of this paper is to be found in the Snowden Collection at Keighley Library.

37. See Keighley ILP records, *op. cit.*, 1905 *passim*.

38. C. Cross, *Philip Snowden*, (London, Barrie and Rockliff, 1966), p.44.

39. Lancaster, *op. cit.*, pp.112–113, 172–173.

40. *Bradford Pioneer* is housed in Bradford Central Library, *Leeds Weekly Citizen* is housed in Leeds Central Library and *Huddersfield Worker* and *Huddersfield Citizen* are housed in Huddersfield Central Library.

41. Deian Hopkin 'The Newspapers of the Independent Labour Party: 1893–1906', unpublished PhD, University College of Wales, Aberystwith, 1981.

42. None of these have survived as a complete run. Copies of the *Bradford Labour Echo* and *Bottom Dog* are in Bradford Central Library. Some copies of *Labour Union Journal* are in the West Yorkshire Archive Service, Bradford.

43. MacDougal, *op. cit.*, pp.408–418.

44. Thompson, *op. cit.*, pp.82–85.

45. James, *op. cit.*, p.175.

46. *Keighley Labour Journal*, 2 Feb 1898.

47. Quoted in Thompson, *op. cit.*, p.138.

48. Pelling, *op. cit.*, p.173.

49. Quoted in Howell, *op. cit.*, p.381.

50. Dowse, *op. cit.*, p.82.

51. National Museum of Labour History, 103 Princess Street, Manchester, M1 6DD.

52. *Keighley News*, 1 Apr 1893.

53. *Ibid.*, 20 July 1895.

54. Bruce Glasier's papers are kept at the Sidney Jones Library, University of Liverpool. Ramsay MacDonald's papers are in the Public Record Office.

55. Strathclyde Regional Archives, Mitchell Library, North Street, Glasgow. The reference number for the Maxton collection is TD956.
56. MacDougall, *op. cit.*, pp.483–485.
57. Bradford District Archives, 15 Canal Road Bradford, BD1 4AT. The reference number for the Hartley papers is 11D85.
58. Held in the British Library of Political and Economic Science.
59. Quoted in Pelling, *op. cit.*, p.167.
60. The papers of John Burns are held by the British Museum, those of Edward Carpenter in Sheffield Archives, and those of Lloyd George in the House of Lords Library.
61. *Op. cit.*
62. Laybourn, *Snowden*, p.194.
63. J. H. Thomas, *My Story* (London, Hutchinson, 1937).
64. Dowse, *op. cit.*, p.219.
65. J. Gilray, 'Early Days of the Socialist Movement in Edinburgh', tss., National Library of Scotland; John Lister, 'The Early History of the ILP Movement in Halifax', mss., West Yorkshire Archive Service, Calderdale; S. Bryher, 'An Account of the Labour and Socialist Movement in Bristol', (Bristol, 1929).
66. Brockway, *op. cit.*; F. Brockway, *Bermondsey Story, the Life of Alfred Salter* (London, George Allen and Unwin, 1949); G. McAllister, *James Maxton, Portrait of a Rebel* (London, 1925).
67. T. Steele, *Alfred Orage and the Leeds Art Club, 1893–1923* (London, Scolar Press, 1990); J. Liddington, *Selina Cooper: a biography* (London, Virago, 1982); J. Liddington, 'Looking for Mrs Cooper' in N. Kirk (ed.), *Women and the Labour Movement* (Manchester, North West Labour History Society Bulletin 7, published in association with the Manchester Women's History Group), 1980–81. This article is a textbook example of how to use a wide variety of sources – archival, printed and oral – in the exploration of a poorly documented research area.
68. The Colne Valley Socialist League and its predecessors minutes run from 1891–1918, and the Colne Valley Divisional Labour Party minutes start in 1917.
69. *Observer*, 16 Apr 1922.
70. Dowse, *op. cit.*, p.42.
71. For example, the West Yorkshire Archive Service, Calderdale, house the records of Pennine Heritage, while the tapes and transcripts of the Bradford Heritage Recording Unit are kept jointly by Bradford Libraries and Museums. Dr R. Perks in his forthcoming article in *Labour History Review* lists the major oral history collections which contain material on labour history.

3. The ILP: a Century for Socialism

Barry Winter

In its struggle for radical social change, the Independent Labour Party has throughout its history been challenging the 'common sense' ideas of the time. Standing out against popular opinion and prejudices in this way has never been easy, however. It takes courage and commitment, some toughness and a great deal of patience.

In the last hundred years, ILPers have been involved in numerous campaigns, sometimes successfully but often not so. On many occasions their arguments on the issues of the day appeared to be making little headway. Yet, at a later date, certain ILP heresies became more widely accepted.

This is not to say that the ILP was always right. No organisation made up of human beings could expect to be. However, the record is worth considering.

When ILPers called for a party of labour separate from the Liberals, they faced the organised wrath of Lib-Lab trade unionists. But in time the Labour party was set up with the trade unions.

Calling for votes for women was also widely derided. Those who took the issue to the streets had to expect a rowdy reception. Sometimes they needed physical protection. But no-one today seriously questions women's right to vote.

When ILPers opposed the First World War they met ferocious hostility. Yet, as the war progressed, large numbers of people turned against the slaughter. And when ILP members resisted compulsory military service to replace the tens of thousands of young men killed or injured, they were attacked as traitors. Yet, later, the right to conscientious objection was recognised.

When ILPers and others argued that men and women should be properly informed about birth control, many people were horrified, claiming that this would encourage immorality. Nowadays such knowledge is seen as right and proper.

When the ILPers supported the independence movements in India and other British colonies, the supporters of the empire were incensed. Yet independence came. When ILPers and other peace activists first campaigned against nuclear weapons they were denounced as communist stooges. Later, large numbers of people were won to the arguments.

Even when people were persuaded by some of the ideas of the socialists, they often recoiled from anything connected with socialism itself. Traditionally, socialism has had a 'bad press'. That is why it was necessary to set up its own.

Helen Crawfurd, married to a vicar in the impoverished Glasgow docklands, put it this way: 'I used to listen to open-air speakers – and would feel they were speaking the truth – but if the word socialism was used I walked away. This was of the Devil.' Later she took up the 'devil's work' by joining the ILP.

Today, the popular view is that socialism is dead. In their separate ways the fourth election defeat for the Labour party and the appalling experiences of 'communism' in Eastern Europe are taken as evidence of this view.

Coming from a different socialist tradition, the ILP disagrees with the received wisdom. We accept that socialism is down but it is not out. For us, much that has been done in the name of socialism has been wrong, very wrong. However, the need for a more equal, just and democratic society remains as important as ever. For a price, capitalism can deliver a multiplicity of goods and service but it is incapable of delivering a fair society.

We live in a world of massive social inequality, where poverty and hunger haunt the lives of millions, where unemployment takes away people's self-respect and condemns them to second-class citizenship, and where the environment is under grave threat. In such conditions, the ILP argues that radical social change remains the best hope for humanity.

But where is the ILP today? Having left the Labour party in 1932, after major battles with Ramsay MacDonald's disastrous government, the ILP had a hard time. It found itself squeezed politically between the Labour Party and the Communist Party. Yet it still managed to play a significant political role in these years – not least in opposing the rise of fascism.

After the Second World War, the ILP went into marked decline. Ironically, it saw the post-war Labour government introduce many of the reforms that the ILP had been advocating without success for 20 years.

Thanks to the efforts and the vision of those ILPers who refused to give up, it survived and has now begun to rebuild. In 1993 it will be celebrating its centenary to uphold the memory of the many thousands of unknown men and women who fought for a better society.

Why did those ILPers keep going? A clue is given in David Howell's book about the ILP in its early years. In *British Workers and the Independent Labour Party, 1888–1906* he writes: 'The ILP was not so much a Party, more a way of life.' In other words they did not give up because for them the ILP embodied a unique socialist and moral vision which they wanted to see live.

In 1975, the ILP became Independent Labour Publications. It was welcomed back into the Labour Party. Through its publications and other activities, the modern ILP has contributed to a wide range of debates on party democracy and policy, including defence cuts, the poll tax, and Northern Ireland.

Often it has stood alone, once again dissenting from the existing mainstream Labour left. In doing so, it has tried to learn the lessons of its own history. It has argued that those who seek social change must face the harsh truth that we live in a conservative culture. This does not mean capitulating to that conservatism but no purpose is served in wishing it away.

Now socialism is in crisis. The once familiar political landscape is changing rapidly. What is taking place in Britain and internationally is every bit as dramatic as the events which gave birth and energy to the early ILP.

For these reasons, the ILP intends to relaunch itself as a political pressure group in its centenary year. The best way to honour the memory of the socialist pioneers is to seek a renewal of socialism that is relevant to our times. Future generations will have to judge whether the ILP today was right do so.

For further information about the ILP and the centenary celebrations contact Barry Winter, ILP, 49 Top Moor Side, Leeds LS11 9LW, or telephone 0532 430613.

Index